中国残疾人事业统计年鉴

China Statistical Yearbook on the Work for Persons with Disabilities

2019

(总第18期 No.18)

中国残疾人联合会 编

Compiled By China Disabled Persons' Federation

中国统计出版社
China Statistics Press

图书在版编目（CIP）数据

中国残疾人事业统计年鉴. 2019 / 中国残疾人联合会编. -- 北京 : 中国统计出版社, 2019.9
ISBN 978-7-5037-8848-2

Ⅰ. ①中… Ⅱ. ①中… Ⅲ. ①残疾人－社会福利事业－统计资料－中国－2019－年鉴 Ⅳ. ①D669.69-66

中国版本图书馆 CIP 数据核字(2019)第 146426 号

中国残疾人事业统计年鉴－2019
China Statistical Yearbook on the Work for Persons with Disabilities-2019

作　　者/中国残疾人联合会
责任编辑/冯燕玲
封面设计/王　鹏
出版发行/中国统计出版社
通信地址/北京市丰台区西三环南路甲 6 号　邮政编码/100073
电　　话/邮购（010）63376909　书店（010）68783171
网　　址/http://www.zgtjcbs.com
印　　刷/河北鑫兆源印刷有限公司
经　　销/新华书店
开　　本/880×1230mm　1/16
印　　张/14.25　彩页 0.5
字　　数/460 千字
版　　别/2019 年 9 月第 1 版
版　　次/2019 年 9 月第 1 次印刷
定　　价/180.00 元

如有印装差错，由本社发行部调换。

《中国残疾人事业统计年鉴—2019》编委会和编辑工作人员

编　委　会

编辑工作人员

编者说明

《中国残疾人事业统计年鉴—2019》收录了全国和各省、自治区、直辖市 2018 年残疾人工作各方面的统计数据，是一部反映中国残疾人事业发展的资料性年刊。

本书内容由六部分组成：第一部分为主要数据图；第二部分为 2018 年中国残疾人事业发展统计公报；第三部分为综合统计资料，是历年统计情况的综合反映；第四部分为 2018 年度分省统计资料，记录 2018 年各省任务指标执行情况和全国汇总情况；第五部分为分省统计报告，包括全国 31 个省（自治区、直辖市）、新疆生产建设兵团和黑龙江垦区的残疾人事业统计公报；第六部分为附录，介绍中国残疾人事业统计有关的政策法规文件。

本年鉴涉及的全国性统计数据均不包括香港、澳门特别行政区和台湾省数据。

本年鉴是根据各地残联报送的统计年报和部分专项业务项目统计结果编制而成。表格中“空格”表示该项统计指标数据不足本表最小单位数、数据不详或无该项数据。

2019 年 7 月

目　录
Contents

第一部分　主要数据图
Part Ⅰ　Charts

第二部分　统计公报
Part Ⅱ　Statistical Communiqué

第三部分　综合统计资料
Part Ⅲ　Overall Statistics

第四部分　分省统计资料
Part Ⅳ　Provincial Statistics

一、康复
Rehabilitation

二、教育
Education

三、就业

Employment

四、扶贫

Poverty Alleviation

五、社会保障

Social Security

六、专门协会

Specialized Associations

七、盲人按摩

Massage by the Blind

八、宣传文化

Publicity and Cultural Activities

九、体育

Sports

十、维权

Rights Protection

十一、组织建设

Disabled Persons' Organizations

十二、残疾人服务设施建设

Service Facilities for Persons with Disabilities

十三、信息化建设

Application of IT

第五部分　分省统计报告
Part Ⅴ　Provincial Statistical Reports

1

主要数据图

Charts

图–1 2018年各类残疾人接受康复服务情况

Chart1 Rehabilitation Services Received by Persons with Different Categories of Disabilities in 2018

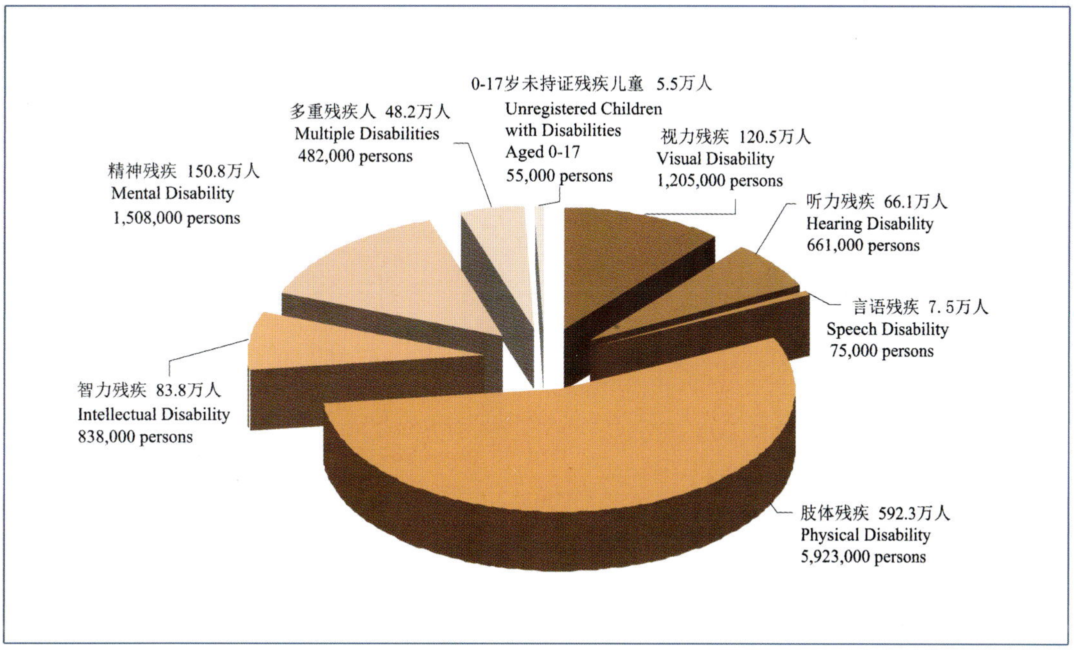

图–2 2014–2018年残疾人康复机构建设情况

Chart2 Development of Rehabilitation Facilities for Persons with Disabilities during 2014-2018

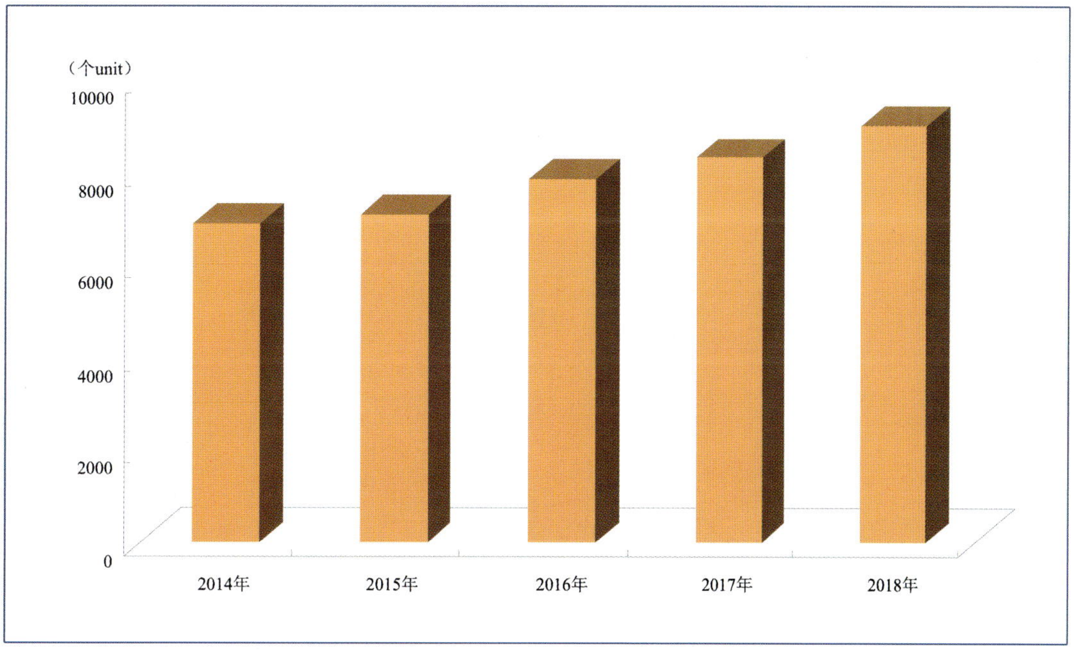

图-3 2014-2018年高等院校录取残疾考生情况

Chart 3 Admission of Disabled Students to Higher Education Institutes during 2014-2018

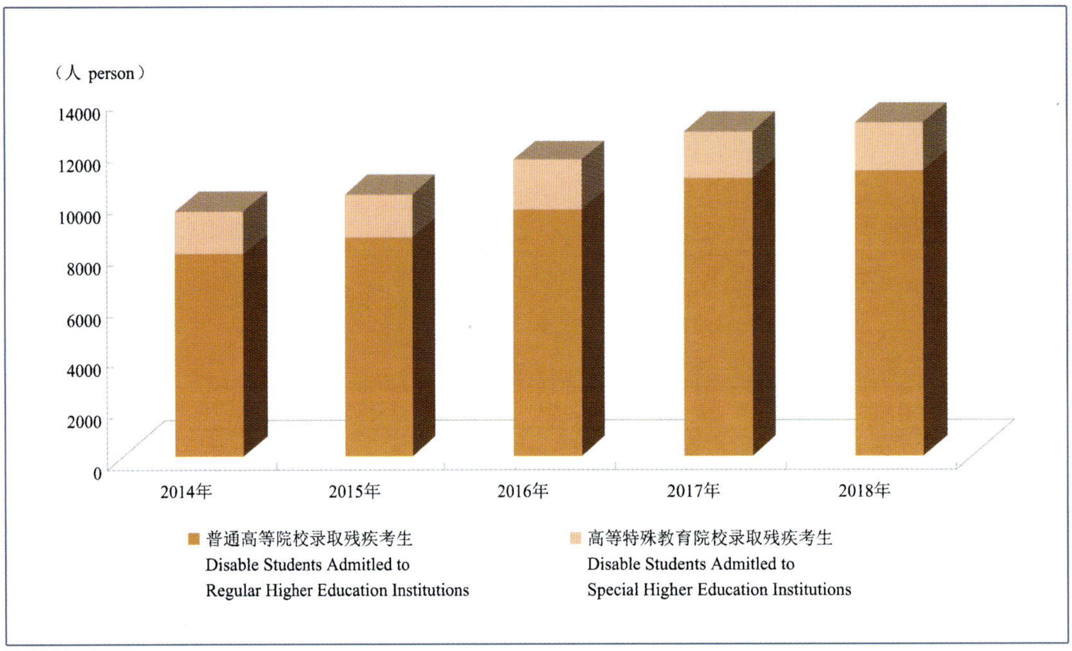

图-4 2018年城乡持证残疾人就业形式

Chart 4 Employment of Registered Persons with Disabilities in Urban and Rural Areas in 2018

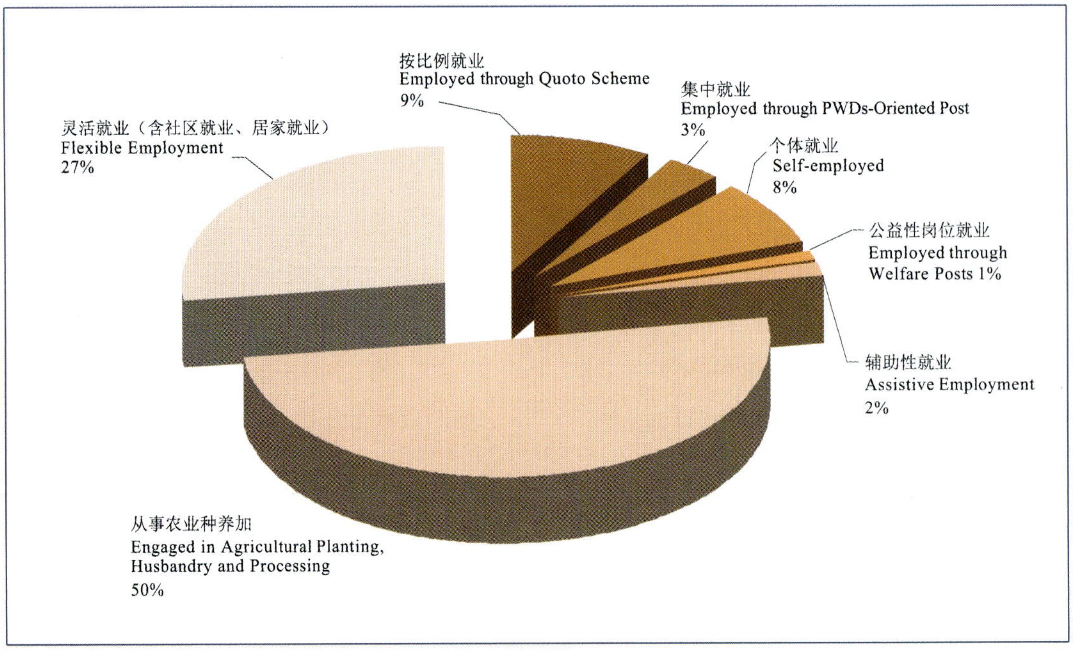

图–5 2014–2018年农村贫困残疾人危房改造情况

Chart 5 House Renovation for Financially Difficult Persons with Disabilities in Rural Areas during 2014-2018

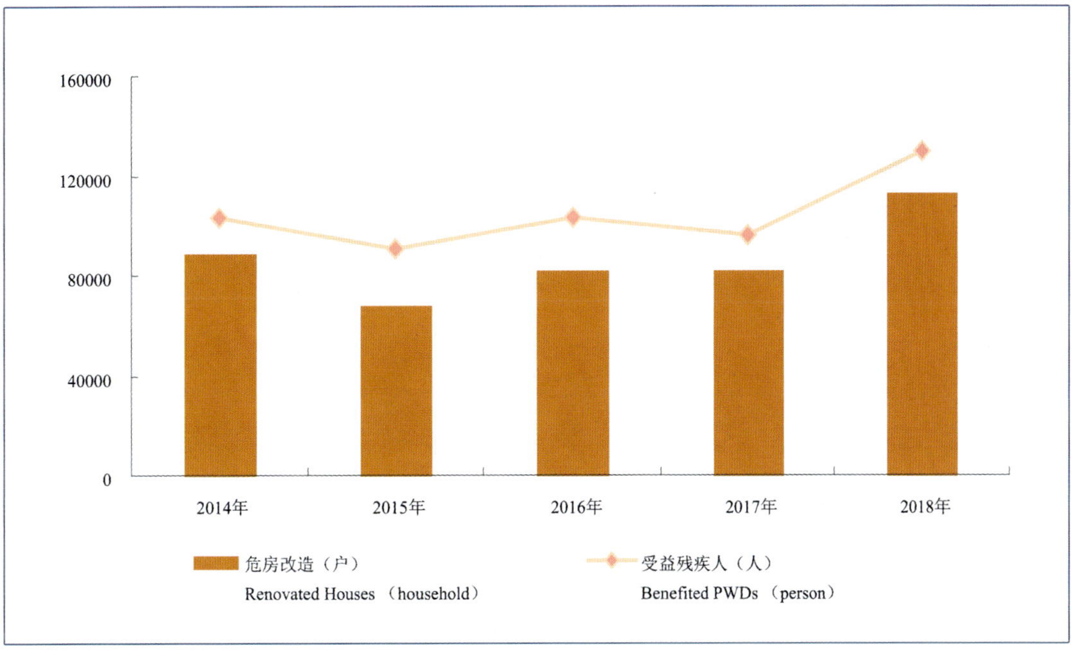

图–6 2014–2018年农村贫困残疾人扶持情况

Chart 6 Poverty Alleviation for Financially Difficult Persons with Disabilities in Rural Areas during 2014-2018

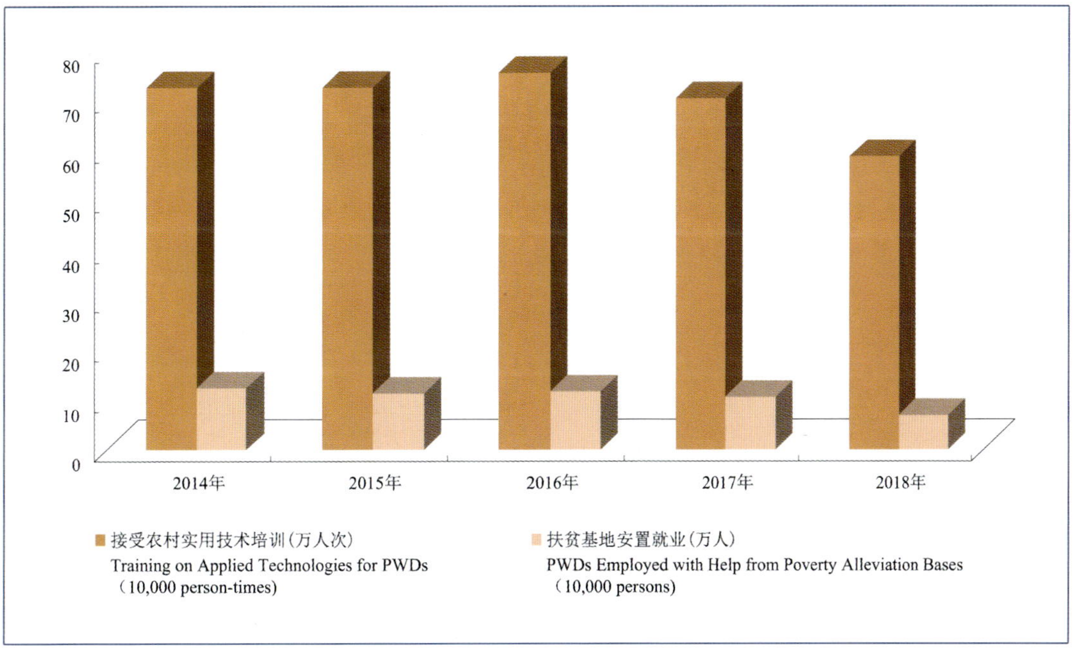

图-7 2014-2018年残疾人接受托养服务情况

Chart 7 Institutional Care Services Received by Persons with Disabilities during 2014-2018

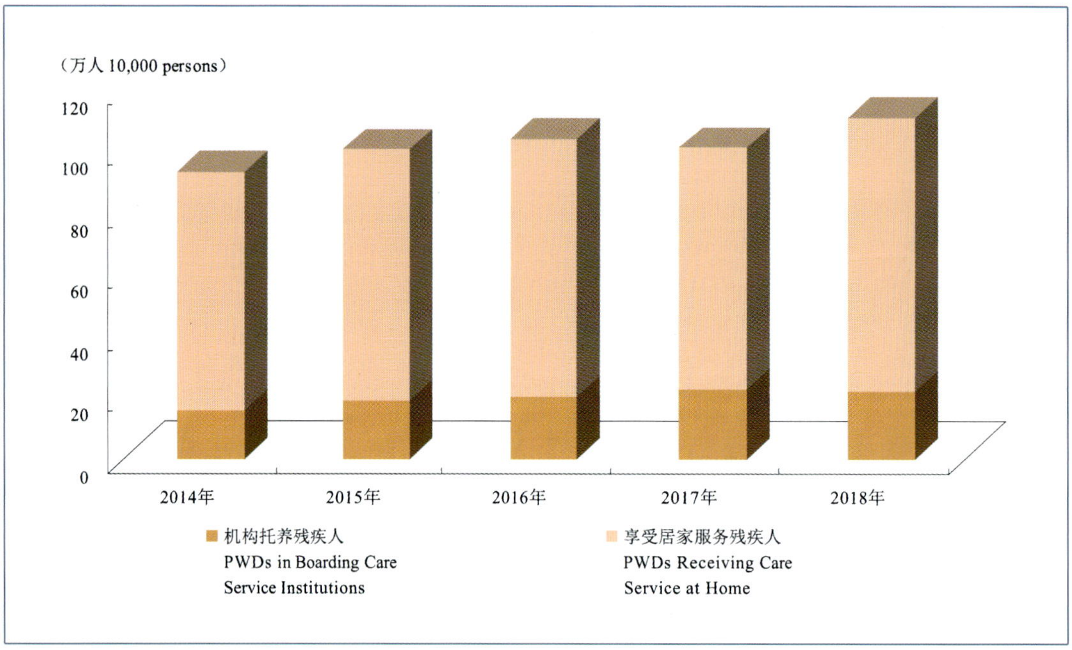

图-8 2014-2018年省、市级电视手语栏目播出情况

Chart 8 Sign Language Displayed in Provincial and Municipal TV Programs during 2014-2018

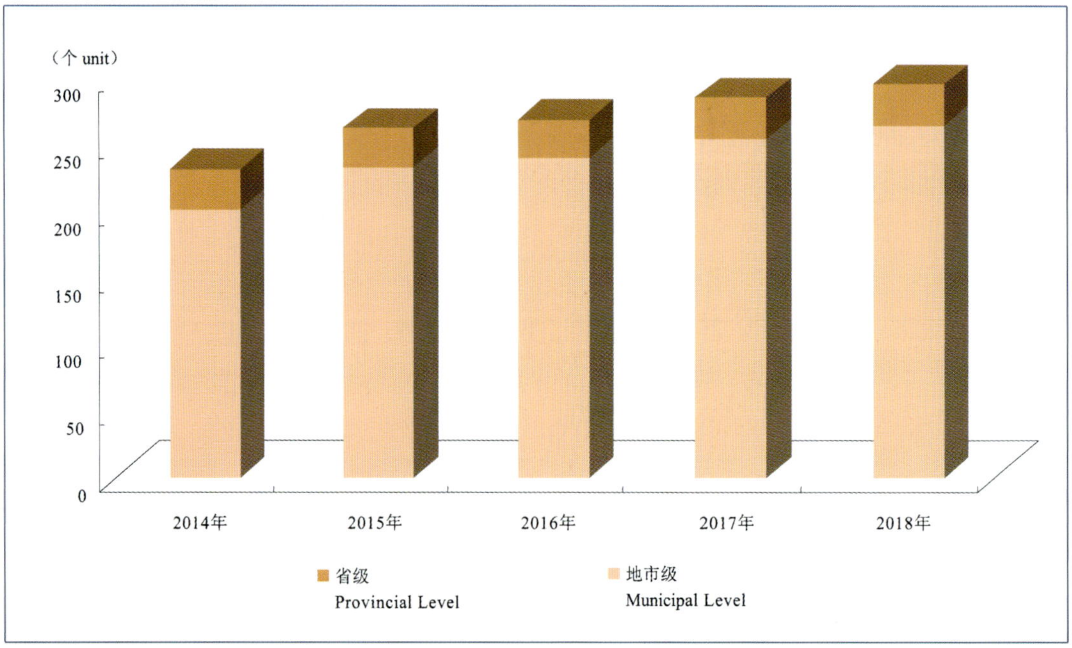

图-9 2014–2018年残疾人机动轮椅车燃油补贴发放情况

Chart 9 Gas Subsidy for Motorized Wheelchairs during 2014-2018

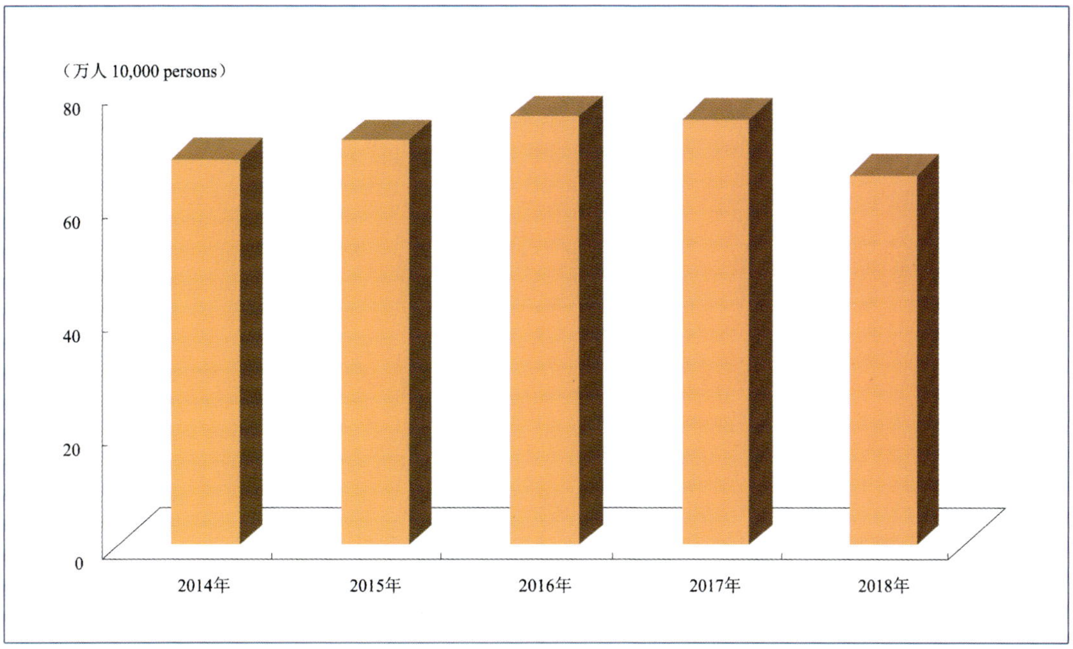

图-10 2014–2018年系统开展无障碍环境建设市、县

Chart 10 Accessible Environments Building in Cities and Counties during 2014-2018

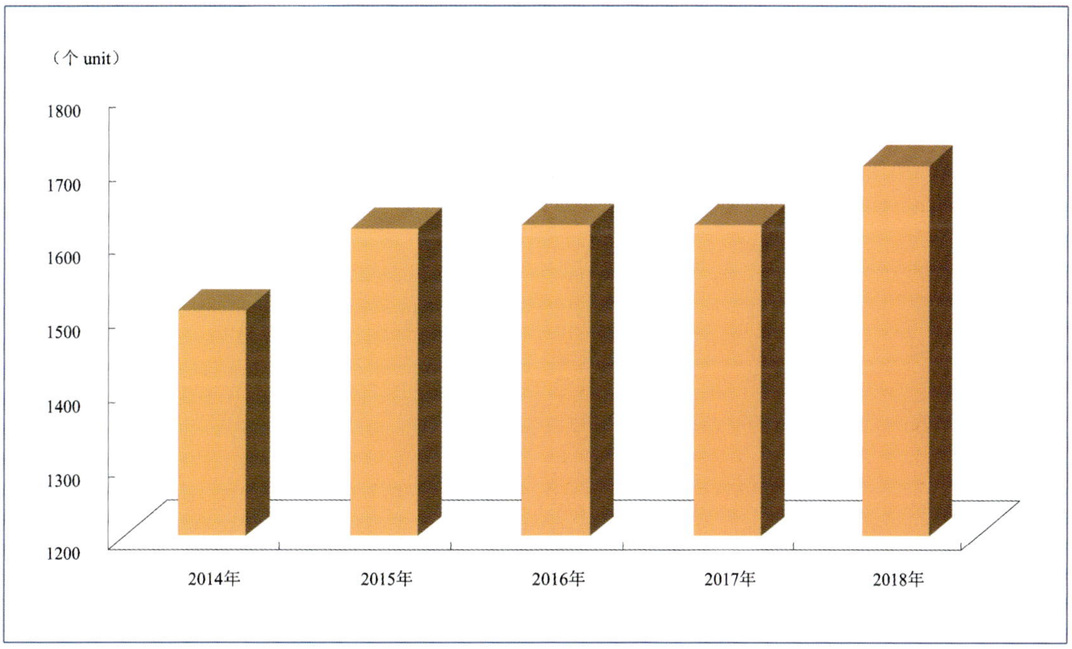

图－11 2014-2018年残疾人专职委员选聘情况

Chart 11 Appointment of Commissioners for Disability Issues at Grass-roots Level during 2014-2018

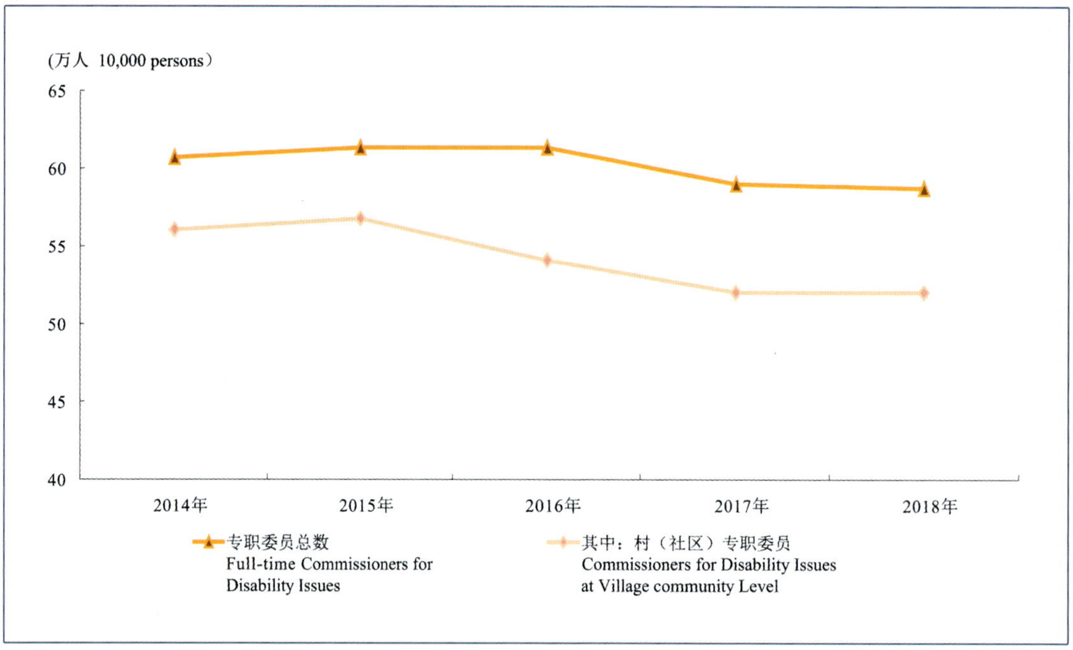

图－12 2018年残疾人服务设施建设情况

Chart 12 Development of Service Facilities for Persons with Disabilities in 2018

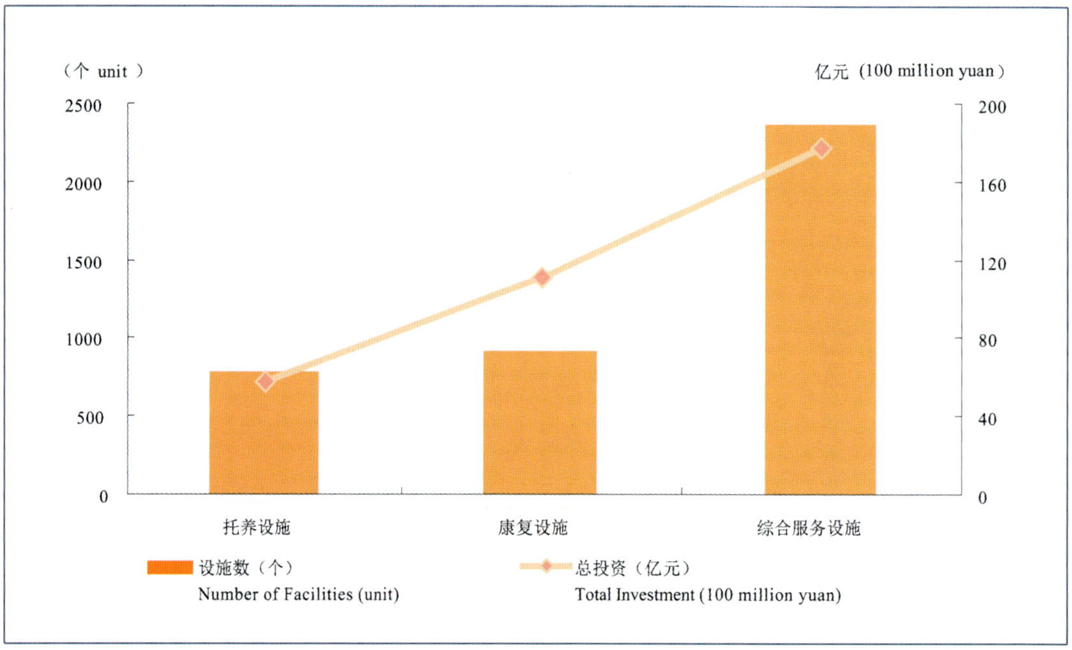

2

统计公报

Statistical Communiqué

2018年残疾人事业发展统计公报

2018年，全国残联系统认真学习习近平总书记关于残疾人事业的重要论述，围绕实现“全面建成小康社会，残疾人一个也不能少”的目标，着力打赢打好贫困残疾人脱贫攻坚战，努力开创新时代残疾人事业发展新局面。

一、康复

2018年，1074.7万残疾儿童及持证残疾人得到基本康复服务，其中0-6岁儿童15.7万人。得到康复服务的持证残疾人中，有视力残疾人120.5万、听力残疾人66.1万、言语残疾人7.5万、肢体残疾人592.3万、智力残疾人83.8万、精神残疾人150.8万、多重残疾人48.2万。全年共为319.1万残疾人提供各类辅助器具适配服务。

截至2018年底，全国已有残疾人康复机构9036个，其中，1346个机构提供视力残疾康复服务，1549个提供听力言语残疾康复服务，3737个提供肢体残疾康复服务，3024个提供智力残疾康复服务，1962个提供精神残疾康复服务，1811个提供孤独症儿童康复服务，1929个提供辅助器具服务。康复机构在岗人员达25.0万人，其中，管理人员2.9万人，专业技术人员17.6万人，其他人员4.5万人。

二、教育

会同教育部指导各省（区、市）出台《第二期特殊教育提升计划（2017-2020年）》实施方案。与教育部、国家发展改革委出台《关于加快发展残疾人职业教育的若干意见》。继续开展残疾人高等融合教育试点工作。《国家通用手语常用词表》《国家通用盲文方案》作为语言文字规范正式发布。会同中央宣传部等部门印发《关于推广国家通用手语和国家通用盲文的通知》，在全国范围内逐步推广使用国家通用手语和国家通用盲文。残疾人受教育权得到了更好保障，进一步提高了特殊教育发展水平。

残疾人事业专项彩票公益金助学项目的实施，为全国1.7万名家庭经济困难的残疾儿童享受普惠性学前教育提供资助。各地多渠道争取资金支持，对4993名残疾儿童给予学前教育资助。

2018年，全国共有特殊教育普通高中班（部）102个，在校生7666人，其中聋生5554人，盲生2056人，其他56人。残疾人中等职业学校（班）133个，在校生19475人，毕业生4837人，毕业生中1199人获得职业资格证书。全国有11154名残疾人被普通高等院校录取，1873名残疾人进入高等特殊教育学院学习。

继续实施《“十三五”残疾青壮年文盲扫盲行动方案》。5.2万名残疾青壮年文盲接受了扫盲教育。

三、就业

2018年城乡持证残疾人新增就业36.7万人，其中，城镇新增就业11.8万人，农村新增就业24.9万人；城乡新增培训残疾人49.4万人。

全国城乡持证残疾人就业人数为948.4万人，其中按比例就业81.3万人，集中就业33.1万人，个体就业71.4万人，公益性岗位就业13.1万人，辅助性就业14.8万人，灵活就业（含社区、居家就业）254.6万人，从事农业种养加480.1万人。

盲人按摩事业稳步发展，按摩机构持续增长。全国共培训盲人保健按摩人员19732名、盲人医疗按摩人员10160名；保健按摩机构16776个，医疗按摩机构1126个；953人获得盲人医疗按摩人员初级职务任职资格，122人获得中级职务任职资格。

四、社会保障

截至2018年底，残疾居民参加城乡社会养老保险人数2561.2万；595.2万60岁以下参保重度残疾人中，576.0万得到政府的参保扶助，享受代缴比例达到96.8%。298.4万非重度残疾人享受了个人缴费资助政策。1024.4万人领取养老金。

残疾人托养服务工作稳步推进，残疾人托养服务机构8435个，其中寄宿制托养服务机构2639个，日间照料机构4099个，综合性托养服务机构1697

个，为22.3万残疾人提供了托养服务。88.8万残疾人接受居家服务。2.2万名托养服务管理和服务人员接受了各级各类专业培训。

五、扶贫开发

贫困残疾人得到有效扶持，116.1万残疾人脱贫退出建档立卡；残疾人接受实用技术培训58.8万人次。

1.3万农村残疾人获得康复扶贫贴息贷款扶持。5490个残疾人扶贫基地安置7.0万残疾人就业，扶持带动13.5万户残疾人家庭。

全国共完成11.3万户农村贫困残疾人危房改造，投入资金13.7亿元。

六、宣传文化

2018年，以“全面建成小康社会，残疾人一个也不能少”为主题，组织第二十八次全国助残日活动，开展“平昌冬季残奥会”“残疾预防日”“2018年国际残疾人日”等系列宣传活动；全年组织记者采访500余人次，进行20次专题新闻发布，结合工作实际组织拍摄微视频4部。各大媒体大力宣传残疾人事业，新华社发表文章128篇，中央电视台播发新闻119条，《人民日报》发表文章71篇。“两微一端”关注、订阅人数近435万人，总阅览量约4896万人次。截至2018年底，全国共有省级残疾人专题广播节目25个、电视手语栏目31个；地市级残疾人专题广播节目205个、电视手语栏目264个。

积极为残疾人提供优秀文化产品和服务。组织开展了全国残疾人文化周等活动，推动创作话剧《但的故事》等反映改革开放40年来党和政府及社会各界对残疾人格外关心、格外关注的文艺作品。对文化进残疾人家庭“五个一”、残疾人特殊艺术人才培养基地建设等项目进行专项扶持。截至2018年底，全国省、市、县三级公共图书馆共设立盲文及盲文有声读物阅览室1124个，共开展残疾人文化周活动7931场次；全国省、市两级残联共举办残疾人文化艺术类的比赛及展览663次，共有各类残疾人艺术团283个。

七、体育

残疾人群众体育活动日益活跃，残疾人竞技体育水平不断提高。继续实施残疾人“康复体育关爱工程”和“自强健身工程”，第八届“残疾人自强健身周”、第三届“中国残疾人冰雪运动季”活动列入国家体育总局全民健身示范活动。特奥融合运动深入开展，残疾人文化体育参与率由2017年的10.9%增长至2018年的12.9%。

雪上项目在国际赛事上获得15枚金牌。在雅加达第三届亚残运会上，中国代表团获得172枚金牌、88枚银牌、59枚铜牌，奖牌总数319枚，破7项世界纪录，位列金牌及奖牌榜首位，实现了远南运动会和亚残运会“九连冠”。全年共举办38项全国残疾人体育赛事，共有5000多名运动员参赛。参加了30项国际赛事，获得了302枚金牌、161枚银牌、116枚铜牌。2022年北京冬残奥会筹办和备战工作进展顺利。2019年天津全国第十届残运会暨第七届特奥会筹办工作稳步推进，完成了9个项目提前比赛，集体项目和群体项目预赛。推动实现了2021年全国残运会与全运会、2022年亚残运会与亚运会同城同年举办，开创了我国残奥会与奥运会、亚残运会与亚运会、全国残运会与全运会全部同城同年举办的新模式。

八、维权

各级残联维权组织建设进一步加强，残疾人事业法律法规体系更加完善，无障碍环境建设取得新突破，残疾人维权工作全面开展。

2018年，制定或修改省级关于残疾人的专门法规、规章15个，地市级9个；制定或修改保障残疾人权益的省级规范性文件19个，地市级61个，县级148个。全国县级以上人大开展《中华人民共和国残疾人保障法》执法检查和专题调研294次；政协开展视察和专题调研280次。全国开展省级普法宣传教育活动309次，35835人参加；举办省级法律培训班59个，4051人参加。

截至2018年底，全国成立残疾人法律救助工作协调机构1988个，建立残疾人法律救助工作站1814个。

残疾人参政议政工作得到加强，各地残联协助人大代表、政协委员提出议案、建议、提案833件，办理议案、建议、提案1081件。

无障碍环境建设法规、标准进一步完善。全国共出台了475个省、地市、县级无障碍环境建设与管理法规、政府令和规范性文件；1702个地市、县系统开展无障碍环境建设；全国开展无障碍环境建设检查 2929 次，无障碍培训 3.7 万人次；为 115.8 万户残疾人家庭实施了无障碍改造，其中包括 16.6 万户贫困重度残疾人；为 65.1 万残疾人发放了残疾人机动轮椅车燃油补贴。

九、组织建设

2018 年，全国省市县乡（除兵团、垦区外）共成立残联 4.2 万个，各省（区、市）、市（地、州）全部建立残联；97.5%的县（市、区）、97.1%的乡镇（街道）已建立残联；94.4%的社区（村）建立残协，共 54.9 万个。

省市县乡残联工作人员达 11.1 万人，乡镇（街道）、村（社区）选聘残疾人专职委员总计 58.7 万人。全部省级残联、69.3%的地市级残联配备了残疾人领导干部，49.8%的县级残联配备了残疾人干部。

全国共建立省级及以下各类残疾人专门协会 1.6 万个，其中省级各类专门协会已建比例为 100%，市级为 96.8%，县级为 92.4%。全国助残社会组织 2562 个。

十、服务设施

残疾人服务设施建设得到全面发展。截至 2018 年底，全国已竣工的各级残疾人综合服务设施 2364 个，总建设规模 578.3 万平方米，总投资 176.9 亿元；已竣工各级残疾人康复设施 914 个，总建设规模 344.9 万平方米，总投资 111.2 亿元；已竣工的各级残疾人托养服务设施 791 个，总建设规模 214.8 万平方米，总投资 57.8 亿元。

十一、信息化建设

截至 2018 年底，全国 31 个省级、261 个地市级、863 个县级残联开通网站。全国残疾人人口基础数据库持证残疾人 3566.2 万人。智能化残疾人证试点成功，正式进入全面换发阶段。北京智能化残疾人证全面换发完成，20 个省区市启动第三代残疾人证的换发工作。北京和上海开展了电子证照的试点应用服务，为“互联网+残疾人服务”奠定技术基础。

Statistical Communiqué on the Development of the Work for Persons with Disabilities in 2018

In 2018, China Disabled Persons' Federation (CDPF) conscientiously studied General Secretary Xi Jinping's important statements about the cause for persons with disabilities (PWDs). To achieve the goal of "no person with disabilities should be left behind on our way to build a moderately prosperous society", CDPF, laying emphasis on empowering PWDs to win the war against poverty, strove to initiate a new stage of the development of the work for PWDs.

I. Rehabilitation

In 2018, 10,747 thousand registered PWDs and unregistered children with disabilities received basic rehabilitation services. Among them, 157 thousand were children aged between 0 and 6 years. Of the registered PWDs, 1,205 thousand had visual disabilities, 661 thousand had hearing disabilities, 75 thousand had speech disabilities, 5,923 thousand had physical disabilities, 838 thousand had intellectual disabilities, 1,508 thousand had mental disabilities, and 482 thousand had multiple disabilities. Particularly, 3,191 thousand PWDs were provided and fitted with assistive devices of various kinds.

By the end of 2018, the number of rehabilitation facilities in China reached 9,036, Among them, 1,346 provided services for persons with visual disabilities, 1,549 for persons with hearing and speech disabilities, 3,737 for persons with physical disabilities, 3,024 for persons with intellectual disabilities, 1,962 for persons with mental disabilities, 1,811 for children with autism, and 1,929 provided assistive technology-related services. Staff in those rehabilitation institutions reached 250 thousand, including 29 thousand managerial personnel, 176 thousand professional personnel, and 45 thousand other staff.

II. Education

CDPF collaborated with the Ministry of Education to guide the governments of all provinces (including municipalities directly under the central government and autonomous regions) in releasing their *Special Education Advancement Program (Phase II) for 2017-2020*. CDPF, the Ministry of Education and the National Development and Reform Commission jointly released the *Opinions on Accelerating the Development of Vocational Education of Persons with Disabilities*, and continued to carry out pilot projects for inclusive higher education of PWDs. *The Basic Vocabulary for Standard Sign Language* and the *Standard Braille Scheme* were officially released as part of the national language standards. CDPF, jointly with the Publicity Department of the CPC Central Committee, issued the *Notice on Promoting the Standard Sign Language and Standard Braille,* so as to promote the use of standard sign language and standard Braille nationwide. PWDs' right to education was better protected and special education was further improved.

The Welfare Lottery for Persons with Disabilities provided financial support to more than 17 thousand disabled children from financially difficult families for their preschool education. Other funding channels were also explored, sponsoring the pre-school education of 4,993 children with disabilities.

By the end of 2018, there were 102 high schools nationwide for special education, with a total of 7,666 students. Among them, 5,554 were deaf, 2,056 were blind, and 56 had other disabilities. There were 133 vocational schools, with 19,475 in school and 4,837 graduates. Among these graduates, 1,199 achieved vocational certificates. Throughout the country, 11,154 students with disabilities were admitted to regular higher education institutions and 1,873 entered special higher education institutions.

CDPF continued to implement the *Action Plan to Eliminate Illiteracy among Young and Middle-aged People with Disabilities during the 13th Five-Year*

Period, thanks to which 52 thousand adults with disabilities received literacy education.

III. Employment

In 2018, 367 thousand registered PWDs were newly employed, including 118 thousand in urban areas and 249 thousand in rural areas. In addition, 494 thousand PWDs received vocational training.

A total of 9,484 thousand registered PWDs were in employment, among whom 813 thousand were employed through the employment quota system of persons with disabilities, 331 thousand through concentrative placement, 714 thousand through self-employment, 131 thousand through welfare job posts, 148 thousand through supportive employment, 2,546 thousand through flexible employment (including community-aided employment and telecommuting), and 4,801 thousand through farming, husbandry and food processing.

The industry of massage by blind people grew steadily, with a continuous increase in the number of massage institutions. In 2018, 19,732 healthcare massagers and 10,160 medical massagers received professional training. The number of healthcare massage institutions reached 16,776, and medical massage institutions 1,126. As many as 953 massagers obtained elementary and 122 massagers secondary professional qualifications respectively.

IV. Social Security

By the end of 2018, 25,612 thousand PWDs in rural and urban areas were covered by the pension scheme. Of the 5,952 thousand persons with severe disabilities under the age of 60, 5,760 thousand (accounting for 96.8% of the total) received governments' subsidies in paying the pension premium. Another 2,984 thousand persons with slight or moderate disabilities were also fully or partially sponsored by the governments to join in the pension scheme. Meanwhile, 10,244 thousand PWDs received their pension.

Institutional care services for PWDs progressed steadily. By the end of 2018, the country housed 8,435 institutional care facilities, providing services to 223 thousand PWDs. Among them, 2,639 were boarding facilities, 4,099 were daycare facilities, and 1,697 provided integrated services. In addition, 888 thousand PWDs received care services at home. Throughout the year, 22 thousand managerial and professional personnel from institutional care facilities received various types of trainings.

V. Poverty Alleviation

In 2018, with effective measures, 1,161 thousand PWDs were lifted out of poverty and 588 thousand PWDs received training on practical skills and technologies.

Moreover, 13 thousand PWDs in rural areas were granted interest-subsidized loans. A total of 5,490 poverty alleviation centers provided jobs to 70 thousand PWDs and created income sources for 135 thousand households with members living with disabilities.

A total of 1.37 billion was invested to renovate dilapidated houses for 113 thousand households with PWDs.

VI. Publicity and Cultural Activities

For the 28th National Day of Helping Persons with Disabilities, a variety of activities were held under the theme of "No Person with Disabilities Will Be Left Behind on Our Way to Build a Moderately Prosperous Society". A series of disability-related events, such as the PyeongChang Winter Paralympic Games, the Disability Prevention Day, and the International Day of People with Disability were widely covered. Regarding disability affairs, more than 500 interviews were conducted by journalists, 20 pieces of featured news were released, and 4 fact-based micro-videos were produced. Disability issues were highlighted by multiple mainstream media agencies. For example, Xinhua News Agency published 128 articles, China Central Television aired 119 pieces of news, and the *People's Daily* published 71 articles pertaining to disability issues. Meanwhile, the influence of CDPF's official accounts of Sina Weibo, WeChat, and news app was increased continuously. By the end of 2018, the number of their followers and subscribers reached 4,350 thousand and the total number of visits approximated 48,960 thousand. At the provincial level, there were 25 radio programs for persons with disabilities and 31 TV programs with sign language interpretation; at the prefectural level, there were 205 radio programs for persons with disabilities and 264 TV programs with sign language interpretation.

CDPF proactively provided PWDs with good cultural products and services. Events including the National Cultural Week of Persons with Disabilities were organized. Works of literature and arts were created, including the drama *The Story of Dan* and other works that reflected the special care and concern of the Communist Party of China, the government and all walks of life for PWDs in the past 40 years of reform and opening-up. Special support was given to particular projects, such as the Five-One Project (which was designed to help persons with disabilities to "read one book, see one movie, visit one park, see one exhibition and join in one cultural event") and the program of building training bases for PWDs who were artistically talented. By the end of 2018, at the provincial-, prefectural- and county-level libraries nationwide, 1,124 reading rooms with Braille and audible reading materials were established and 7,931 activities echoing the Cultural Week of Persons with Disabilities were held. Provincial and prefectural Disabled Persons' Federation (DPFs) held 663 cultural and artistic competitions and exhibitions. Meanwhile, the number of arts groups of PWDs in the country reached 283.

VII. Sports

Fitness sports of PWDs became increasingly popular, and their performance in competitive sports kept improving. Programs such as "Rehabilitative Sports for Persons with Disabilities" and "Self-empowering Fitness Sports for Persons with Disabilities" were further implemented. The 8th Fitness Sports Week of Persons with Disabilities and the 3rd Winter Sports Season for Persons with Disabilities were identified as demonstrative public fitness programs by the General Administration of Sport of China (GASC). The Special Olympics movement went further, and the participation of PWDs in cultural and sports activities increased from 10.9% in 2017 to 12.9% in 2018.

In international snow sports, Chinese athletes won 15 gold medals. In the Third Asian Para Games held in Jakarta, Chinese athletes won a total of 319 medals, including 172 gold, 88 silver and 59 bronze medals, and broke 7 world records, ranking first in the medal and gold medal table. This was China 9th consecutive championship in the Far East and South Pacific Games for the Disabled (FESPIC) and Asian Para Games. A total of 38 national sports events for persons with disabilities were organized, with over 5,000 participating athletes. Chinese athletes took part in 30 international sports games, won 302 gold, 161 silver and 116 bronze medals. The preparation for the 2022 Paralympic Winter Games went well. The preparation for the 10th National Games for Persons with Disabilities and the 7th Special Olympic Games in Tianjin was steadily advanced, with 9 events already held, as well as the preliminary contests of group sports and grassroot sports. It was settled that the China National Games for Persons with Disabilities will be held in the same city as the China National Games in 2021, and that the Asian Para Games in the same city as the Asian Games in 2022, initiating a new model of hosting Paralympic Games, Asian Para Games, and National Games for Persons with Disabilities in the same city and the same year as their counterpart sport events.

VIII. Rights Protection

DPFs at various levels continued to strengthen the rights protection of persons with disabilities. The legal and regulatory system regarding disability affairs was further improved, new achievements were made in building accessible environments, and the work on rights protection of PWDs was carried out in an all-round way.

In 2018, 15 provincial- and 9 prefectural-level disability-specific laws and regulations were formulated or amended; 19 provincial-, 61 prefectural- and 148 county-level normative documents on rights protection of PWDs were formulated or amended. The People's Congress at and above the county level carried out 294 inspections and researches on the enforcement of the Law on Protection of Persons with Disabilities. The Political Consultative Conference at all levels carried out 280 inspections and researches on disability issues. Moreover, 309 events were held at the provincial level to publicize disability-related laws and regulations, attracting 35,835 participants, while 59 legal training sessions were organized at the provincial level and joined by 4,051 audiences.

By the end of 2018, 1,988 coordinating agencies were established to render legal assistance to PWDs, and 1,814 legal assistance stations were set up.

PWDs took a stronger part in political affairs. With assistance from DPFs, members of the People's Congress and the Political Consultative Conferences submitted 833 and handled 1,081 motions and proposals.

Legislation and standardization on building accessible environments were further improved. As many as 475 provincial-, prefectural- and county-level rules, regulations, government decrees and guidelines on accessibility were issued, while 1,702 cities, counties and districts were in the process of building accessible environments systematically. A total of 2,929 accessibility inspections were carried out, and 37 thousand persons received trainings on accessibility. The homes of 1,158 thousand households with PWDs were renovated to improve their accessibility, of which 166 thousand were financially difficult families with severely disabled members. Meanwhile, 651 thousand PWDs received subsidies to fuel their motorized wheelchairs.

IX. Organizational Building

By the end of 2018, there were as many as 42 thousand DPFs at provincial, prefectural, county and township levels (excluding DPFs in production and construction corps and reclamation areas). All provinces, prefectures and cities had DPFs; 97.5% counties (and districts) and 97.1% townships (sub-districts) had DPFs; 94.4% communities (and villages) had disabled persons' associations, amounting to 549 thousand.

There were about 111 thousand staff in provincial-, prefectural-, county- or township-level DPFs, while 587 thousand people were designated as disability commissioners in townships, sub-districts, villages and communities. All provincial and 69.3% prefectural DPFs had leading members with disabilities and 49.8% of the county-level DPFs had members with disabilities playing an important role.

There were 16 thousand specialized disability associations at the provincial level and below. All provinces, 96.8% cities and prefectures, and 92.4% counties established their local specialized disability associations. Meanwhile, there were 2,562 social organizations nationwide dedicated to helping persons with disabilities.

X. Service Facilities for PWDs

Service facilities for PWDs saw extensive development. By the end of 2018, there were 2,364 comprehensive service facilities for persons with disabilities at different administrative levels, with a construction area of 5,783 thousand square meters and an investment of RMB17.69 billion in total. There were 914 rehabilitation facilities, with a construction area of 3,449 thousand square meters and an investment of RMB11.12 billion. And there were 791 institutional care facilities, with a construction area of 2,148 thousand square meters and an investment of RMB5.78 billion.

XI. Application of Information Technology

By the end of 2018, 31 provincial-level, 261 prefectural-level and 863 county-level DPFs had launched their websites. The National Basic Database of Disabled Population covered 356,62 thousand registered PWDs. Following successful pilot projects, intelligent disability certificates were being distributed on a nationwide scale. Beijing already replaced all traditional disability certificates with the intelligent version, while over 20 other provinces, provincial-level municipalities and autonomous regions were carrying out the replacement. In addition, Beijing and Shanghai ran pilot projects on electronic disability certificates, laying a technical foundation for the application of "Internet+ Services" for PWDs

3

综合统计资料

Overall Statistics

3-1 中国残疾人事业主要业务进展情况 (2014－2018)

指 标 名 称		Item	
康 复		**Rehabilitation**	
1. 残疾人精准康复服务		**Provision of Targeted Rehabilitation Service**	
视力残疾人	(万人)	Visual Disability	(10,000 persons)
听力残疾人	(万人)	Hearing Disability	(10,000 persons)
言语残疾人	(万人)	Speech Disability	(10,000 persons)
肢体残疾人	(万人)	Physical Disability	(10,000 persons)
智力残疾人	(万人)	Intellectual Disability	(10,000 persons)
精神残疾人	(万人)	Mental Disability	(10,000 persons)
多重残疾人	(万人)	Multiple Disabilities	(10,000 persons)
2. 残疾人辅助器具供应服务		**Provision of Assistive Devices**	
辅助器具供应	(万人)	Assistive Devices Provided	(10,000 persons)
3. 康复机构建设		**Construction of Rehabilitation Institution**	
残疾人康复机构	(个)	Rehabilitation Institutions for PWDs	(unit)
康复机构在岗人员	(万人)	Staff of Rehabilitation Institutions	(10,000 persons)
4. 社区康复		**Community-Based Rehabilitation (CBR)**	
开展社区康复服务的县(市、区)*	(个)	Counties and Districts Providing CBR	(unit)
社区康复协调员	(万人)	CBR Coordinators	(10,000 persons)
教 育		**Education**	
1. 学前教育		**Pre-school Education**	
残疾人事业专项彩票公益金助学项目资助	(人)	Students Supported by Educational Projects Funded by Welfare Lottery Fund for PWDs	(person)
其他残疾儿童学前教育助学项目资助	(人)	Students supported by Other Pre-School Educational Projects for Disabled Children	(person)
2. 残疾人高级中等教育		**Senior Secondary Education for PWDs**	
特教普通高中	(个)	Special Education Senior High Schools	(unit)
特教普通高中在校学生	(人)	Students in Special Education Senior High Schools	(person)
中等职业教育机构	(个)	Secondary Vocational Schools	(unit)
中等职业教育在校学生	(人)	Students in Secondary Vocational Schools	(person)
3. 残疾人高等教育		**Higher Education for PWDs**	
高等特殊教育院校	(个)	Special Higher Education Institutions	(unit)
高等特殊教育院校录取残疾考生	(人)	Disable Students Admitted to Special Higher Education Institutions	(person)
普通高等院校录取残疾考生	(人)	Disable Students Admitted to Regular Higher Education Institutions	(person)
4. 扫盲教育	(人)	**Anti-Illiteracy Education**	**(person)**

注：*"开展社区康复服务的县(市、区)"包含正式行政区划单位和开发区、管委会等非正式行政区划，以及新疆兵团、黑龙江垦区下属县级单位。

Counties (cities and districts) providing community rehabilitation service include formal administrative divisions and development zones, informal administrative divisions such as management committees, and county-level units subordinate to the Xinjiang Production and Construction Corps and Heilongjiang Reclamation Area.

Summary on the Development of the Work for Persons with Disabilities (2014－2018)

2014-2018年完成情况 Implementation (2014-2018)				
2014	2015	2016	2017	2018
-	-	40.0	88.3	120.5
-	-	18.5	40.7	66.1
-	-	-	4.3	7.5
-	-	135.7	484.6	592.3
-	-	23.1	71.3	83.8
-	-	62.6	125.9	150.8
-	-	-	35.5	48.2
-	-	132.2	244.4	319.1
6914	7111	7858	8334	9036
23.4	23.2	22.3	24.6	25.0
2937	2956	2962	2988	2750
39.2	40.6	45.4	47.9	47.8
11528	12127	14412	18685	17216
2908	1767	2607	2971	4993
187	109	111	112	102
7227	7488	7686	8466	7666
197	100	118	132	133
11671	8134	11209	12968	19475
18	20	21	21	23
1678	1678	1942	1845	1873
7864	8508	9592	10818	11154
-	-	43408	42782	52462

3-1 续表 1

指 标 名 称		Item	
就 业		**Employment**	
1. 城乡持证残疾人就业状况		**Employment of PWDs in Urban and Rural Areas**	
按比例就业	(万人)	Employed through Quoto Scheme	(10,000 persons)
集中就业	(万人)	Employed through PWDs-Oriented Post	(10,000 persons)
个体就业	(万人)	Self-Employed	(10,000 persons)
公益性岗位就业	(万人)	Employed through Welfare Post	(10,000 persons)
辅助性就业	(万人)	Assistive Employment	(10,000 persons)
灵活就业(含社区就业、居家就业)	(万人)	Flexible Employment	(10,000 persons)
从事农业种养加	(万人)	Engaged in Agricultural Planting, Husbandry and Processing	(10,000 persons)
2. 盲人按摩		**Massage by the Blind**	
按摩人员培训		Massage Training	
保健按摩人员	(人)	Training for Health-Care Masseurs	(person)
医疗按摩人员	(人)	Training for Therapeutical Masseurs	(person)
按摩机构		Institutions of Blind Massage	
医疗按摩机构	(个)	Therapeutical Massage Clinics	(unit)
保健按摩机构	(个)	Health-Care Massage Houses	(unit)
社会保障		**Social Security**	
1. 社会保险		**Social Insurance**	
残疾居民参加城乡社会养老保险	(万人)	PWDs Covered by Pension Scheme	(10,000 persons)
2. 托养服务		**Institutional Care Services**	
托养服务机构	(个)	Institutional Care Service Facilities	(unit)
托养残疾人	(万人)	PWDs Receiving Institutional Care Service	(10,000 persons)
扶 贫		**Poverty Alleviation**	
1. 扶贫效果		**Outcome of Poverty Alleviation**	
退出建档立卡贫困残疾户	(万户)	Families with Disabled Member Lifted Out of Poverty	(10,000 households)
退出建档立卡贫困残疾人	(万人)	Persons with Disabilities Lifted Out of Poverty	(10,000 persons)
实用技术培训	(万人次)	Training on Practical Skills and Technologies for PWDs	(10,000 person-times)
2. 残疾人扶贫资金落实情况		**Poverty Alleviation Fund for PWDs**	
贷款实际落实	(亿元)	Actual Implementation of The Loan	(100 million yuan)
项目贷款扶持贫困残疾人	(万人)	Financially Difficult Disabled Persons Supported by Loans for Project	(10,000 persons)
到户贷款扶持贫困残疾人	(万人)	Financially Difficult Disabled Persons Supported by Loans to Househdds	(10,000 persons)
3. 残疾人扶贫基地建设		**Poverty Alleviation Bases for PWDs in Rural Areas**	
残疾人扶贫基地	(个)	Poverty Alleviation Bases for PWDs	(unit)
安置残疾人就业	(万人)	PWDs Provided with Employment Opportunities	(10,000 persons)
扶持带动贫困残疾人	(万户)	Benefited PWDs with Financial Difficult	(10,000 households)
4. 农村贫困残疾人危房改造		**House Renovation for Financially Difficult PWDs in Rural Areas**	
危房改造	(万户)	Houses Renovated for PWDs	(10,000 households)
受益残疾人	(万人)	Benefited PWDs	(10,000 persons)
宣传文化		**Publicity and Cultural Activities**	
1. 宣传		**Publicity at Provincial and Municipal Level**	
省、市级广播电台残疾人专题节目	(个)	Radio Programs on Disability	(unit)

Continued 1

2014–2018年完成情况　Implementation(2014-2018)				
2014	2015	2016	2017	2018
-	-	66.9	72.7	81.3
-	-	29.3	30.2	33.1
-	-	63.9	70.6	71.4
-	-	7.9	9.0	13.1
-	-	13.9	14.4	14.8
-	-	262.9	272.6	254.6
-	-	451.2	472.5	480.1
21296	19979	18997	20796	19732
5623	5165	5267	7217	10160
1018	1025	1211	1255	1126
15609	17171	18605	19257	16776
2180.0	2229.6	2370.6	2614.7	2561.2
5917	6352	6740	7923	8435
93.2	100.5	104.2	101.1	111.1
-	-	66.4	66.4	92.4
-	-	87.8	92.5	116.1
72.6	72.7	75.6	70.6	58.8
9.4	7.6	6.6	4.1	3.1
2.4	1.2	0.9	1.2	0.7
3.7	1.6	1.4	0.9	0.7
6593	6693	7111	6692	5490
12.4	11.4	11.6	10.5	7.0
25.8	25.0	24.9	21.8	13.5
9.0	6.9	8.2	8.2	11.3
10.3	9.1	10.4	9.6	13.0
258	235	223	223	230

3-1 续表 2

指 标 名 称		Item	
省、市级电视手语栏目	(个)	TV Programmes with Sign Language	(unit)
2. 文化		**Cultural Activities at Provincial and Municipal Level**	
省、市级盲文及盲人有声读物阅览室	(个)	Reading Rooms with Braille and Audio Reading Materials	(unit)
省、市级残疾人文化周	(场次)	Cultural Week for PWDs	(session)
省、市级残疾人文化艺术类比赛及展览	(次)	Cultural or Artistic Competitions and Exhibitions for PWDs	(time)
维 权		**Rights Protection**	
1. 法规体系和政策文件		**Legal System**	
制定或修改关于残疾人的专门法规、规章	(个)	Disability-Specific Laws and Regulations Formulated or Amended	(unit)
制定或修改保障残疾人权益的规范性文件	(个)	Normative Documents on Rights of PWDs Formulated or Amended	(unit)
2. 执法检查		**Inspections on Law Enforcement**	
人大执法检查或专题调研	(次)	Inspections and Researches by People’s Congresses	(time)
政协视察或专题调研	(次)	Inspections and Researches by Political Consultative Conferences	(time)
3. 法律救助		**Legal Aid**	
残疾人法律救助工作站	(个)	Legal Assistance Stations for PWDs	(unit)
4. 参政议政		**PWDs Participating in Administration and Discussion of State Affairs**	
协助人大代表、政协委员提出议案、建议、提案	(件)	Bills, Suggestions and Proposals Submitted with Assistance of Disabled Persons' Federations	(case)
办理人大、政协交办的议案、建议、提案	(件)	Suggestions and Proposals Handled by Disabled Persons' Federations	(case)
5. 无障碍环境建设		**Accessible Environments Building**	
无障碍环境建设与管理法规、政府令	(个)	Regulations and Decrees on Accessible Environments Building and Management	(unit)
残疾人家庭无障碍改造	(万户)	Accessibility Renovation for Homes of PWDs	(10,000 households)
6. 残疾人机动轮椅车燃油补贴	(万人)	**Gas Subsidy for Motorized Wheelchairs of PWDs**	**(10,000 persons)**

Continued 2

2014–2018年完成情况　Implementation (2014-2018)				
2014	2015	2016	2017	2018
231	262	269	285	295
462	420	267	282	301
1356	1062	1002	1037	940
959	803	719	640	663
18	13	19	21	24
427	338	285	217	228
649	548	392	290	294
635	565	370	267	280
1348	1542	1670	1746	1814
1538	1406	956	753	833
1374	1238	988	993	1081
451	451	451	451	475
-	-	93.6	89.2	115.8
67.9	71.3	75.3	74.9	65.1

3-1 续表 3

指 标 名 称		Item	
组织建设		**Organizational Structure**	
1. 省市县乡残联实有人员	(万人)	**Staff of Disabled Persons' Federations at Provincial, Municipal, County and Township Level**	**(10,000 persons)**
2. 市级残联		**Disabled Persons' Federations at Municipal Level**	
配备残疾人领导干部的残联	(个)	Disabled Persons' Federations Whose Leadership Include PWDs	(unit)
残疾人干部	(人)	Staff with Disability	(person)
3. 县级残联		**Disabled Persons' Federations at County Level**	
配备残疾人干部的残联	(个)	Disabled Persons' Federations Whose Leadership Include PWDs	(unit)
残疾人干部	(人)	Staff with Disability	(person)
4. 乡级残联与村级残疾人协会		**Disabled Persons' Federations in Township (Town, Sub-distric) and Villages (Communities)**	
已建乡、镇、街道残联	(万个)	Disabled Persons' Federation Established	(10,000 units)
其中：已配专兼职理事长	(万人)	Disabled Persons' Federation with Full-Time (Part-Time) President	(10,000 persons)
已建村(社区)残疾人协会	(万个)	Associations of Disabled Persons Established in Villages (Communities)	(10,000 units)
选聘残疾人专职委员	(万人)	Full-time Commissioners for Disability Issues	(10,000 persons)
5. 省级以下各类专门协会		**Special Associations below Provincial Level**	
盲人协会	(个)	Associations of Persons with Visual Disability	(unit)
聋人协会	(个)	Associations of Persons with Hearing Disability	(unit)
肢残人协会	(个)	Associations of Persons with Physical Disability	(unit)
智力残疾人及亲友协会	(个)	Associations of Persons with Intellectual Disability and Their Relatives and Friends	(unit)
精神残疾人及亲友协会	(个)	Associations of Persons with Psychosocial Disability and Their Relatives and Friends	(unit)
智力残疾人及亲友协会和精神残疾人及亲友协会合一的协会	(个)	Joint Associations of Persons with Intellectual or Psychosocial Disability and Their Relatives and Friends	(unit)
残疾人服务设施建设		**Service Facilities for PWDs**	
1. 残疾人综合服务设施		**Comprehensive Service Facilities for PWDs**	
已竣工	(个)	Completed Projects	(unit)
总建设规模	(万平米)	Construction Area	(10,000 sq.m)
2. 残疾人康复设施		**Rehabilitation Service Facilities for PWDs**	
已竣工	(个)	Completed Projects	(unit)
总建设规模	(万平米)	Construction Area	(10,000 sq.m)
3. 残疾人托养设施		**Institutional Care Service Facilities for PWDs**	
已竣工	(个)	Completed Projects	(unit)
总建设规模	(万平米)	Construction Area	(10,000 sq.m)
信息化建设		**Application of IT**	
1. 残疾人人口基础库数据	(万人)	**Data of the National Basic Database of Persons with Disabilities**	**(10,000 persons)**
2. 省、市、县各级残联网站	(个)	**Websites at Provincial, Municipal, and County Levels**	**(unit)**

Continued 3

2014–2018年完成情况 Implementation (2014-2018)				
2014	2015	2016	2017	2018
11.5	11.1	11.3	11.3	11.1
246	244	235	229	236
433	423	409	418	429
1631	1630	1584	1572	1499
2234	2211	2180	2165	2195
4.0	4.0	4.0	4.0	3.9
2.8	2.6	2.4	2.4	2.1
59.0	58.6	58.4	58.6	54.9
60.7	61.4	61.3	59.0	58.7
3128	3120	3147	3145	3140
3113	3107	3133	3130	3121
3139	3127	3159	3155	3154
2958	2953	2986	3003	2991
2954	2951	2982	3003	2992
177	171	169	117	128
2231	2281	2294	2340	2364
460.3	491.4	504.7	533.0	578.3
613	682	762	833	914
130.0	165.7	213.4	261.4	344.9
442	500	566	649	791
101.4	115.4	129.6	161.2	214.8
2946.7	3145.7	3219.4	3404.0	3566.2
1660	1694	1634	1504	1155

3–2 全国残疾人人口基础库主要数据
Statistics of the National Basic Information Database of Persons with Disabilities

单位：人 (截止时间：2018年12月31日) (person)

地 区	Region	已办理残疾人证 Registered Persons with Disabilities	0–14岁 Aged 0-14	15–59岁 Aged 15-59	60岁及以上 Aged 60 and above
全 国	**Nationwide**	**35661962**	**1045038**	**19331278**	**15285646**
北 京	Beijing	525941	6481	242494	276966
天 津	Tianjin	337043	4217	166962	165864
河 北	Hebei	1891286	54101	1004512	832673
山 西	Shanxi	964079	22774	549474	391831
内蒙古	Inner Mongolia	819796	16028	491451	312317
辽 宁	Liaoning	1058225	17963	634157	406105
吉 林	Jilin	850639	15825	513246	321568
黑龙江	Heilongjiang	1080882	17607	694940	368335
上 海	Shanghai	564945	3202	196124	365619
江 苏	Jiangsu	1624718	39582	879861	705275
浙 江	Zhejiang	1269003	25359	617653	625991
安 徽	Anhui	1779266	51759	957736	769771
福 建	Fujian	924869	29049	446542	449278
江 西	Jiangxi	1118003	46191	687375	384437
山 东	Shandong	2263445	72957	1183336	1007152
河 南	Henan	2738316	99025	1428112	1211179
湖 北	Hubei	1534589	34370	873334	626885
湖 南	Hunan	1726675	53522	959947	713206
广 东	Guangdong	1544414	74059	860857	609498
广 西	Guangxi	1352610	49876	633857	668877
海 南	Hainan	178425	8133	107591	62701
重 庆	Chongqing	876701	27340	485888	363473
四 川	Sichuan	2750518	70628	1362984	1316906
贵 州	Guizhou	1215661	45649	688184	481828
云 南	Yunnan	1393353	45291	830043	518019
西 藏	Tibet	103004	8860	66867	27277
陕 西	Shaanxi	1357022	23382	642661	690979
甘 肃	Gansu	783949	25549	460109	298291
青 海	Qinghai	180506	9074	112550	58882
宁 夏	Ningxia	235723	7827	131870	96026
新 疆	Xinjiang	514845	37452	346232	131161
新疆兵团	Xinjiang Corps	66401	1425	48501	16475
黑龙江垦区	Heilongjiang Land Reclamation	37110	481	25828	10801

3-2 续表 1 Continued 1

单位：人 (person)

地 区	Region	已办理证件残疾人 Registered Persons with Disabilities					
		性 别 Gender		残疾等级 Disability Grading			
		男 性 Male	女 性 Female	残疾一级 Grade-1	残疾二级 Grade-2	残疾三级 Grade-3	残疾四级 Grade-4
全 国	**Nationwide**	**20894691**	**14767271**	**4733819**	**10519444**	**9260485**	**11148214**
北 京	Beijing	283740	242201	64615	114582	130729	216015
天 津	Tianjin	187677	149366	35873	97775	99367	104028
河 北	Hebei	1108024	783262	236782	528404	418123	707977
山 西	Shanxi	594137	369942	127249	263255	236076	337499
内蒙古	Inner Mongolia	487328	332468	84021	227254	236061	272460
辽 宁	Liaoning	649599	408626	135810	305864	299674	316877
吉 林	Jilin	512359	338280	99586	265848	247511	237694
黑龙江	Heilongjiang	667255	413627	129335	302799	316944	331804
上 海	Shanghai	291305	273640	82805	109619	136775	235746
江 苏	Jiangsu	898809	725909	214404	517751	483615	408948
浙 江	Zhejiang	738679	530324	168055	254163	385308	461477
安 徽	Anhui	1006274	772992	221986	770640	426879	359761
福 建	Fujian	528574	396295	128043	283873	221754	291199
江 西	Jiangxi	682222	435781	123912	322792	302831	368468
山 东	Shandong	1359966	903479	325425	723205	573086	641729
河 南	Henan	1574420	1163896	348100	919449	713704	757063
湖 北	Hubei	904369	630220	231801	521088	364417	417283
湖 南	Hunan	1057155	669520	230513	613012	382841	500309
广 东	Guangdong	910973	633441	290519	562031	360797	331067
广 西	Guangxi	767696	584914	160066	357030	315446	520068
海 南	Hainan	104432	73993	65267	39585	38194	35379
重 庆	Chongqing	527269	349432	99306	242436	224232	310727
四 川	Sichuan	1604250	1146268	382681	787652	690108	890077
贵 州	Guizhou	748881	466780	137927	220468	307532	549734
云 南	Yunnan	828111	565242	166784	312649	326317	587603
西 藏	Tibet	53336	49668	13165	21594	26088	42157
陕 西	Shaanxi	761717	595305	156508	292469	505720	402325
甘 肃	Gansu	454682	329267	144255	214059	204553	221082
青 海	Qinghai	101738	78768	26751	69888	43405	40462
宁 夏	Ningxia	129991	105732	27854	82819	59302	65748
新 疆	Xinjiang	306534	208311	63643	147363	152700	151139
新疆兵团	Xinjiang Corps	39896	26505	6423	19531	19523	20924
黑龙江垦区	Heilongjiang Land Reclamation	23293	13817	4355	8497	10873	13385

3-2 续表 2 Continued 2

单位：人 (person)

地区	Region	已办理证件残疾人 Registered Persons with Disabilities 残疾类别 Disability Category 视力残疾人 Persons with Visual Disability	听力残疾人 Persons with Hearing Disability	言语残疾人 Persons with Speech Disability	肢体残疾人 Persons with Physical Disability	智力残疾人 Persons with Intellectual Disability
全国	**Nationwide**	**4108353**	**2883649**	**623691**	**19886774**	**3081281**
北京	Beijing	56688	38768	2938	296993	50770
天津	Tianjin	27941	23008	4186	220834	29149
河北	Hebei	175554	133541	36455	1179952	157692
山西	Shanxi	102921	85559	21351	565476	90830
内蒙古	Inner Mongolia	86359	75891	16603	478414	67670
辽宁	Liaoning	111565	84956	10963	584429	115257
吉林	Jilin	93814	74674	14230	479511	75283
黑龙江	Heilongjiang	114362	88482	13622	654274	89989
上海	Shanghai	95772	68739	5315	268027	59887
江苏	Jiangsu	194360	108682	9805	876930	205894
浙江	Zhejiang	128409	190361	17857	610919	124959
安徽	Anhui	196792	112203	30461	932562	165449
福建	Fujian	117909	120610	12609	441637	90884
江西	Jiangxi	121686	79387	17188	607123	104304
山东	Shandong	179015	141633	25315	1386839	204297
河南	Henan	262994	200771	71809	1646951	264817
湖北	Hubei	206047	109094	37590	769988	127199
湖南	Hunan	226994	106744	33483	935173	141125
广东	Guangdong	137152	127992	27510	739091	160885
广西	Guangxi	167832	104715	24503	763524	93642
海南	Hainan	17985	9702	3230	95112	16293
重庆	Chongqing	135271	58386	14876	468181	78328
四川	Sichuan	417900	224849	44145	1545219	184099
贵州	Guizhou	146922	77424	28351	762362	64624
云南	Yunnan	176350	109106	31823	806499	80243
西藏	Tibet	17373	10983	5127	52093	2978
陕西	Shaanxi	168352	142793	26705	738536	81874
甘肃	Gansu	85993	68127	12153	433120	65993
青海	Qinghai	23764	24957	4104	95710	14914
宁夏	Ningxia	30264	24659	4526	129683	19283
新疆	Xinjiang	71503	49188	13393	266907	42545
新疆兵团	Xinjiang Corps	8444	4684	851	34501	6635
黑龙江垦区	Heilongjiang Land Reclamation	4066	2981	614	20204	3490

3-2 续表 3 Continued 3

单位：人 (person)

地区	Region	已办理证件残疾人 Registered Persons with Disabilities			
		残疾类别 Disability Category		户口性质 Registered Permanent Residence	
		精神残疾人 Persons with Mental Disability	多重残疾人 Persons with Multiple Disabilities	农业 Rural	非农业 Urban
全　国	**Nationwide**	**3403156**	**1675058**	**27093961**	**8568001**
北　京	Beijing	52973	26811	204425	321516
天　津	Tianjin	25683	6242	131466	205577
河　北	Hebei	113307	94785	1623384	267902
山　西	Shanxi	60586	37356	776201	187878
内蒙古	Inner Mongolia	59278	35581	553257	266539
辽　宁	Liaoning	111151	39904	592520	465705
吉　林	Jilin	82319	30808	496416	354223
黑龙江	Heilongjiang	85132	35021	569896	510986
上　海	Shanghai	54401	12804	98019	466926
江　苏	Jiangsu	178176	50871	314075	1310643
浙　江	Zhejiang	151782	44716	1019860	249143
安　徽	Anhui	230994	110805	1505142	274124
福　建	Fujian	91503	49717	777825	147044
江　西	Jiangxi	127028	61287	899416	218587
山　东	Shandong	217007	109339	1972577	290868
河　南	Henan	206804	84170	2449528	288788
湖　北	Hubei	197728	86943	1237173	297416
湖　南	Hunan	186762	96394	1475250	251425
广　东	Guangdong	258896	92888	1155161	389253
广　西	Guangxi	124592	73802	1219728	132882
海　南	Hainan	28414	7689	133005	45420
重　庆	Chongqing	88609	33050	669113	207588
四　川	Sichuan	234877	99429	2323096	427422
贵　州	Guizhou	59973	76005	1089520	126141
云　南	Yunnan	126301	63031	1231822	161531
西　藏	Tibet	5867	8583	95125	7879
陕　西	Shaanxi	112209	86553	1153838	203184
甘　肃	Gansu	55373	63190	662672	121277
青　海	Qinghai	5641	11416	142471	38035
宁　夏	Ningxia	16287	11021	167716	68007
新　疆	Xinjiang	39795	31514	352021	162824
新疆兵团	Xinjiang Corps	8982	2304	1635	64766
黑龙江垦区	Heilongjiang Land Reclamation	4726	1029	608	36502

3-2 续表 4 Continued 4

单位：人 (person)

地区	Region	已办理证件残疾人 Registered Persons with Disabilities 受教育程度 Education 文盲 Illiterate	小学 Primary School	初中 Junior High School	高中及中专 Senior High or Vocational School	大学专科及以上 Junior College and Above	其他 Others
全国	**Nationwide**	**6629794**	**13969188**	**10727366**	**2965721**	**597332**	**772561**
北京	Beijing	58621	92031	204795	115119	48114	7261
天津	Tianjin	5232	12589	20493	9758	2856	286115
河北	Hebei	226030	767021	670578	162405	28599	36653
山西	Shanxi	125586	329407	389394	89646	18069	11977
内蒙古	Inner Mongolia	137919	281384	288371	88537	17470	6115
辽宁	Liaoning	110972	331775	471703	112459	24326	6990
吉林	Jilin	95995	274892	340059	120441	14944	4308
黑龙江	Heilongjiang	88230	369408	458303	131899	22582	10460
上海	Shanghai	49696	117529	234568	122524	40019	609
江苏	Jiangsu	531927	501170	436218	123656	31442	305
浙江	Zhejiang	269747	560905	327958	72901	21239	16253
安徽	Anhui	513206	706822	436289	85241	20130	17578
福建	Fujian	167308	445968	220021	58627	10887	22058
江西	Jiangxi	147591	480580	360795	85539	12351	31147
山东	Shandong	406909	814669	760409	213868	32857	34733
河南	Henan	721609	923439	814675	200086	29738	48769
湖北	Hubei	319122	500254	505004	170082	25577	14550
湖南	Hunan	230761	722547	548732	184446	19080	21109
广东	Guangdong	241066	640158	452177	129187	24819	57007
广西	Guangxi	167381	686485	372811	77218	11659	37056
海南	Hainan	35158	56090	64814	17497	2634	2232
重庆	Chongqing	93906	451675	246672	54927	10533	18988
四川	Sichuan	438478	1457777	668608	137768	27040	20847
贵州	Guizhou	354887	528709	262992	46400	13507	9166
云南	Yunnan	369413	661566	269206	63411	19042	10715
西藏	Tibet	59559	35985	4765	1216	627	852
陕西	Shaanxi	257886	504165	441961	122757	20726	9527
甘肃	Gansu	232148	298043	175214	61976	11929	4639
青海	Qinghai	43760	91944	28041	11490	3604	1667
宁夏	Ningxia	60991	87488	59349	18875	6558	2462
新疆	Xinjiang	61947	210927	147679	55954	19297	19041
新疆兵团	Xinjiang Corps	4781	18167	26819	11952	3679	1003
黑龙江垦区	Heilongjiang Land Reclamation	1972	7619	17893	7859	1398	369

4

分省统计资料

Provincial Statistics

一、康复
Rehabilitation

4-1-1 社区康复
Community-Based Rehabilitation(CBR)

地 区	Region	开展社区康复服务的市辖区* Districts Delivering CBR Services	开展社区康复服务的县(市)* Counties Delivering CBR Services	社区康复协调员 CBR Coordinators
		个 unit	个 unit	人 person
全 国	**Nationwide**	**1001**	**1749**	**477971**
北 京	Beijing	16		6107
天 津	Tianjin	16		3970
河 北	Hebei	47	108	44967
山 西	Shanxi	23	96	24300
内蒙古	Inner Mongolia	26	82	11473
辽 宁	Liaoning	68	42	14548
吉 林	Jilin	31	38	11149
黑龙江	Heilongjiang	70	63	6757
上 海	Shanghai	16		5138
江 苏	Jiangsu	60	36	19534
浙 江	Zhejiang	42	52	25520
安 徽	Anhui	50	59	16541
福 建	Fujian	28	58	14621
江 西	Jiangxi	31	76	13498
山 东	Shandong	62	62	45524
河 南	Henan	62	103	47172
湖 北	Hubei	38	66	10339
湖 南	Hunan	37	78	24827
广 东	Guangdong	70	53	23366
广 西	Guangxi	38	61	14696
海 南	Hainan	4	9	2089
重 庆	Chongqing	28	12	11232
四 川	Sichuan	38	106	23544
贵 州	Guizhou	9	72	9485
云 南	Yunnan	15	101	12963
西 藏	Tibet	4	10	103
陕 西	Shaanxi	28	89	14953
甘 肃	Gansu	17	69	12159
青 海	Qinghai	6	40	2378
宁 夏	Ningxia	9	13	1703
新 疆	Xinjiang	11	53	2750
新疆兵团	Xinjiang Production and Construction Corps		5	443
黑龙江垦区	Heilongjiang Land Reclamation Area	1	37	122

注：*“开展社区康复服务的县(市、区)”包含正式行政区划单位和开发区、管委会等非正式行政区划，以及新疆兵团、黑龙江垦区下属县级单位。

The data in "Counties Delivering CBR Services" covered formal administrative units and informal administrative units such as development zones, as well as county-level units under the jurisdiction of Xinjiang Production and Construction Corps and Heilongjiang Land Reclamation Area.

4-1-2 残疾人接受基本康复服务总体情况
Basic Rehabilitation Services Received by Persons with Disabilities

地 区	Region	合 计 Total	其中：0-6岁残疾儿童 Disabled Children Aged 0-6	视力残疾 Persons with Visual Disability	听力残疾 Persons with Hearing Disability	言语残疾 Persons with Speech Disability	肢体残疾 Persons with Physical Disability
		人 person	人 person	人 person	人 person	人 person	人 person
全 国	**Nationwide**	**10746860**	**157002**	**1204542**	**661447**	**75483**	**5923451**
北 京	Beijing	258653	1420	26075	18460	513	153448
天 津	Tianjin	52564	199	3436	2433	167	31865
河 北	Hebei	493290	4737	40973	26397	3198	332435
山 西	Shanxi	216779	3135	17328	9959	9	136610
内蒙古	Inner Mongolia	134165	1419	12433	11606	92	80654
辽 宁	Liaoning	252247	2466	29012	13823	1015	136266
吉 林	Jilin	216952	1915	21924	10631	525	140027
黑龙江	Heilongjiang	160552	2716	18061	7143	13	105119
上 海	Shanghai	159190	142	29016	14946	1092	75703
江 苏	Jiangsu	359064	22777	35621	13008	110	177661
浙 江	Zhejiang	662057	6222	66380	73359	5448	266104
安 徽	Anhui	813806	7601	90915	37292	5320	410208
福 建	Fujian	169167	7956	5739	9645	156	77705
江 西	Jiangxi	246463	3780	24786	10578	113	137293
山 东	Shandong	777781	15782	59190	35861	2333	497142
河 南	Henan	640899	13340	64893	31212	3553	420964
湖 北	Hubei	506081	6338	70593	35016	13571	223370
湖 南	Hunan	541524	8275	69156	23321	966	316358
广 东	Guangdong	310671	12370	16916	14478	1087	116614
广 西	Guangxi	236587	5145	25178	8799	741	134301
海 南	Hainan	61386	1231	7006	1649	100	30094
重 庆	Chongqing	212193	3389	26726	9085	380	93924
四 川	Sichuan	1706414	5275	258065	137806	27252	959341
贵 州	Guizhou	234504	3910	28262	12633	1074	148350
云 南	Yunnan	387505	3993	47600	26663	3188	205641
西 藏	Tibet	1153	28	93	152		783
陕 西	Shaanxi	396541	3556	46023	20981	407	218006
甘 肃	Gansu	267980	2706	30262	17363	398	156915
青 海	Qinghai	77398	1226	11015	9430	851	43341
宁 夏	Ningxia	102905	1511	13482	10102	1391	50237
新 疆	Xinjiang	78442	2342	7698	7131	420	41729
新疆兵团	Xinjiang Production and Construction Corps	10908	98	661	467		4606
黑龙江垦区	Heilongjiang Land Reclamation Area	1039	2	24	18		637

4-1-2 续表 Continued

地 区	Region	智力残疾 Persons with Intellectual Disability	精神残疾 Persons with Mental Disability	多重残疾 Persons with Multiple Disabilities	0-17岁未持证残疾儿 Unregistered Disabled Children Aged 0-17
		人 person	人 person	人 person	人 person
全 国	**Nationwide**	**838470**	**1507742**	**482451**	**53274**
北 京	Beijing	17496	27493	15165	3
天 津	Tianjin	5784	7139	1673	67
河 北	Hebei	31303	35558	22711	715
山 西	Shanxi	18832	25003	7890	1148
内蒙古	Inner Mongolia	7062	16218	5791	309
辽 宁	Liaoning	20378	37151	13833	769
吉 林	Jilin	13578	23649	6024	594
黑龙江	Heilongjiang	9655	15633	3557	1371
上 海	Shanghai	15353	18427	4653	
江 苏	Jiangsu	30624	76140	8084	17816
浙 江	Zhejiang	94654	126956	28018	1138
安 徽	Anhui	74533	147039	47606	893
福 建	Fujian	23150	40792	8253	3727
江 西	Jiangxi	13556	49001	10672	464
山 东	Shandong	58564	85818	37557	1316
河 南	Henan	51088	47233	16895	5061
湖 北	Hubei	39700	90024	31526	2281
湖 南	Hunan	29795	77650	20881	3397
广 东	Guangdong	23394	118183	16882	3117
广 西	Guangxi	20156	33917	11753	1742
海 南	Hainan	4780	15123	2386	248
重 庆	Chongqing	19507	53781	7685	1105
四 川	Sichuan	114225	145414	61374	2937
贵 州	Guizhou	11490	15773	16363	559
云 南	Yunnan	25561	58167	20390	295
西 藏	Tibet	13	12	100	
陕 西	Shaanxi	16875	75181	17551	1517
甘 肃	Gansu	23490	18071	21350	131
青 海	Qinghai	5627	2408	4702	24
宁 夏	Ningxia	9899	11112	6327	355
新 疆	Xinjiang	7300	9536	4453	175
新疆兵团	Xinjiang Production and Construction Corps	1038	3811	325	
黑龙江垦区	Heilongjiang Land Reclamation Area	10	329	21	

4-1-3 视力残疾基本康复服务
Basic Rehabilitation Services for Persons with Visual Disability

地 区	Region	复明手术、定向行走等训练 Sight-Restoring Surgeries and Orientation and Mobility Trainings	盲杖、助视器等辅具适配服务 Fitting of Assistive Devices such as Tactle Sticks and Visual Aids	其他 Others
		人 person	人 person	人 person
全 国	**Nationwide**	**156874**	**421629**	**736699**
北 京	Beijing	15812	13271	
天 津	Tianjin	306	1930	1332
河 北	Hebei	5907	16251	22562
山 西	Shanxi	2264	12353	3977
内蒙古	Inner Mongolia	2282	6803	4072
辽 宁	Liaoning	1647	13241	17146
吉 林	Jilin	1637	7880	14535
黑龙江	Heilongjiang	4917	13545	1283
上 海	Shanghai	20	498	32945
江 苏	Jiangsu	10096	22378	9610
浙 江	Zhejiang	2598	17713	69599
安 徽	Anhui	10843	30151	64435
福 建	Fujian	558	2814	2700
江 西	Jiangxi	2967	19924	2949
山 东	Shandong	1544	14722	43756
河 南	Henan	9598	34156	24469
湖 北	Hubei	4256	19713	44287
湖 南	Hunan	12493	46058	12808
广 东	Guangdong	2271	9432	6147
广 西	Guangxi	2397	13584	11843
海 南	Hainan	950	2509	4141
重 庆	Chongqing	2532	12466	13590
四 川	Sichuan	10119	17031	241803
贵 州	Guizhou	4745	15193	9761
云 南	Yunnan	5311	13286	31205
西 藏	Tibet	4	88	4
陕 西	Shaanxi	29853	16924	13402
甘 肃	Gansu	6346	12031	13622
青 海	Qinghai	883	4994	6520
宁 夏	Ningxia	497	6453	9093
新 疆	Xinjiang	994	3799	3057
新疆兵团	Xinjiang Production and Construction Corps	221	420	46
黑龙江垦区	Heilongjiang Land Reclamation Area	6	18	

4-1-4 听力残疾基本康复服务
Basic Rehabilitation Services for Persons with Hearing Disability

地 区	Region	人工耳蜗植入手术及服务、助听器适配 Artificial Cochlea Implant Surgeries and Fitting of Hearing Aids	听觉言语功能训练 Hearing and Speech Trainings	其他 Others
		人 person	人 person	人 person
全 国	**Nationwide**	**420172**	**12152**	**524706**
北 京	Beijing	14197	354	4422
天 津	Tianjin	1906		1028
河 北	Hebei	22453	252	23398
山 西	Shanxi	11220	240	589
内蒙古	Inner Mongolia	13146	57	621
辽 宁	Liaoning	8943	172	21288
吉 林	Jilin	5761	54	7725
黑龙江	Heilongjiang	8294	210	124
上 海	Shanghai	338		21281
江 苏	Jiangsu	11464	2391	3036
浙 江	Zhejiang	36480	623	61691
安 徽	Anhui	26622	465	42176
福 建	Fujian	10302	650	643
江 西	Jiangxi	13776	397	1121
山 东	Shandong	13302	1230	38579
河 南	Henan	31190	836	10966
湖 北	Hubei	12320	590	54960
湖 南	Hunan	30482	356	3507
广 东	Guangdong	13496	1594	4528
广 西	Guangxi	7855	272	4484
海 南	Hainan	1325	35	1174
重 庆	Chongqing	10195	129	2907
四 川	Sichuan	7421	502	166022
贵 州	Guizhou	18402	353	4431
云 南	Yunnan	21858	99	16495
西 藏	Tibet	194		
陕 西	Shaanxi	21503	80	4557
甘 肃	Gansu	26225	69	2590
青 海	Qinghai	7550	32	6482
宁 夏	Ningxia	5598	71	11218
新 疆	Xinjiang	5821	35	2637
新疆兵团	Xinjiang Production and Construction Corps	514	4	14
黑龙江垦区	Heilongjiang Land Reclamation Area	19		12

4-1-5 肢体残疾基本康复服务
Basic Rehabilitation Services for Persons with Physical Disability

地 区	Region	矫治手术、运动功能训练等 Orthopedic Surgeries and Physical Function Trainings	假肢、矫形器等辅具适配服务 Fitting of Assistive Devices such as Prosthetics and Orthotics	其他 Others
		人 person	人 person	人 person
全 国	**Nationwide**	**594737**	**2135216**	**3996738**
北 京	Beijing	6838	151818	16326
天 津	Tianjin	710	12587	20720
河 北	Hebei	67006	106408	197947
山 西	Shanxi	16737	92007	43478
内蒙古	Inner Mongolia	11427	48091	26516
辽 宁	Liaoning	12444	51179	85741
吉 林	Jilin	9616	42737	100847
黑龙江	Heilongjiang	38762	58943	18050
上 海	Shanghai	16	643	84451
江 苏	Jiangsu	23668	116557	54258
浙 江	Zhejiang	16884	72309	325317
安 徽	Anhui	40571	107393	361293
福 建	Fujian	3302	21407	62693
江 西	Jiangxi	18554	102426	22681
山 东	Shandong	22873	125630	406193
河 南	Henan	71834	181518	199028
湖 北	Hubei	16202	73294	187463
湖 南	Hunan	46016	215524	68453
广 东	Guangdong	11707	48380	76536
广 西	Guangxi	11256	58673	79609
海 南	Hainan	1117	13489	17853
重 庆	Chongqing	9382	35744	56199
四 川	Sichuan	2616	73533	913949
贵 州	Guizhou	10890	55288	93858
云 南	Yunnan	17475	51909	155867
西 藏	Tibet	23	597	219
陕 西	Shaanxi	74176	94505	142068
甘 肃	Gansu	16581	54362	98714
青 海	Qinghai	2737	17872	29220
宁 夏	Ningxia	3081	27258	31206
新 疆	Xinjiang	8376	20325	19204
新疆兵团	Xinjiang Production and Construction Corps	1800	2231	766
黑龙江垦区	Heilongjiang Land Reclamation Area	60	579	15

4-1-6 智力残疾基本康复服务
Basic Rehabilitation Services for Persons with Intellectual Disability

地区	Region	认知及适应训练 Cognitive and Adaptive Trainings	其他 Others
		人 person	人 person
全 国	**Nationwide**	**140329**	**835280**
北 京	Beijing	7292	10204
天 津	Tianjin	104	5924
河 北	Hebei	6339	29814
山 西	Shanxi	4482	16909
内蒙古	Inner Mongolia	2412	5496
辽 宁	Liaoning	2469	19672
吉 林	Jilin	863	13708
黑龙江	Heilongjiang	4089	6930
上 海	Shanghai	88	16953
江 苏	Jiangsu	14670	21364
浙 江	Zhejiang	3273	133217
安 徽	Anhui	7230	82621
福 建	Fujian	3190	23570
江 西	Jiangxi	6120	9587
山 东	Shandong	5977	56850
河 南	Henan	11151	45187
湖 北	Hubei	5894	33723
湖 南	Hunan	13048	21662
广 东	Guangdong	7470	19066
广 西	Guangxi	2696	21104
海 南	Hainan	595	4908
重 庆	Chongqing	3168	18292
四 川	Sichuan	1524	119591
贵 州	Guizhou	3168	10915
云 南	Yunnan	3005	26429
西 藏	Tibet	6	13
陕 西	Shaanxi	10462	16169
甘 肃	Gansu	5182	21752
青 海	Qinghai	748	5456
宁 夏	Ningxia	1247	11266
新 疆	Xinjiang	1703	6450
新疆兵团	Xinjiang Production and Construction Corps	658	472
黑龙江垦区	Heilongjiang Land Reclamation Area	6	6

4-1-7 精神残疾基本康复服务
Basic Rehabilitation Services for Persons with Mental Disability

地 区	Region	孤独症沟通及适应训练 Communication and Adaptive Trainings for People with Autism	药物治疗及作业疗法训练 Medical Treatments and Occupational Therapies	其他 Others
		人 person	人 person	人 person
全 国	**Nationwide**	**32855**	**804311**	**819395**
北 京	Beijing	410	16574	10509
天 津	Tianjin	65	5126	2762
河 北	Hebei	303	15684	29156
山 西	Shanxi	308	10952	16178
内蒙古	Inner Mongolia	294	10902	5624
辽 宁	Liaoning	713	19794	31020
吉 林	Jilin	459	8835	17522
黑龙江	Heilongjiang	1033	10166	6059
上 海	Shanghai		79	1879
江 苏	Jiangsu	5067	60545	17969
浙 江	Zhejiang	1126	74396	19377
安 徽	Anhui	1313	65041	110577
福 建	Fujian	2347	27544	16009
江 西	Jiangxi	939	39656	11309
山 东	Shandong	2283	37833	53865
河 南	Henan	681	20059	33127
湖 北	Hubei	652	36750	75627
湖 南	Hunan	1632	56860	23446
广 东	Guangdong	4960	91312	30770
广 西	Guangxi	391	5357	29543
海 南	Hainan	376	7178	9596
重 庆	Chongqing	457	38275	20105
四 川	Sichuan	175	43201	108927
贵 州	Guizhou	396	7211	12396
云 南	Yunnan	238	25684	38138
西 藏	Tibet		1	11
陕 西	Shaanxi	5829	49235	51737
甘 肃	Gansu	134	5618	14130
青 海	Qinghai	15	488	3749
宁 夏	Ningxia	149	5675	12611
新 疆	Xinjiang	73	4729	4986
新疆兵团	Xinjiang Production and Construction Corps	36	3317	585
黑龙江垦区	Heilongjiang Land Reclamation Area	1	234	96

4−1−8 辅助器具供应服务
Provision of Assistive Devices

地 区	Region	接受辅助器具适配服务的残疾人 Persons with Disablities Fitted with Assistive Devices	接受盲杖及助视器适配服务 Persons with Disablities Fitted with Tactile Sticks and Visual Aids	接受人工耳蜗及助听器适配服务 Persons with Disablities Fitted with Cochlears and Hearing Aids	接受假肢、矫形器、轮椅等主要肢体残疾辅助器具适配服务 Persons with Disablities Fitted with Prosthetics, Orthotics, Wheelchairs, and Other Mobility Aids	接受其他各类辅助器具适配服务 Persons with Disablities Fitted with Other Assistive Devices
		人 person	人次 person-time	人次 person-time	人次 person-time	人次 person-time
全 国	**Nationwide**	**3190814**	**198269**	**247037**	**2552322**	**745075**
北 京	Beijing	198838	13271	14197	151818	19552
天 津	Tianjin	16393	904	741	12995	2388
河 北	Hebei	153604	9701	13396	112158	23014
山 西	Shanxi	115400	7038	8573	92330	9610
内蒙古	Inner Mongolia	68002	3486	9901	48742	7732
辽 宁	Liaoning	74305	2587	3155	54373	18170
吉 林	Jilin	56234	2990	3679	44533	7609
黑龙江	Heilongjiang	80378	4823	7226	38628	29954
上 海	Shanghai	60687	3985	2647	42514	23993
江 苏	Jiangsu	149836	7531	5252.5	132194	23502
浙 江	Zhejiang	127420	6060	20255.5	75964	35757
安 徽	Anhui	164221	14090	10273	109688	36418
福 建	Fujian	34787	1030	8762	23251	3893
江 西	Jiangxi	135679	7156	5784	103354	24780
山 东	Shandong	158610	7215	7647	129963	17738
河 南	Henan	252864	15644	16207	184813	44845
湖 北	Hubei	105042	10611	7120	80818	26055
湖 南	Hunan	291970	21549	15032	213881	52232
广 东	Guangdong	71049	2591	9769	55175	13697
广 西	Guangxi	84177	6487	6239	60889	14937
海 南	Hainan	17296	632	858	13934	2921
重 庆	Chongqing	58041	6467	6720	36881	11206
四 川	Sichuan	198724	15435	6692	382566	174415
贵 州	Guizhou	89351	5623	7424	56647	23325
云 南	Yunnan	88127	4185	11415	53045	22212
西 藏	Tibet	899	55	179	774	62
陕 西	Shaanxi	139865	4918	12265	107532	27006
甘 肃	Gansu	93004	4700	12659	53692	24176
青 海	Qinghai	31136	2181	6076	19054	7012
宁 夏	Ningxia	40575	3481	3427	34248	7861
新 疆	Xinjiang	30523	1685	3228	23431	6786
新疆兵团	Xinjiang Production and Construction Corps	3161	140	210	1239	2181
黑龙江垦区	Heilongjiang Land Reclamation Area	616	18	28	1198	36

4–1–9 康复机构
Rehabilitation Institutions

地 区	Region	残疾人康复机构 Rehabilitation Institutions for Persons with Disabilities	各类康复机构 Specialized Rehabilitation Institutions		
			视力残疾康复机构 Rehabilitation Institution for Visual Disabilities	听力言语残疾康复机构 Rehabilitation Institutions for Hearing and Speech Disabilities	肢体残疾康复机构 Rehabilitation Institutions for Physical Disabilities
		个 unit	个 unit	个 unit	个 unit
全 国	**Nationwide**	**9036**	**1346**	**1549**	**3737**
北 京	Beijing	127	10	26	25
天 津	Tianjin	89	10	9	16
河 北	Hebei	431	41	97	185
山 西	Shanxi	327	48	51	164
内蒙古	Inner Mongolia	211	46	52	100
辽 宁	Liaoning	376	52	57	164
吉 林	Jilin	294	82	29	155
黑龙江	Heilongjiang	252	46	39	154
上 海	Shanghai	1071	93	58	305
江 苏	Jiangsu	435	93	83	149
浙 江	Zhejiang	206	21	41	84
安 徽	Anhui	237	12	79	86
福 建	Fujian	274	23	29	64
江 西	Jiangxi	210	15	46	65
山 东	Shandong	564	46	75	247
河 南	Henan	385	40	108	183
湖 北	Hubei	214	18	34	67
湖 南	Hunan	401	55	75	105
广 东	Guangdong	733	115	127	302
广 西	Guangxi	363	79	51	211
海 南	Hainan	34	5	4	15
重 庆	Chongqing	265	71	62	91
四 川	Sichuan	278	51	65	131
贵 州	Guizhou	194	45	48	62
云 南	Yunnan	257	47	52	78
西 藏	Tibet	6	1	1	4
陕 西	Shaanxi	358	74	49	246
甘 肃	Gansu	129	39	39	64
青 海	Qinghai	31	9	11	20
宁 夏	Ningxia	30	8	7	22
新 疆	Xinjiang	148	34	27	89
新疆兵团	Xinjiang Production and Construction Corps	35	17	17	30
黑龙江垦区	Heilongjiang Land Reclamation Area	71		1	54

4-1-9 续表 Continued

地 区	Region	各类康复机构 Specialized Rehabilitation Institutions			
		智力残疾康复机构 Rehabilitation Institutions for Intellectual Disabilities	精神残疾康复机构 Rehabilitation Institutions for Mental Disabilities	孤独症儿童康复机构 Rehabilitation Institutions for Children with Autism	辅助器具服务机构 Assistive Technology Institutions Providing
		个 unit	个 unit	个 unit	个 unit
全 国	**Nationwide**	**3024**	**1962**	**1811**	**1929**
北 京	Beijing	43	20	32	8
天 津	Tianjin	19	12	36	21
河 北	Hebei	157	87	79	62
山 西	Shanxi	134	73	50	64
内蒙古	Inner Mongolia	59	26	42	66
辽 宁	Liaoning	94	79	73	115
吉 林	Jilin	93	89	43	46
黑龙江	Heilongjiang	70	24	51	24
上 海	Shanghai	318	273	61	258
江 苏	Jiangsu	127	78	111	74
浙 江	Zhejiang	96	39	85	56
安 徽	Anhui	127	10	109	42
福 建	Fujian	97	56	104	55
江 西	Jiangxi	70	58	35	35
山 东	Shandong	182	102	148	67
河 南	Henan	160	73	65	80
湖 北	Hubei	62	59	35	55
湖 南	Hunan	123	68	83	112
广 东	Guangdong	281	191	224	106
广 西	Guangxi	156	127	53	93
海 南	Hainan	8	7	12	3
重 庆	Chongqing	96	72	31	39
四 川	Sichuan	117	85	57	78
贵 州	Guizhou	54	62	31	42
云 南	Yunnan	72	61	26	101
西 藏	Tibet	3	1	2	5
陕 西	Shaanxi	72	53	42	47
甘 肃	Gansu	46	26	39	66
青 海	Qinghai	19	6	16	15
宁 夏	Ningxia	23	9	15	10
新 疆	Xinjiang	39	23	17	40
新疆兵团	Xinjiang Production and Construction Corps	7	10	4	7
黑龙江垦区	Heilongjiang Land Reclamation Area		3		37

4-1-10 康复人才
Rehabilitation Professionals

地区	Region	康复机构在岗人员 Staff in Rehabilitation Institutions	业务人员 Professionals	管理人员 Managerial Personnel	其他人员 Other Staff
		人 person	人 person	人 person	人 person
全 国	**Nationwide**	**250469**	**176471**	**29087**	**44911**
北 京	Beijing	3774	2592	534	648
天 津	Tianjin	2228	1457	230	541
河 北	Hebei	12570	8893	1611	2066
山 西	Shanxi	9784	7266	929	1589
内蒙古	Inner Mongolia	5067	3262	740	1065
辽 宁	Liaoning	9682	6829	1297	1556
吉 林	Jilin	11225	7276	1551	2398
黑龙江	Heilongjiang	6130	4448	663	1019
上 海	Shanghai	8956	4712	1306	2938
江 苏	Jiangsu	13677	9699	1513	2465
浙 江	Zhejiang	6434	4454	663	1317
安 徽	Anhui	5800	4449	645	706
福 建	Fujian	6244	4236	828	1180
江 西	Jiangxi	5982	3714	834	1434
山 东	Shandong	22291	17291	2063	2937
河 南	Henan	13729	10792	1392	1545
湖 北	Hubei	7256	4828	732	1696
湖 南	Hunan	12121	8638	1362	2121
广 东	Guangdong	24871	17706	2437	4728
广 西	Guangxi	8700	6211	1048	1441
海 南	Hainan	1065	810	122	133
重 庆	Chongqing	7415	4982	991	1442
四 川	Sichuan	10608	7157	1298	2153
贵 州	Guizhou	7014	4687	880	1447
云 南	Yunnan	6929	4826	794	1309
西 藏	Tibet	63	39	14	10
陕 西	Shaanxi	12597	9482	1398	1717
甘 肃	Gansu	3094	2162	458	474
青 海	Qinghai	405	242	73	90
宁 夏	Ningxia	567	390	89	88
新 疆	Xinjiang	2486	1737	347	402
新疆兵团	Xinjiang Production and Construction Corps	810	588	105	117
黑龙江垦区	Heilongjiang Land Reclamation Area	895	616	140	139

4-1-10 续表 1 Continued 1

地 区	Region	康复机构在岗人员 Staff in Rehabilitation Institutions			
		视力残疾康复在岗人员 Staff for Vision Rehabilitation	业务人员 Professionals	管理人员 Managerial Personnels	其他人员 Other Staff
		人 person	人 person	人 person	人 person
全 国	**Nationwide**	**21090**	**14282**	**2582**	**4226**
北 京	Beijing	93	74	16	3
天 津	Tianjin	84	62	12	10
河 北	Hebei	516	385	51	80
山 西	Shanxi	815	452	115	248
内蒙古	Inner Mongolia	818	586	130	102
辽 宁	Liaoning	1119	720	101	298
吉 林	Jilin	1620	1061	261	298
黑龙江	Heilongjiang	378	304	49	25
上 海	Shanghai	622	418	91	113
江 苏	Jiangsu	1932	1356	237	339
浙 江	Zhejiang	66	39	15	12
安 徽	Anhui	288	189	43	56
福 建	Fujian	398	181	91	126
江 西	Jiangxi	118	48	22	48
山 东	Shandong	1012	699	125	188
河 南	Henan	473	356	60	57
湖 北	Hubei	184	92	23	69
湖 南	Hunan	1854	1071	215	568
广 东	Guangdong	1664	1161	182	321
广 西	Guangxi	780	558	94	128
海 南	Hainan	102	61	15	26
重 庆	Chongqing	1123	694	166	263
四 川	Sichuan	489	309	79	101
贵 州	Guizhou	936	681	85	170
云 南	Yunnan	549	429	45	75
西 藏	Tibet	3	2	1	
陕 西	Shaanxi	2286	1778	132	376
甘 肃	Gansu	287	202	47	38
青 海	Qinghai	51	38	9	4
宁 夏	Ningxia	28	21	7	
新 疆	Xinjiang	323	209	51	63
新疆兵团	Xinjiang Production and Construction Corps	79	46	12	21
黑龙江垦区	Heilongjiang Land Reclamation Area				

4-1-10 续表 2 Continued 2

地 区	Region	康复机构在岗人员 Staff in Rehabilitation Institutions			
		听力言语康复在岗人员 Staff for Hearing and Speech Rehabilitation	业务人员 Professionals	管理人员 Managerial Personnel	其他人员 Other Staff
		人 person	人 person	人 person	人 person
全 国	**Nationwide**	**16678**	**10852**	**2206**	**3620**
北 京	Beijing	445	293	66	86
天 津	Tianjin	72	63	8	1
河 北	Hebei	1144	867	130	147
山 西	Shanxi	470	315	74	81
内蒙古	Inner Mongolia	797	182	64	551
辽 宁	Liaoning	471	255	78	138
吉 林	Jilin	486	243	81	162
黑龙江	Heilongjiang	240	158	56	26
上 海	Shanghai	337	135	64	138
江 苏	Jiangsu	1079	783	149	147
浙 江	Zhejiang	413	298	48	67
安 徽	Anhui	835	613	101	121
福 建	Fujian	325	249	34	42
江 西	Jiangxi	502	287	78	137
山 东	Shandong	1080	831	120	129
河 南	Henan	1647	1307	189	151
湖 北	Hubei	453	279	65	109
湖 南	Hunan	756	507	121	128
广 东	Guangdong	1595	864	145	586
广 西	Guangxi	404	259	65	80
海 南	Hainan	54	46	6	2
重 庆	Chongqing	444	258	82	104
四 川	Sichuan	516	383	63	70
贵 州	Guizhou	400	261	58	81
云 南	Yunnan	493	317	63	113
西 藏	Tibet	8	5	3	
陕 西	Shaanxi	485	331	84	70
甘 肃	Gansu	391	241	62	88
青 海	Qinghai	25	10	5	10
宁 夏	Ningxia	56	48	5	3
新 疆	Xinjiang	217	143	32	42
新疆兵团	Xinjiang Production and Construction Corps	37	20	7	10
黑龙江垦区	Heilongjiang Land Reclamation Area	1	1		

4-1-10 续表 3 Continued 3

地　区	Region	康复机构在岗人员 Staff in Rehabilitation Institutions			
		肢体残疾康复在岗人员 Staff for Physical Rehabilitation	业务人员 Professionals	管理人员 Managerial Personnel	其他人员 Other Staff
		人 person	人 person	人 person	人 person
全　国	**Nationwide**	**70632**	**55497**	**5992**	**9143**
北　京	Beijing	579	449	60	70
天　津	Tianjin	401	283	31	87
河　北	Hebei	3925	2976	366	583
山　西	Shanxi	3465	2865	246	354
内蒙古	Inner Mongolia	1257	1019	132	106
辽　宁	Liaoning	2450	1885	314	251
吉　林	Jilin	2397	1726	241	430
黑龙江	Heilongjiang	2293	1838	191	264
上　海	Shanghai	3485	2058	285	1142
江　苏	Jiangsu	3529	2898	263	368
浙　江	Zhejiang	2010	1474	143	393
安　徽	Anhui	1801	1583	117	101
福　建	Fujian	1200	1022	94	84
江　西	Jiangxi	729	525	99	105
山　东	Shandong	7678	6488	475	715
河　南	Henan	4482	3878	299	305
湖　北	Hubei	1557	1274	107	176
湖　南	Hunan	2495	2024	195	276
广　东	Guangdong	7182	5548	562	1072
广　西	Guangxi	2984	2353	288	343
海　南	Hainan	286	223	36	27
重　庆	Chongqing	1764	1296	182	286
四　川	Sichuan	1973	1627	181	165
贵　州	Guizhou	2189	1606	164	419
云　南	Yunnan	1457	1141	103	213
西　藏	Tibet	20	15	3	2
陕　西	Shaanxi	4771	3676	557	538
甘　肃	Gansu	744	568	76	100
青　海	Qinghai	120	70	17	33
宁　夏	Ningxia	158	117	21	20
新　疆	Xinjiang	804	643	88	73
新疆兵团	Xinjiang Production and Construction Corps	248	211	25	12
黑龙江垦区	Heilongjiang Land Reclamation Area	199	138	31	30

4-1-10 续表 4 Continued 4

地 区	Region	康复机构在岗人员 Staff in Rehabilitation Institutions			
		智力残疾康复在岗人员 Staff for Intellectual Rehabilitation	业务人员 Professionals	管理人员 Managerial Personnel	其他人员 Other Staff
		人 person	人 person	人 person	人 person
全 国	**Nationwide**	**39166**	**28572**	**4388**	**6206**
北 京	Beijing	756	534	118	104
天 津	Tianjin	343	270	31	42
河 北	Hebei	2534	1872	284	378
山 西	Shanxi	1818	1484	136	198
内蒙古	Inner Mongolia	641	515	74	52
辽 宁	Liaoning	1002	765	108	129
吉 林	Jilin	771	513	88	170
黑龙江	Heilongjiang	844	696	71	77
上 海	Shanghai	1393	474	275	644
江 苏	Jiangsu	1848	1305	192	351
浙 江	Zhejiang	1073	754	122	197
安 徽	Anhui	1310	957	154	199
福 建	Fujian	1310	839	176	295
江 西	Jiangxi	1133	766	162	205
山 东	Shandong	3462	2691	291	480
河 南	Henan	3095	2591	291	213
湖 北	Hubei	1206	863	116	227
湖 南	Hunan	1833	1377	218	238
广 东	Guangdong	3541	2592	351	598
广 西	Guangxi	1455	973	196	286
海 南	Hainan	190	169	8	13
重 庆	Chongqing	1014	717	145	152
四 川	Sichuan	1899	1292	242	365
贵 州	Guizhou	762	560	84	118
云 南	Yunnan	1186	840	150	196
西 藏	Tibet	5	3	1	1
陕 西	Shaanxi	1334	1098	129	107
甘 肃	Gansu	593	470	74	49
青 海	Qinghai	104	62	15	27
宁 夏	Ningxia	126	88	16	22
新 疆	Xinjiang	394	289	54	51
新疆兵团	Xinjiang Production and Construction Corps	191	153	16	22
黑龙江垦区	Heilongjiang Land Reclamation Area				

4-1-10 续表 5 Continued 5

地 区	Region	康复机构在岗人员 Staff in Rehabilitation Institutions			
		精神残疾康复在岗人员 Staff for Mental Rehabilitation	业务人员 Professionals	管理人员 Managerial Personnel	其他人员 Other Staff
		人 person	人 person	人 person	人 person
全 国	**Nationwide**	**72688**	**48218**	**8695**	**15775**
北 京	Beijing	1338	844	171	323
天 津	Tianjin	736	389	52	295
河 北	Hebei	3225	2025	568	632
山 西	Shanxi	2583	1816	202	565
内蒙古	Inner Mongolia	1012	664	197	151
辽 宁	Liaoning	3276	2455	442	379
吉 林	Jilin	5281	3294	774	1213
黑龙江	Heilongjiang	1709	966	206	537
上 海	Shanghai	1853	1175	287	391
江 苏	Jiangsu	3231	1949	352	930
浙 江	Zhejiang	1693	1112	150	431
安 徽	Anhui	245	193	22	30
福 建	Fujian	1334	882	183	269
江 西	Jiangxi	3040	1808	369	863
山 东	Shandong	6205	4588	662	955
河 南	Henan	2689	1771	337	581
湖 北	Hubei	3056	1876	300	880
湖 南	Hunan	3888	2824	362	702
广 东	Guangdong	6573	4628	605	1340
广 西	Guangxi	2192	1544	249	399
海 南	Hainan	128	100	15	13
重 庆	Chongqing	2475	1679	291	505
四 川	Sichuan	5034	3140	555	1339
贵 州	Guizhou	2202	1280	379	543
云 南	Yunnan	2750	1825	302	623
西 藏	Tibet	1			1
陕 西	Shaanxi	2979	2057	374	548
甘 肃	Gansu	503	350	74	79
青 海	Qinghai	8	3	4	1
宁 夏	Ningxia	114	65	23	26
新 疆	Xinjiang	476	312	63	101
新疆兵团	Xinjiang Production and Construction Corps	217	144	34	39
黑龙江垦区	Heilongjiang Land Reclamation Area	642	460	91	91

4-1-10 续表 6 Continued 6

地 区	Region	康复机构在岗人员 Staff in Rehabilitation Institutions			
		孤独症儿童康复在岗人员 Staff for Rehabilitation of Children with Autism	业务人员 Professionals	管理人员 Managerial Personnel	其他人员 Other Staff
		人 person	人 person	人 person	人 person
全 国	**Nationwide**	**22243**	**15513**	**3038**	**3692**
北 京	Beijing	503	358	91	54
天 津	Tianjin	512	354	65	93
河 北	Hebei	969	665	145	159
山 西	Shanxi	387	233	83	71
内蒙古	Inner Mongolia	320	233	52	35
辽 宁	Liaoning	823	538	120	165
吉 林	Jilin	439	315	51	73
黑龙江	Heilongjiang	587	450	70	67
上 海	Shanghai	351	197	74	80
江 苏	Jiangsu	1538	1113	211	214
浙 江	Zhejiang	1009	713	130	166
安 徽	Anhui	1182	852	170	160
福 建	Fujian	1480	944	199	337
江 西	Jiangxi	335	235	64	36
山 东	Shandong	2462	1766	308	388
河 南	Henan	718	501	101	116
湖 北	Hubei	633	371	66	196
湖 南	Hunan	878	647	118	113
广 东	Guangdong	3771	2672	443	656
广 西	Guangxi	558	422	77	59
海 南	Hainan	289	199	39	51
重 庆	Chongqing	398	260	57	81
四 川	Sichuan	354	241	69	44
贵 州	Guizhou	409	269	52	88
云 南	Yunnan	171	133	23	15
西 藏	Tibet	3	1	1	1
陕 西	Shaanxi	454	361	49	44
甘 肃	Gansu	388	270	57	61
青 海	Qinghai	68	45	12	11
宁 夏	Ningxia	61	42	7	12
新 疆	Xinjiang	165	101	26	38
新疆兵团	Xinjiang Production and Construction Corps	28	12	8	8
黑龙江垦区	Heilongjiang Land Reclamation Area				

4-1-10 续表 7 Continued 7

地 区	Region	康复机构在岗人员 Staff in Rehabilitation Institutions				培训康复管理人员 Rehabilitation Managerial Staff Trained	培训康复业务人员 Rehabilitation Professionals Trained
		辅助器具残疾康复在岗人员 Staff for Rehabilition with Assistive Devices	业务人员 Professionals	管理人员 Managerial Personnel	其他人员 Other Staff		
		人 person	人 person	人 person	人 person	人次 person-time	人次 person-time
全 国	**Nationwide**	**7972**	**3537**	**2186**	**2249**	**65205**	**282580**
北 京	Beijing	60	40	12	8	1065	8540
天 津	Tianjin	80	36	31	13	375	1516
河 北	Hebei	257	103	67	87	1618	5302
山 西	Shanxi	246	101	73	72	1094	9102
内蒙古	Inner Mongolia	222	63	91	68	2724	2324
辽 宁	Liaoning	541	211	134	196	3025	15203
吉 林	Jilin	231	124	55	52	4928	9779
黑龙江	Heilongjiang	79	36	20	23	616	4195
上 海	Shanghai	915	255	230	430	2653	15375
江 苏	Jiangsu	520	295	109	116	4484	20042
浙 江	Zhejiang	170	64	55	51	1794	13208
安 徽	Anhui	139	62	38	39	1412	4366
福 建	Fujian	197	119	51	27	1318	5260
江 西	Jiangxi	125	45	40	40	837	2530
山 东	Shandong	392	228	82	82	5042	28412
河 南	Henan	625	388	115	122	3805	29328
湖 北	Hubei	167	73	55	39	1968	12230
湖 南	Hunan	417	188	133	96	2185	7676
广 东	Guangdong	545	241	149	155	5538	34548
广 西	Guangxi	327	102	79	146	1453	4727
海 南	Hainan	16	12	3	1	161	604
重 庆	Chongqing	197	78	68	51	1108	5729
四 川	Sichuan	343	165	109	69	8056	16095
贵 州	Guizhou	116	30	58	28	2478	3944
云 南	Yunnan	323	141	108	74	1765	5834
西 藏	Tibet	23	13	5	5	17	30
陕 西	Shaanxi	288	181	73	34	2187	9603
甘 肃	Gansu	188	61	68	59	560	2047
青 海	Qinghai	29	14	11	4	178	330
宁 夏	Ningxia	24	9	10	5	209	1412
新 疆	Xinjiang	107	40	33	34	349	2442
新疆兵团	Xinjiang Production and Construction Corps	10	2	3	5	111	695
黑龙江垦区	Heilongjiang Land Reclamation Area	53	17	18	18	92	152

二、教育
Education

4-2-1 学前教育阶段
Pre-School Education

地区	Region	残疾人事业专项彩票公益金助学项目资助 Students Supported by Educational Projects Funded by Welfare Lottery Fund for PWDs	视力残疾 Children with Visual Disability	听力残疾 Children with Hearing Disability	言语残疾 Children with Speech Disability	肢体残疾 Children with Physical Disability
		人 person	人 person	人 person	人 person	人 person
全国	**Nationwide**	**17216**	**332**	**3225**	**830**	**3234**
北京	Beijing	6				
天津	Tianjin					
河北	Hebei	914	6	169	33	47
山西	Shanxi	793	4	206	35	104
内蒙古	Inner Mongolia	214	5	31	14	75
辽宁	Liaoning	1082	10	169	52	128
吉林	Jilin	204		1	2	30
黑龙江	Heilongjiang	326		40	2	16
上海	Shanghai					
江苏	Jiangsu	586	31	109	19	132
浙江	Zhejiang	433	12	117	7	74
安徽	Anhui	871	18	236	19	174
福建	Fujian	420	18	78	23	119
江西	Jiangxi	525	3	94	12	53
山东	Shandong	957	7	192	19	219
河南	Henan	1536	32	314	89	325
湖北	Hubei	682	10	104	59	92
湖南	Hunan	995	7	150	66	113
广东	Guangdong	1255	23	191	78	316
广西	Guangxi	1266	10	290	61	123
海南	Hainan	368	9	63	13	74
重庆	Chongqing	373	6	43	34	46
四川	Sichuan	311	7	59	17	49
贵州	Guizhou	584	31	66	51	202
云南	Yunnan	465	18	107	35	104
西藏	Tibet	102	11	11	16	31
陕西	Shaanxi	131	1	28	5	32
甘肃	Gansu	1137	28	202	44	350
青海	Qinghai	205	8	46	8	80
宁夏	Ningxia	250	11	33	8	90
新疆	Xinjiang	180	3	65	7	23
新疆兵团	Xinjiang Production and Construction Corps	45	3	11	2	13
黑龙江垦区	Heilongjiang Land Reclamation Area					

4-2-1 续表 Continued

地 区	Region	智力残疾 Chidren with Intellectual Disability	精神残疾 Children with Mental Disability	多重残疾 Children with Multiple Disabilities	其他残疾儿童学前教育助学项目资助 Students Supported by Other Pre-School Educational Projects for Disabled Children
		人 person	人 person	人 person	人 person
全 国	**Nationwide**	**5395**	**1723**	**2477**	**4993**
北 京	Beijing	3		3	315
天 津	Tianjin				85
河 北	Hebei	372	136	151	2
山 西	Shanxi	255	52	137	10
内蒙古	Inner Mongolia	44	27	18	64
辽 宁	Liaoning	310	282	131	12
吉 林	Jilin	69	81	21	16
黑龙江	Heilongjiang	115	117	36	
上 海	Shanghai				
江 苏	Jiangsu	157	76	62	401
浙 江	Zhejiang	137	35	51	326
安 徽	Anhui	222	95	107	144
福 建	Fujian	122	18	42	274
江 西	Jiangxi	202	69	92	1287
山 东	Shandong	279	95	146	198
河 南	Henan	545	65	166	15
湖 北	Hubei	279	63	75	43
湖 南	Hunan	459	68	132	3
广 东	Guangdong	327	122	198	552
广 西	Guangxi	451	84	247	31
海 南	Hainan	101	79	29	11
重 庆	Chongqing	185	15	44	46
四 川	Sichuan	108	12	59	690
贵 州	Guizhou	92	46	96	14
云 南	Yunnan	125	8	68	4
西 藏	Tibet	8	2	23	4
陕 西	Shaanxi	38	8	19	118
甘 肃	Gansu	208	48	257	182
青 海	Qinghai	51		12	6
宁 夏	Ningxia	69	16	23	34
新 疆	Xinjiang	50	2	30	92
新疆兵团	Xinjiang Production and Construction Corps	12	2	2	14
黑龙江垦区	Heilongjiang Land Reclamation Area				

4-2-2 高中教育阶段
Senior High Education

地 区	Region	特殊教育普通高中学校(班) Special Education Senior High Schools/Classes				学生 Students		
			盲普通高中 Senior High Schools for Blind Students	聋普通高中 Senior High Schools for Deaf Students	其他 Others	招生 Newly Enrolled Students with Disabilities	盲 Students with Visual Disability	聋 Students with Hearing Disability
		个 unit	个 unit	个 unit	个 unit	人 person	人 person	人 person
全 国	**Nationwide**	**102**	**14**	**75**	**13**	**2274**	**575**	**1699**
北 京	Beijing	2	1	1		36	11	25
天 津	Tianjin	2	1	1		32	10	22
河 北	Hebei	10	1	6	3	364	45	319
山 西	Shanxi	7	1	5	1	99	15	84
内蒙古	Inner Mongolia	6	2	4		58		58
辽 宁	Liaoning	5		5		20		20
吉 林	Jilin	5		5		40		40
黑龙江	Heilongjiang	1		1		25		25
上 海	Shanghai	1	1			5	5	
江 苏	Jiangsu	4		2	2	147	7	140
浙 江	Zhejiang	6	1	5		93	47	46
安 徽	Anhui	1		1				
福 建	Fujian	4		3	1	85	9	76
江 西	Jiangxi	2		1	1	32		32
山 东	Shandong	5	1	3	1	156	60	96
河 南	Henan	4		3	1	28		28
湖 北	Hubei	6	1	5		63		63
湖 南	Hunan	3		3		40		40
广 东	Guangdong	6	1	4	1	154	16	138
广 西	Guangxi	2		2		49		49
海 南	Hainan	1		1				
重 庆	Chongqing	2	1	1		59	59	
四 川	Sichuan	3		2	1	212	50	162
贵 州	Guizhou	6	1	5		303	165	138
云 南	Yunnan							
西 藏	Tibet							
陕 西	Shaanxi	3		3		42		42
甘 肃	Gansu	2		2		6		6
青 海	Qinghai	1	1			56	56	
宁 夏	Ningxia	1			1	70	20	50
新 疆	Xinjiang	1		1				
新疆兵团	Xinjiang Production and Construction Corps							
黑龙江垦区	Heilongjiang Land Reclamation Area							

4-2-2 续表 1 Continued 1

地 区	Region	学生 Students					
		在校生 Students in School	盲 Students with Visual Disability	聋 Students with Hearing Disability	毕业生 Graduates	盲 Students with Visual Disability	聋 Students with Hearing Disability
		人 person	人 person	人 person	人 person	人 person	人 person
全 国	**Nationwide**	**7666**	**2056**	**5554**	**1563**	**364**	**1199**
北 京	Beijing	287	89	198	65	30	35
天 津	Tianjin	105	31	74	43	11	32
河 北	Hebei	804	185	578	149	51	98
山 西	Shanxi	588	59	529	112	11	101
内蒙古	Inner Mongolia	329		329	3		3
辽 宁	Liaoning	74		74	12		12
吉 林	Jilin	227		227	57		57
黑龙江	Heilongjiang	25		25			
上 海	Shanghai	172	172		8	8	
江 苏	Jiangsu	588	23	550	143		143
浙 江	Zhejiang	370	283	87	193	30	163
安 徽	Anhui	10		10			
福 建	Fujian	144	22	122	80	8	72
江 西	Jiangxi	355	29	326	27		27
山 东	Shandong	658	319	339	179	103	76
河 南	Henan	268	66	202	23	5	18
湖 北	Hubei	170		170	5		5
湖 南	Hunan	120		120	45		45
广 东	Guangdong	444	49	395	162	15	147
广 西	Guangxi	91		91	1		1
海 南	Hainan						
重 庆	Chongqing	285	285		51	51	
四 川	Sichuan	79		79	13		13
贵 州	Guizhou	718	165	553	110		110
云 南	Yunnan						
西 藏	Tibet						
陕 西	Shaanxi	274		274	18		18
甘 肃	Gansu	18		18	7		7
青 海	Qinghai	179	179		35	35	
宁 夏	Ningxia	284	100	184	22	6	16
新 疆	Xinjiang						
新疆兵团	Xinjiang Production and Construction Corps						
黑龙江垦区	Heilongjiang Land Reclamation Area						

4-2-2 续表 2 Continued 2

地 区	Region	残疾人中等职业学校(班) Secondary Vocational Schools/Classes for PWDs	教育部门办 Supervised by Educational Departments	残联部门办 Supervised by Disabled Persons' Federations	其他 Others
		个 unit	个 unit	个 unit	个 unit
全 国	**Nationwide**	**133**	**118**	**11**	**4**
北 京	Beijing	3	3		
天 津	Tianjin				
河 北	Hebei	4	3		1
山 西	Shanxi	2	2		
内蒙古	Inner Mongolia	2	1	1	
辽 宁	Liaoning	6	6		
吉 林	Jilin	3	2	1	
黑龙江	Heilongjiang	5	5		
上 海	Shanghai	17	16		1
江 苏	Jiangsu	11	10	1	
浙 江	Zhejiang	12	12		
安 徽	Anhui	4	3	1	
福 建	Fujian	7	7		
江 西	Jiangxi	5	4		1
山 东	Shandong	5	4	1	
河 南	Henan	7	7		
湖 北	Hubei	5	5		
湖 南	Hunan	6	5	1	
广 东	Guangdong	11	9	2	
广 西	Guangxi				
海 南	Hainan				
重 庆	Chongqing	1	1		
四 川	Sichuan	2	2		
贵 州	Guizhou	1		1	
云 南	Yunnan	4	4		
西 藏	Tibet				
陕 西	Shaanxi	3	2	1	
甘 肃	Gansu	4	3		1
青 海	Qinghai	1	1		
宁 夏	Ningxia				
新 疆	Xinjiang	2	1	1	
新疆兵团	Xinjiang Production and Construction Corps				
黑龙江垦区	Heilongjiang Land Reclamation Area				

4-2-2 续表 3 Continued 3

地 区	Region	残疾人中等职业学校(班)学生 Students of Secondary Vocational Schools/Classes for PWDs			
		招生 Newly Enrolled Students	盲 Students with Visual Disability	聋 Students with Hearing Disability	肢残 Students with Physical Disability
		人 person	人 person	人 person	人 person
全 国	**Nationwide**	**7010**	**1496**	**2096**	**1251**
北 京	Beijing	77		16	
天 津	Tianjin				
河 北	Hebei	200	36	18	22
山 西	Shanxi	25		25	
内蒙古	Inner Mongolia	21	21		
辽 宁	Liaoning	92	36	28	
吉 林	Jilin	274	19	112	64
黑龙江	Heilongjiang	71	22	35	1
上 海	Shanghai	249	5	19	12
江 苏	Jiangsu	398	113	105	34
浙 江	Zhejiang	149		15	8
安 徽	Anhui	461	130	164	110
福 建	Fujian	53	5	18	
江 西	Jiangxi	377	38	77	
山 东	Shandong	182	81	33	48
河 南	Henan	227	66	127	
湖 北	Hubei	1354	340	548	401
湖 南	Hunan	455	139	131	100
广 东	Guangdong	498	85	139	71
广 西	Guangxi				
海 南	Hainan				
重 庆	Chongqing	32		32	
四 川	Sichuan	29	11	7	
贵 州	Guizhou	128	60	50	18
云 南	Yunnan	850	123	166	108
西 藏	Tibet				
陕 西	Shaanxi	437	104	76	175
甘 肃	Gansu	113	9	58	18
青 海	Qinghai	118	40	48	
宁 夏	Ningxia				
新 疆	Xinjiang	140	13	49	61
新疆兵团	Xinjiang Production and Construction Corps				
黑龙江垦区	Heilongjiang Land Reclamation Area				

4-2-2 续表 4 Continued 4

地 区	Region	残疾人中等职业学校(班)学生 Students of Secondary Vocational Schools/classes for PWDs			
		在校学生 Students in Schools	盲 Students with Visual Disability	聋 Students with Hearing Disability	肢残 Students with Physical Disability
		人 person	人 person	人 person	人 person
全 国	**Nationwide**	**19475**	**3914**	**7176**	**3012**
北 京	Beijing	340		85	
天 津	Tianjin				
河 北	Hebei	376	82	102	35
山 西	Shanxi	163	6	80	3
内蒙古	Inner Mongolia	65	65		
辽 宁	Liaoning	444	182	151	2
吉 林	Jilin	567	22	272	92
黑龙江	Heilongjiang	210	64	106	1
上 海	Shanghai	515	161	80	16
江 苏	Jiangsu	1544	326	747	101
浙 江	Zhejiang	458		66	10
安 徽	Anhui	1572	252	652	345
福 建	Fujian	213	12	57	
江 西	Jiangxi	715	130	105	
山 东	Shandong	392	169	120	37
河 南	Henan	305	103	168	
湖 北	Hubei	4673	1078	2135	1159
湖 南	Hunan	1414	262	457	231
广 东	Guangdong	1307	261	332	211
广 西	Guangxi				
海 南	Hainan				
重 庆	Chongqing	251		251	
四 川	Sichuan	135	16	26	
贵 州	Guizhou	355	135	200	20
云 南	Yunnan	1545	203	348	276
西 藏	Tibet				
陕 西	Shaanxi	1051	276	199	394
甘 肃	Gansu	371	29	249	18
青 海	Qinghai	354	67	139	
宁 夏	Ningxia				
新 疆	Xinjiang	140	13	49	61
新疆兵团	Xinjiang Production and Construction Corps				
黑龙江垦区	Heilongjiang Land Reclamation Area				

4-2-2 续表 5 Continued 5

地　区	Region	残疾人中等职业学校(班)学生 Students of Secondary Vocational Schools/Classes for PWDs			
		毕业生 Graduates	盲 Students with Visual Disability	聋 Students with Hearing Disability	肢残 Students with Physical Disability
		人 person	人 person	人 person	人 person
全　国	**Nationwide**	**4837**	**1060**	**1628**	**1074**
北　京	Beijing	72		17	
天　津	Tianjin				
河　北	Hebei	153	31	6	14
山　西	Shanxi	21		21	
内蒙古	Inner Mongolia	23	23		
辽　宁	Liaoning	86	34	35	
吉　林	Jilin	187	18	87	48
黑龙江	Heilongjiang	76	24	19	1
上　海	Shanghai	82	6	27	
江　苏	Jiangsu	442	62	94	29
浙　江	Zhejiang	123		27	10
安　徽	Anhui	347	81	164	85
福　建	Fujian	39	8	18	
江　西	Jiangxi	76	35	5	
山　东	Shandong	130	51	33	36
河　南	Henan	65	18	41	
湖　北	Hubei	1290	337	529	374
湖　南	Hunan	207	57	62	75
广　东	Guangdong	376	58	61	90
广　西	Guangxi				
海　南	Hainan				
重　庆	Chongqing	31		31	
四　川	Sichuan	38	5	21	
贵　州	Guizhou				
云　南	Yunnan	289	48	119	100
西　藏	Tibet				
陕　西	Shaanxi	474	125	115	157
甘　肃	Gansu	71	14	57	
青　海	Qinghai	47	12	15	
宁　夏	Ningxia				
新　疆	Xinjiang	92	13	24	55
新疆兵团	Xinjiang Production and Construction Corps				
黑龙江垦区	Heilongjiang Land Reclamation Area				

4-2-2 续表 6 Continued 6

地区	Region	残疾人中等职业学校(班)学生 Students of Secondary Vocational Schools/Classes for PWDs			
		毕业生获得职业资格证书 Graduates Granted Professional Qualification Certificates	盲 Students with Visual Disability	聋 Students with Hearing Disability	肢残 Students with Physical Disability
		人 person	人 person	人 person	人 person
全国	**Nationwide**	**1199**	**249**	**420**	**319**
北京	Beijing				
天津	Tianjin				
河北	Hebei	37	8	2	5
山西	Shanxi	4		4	
内蒙古	Inner Mongolia				
辽宁	Liaoning	23	23		
吉林	Jilin				
黑龙江	Heilongjiang	32	7	3	1
上海	Shanghai	35		27	
江苏	Jiangsu	142	43	54	14
浙江	Zhejiang	46		27	
安徽	Anhui				
福建	Fujian				
江西	Jiangxi	5		5	
山东	Shandong	30	10	14	6
河南	Henan	26	6	20	
湖北	Hubei	38		6	20
湖南	Hunan				
广东	Guangdong	118		49	48
广西	Guangxi				
海南	Hainan				
重庆	Chongqing	27		27	
四川	Sichuan	12	5	7	
贵州	Guizhou				
云南	Yunnan	196	48	68	80
西藏	Tibet				
陕西	Shaanxi	414	99	93	145
甘肃	Gansu	14		14	
青海	Qinghai				
宁夏	Ningxia				
新疆	Xinjiang				
新疆兵团	Xinjiang Production and Construction Corps				
黑龙江垦区	Heilongjiang Land Reclamation Area				

4-2-3 高等教育
Higher Education

地 区	Region	高等特殊教育学院 Special Higher Education Institutions 机构 Institutions	录取残疾考生 Newly Enrolled Students	本科 Under-graduates	盲 Students with Visual Disability	聋 Students with Hearing Disability
		个 unit	人 person	人 person	人 person	人 person
全 国	**Nationwide**	**23**	**1873**	**776**	**165**	**386**
北 京	Beijing	1	122	122	33	89
天 津	Tianjin	1	121	121		70
河 北	Hebei					
山 西	Shanxi					
内蒙古	Inner Mongolia					
辽 宁	Liaoning	1	19			
吉 林	Jilin	1	200	200	88	61
黑龙江	Heilongjiang	1				
上 海	Shanghai	1	15	15		15
江 苏	Jiangsu	3	124	95	21	36
浙 江	Zhejiang	1	317			
安 徽	Anhui					
福 建	Fujian	1	35			
江 西	Jiangxi					
山 东	Shandong	2	261	31	23	8
河 南	Henan	3	386	137		59
湖 北	Hubei					
湖 南	Hunan	1	117			
广 东	Guangdong	2	76			
广 西	Guangxi					
海 南	Hainan					
重 庆	Chongqing	1	25	25		18
四 川	Sichuan	1	30	30		30
贵 州	Guizhou					
云 南	Yunnan	1	25			
西 藏	Tibet					
陕 西	Shaanxi	1				
甘 肃	Gansu					
青 海	Qinghai					
宁 夏	Ningxia					
新 疆	Xinjiang					
新疆兵团	Xinjiang Production and Construction Corps					
黑龙江垦区	Heilongjiang Land Reclamation Area					

4-2-3 续表 1 Continued 1

地 区	Region				普通高等院校 Regular Higher Education Institutions			
		专科(高职) Students of Vocational College	盲 Students with Visual Disability	聋 Students with Hearing Disability	残疾考生达到录取分数线 Students above Admission Line	录取人数 Students Enrolled	研究生 Postgraduates	盲 Students with Visual Disability
		人 person	人 person	人 person	人 person	人 person	人 person	人 person
全 国	**Nationwide**	**1097**	**226**	**468**	**11832**	**11154**	**137**	**10**
北 京	Beijing				97	97		
天 津	Tianjin				65	65		
河 北	Hebei				194	187	4	
山 西	Shanxi				393	377		
内蒙古	Inner Mongolia				436	436	5	
辽 宁	Liaoning	19	3	6	245	243	8	1
吉 林	Jilin				273	268	9	
黑龙江	Heilongjiang				206	206	3	
上 海	Shanghai				77	77	5	
江 苏	Jiangsu	29		9	391	368	22	1
浙 江	Zhejiang	317	50	95	430	418	1	
安 徽	Anhui				599	545	22	1
福 建	Fujian	35	1	17	220	216	3	
江 西	Jiangxi				452	452	5	2
山 东	Shandong	230	44	159	596	511	12	2
河 南	Henan	249	104	32	861	861	7	1
湖 北	Hubei				419	419	12	
湖 南	Hunan	117		117	482	444	4	1
广 东	Guangdong	76	24	30	690	565	1	
广 西	Guangxi				306	297	3	1
海 南	Hainan				76	54		
重 庆	Chongqing				470	393		
四 川	Sichuan				651	583	4	
贵 州	Guizhou				731	731	3	
云 南	Yunnan	25		3	815	773		
西 藏	Tibet				67	48		
陕 西	Shaanxi				256	217		
甘 肃	Gansu				594	594	1	
青 海	Qinghai				158	150		
宁 夏	Ningxia				166	166	1	
新 疆	Xinjiang				375	360	2	
新疆兵团	Xinjiang Production and Construction Corps				35	27		
黑龙江垦区	Heilongjiang Land Reclamation Area				6	6		

4-2-3 续表 2 Continued 2

地　区	Region	普通高等院校 Regular Higher Education Institutions					
		聋 Students with Hearing Disability	肢残 Students with Physical Disability	本科 Under-graduates	盲 Students with Visual Disability	聋 Students with Hearing Disability	肢残 Students with Physical Disability
		人 person	人 person	人 person	人 person	人 person	人 person
全　国	**Nationwide**	**20**	**103**	**5200**	**687**	**843**	**3211**
北　京	Beijing			69	8	19	39
天　津	Tianjin			50	2	16	29
河　北	Hebei	1	3	87	11	21	42
山　西	Shanxi			184	17	21	135
内蒙古	Inner Mongolia	1	4	184	26	30	107
辽　宁	Liaoning	1	6	134	10	40	81
吉　林	Jilin	2	7	152	20	41	71
黑龙江	Heilongjiang		3	118	19	33	60
上　海	Shanghai	4	1	46	7	15	23
江　苏	Jiangsu	3	18	175	19	33	113
浙　江	Zhejiang		1	178	21	56	94
安　徽	Anhui	2	18	291	30	59	156
福　建	Fujian	1	2	112	18	28	52
江　西	Jiangxi		2	189	25	31	118
山　东	Shandong		10	233	26	55	135
河　南	Henan	1	4	413	62	54	272
湖　北	Hubei	2	10	182	22	29	111
湖　南	Hunan		3	192	18	37	112
广　东	Guangdong		1	177	21	35	111
广　西	Guangxi		2	126	17	14	82
海　南	Hainan			27	3	2	21
重　庆	Chongqing			251	45	24	160
四　川	Sichuan	1	3	272	51	36	157
贵　州	Guizhou		3	389	55	16	273
云　南	Yunnan			328	49	22	242
西　藏	Tibet			11	1	1	9
陕　西	Shaanxi			142	14	26	84
甘　肃	Gansu			211	29	28	134
青　海	Qinghai			62	7	3	47
宁　夏	Ningxia		1	71	12	6	40
新　疆	Xinjiang	1	1	130	19	12	91
新疆兵团	Xinjiang Production and Construction Corps			8	3		4
黑龙江垦区	Heilongjiang Land Reclamation Area			6			6

4-2-3 续表 3 Continued 3

地 区	Region	普通高等院校 Regular Higher Education Institutions			
		录取残疾考生 Students Enrolled			
		专科(高职) Students of Vocational College	盲 Students with Visual Disability	聋 Students with Hearing Disability	肢残 Students with Physical Disability
		人 person	人 person	人 person	人 person
全 国	**Nationwide**	**5817**	**665**	**774**	**3629**
北 京	Beijing	28	2	7	13
天 津	Tianjin	15		4	10
河 北	Hebei	96	11	22	55
山 西	Shanxi	193	11	30	130
内蒙古	Inner Mongolia	247	29	29	133
辽 宁	Liaoning	101	9	20	64
吉 林	Jilin	107	19	22	54
黑龙江	Heilongjiang	85	6	9	56
上 海	Shanghai	26	2	5	17
江 苏	Jiangsu	171	20	31	101
浙 江	Zhejiang	239	24	64	135
安 徽	Anhui	232	14	23	146
福 建	Fujian	101	12	22	49
江 西	Jiangxi	258	26	29	168
山 东	Shandong	266	27	46	172
河 南	Henan	441	44	46	315
湖 北	Hubei	225	28	30	138
湖 南	Hunan	248	33	24	158
广 东	Guangdong	387	33	56	264
广 西	Guangxi	168	13	16	120
海 南	Hainan	27	7	4	10
重 庆	Chongqing	142	16	20	85
四 川	Sichuan	307	42	44	166
贵 州	Guizhou	339	64	22	211
云 南	Yunnan	445	53	45	319
西 藏	Tibet	37	5	3	26
陕 西	Shaanxi	75	3	8	49
甘 肃	Gansu	382	49	33	230
青 海	Qinghai	88	14	12	54
宁 夏	Ningxia	94	13	17	37
新 疆	Xinjiang	228	32	29	135
新疆兵团	Xinjiang Production and Construction Corps	19	4	2	9
黑龙江垦区	Heilongjiang Land Reclamation Area				

三、就业
Employment

4-3-1 残疾人就业状况
Employment of Persons with Disabilities

地区	Region	就业合计 Employed PWDs	按比例就业 Employed through Quoto Scheme	集中就业 Employed through PWDs-Oriented Post	个体就业 Self-Employed
		人 person	人 person	人 person	人 person
全 国	**Nationwide**	**9484375**	**812713**	**330978**	**714285**
北 京	Beijing	112358	43875	5586	5129
天 津	Tianjin	83272	49558	533	11500
河 北	Hebei	613526	16856	7378	19432
山 西	Shanxi	285137	5973	6158	10392
内蒙古	Inner Mongolia	235801	11493	6795	23467
辽 宁	Liaoning	282631	40713	15952	17789
吉 林	Jilin	201192	6124	5631	21783
黑龙江	Heilongjiang	253914	15891	6659	27750
上 海	Shanghai	86035	44013	18428	812
江 苏	Jiangsu	452416	91242	43140	1841
浙 江	Zhejiang	338248	88551	45498	46853
安 徽	Anhui	497301	12002	7009	36747
福 建	Fujian	215669	15621	5572	23714
江 西	Jiangxi	360113	12276	20868	46314
山 东	Shandong	576786	63983	20248	30840
河 南	Henan	597242	27192	15668	132615
湖 北	Hubei	429057	34423	22894	26975
湖 南	Hunan	417008	25574	14857	35224
广 东	Guangdong	288867	60986	7087	12974
广 西	Guangxi	326384	9631	1953	14395
海 南	Hainan	36324	5222	399	1136
重 庆	Chongqing	246415	16515	10651	19950
四 川	Sichuan	884004	21713	12125	52517
贵 州	Guizhou	343664	9212	6137	19132
云 南	Yunnan	449433	18259	7561	17434
西 藏	Tibet	16883	344	300	619
陕 西	Shaanxi	263278	12292	4603	14083
甘 肃	Gansu	269325	7561	2110	17555
青 海	Qinghai	48220	1880	1999	2976
宁 夏	Ningxia	62115	7306	1782	5002
新 疆	Xinjiang	177745	21378	4236	13473
新疆兵团	Xinjiang Production and Construction Corps	23827	10805	1064	2817
黑龙江垦区	Heilongjiang Land Reclamation Area	10185	4249	97	1045

4-3-1 续表 Continued

地 区	Region	公益性岗位就业 Employed through Welfare Post	辅助性就业 Assistive Employment	灵活就业（含社区、居家就业） Flexible Employment	从事农业种养加 Engaged in Agricultural Planting, Husbandry and Processing
		人 person	人 person	人 person	人 person
全 国	**Nationwide**	**130647**	**147789**	**2546136**	**4801827**
北 京	Beijing	3086	1792	37357	15533
天 津	Tianjin	1275	1	1180	19225
河 北	Hebei	1567	3352	131799	433142
山 西	Shanxi	1104	1092	40207	220211
内蒙古	Inner Mongolia	1625	1209	66197	125015
辽 宁	Liaoning	7417	7677	42998	150085
吉 林	Jilin	2718	1177	46962	116797
黑龙江	Heilongjiang	6505	2325	80399	114385
上 海	Shanghai	3532	4663	8888	5699
江 苏	Jiangsu	39528	9080	152531	115054
浙 江	Zhejiang	5125	9456	83894	58871
安 徽	Anhui	2634	10438	151913	276558
福 建	Fujian	2440	3479	65821	99022
江 西	Jiangxi	7672	8281	139410	125292
山 东	Shandong	3015	4600	100838	353262
河 南	Henan	3624	15834	71881	330428
湖 北	Hubei	3849	8004	131534	201378
湖 南	Hunan	2375	5905	132696	200377
广 东	Guangdong	5442	5984	64112	132282
广 西	Guangxi	1948	2448	67008	229001
海 南	Hainan	412	154	6927	22074
重 庆	Chongqing	2245	3073	72071	121910
四 川	Sichuan	7000	17048	418220	355381
贵 州	Guizhou	1645	2986	100638	203914
云 南	Yunnan	1091	4994	98505	301589
西 藏	Tibet	115	54	9156	6295
陕 西	Shaanxi	4101	5281	72481	150437
甘 肃	Gansu	2691	3886	65279	170243
青 海	Qinghai	948	582	14936	24899
宁 夏	Ningxia	646	1266	20631	25482
新 疆	Xinjiang	2752	1343	41974	92589
新疆兵团	Xinjiang Production and Construction Corps	384	305	5134	3318
黑龙江垦区	Heilongjiang Land Reclamation Area	136	20	2559	2079

四、扶贫
Poverty Alleviation

4-4-1 农村贫困残疾人扶持效果
Poverty Alleviation for Persons with Disabilities in Rural Areas

地区	Region	本年度退出建档立卡贫困残疾户 Families with Disabled Member(s) Lifted Out of Poverty	本年度退出建档立卡贫困残疾人 PWDs Lifted Out of Poverty	本年返贫 Reimpoverished PWDs in 2018	残疾人实用技术培训 Training on Practical Skills and Technologies for PWDs		
					本年度培训残疾人 Training on Practical Skills and Technologies for PWDs in 2018	扫盲教育 Anti-Illiteracy Education	本年度培训投入经费 Fund for Training on Practical Skills and Technologies for PWDs in 2018
		万户 10,000 households	万人 10,000 persons	人 persons	万人次 10,000 person-times	人 person	万元 10,000 yuan
全　国	**Nationwide**	**92.4**	**116.1**	**15773**	**58.8**	**52462**	**29681.0**
北　京	Beijing				0.3		6.4
天　津	Tianjin						
河　北	Hebei	4.8	6.0	1214	3.0	871	2175.7
山　西	Shanxi	3.3	4.5	394	1.2	548	534.7
内蒙古	Inner Mongolia	3.0	3.4	1208	2.0	791	674.3
辽　宁	Liaoning	2.0	2.8	306	1.2	172	360.9
吉　林	Jilin	2.3	2.7	326	1.2	626	461.2
黑龙江	Heilongjiang	2.4	3.1	38	1.0	671	418.0
上　海	Shanghai				2.2		136.3
江　苏	Jiangsu				0.8	2178	264.1
浙　江	Zhejiang				1.3	2170	399.3
安　徽	Anhui	7.4	10.0	367	2.1	1613	809.3
福　建	Fujian	0.0	0.0		0.6	797	316.8
江　西	Jiangxi	5.3	6.8	221	0.8	538	460.7
山　东	Shandong	4.1	4.5		1.7	1081	2218.0
河　南	Henan	5.6	7.9	619	3.5	1355	1500.2
湖　北	Hubei	7.8	10.3	314	2.2	1921	810.9
湖　南	Hunan	7.7	9.7	739	2.1	1463	2356.1
广　东	Guangdong				1.3	3034	727.8
广　西	Guangxi	5.0	5.7	826	2.6	1053	1518.5
海　南	Hainan	0.3	0.4	80	0.6	536	3462.5
重　庆	Chongqing	1.2	1.4	254	1.2	2412	604.7
四　川	Sichuan	4.8	5.4	219	12.8	12065	4416.9
贵　州	Guizhou	6.7	8.9	1342	1.2	1399	617.7
云　南	Yunnan	6.9	8.0	2574	3.3	3419	1131.9
西　藏	Tibet	0.7	0.8	22	0.1	544	110.5
陕　西	Shaanxi	4.7	6.1	3928	2.5	2086	752.2
甘　肃	Gansu	3.2	4.2	372	2.3	3645	1170.0
青　海	Qinghai	0.7	0.9	39	0.7	1869	230.3
宁　夏	Ningxia	0.8	0.9	318	0.6	683	202.2
新　疆	Xinjiang	1.5	1.7	51	1.8	2767	699.2
新疆兵团	Xinjiang Production and Construction Corps	0.1	0.1	2	0.5	155	64.5
黑龙江垦区	Heilongjiang Land Reclamation Area				0.1		69.3

4−4−2 扶贫资金与残疾人扶贫贷款
Poverty Alleviation Funds and Loans

地 区	Region	扶贫资金 Poverty Alleviation Funds		残疾人扶贫贷款 Poverty Alleviation Funds and Loans		
				康复扶贫贴息贷款 Interest-subsidized Loans for Rehabilitation		
		省级财政投入 Poverty Alleviation Fund from the Provincial Budget	社会募集 Fund Raised from Society	本年度贷款实际落实 Allocated Loans in 2018	本年度贷款财政贴息资金数额 Amount of Interest Subsidy by Government Finance for Loans in 2018	本年度项目贷款扶持贫困残疾人 Financially Difficult PWDs Supported by Loans for Project in 2018
		万元 10,000 yuan	万元 10,000 yuan	万元 10,000 yuan	万元 10,000 yuan	人 person
全 国	**Nationwide**	**64116.3**	**2440.3**	**30503.3**	**1785.7**	**6605**
北 京	Beijing					
天 津	Tianjin					
河 北	Hebei	1698.7	17.3	445.2	35.4	44
山 西	Shanxi	580.8				
内蒙古	Inner Mongolia		51.1	2399.2	163.1	940
辽 宁	Liaoning	2000.0	8.2			
吉 林	Jilin	391.3		25.3	1.4	4
黑龙江	Heilongjiang	407.2	29.0			
上 海	Shanghai					
江 苏	Jiangsu	1713.6	28.0	2439.8	145.3	265
浙 江	Zhejiang	13092.8	135.0	6935.8	419.5	849
安 徽	Anhui	5044.9		1467.0	58.2	139
福 建	Fujian	2232.4	54.8	5540.3	245.8	1115
江 西	Jiangxi	885.0	722.0	85.0	5.5	58
山 东	Shandong	1247.4	20.0			
河 南	Henan	520.0	4.2			
湖 北	Hubei	2613.2	360.9	423.0	25.5	609
湖 南	Hunan	2348.7	295.6	5985.3	415.1	1528
广 东	Guangdong	37.0	1.5	30.0	2.1	42
广 西	Guangxi	10695.8	3.3			
海 南	Hainan	213.9				
重 庆	Chongqing	2507.0	0.5			
四 川	Sichuan	1134.2	25.0	149.2	7.7	1
贵 州	Guizhou	589.7	20.0	1460.0	101.4	128
云 南	Yunnan	1652.9	161.0	54.0	3.0	
西 藏	Tibet					
陕 西	Shaanxi	11655.1	10.0	12.0	0.6	
甘 肃	Gansu	552.9	216.0	16.0	0.7	15
青 海	Qinghai	121.4	128.0	31.0	5.0	33
宁 夏	Ningxia	142.6	146.0	3005.2	150.7	834
新 疆	Xinjiang	14.7	2.9			1
新疆兵团	Xinjiang Production and Construction Corps	23.0				
黑龙江垦区	Heilongjiang Land Reclamation Area					

4-4-3 社会帮扶与残疾人扶贫基地建设
Social Assistance and Poverty Alleviation Bases

地区	Region	社会帮扶 Social Assistance for PWDs	残疾人扶贫基地建设 Poverty Alleviation Bases for PWDs		
		结对帮扶受益残疾人 Individuals who Assisted PWDs in One-to-one Way	残疾人扶贫基地 Poverty Alleviation Bases for PWDs	安置残疾人就业 PWDs Provided with Employment Opportunities	扶持带动贫困残疾人 Benefited PWDs
		人 person	个 unit	人 person	户 household
全 国	**Nationwide**	**563063**	**5490**	**70198**	**134767**
北 京	Beijing		32	659	401
天 津	Tianjin	240			
河 北	Hebei	2707	187	2657	6939
山 西	Shanxi	7515	49	1184	1350
内蒙古	Inner Mongolia	2956	116	1363	1719
辽 宁	Liaoning	4355	19	234	359
吉 林	Jilin	4695	192	1396	4216
黑龙江	Heilongjiang	3867	82	1454	1749
上 海	Shanghai		267	4145	4189
江 苏	Jiangsu	16225	207	3851	4353
浙 江	Zhejiang	17635	965	5853	15942
安 徽	Anhui	59194	146	2017	2302
福 建	Fujian	16946	75	999	1192
江 西	Jiangxi	20298	333	2148	1895
山 东	Shandong	16095	421	6485	9232
河 南	Henan	46149	170	4562	8073
湖 北	Hubei	39754	89	1346	6351
湖 南	Hunan	36243	368	6005	9421
广 东	Guangdong	863	67	2000	1653
广 西	Guangxi	28067	125	3184	13626
海 南	Hainan	3	32	187	143
重 庆	Chongqing	17815	120	1144	1235
四 川	Sichuan	62706	255	4102	5931
贵 州	Guizhou	28313	171	1602	2673
云 南	Yunnan	43111	353	2703	13811
西 藏	Tibet	2396			
陕 西	Shaanxi	16661	136	1990	4354
甘 肃	Gansu	54568	182	2857	5312
青 海	Qinghai	2083	60	877	960
宁 夏	Ningxia	3942	36	496	1676
新 疆	Xinjiang	5387	182	2078	2557
新疆兵团	Xinjiang Production and Construction Corps	2018	50	606	1150
黑龙江垦区	Heilongjiang Land Reclamation Area	256	3	14	3

4-4-4 农村贫困残疾人危房改造
House Renovation for Financially Difficnlt Persons with Disabilities in Rural Areas

地 区	Region	本年度危房改造实际完成 Houses Renovated for PWDs in 2018	本年度危房改造项目受益贫困残疾人 Financially Difficnlt PWDs Benefited from House Renovation Projects in 2018	本年度投入资金 Fund Input in Houses Renovation in 2018	省级投入资金 Fund from Provincial Budgets	地市级投入资金 Fund from the Municipal Budgets	县级投入资金 Fund from County-Level Budgets
		户 household	人 person	万元 10,000 yuan	万元 10,000 yuan	万元 10,000 yuan	万元 10,000 yuan
全 国	**Nationwide**	**113263**	**129508**	**137051.8**	**91338.3**	**6336.7**	**39376.9**
北 京	Beijing	124	131	37.2			37.2
天 津	Tianjin	459	459	1217.8	809.5		408.3
河 北	Hebei	1590	1847	1234.4	969.2	92.5	172.7
山 西	Shanxi	298	312	107.0	67.6	19.3	20.0
内蒙古	Inner Mongolia	1477	1562	647.9	20.8	0.1	627.0
辽 宁	Liaoning	3730	3945	5764.1	3440.5	642.7	1680.8
吉 林	Jilin	262	407	25.6	25.6		
黑龙江	Heilongjiang	6155	6763	7787.7	6832.6	98.0	857.1
上 海	Shanghai	114	162	106.5	12.1		94.4
江 苏	Jiangsu	839	930	1101.9	500.0	136.2	465.7
浙 江	Zhejiang	2274	2542	2121.6	621.7	233.8	1266.1
安 徽	Anhui	15447	16895	16923.3	6291.8	153.7	10477.8
福 建	Fujian	1876	2056	3624.9	1398.7	395.9	1830.3
江 西	Jiangxi	3233	3564	3862.6	3327.9	47.9	486.8
山 东	Shandong	563	582	183.4	35.7	99.1	48.6
河 南	Henan	4139	5155	3091.3	1375.0	202.7	1513.7
湖 北	Hubei	2992	3589	1849.4	1247.0		602.4
湖 南	Hunan	8704	9489	11050.1	6810.7	1149.0	3090.4
广 东	Guangdong	2195	2523	2874.7	1908.9	402.6	563.2
广 西	Guangxi	3184	3779	1928.2	1057.5	224.0	646.6
海 南	Hainan	894	926	775.5	28.0		747.5
重 庆	Chongqing	3418	3740	4871.8	1062.0		3809.8
四 川	Sichuan	7162	9297	7125.3	4827.3	16.3	2281.7
贵 州	Guizhou	632	660	170.6	106.2	13.0	51.4
云 南	Yunnan	19516	22480	23464.0	19677.1	408.2	3378.7
西 藏	Tibet	39	41	3.6			3.6
陕 西	Shaanxi	2968	3197	4177.7	1899.5	1333.6	944.6
甘 肃	Gansu	6340	7608	13223.2	12550.0	55.1	618.1
青 海	Qinghai	1307	2156	1070.7	886.5	61.6	122.6
宁 夏	Ningxia	609	614	1554.6	664.0		890.6
新 疆	Xinjiang	10723	12097	15075.1	12884.7	551.3	1639.1
新疆兵团	Xinjiang Production and Construction Corps						
黑龙江垦区	Heilongjiang Land Reclamation Area						

五、社会保障
Social Security

4-5-1 残疾人参加社会保险情况
Social Insurance Coverage of Persons with Disabilities

地 区	Region	残疾居民参加城乡社会养老保险 Residents with Disabilities Covered by Pension Insurance	享受养老保金 PWDs Drawing Pension	重度残疾人 Persons with Severe Disability
		万人 10,000 persons	万人 10,000 persons	万人 10,000 persons
全 国	**Nationwide**	**2561.2**	**1024.4**	**377.1**
北 京	Beijing	9.0	2.1	0.7
天 津	Tianjin	7.6	5.1	2.1
河 北	Hebei	143.1	51.3	19.7
山 西	Shanxi	94.6	43.6	10.1
内蒙古	Inner Mongolia	45.1	20.2	7.9
辽 宁	Liaoning	43.0	18.1	7.6
吉 林	Jilin	32.8	10.4	3.5
黑龙江	Heilongjiang	41.9	15.9	4.1
上 海	Shanghai	7.5	2.3	0.6
江 苏	Jiangsu	114.7	48.0	21.3
浙 江	Zhejiang	66.4	30.4	11.6
安 徽	Anhui	146.1	54.4	26.6
福 建	Fujian	70.5	34.2	13.7
江 西	Jiangxi	88.0	33.2	9.7
山 东	Shandong	158.6	60.9	28.5
河 南	Henan	290.9	127.1	33.5
湖 北	Hubei	119.4	41.5	17.1
湖 南	Hunan	126.8	50.0	22.9
广 东	Guangdong	96.7	36.2	20.3
广 西	Guangxi	102.0	52.0	15.9
海 南	Hainan	20.6	10.1	3.1
重 庆	Chongqing	56.0	22.8	8.5
四 川	Sichuan	229.8	82.0	35.4
贵 州	Guizhou	83.1	40.7	9.3
云 南	Yunnan	92.2	33.6	12.1
西 藏	Tibet	3.8	0.8	0.3
陕 西	Shaanxi	87.6	35.5	9.6
甘 肃	Gansu	108.6	34.8	8.5
青 海	Qinghai	13.1	5.2	2.7
宁 夏	Ningxia	21.5	10.2	5.3
新 疆	Xinjiang	38.0	11.5	4.9
新疆兵团	Xinjiang Production and Construction Corps	2.2	0.3	0.2
黑龙江垦区	Heilongjiang Land Reclamation Area			

4-5-1 续表 Continued

地 区	Region	残疾居民参加城乡社会养老保险 Residents with Disabilities Covered by Pension Insurance				
		60周岁以下参保残疾人 PWDs under 60	重度残疾人 Persons with Severe Disability	全部或部分代缴 PWDs Whose Pension Premium Were Fully or Partially Covered by Government	其他残疾人 Other PWDs	全部或部分代缴 PWDs Whose Pension Premium Were Fully or Partially Covered by Government
		万人 10,000 persons	万人 10,000 persons	万人 10,000 persons	万人 10,000 persons	万人 10,000 persons
全 国	**Nationwide**	**1536.8**	**595.2**	**576.0**	**941.7**	**298.4**
北 京	Beijing	6.9	4.2	4.2	2.7	2.4
天 津	Tianjin	2.5	2.0	2.0	0.4	0.4
河 北	Hebei	91.8	31.0	30.1	60.8	19.4
山 西	Shanxi	51.0	16.9	15.6	34.1	7.5
内蒙古	Inner Mongolia	24.9	10.9	10.2	14.0	4.7
辽 宁	Liaoning	24.9	9.6	8.8	15.3	3.1
吉 林	Jilin	22.4	10.1	9.9	12.3	7.0
黑龙江	Heilongjiang	26.0	8.1	7.8	17.9	5.0
上 海	Shanghai	5.2	4.0	4.0	1.2	0.5
江 苏	Jiangsu	66.7	30.0	29.4	36.8	21.0
浙 江	Zhejiang	35.9	13.2	13.2	22.7	20.0
安 徽	Anhui	91.7	41.0	40.3	50.7	5.5
福 建	Fujian	36.3	17.2	17.1	19.1	15.5
江 西	Jiangxi	54.7	19.4	19.0	35.3	12.3
山 东	Shandong	97.7	41.7	40.8	55.9	11.0
河 南	Henan	163.8	50.5	48.4	113.3	6.0
湖 北	Hubei	77.8	32.6	32.4	45.2	16.0
湖 南	Hunan	76.8	37.6	36.2	39.2	15.1
广 东	Guangdong	60.6	36.4	35.3	24.2	11.2
广 西	Guangxi	50.0	19.2	18.6	30.8	8.5
海 南	Hainan	10.5	5.4	4.9	5.1	1.2
重 庆	Chongqing	33.2	13.3	13.3	19.9	4.2
四 川	Sichuan	147.8	44.4	43.7	103.4	29.0
贵 州	Guizhou	42.4	15.3	12.3	27.0	5.2
云 南	Yunnan	58.7	20.7	20.2	38.0	21.1
西 藏	Tibet	3.0	1.0	0.7	2.0	0.4
陕 西	Shaanxi	52.1	14.5	14.0	37.6	20.8
甘 肃	Gansu	73.8	24.7	24.2	49.1	10.9
青 海	Qinghai	7.9	4.4	4.3	3.5	3.0
宁 夏	Ningxia	11.3	5.7	5.7	5.6	3.1
新 疆	Xinjiang	26.6	9.3	8.6	17.2	7.0
新疆兵团	Xinjiang Production and Construction Corps	1.8	0.8	0.8	1.0	0.3
黑龙江垦区	Heilongjiang Land Reclamation Area					

4-5-2 托养服务
Institutional Care Services

地 区	Region	托养服务机构合计 Institutions Providing Care Services	寄宿制托养服务 Boarding Institutions Providing Care Services	日间照料托养服务机构 Institutions Providing Day-Care Service	综合托养服务机构 Institutions Providing Combined Care Services	托养残疾人 PWDs Receiving Care Services	寄宿制机构中托养残疾人 PWDs in Boarding Care Institutions
		个 unit	个 unit	个 unit	个 unit	人 person	人 person
全 国	**Nationwide**	**8435**	**2639**	**4099**	**1697**	**1111278**	**73623**
北 京	Beijing	99	85		14	118521	1201
天 津	Tianjin	60	12	47	1	40534	224
河 北	Hebei	214	116	35	63	17374	5580
山 西	Shanxi	115	32	52	31	13420	691
内蒙古	Inner Mongolia	169	110	12	47	9595	2483
辽 宁	Liaoning	180	100	54	26	19906	4624
吉 林	Jilin	71	49	14	8	8611	1197
黑龙江	Heilongjiang	96	59	8	29	8644	975
上 海	Shanghai	796	364	432		41533	6247
江 苏	Jiangsu	1756	81	1130	545	37741	1788
浙 江	Zhejiang	1197	444	537	216	394487	8140
安 徽	Anhui	305	175	40	90	21464	2279
福 建	Fujian	102	43	49	10	15173	1232
江 西	Jiangxi	64	22	23	19	8320	1326
山 东	Shandong	377	207	58	112	38521	6554
河 南	Henan	295	181	21	93	16328	6955
湖 北	Hubei	192	71	98	23	12334	2527
湖 南	Hunan	150	37	80	33	21708	1418
广 东	Guangdong	1169	40	1078	51	36350	1449
广 西	Guangxi	90	42	26	22	38498	2727
海 南	Hainan	15	14		1	24270	531
重 庆	Chongqing	81	26	30	25	22689	570
四 川	Sichuan	164	57	76	31	44199	2130
贵 州	Guizhou	34	13	4	17	8834	1144
云 南	Yunnan	62	36	10	16	17793	1361
西 藏	Tibet	2	1		1	684	17
陕 西	Shaanxi	141	72	18	51	19979	2902
甘 肃	Gansu	94	46	22	26	29861	1230
青 海	Qinghai	45	15	10	20	2533	321
宁 夏	Ningxia	67	21	42	4	7284	708
新 疆	Xinjiang	173	36	86	51	9769	1807
新疆兵团	Xinjiang Production and Construction Corps	49	24	6	19	3916	966
黑龙江垦区	Heilongjiang Land Reclamation Area	11	8	1	2	405	319

4-5-2 续表 1 Continued 1

地区	Region	托养残疾人 PWDs Receiving Institutional Care Services							
		智力残疾人 Persons with Intellectual Disability	精神残疾人 Persons with Mental Disability	重度肢体残疾人 Persons with Severe Physical Disability	日间照料机构中托养残疾人 PWDs Receiving Day Care	智力残疾人 Persons with Intellectual Disability	精神残疾人 Persons with Mental Disability	重度肢体残疾人 Persons with Severe Physical Disability	综合托养服务机构中托养残疾人 PWDs in Institutions Providing Combined Services
		人 person	人 person	人 person	人 person	人 person	人 person	人 person	人 person
全 国	**Nationwide**	**14720**	**34195**	**13899**	**88689**	**35017**	**23852**	**15985**	**60869**
北 京	Beijing	403	326	234					182
天 津	Tianjin	123	41	40	584	411	107	33	26
河 北	Hebei	785	2855	645	2162	682	390	678	4562
山 西	Shanxi	112	501	55	2078	558	400	899	1971
内蒙古	Inner Mongolia	551	616	619	263	57	62	92	942
辽 宁	Liaoning	943	2342	721	882	763	45	29	1248
吉 林	Jilin	156	656	316	215	77	46	85	388
黑龙江	Heilongjiang	213	283	258	60	22	4	25	1272
上 海	Shanghai	2139	2141	855	10315	6278	3671	75	
江 苏	Jiangsu	592	407	447	17337	5741	3005	3690	11270
浙 江	Zhejiang	1842	2890	2394	10652	4909	3742	1011	8029
安 徽	Anhui	433	1093	461	1097	371	363	140	3894
福 建	Fujian	88	723	288	1195	517	88	51	231
江 西	Jiangxi	221	593	322	1081	397	269	195	1400
山 东	Shandong	1225	3867	759	855	472	154	136	3413
河 南	Henan	977	2607	2596	640	114	342	157	4187
湖 北	Hubei	609	1508	221	2170	941	549	532	1307
湖 南	Hunan	479	480	260	2820	1199	817	641	1675
广 东	Guangdong	641	502	179	24732	8505	7364	4845	1961
广 西	Guangxi	90	2375	75	1637	652	523	374	622
海 南	Hainan	35	483	2					55
重 庆	Chongqing	91	416	45	653	172	243	226	876
四 川	Sichuan	382	1294	278	2774	812	456	885	1631
贵 州	Guizhou	77	902	79	202	20	150	15	824
云 南	Yunnan	145	1062	101	83	35	8	23	374
西 藏	Tibet	1							52
陕 西	Shaanxi	412	1515	548	777	342	213	174	2918
甘 肃	Gansu	279	256	349	301	94	64	52	1314
青 海	Qinghai	68	20	73	208	77	16	70	829
宁 夏	Ningxia	192	306	115	958	196	408	265	109
新 疆	Xinjiang	307	285	370	1862	561	303	585	2745
新疆兵团	Xinjiang Production and Construction Corps	87	621	169	94	42	50	1	503
黑龙江垦区	Heilongjiang Land Reclamation Area	22	229	25	2			1	59

4-5-2 续表 2 Continued 2

地　区	Region	托养残疾人 PWDs in the Institutions 以寄宿制方式托养的残疾人 PWDs in Boarding Institutions	智　力残疾人 Persons with Intellectual Disability	精　神残疾人 Persons with Mental Disability	重度肢体残疾人 Persons with Severe Physical Disability	以日间照料方式托养的残疾人 PWDs Receiving Day Care	智　力残疾人 Persons with Intellectual Disability	精　神残疾人 Persons with Mental Disability	重度肢体残疾人 Persons with Severe Physical Disability	享受居家托养服务残疾人 PWDs Recieving Care Service at Home
		人 person	人 person	人 person	人 person	人 person	人 person	人 person	人 person	人 person
全　国	**Nationwide**	**28700**	**6644**	**10048**	**5845**	**32169**	**9023**	**8399**	**7250**	**888097**
北　京	Beijing	163	82	3	56	19	11	1	6	117138
天　津	Tianjin	19	9	3		7	5	2		39700
河　北	Hebei	1496	351	429	346	3066	599	766	575	5070
山　西	Shanxi	733	140	447	126	1238	354	322	413	8680
内蒙古	Inner Mongolia	467	84	38	119	475	62	26	83	5907
辽　宁	Liaoning	934	168	464	117	314	132	43	53	13152
吉　林	Jilin	191	53	97	22	197	39	65	27	6811
黑龙江	Heilongjiang	1013	155	562	97	259	69	68	62	6337
上　海	Shanghai									24971
江　苏	Jiangsu	4062	1178	757	853	7208	2090	963	1518	7346
浙　江	Zhejiang	4019	1154	1345	907	4010	1538	1368	732	367666
安　徽	Anhui	2199	442	532	689	1695	342	465	439	14194
福　建	Fujian	121	71	21	7	110	59	17	3	12515
江　西	Jiangxi	700	141	192	197	700	131	223	186	4513
山　东	Shandong	1942	433	501	381	1471	374	437	405	27699
河　南	Henan	2456	329	1113	651	1731	323	464	723	4546
湖　北	Hubei	770	100	440	128	537	72	296	91	6330
湖　南	Hunan	640	207	247	148	1035	414	346	207	15795
广　东	Guangdong	984	473	342	86	977	389	298	229	8208
广　西	Guangxi	262	19	177	22	360	84	196	55	33512
海　南	Hainan	55	1	52						23684
重　庆	Chongqing	452	124	281	31	424	264	97	51	20590
四　川	Sichuan	836	141	382	220	795	241	231	172	37664
贵　州	Guizhou	409	89	202	19	415	102	164	46	6664
云　南	Yunnan	144	6	130	1	230	50	108	40	15975
西　藏	Tibet	26	4		5	26	4		5	615
陕　西	Shaanxi	1124	212	330	224	1794	478	577	388	13382
甘　肃	Gansu	611	149	301	64	703	192	250	155	27016
青　海	Qinghai	235	87	26	67	594	193	68	162	1175
宁　夏	Ningxia					109	25	37	37	5509
新　疆	Xinjiang	1309	189	537	177	1436	312	433	345	3355
新疆兵团	Xinjiang Production and Construction Corps	286	46	67	83	217	62	67	40	2353
黑龙江垦区	Heilongjiang Land Reclamation Area	42	7	30	2	17	13	1	2	25

六、专门协会
Specialized Associations

4-6-1 省(自治区、直辖市)专门协会建立情况
Establishment of Special Associations at Provincial Level

地 区	Region	盲人协会 Associations of Persons with Visual Disability	聋人协会 Associations of Persons with Hearing Disability	肢残人协会 Associations of Persons with Physical Disability	智力残疾人及亲友协会 Associations of Persons with Intellectual Disability and Their Relatives and Friends	精神残疾人及亲友协会 Associations of Persons with Psychosocial Disability and Their Relatives and Friends
		个 unit	个 unit	个 unit	个 unit	个 unit
全 国	**Nationwide**	**33**	**33**	**33**	**32**	**32**
北 京	Beijing	1	1	1	1	1
天 津	Tianjin	1	1	1	1	1
河 北	Hebei	1	1	1	1	1
山 西	Shanxi	1	1	1	1	1
内蒙古	Inner Mongolia	1	1	1	1	1
辽 宁	Liaoning	1	1	1	1	1
吉 林	Jilin	1	1	1	1	1
黑龙江	Heilongjiang	1	1	1	1	1
上 海	Shanghai	1	1	1	1	1
江 苏	Jiangsu	1	1	1	1	1
浙 江	Zhejiang	1	1	1	1	1
安 徽	Anhui	1	1	1	1	1
福 建	Fujian	1	1	1	1	1
江 西	Jiangxi	1	1	1	1	1
山 东	Shandong	1	1	1	1	1
河 南	Henan	1	1	1	1	1
湖 北	Hubei	1	1	1	1	1
湖 南	Hunan	1	1	1	1	1
广 东	Guangdong	1	1	1	1	1
广 西	Guangxi	1	1	1	1	1
海 南	Hainan	1	1	1	1	1
重 庆	Chongqing	1	1	1	1	1
四 川	Sichuan	1	1	1	1	1
贵 州	Guizhou	1	1	1	1	1
云 南	Yunnan	1	1	1	1	1
西 藏	Tibet	1	1	1		
陕 西	Shaanxi	1	1	1	1	1
甘 肃	Gansu	1	1	1	1	1
青 海	Qinghai	1	1	1	1	1
宁 夏	Ningxia	1	1	1	1	1
新 疆	Xinjiang	1	1	1	1	1
新疆兵团	Xinjiang Production and Construction Corps	1	1	1	1	1
黑龙江垦区	Heilongjiang Land Reclamation Area	1	1	1	1	1

4-6-2　市(地、州、盟)专门协会建立情况
Establishment of Specialized Associations at Municipal Level

地　区	Region	盲人协会 Associations of Persons with Visual Disability	聋人协会 Associations of Persons with Hearing Disability	肢残人协会 Associations of Persons with Physical Disability	智力残疾人及亲友协会 Associations of Persons with Intellectual Disability and Their Relatives and Friends	精神残疾人及亲友协会 Associations of Persons with Psychosocial Disability and Their Relatives and Friends	智力残疾人及亲友协会和精神残疾人及亲友协会合一的协会 Associations of Persons with Intellectual Disability and Psychosocial Disability and Their Relatives and Friends
		个 unit	个 unit	个 unit	个 unit	个 unit	个 unit
全　国	**Nationwide**	**342**	**341**	**343**	**335**	**336**	**6**
北　京	Beijing						
天　津	Tianjin						
河　北	Hebei	11	11	11	11	11	
山　西	Shanxi	11	11	11	11	11	
内蒙古	Inner Mongolia	12	12	12	12	12	
辽　宁	Liaoning	14	14	14	14	14	
吉　林	Jilin	10	10	9	10	10	
黑龙江	Heilongjiang	13	13	13	13	13	
上　海	Shanghai						
江　苏	Jiangsu	13	13	13	13	13	
浙　江	Zhejiang	11	11	11	11	11	
安　徽	Anhui	15	15	15	15	15	
福　建	Fujian	9	9	9	9	9	
江　西	Jiangxi	11	11	11	11	11	
山　东	Shandong	17	17	17	15	15	1
河　南	Henan	18	18	18	18	18	
湖　北	Hubei	13	13	13	13	13	
湖　南	Hunan	14	14	14	14	14	
广　东	Guangdong	21	21	21	21	21	
广　西	Guangxi	14	14	14	14	14	
海　南	Hainan	3	3	3	3	3	
重　庆	Chongqing						
四　川	Sichuan	20	20	20	20	20	
贵　州	Guizhou	9	9	9	9	9	
云　南	Yunnan	16	15	16	15	15	1
西　藏	Tibet						
陕　西	Shaanxi	10	10	10	10	10	
甘　肃	Gansu	15	15	15	15	15	
青　海	Qinghai	8	8	8	8	8	
宁　夏	Ningxia	5	5	5	5	5	
新　疆	Xinjiang	14	14	14	12	12	2
新疆兵团	Xinjiang Production and Construction Corps	6	6	8	4	5	2
黑龙江垦区	Heilongjiang Land Reclamation Area	9	9	9	9	9	

4-6-3 县(县级市、市辖区)专门协会建立情况
Establishment of Specialized Associations at County/District Level

地 区	Region	盲人协会 Associations of Persons with Visual Disability	聋人协会 Associations of Persons with Hearing Disability	肢残人协会 Associations of Persons with Physical Disability	智力残疾人及亲友协会 Associations of Persons with Intellectual Disability and Their Relatives and Friends	精神残疾人及亲友协会 Associations of Persons with Psychosocial Disability and Their Relatives and Friends	智力残疾人及亲友协会和精神残疾人及亲友协会合一的协会 Associations of Persons with Intellectual Disability and Psychosocial Disability and Their Relatives and Friends
		个 unit	个 unit	个 unit	个 unit	个 unit	个 unit
全 国	**Nationwide**	**2798**	**2780**	**2811**	**2656**	**2656**	**122**
北 京	Beijing	16	16	16	16	16	
天 津	Tianjin	16	16	16	16	16	
河 北	Hebei	168	168	168	166	166	2
山 西	Shanxi	117	117	117	110	110	12
内蒙古	Inner Mongolia	103	103	103	87	87	16
辽 宁	Liaoning	105	105	105	105	105	
吉 林	Jilin	63	63	63	62	62	
黑龙江	Heilongjiang	130	130	131	129	129	1
上 海	Shanghai	16	16	16	16	16	
江 苏	Jiangsu	98	98	98	91	91	6
浙 江	Zhejiang	90	89	91	76	76	13
安 徽	Anhui	98	96	101	92	89	5
福 建	Fujian	83	81	83	74	74	9
江 西	Jiangxi	81	81	81	80	80	
山 东	Shandong	132	127	130	122	124	3
河 南	Henan	159	158	159	158	158	
湖 北	Hubei	93	91	94	80	82	10
湖 南	Hunan	122	121	124	113	113	6
广 东	Guangdong	119	119	119	112	113	6
广 西	Guangxi	111	111	111	109	109	2
海 南	Hainan	18	18	18	17	17	1
重 庆	Chongqing	39	39	39	38	38	1
四 川	Sichuan	165	164	168	162	161	2
贵 州	Guizhou	78	76	77	72	72	3
云 南	Yunnan	125	126	127	111	111	15
西 藏	Tibet						
陕 西	Shaanxi	106	105	107	104	106	
甘 肃	Gansu	86	86	86	86	86	
青 海	Qinghai	44	44	45	44	44	1
宁 夏	Ningxia	21	21	21	19	20	1
新 疆	Xinjiang	89	88	90	82	78	7
新疆兵团	Xinjiang Production and Construction Corps						
黑龙江垦区	Heilongjiang Land Reclamation Area	107	107	107	107	107	

七、盲人按摩
Massage by the Blind

4-7-1 盲人按摩
Massage by the Blind

地 区	Region	保健按摩人员本年度培训 Blind Health-Care Masseurs Trained in 2018	医疗按摩人员本年度培训 Blind Therapeutical Masseurs Trained in 2018	按摩机构 Institutions of Blind Massage	
				医疗按摩机构 Therapeutical Massage Institrations	保健按摩机构 Health-Care Massage Institrations
		人 person	人 person	人 person	人 person
全 国	**Nationwide**	**19732**	**10160**	**1126**	**16776**
北 京	Beijing	153	119	3	434
天 津	Tianjin	90	72	5	162
河 北	Hebei	963	1349	56	397
山 西	Shanxi	826	867	44	551
内蒙古	Inner Mongolia	514	179	108	297
辽 宁	Liaoning	568	218	27	564
吉 林	Jilin	375	608	84	713
黑龙江	Heilongjiang	415	373	48	272
上 海	Shanghai	185	73	1	84
江 苏	Jiangsu	705	602	39	1054
浙 江	Zhejiang	431	196	85	954
安 徽	Anhui	1557	216	65	493
福 建	Fujian	432	148	33	290
江 西	Jiangxi	716	238	75	521
山 东	Shandong	936	949	95	944
河 南	Henan	2320	977	84	901
湖 北	Hubei	432	60	43	881
湖 南	Hunan	1437	259	20	1212
广 东	Guangdong	578	674	10	667
广 西	Guangxi	599	109	4	250
海 南	Hainan	192	31	1	217
重 庆	Chongqing	273	133	18	789
四 川	Sichuan	703	131	28	1191
贵 州	Guizhou	717	169	23	571
云 南	Yunnan	1304	357	7	889
西 藏	Tibet	20	4		
陕 西	Shaanxi	1279	275	54	589
甘 肃	Gansu	486	217	23	334
青 海	Qinghai	214	105	10	146
宁 夏	Ningxia	119	164	12	271
新 疆	Xinjiang	191	285	19	120
新疆兵团	Xinjiang Production and Construction Corps	2	3	2	17
黑龙江垦区	Heilongjiang Land Reclamation Area				1

4-7-1 续表 Continued

地 区	Region	盲人医疗按摩人员专业技术职务任职资格评审 Vocational Qualification Appraisal for Blind Therapeutical Masseurs		盲人保健按摩人员就业 Employed Blind Health-Care Masseurs	盲人医疗按摩人员就业 Employed Blind Therapeutical Masseurs
		中级 Middle-Level Blind Therapeutical Masseurs	初级 Junior-Level Blind Therapeutical Masseurs		
		人 person	人 person	人 person	人 person
全 国	**Nationwide**	**122**	**953**	**22161**	**3021**
北 京	Beijing	10	24	330	98
天 津	Tianjin		10	485	25
河 北	Hebei	14	148	1202	260
山 西	Shanxi	13	5	400	65
内蒙古	Inner Mongolia		65	548	208
辽 宁	Liaoning	8	8	257	118
吉 林	Jilin		67	449	57
黑龙江	Heilongjiang	4	18	455	134
上 海	Shanghai		5	59	25
江 苏	Jiangsu		44	624	110
浙 江	Zhejiang		27	1316	196
安 徽	Anhui			1414	158
福 建	Fujian	21	10	466	63
江 西	Jiangxi			1074	117
山 东	Shandong	6	89	980	277
河 南	Henan	4	13	985	85
湖 北	Hubei	1	64	472	131
湖 南	Hunan		23	1009	95
广 东	Guangdong	4	68	1157	57
广 西	Guangxi			616	31
海 南	Hainan	2	10	724	15
重 庆	Chongqing	6	5	771	75
四 川	Sichuan		50	2566	59
贵 州	Guizhou	8	75	1088	63
云 南	Yunnan	2	34	279	12
西 藏	Tibet			2	
陕 西	Shaanxi		50	1309	103
甘 肃	Gansu			395	230
青 海	Qinghai	3	18	98	42
宁 夏	Ningxia		2	438	75
新 疆	Xinjiang	10	16	175	33
新疆兵团	Xinjiang Production and Construction Corps	5		13	4
黑龙江垦区	Heilongjiang Land Reclamation Area	1	5	5	

八、宣传文化
Publicity and Cultural Activities

4-8-1　宣传文化
Publicity and Cultureal Activities

地区	Region	宣传 Publicity 省级 At Provincial Level 组织新闻发布会 Press Conferences about Disability 次 time	广播电台残疾人专题栏目 Radio Programs on Disability 个 unit	电视手语栏目 TV Programmes with Sign Language 个 unit
全　国	**Nationwide**	**76**	**25**	**31**
北　京	Beijing	2	1	2
天　津	Tianjin	2	1	1
河　北	Hebei	19	1	
山　西	Shanxi	1	1	1
内蒙古	Inner Mongolia	2		1
辽　宁	Liaoning	2	1	1
吉　林	Jilin	1	1	1
黑龙江	Heilongjiang		1	2
上　海	Shanghai	10	1	1
江　苏	Jiangsu		1	2
浙　江	Zhejiang	2	1	3
安　徽	Anhui	1	1	1
福　建	Fujian			1
江　西	Jiangxi	1		
山　东	Shandong	3	1	
河　南	Henan		1	1
湖　北	Hubei	1	1	
湖　南	Hunan	3		
广　东	Guangdong	2	1	1
广　西	Guangxi		1	1
海　南	Hainan	8	1	1
重　庆	Chongqing	1	1	1
四　川	Sichuan	1	1	1
贵　州	Guizhou	2	2	1
云　南	Yunnan			1
西　藏	Tibet			
陕　西	Shaanxi	1	1	1
甘　肃	Gansu	2	1	1
青　海	Qinghai		1	1
宁　夏	Ningxia	8	1	1
新　疆	Xinjiang	1		1
新疆兵团	Xinjiang Production and Construction Corps			1
黑龙江垦区	Heilongjiang Land Reclamation Area			

4-8-1 续表 1 Continued 1

地区	Region	宣传 Publicity 省级 At Provincial Level 新促会 Disability Affairs Publicity Commissions 个 unit	官方微博 Official Blog 个 unit	官方微信 Official WeChat 个 unit	入驻政务客户端平台 Government Administrative Platforms Incorporated with Disability Affairs 个 unit
全　国	**Nationwide**	**19**	**14**	**28**	**17**
北　京	Beijing	1	3	1	1
天　津	Tianjin		1	2	1
河　北	Hebei	1	1	1	
山　西	Shanxi				
内蒙古	Inner Mongolia			1	
辽　宁	Liaoning			1	
吉　林	Jilin	1	1	1	1
黑龙江	Heilongjiang	1		1	1
上　海	Shanghai	1		1	1
江　苏	Jiangsu	1		1	
浙　江	Zhejiang	1		1	
安　徽	Anhui			1	
福　建	Fujian			1	
江　西	Jiangxi		1	1	
山　东	Shandong				1
河　南	Henan	1		1	
湖　北	Hubei			1	1
湖　南	Hunan	1			
广　东	Guangdong	1		1	5
广　西	Guangxi	1	1	1	1
海　南	Hainan	1	2	2	1
重　庆	Chongqing	1	1	1	1
四　川	Sichuan	1	2	1	1
贵　州	Guizhou			1	
云　南	Yunnan	1		1	1
西　藏	Tibet		1	1	
陕　西	Shaanxi			1	
甘　肃	Gansu	1		1	
青　海	Qinghai	1			
宁　夏	Ningxia	1		1	
新　疆	Xinjiang	1			
新疆兵团	Xinjiang Production and Construction Corps				
黑龙江垦区	Heilongjiang Land Reclamation Area				

4-8-1 续表 2 Continued 2

地 区	Region	宣传 Publicity			
		地市级 At Municipal Level			
		组织新闻发布会 Press Conferences about Disability	广播电台残疾人专题栏目 Radio Programs on Disability	电视手语栏目 TV Programmes with Sign Language	新促会 Societies for Promoting News Relating to PWDs
		次 time	个 unit	个 unit	个 unit
全 国	**Nationwide**	**86**	**205**	**264**	**88**
北 京	Beijing	1		3	1
天 津	Tianjin		1	6	1
河 北	Hebei	2	8	10	6
山 西	Shanxi	1	11	7	3
内蒙古	Inner Mongolia		2	8	1
辽 宁	Liaoning	6	11	16	4
吉 林	Jilin	3	2	7	5
黑龙江	Heilongjiang		10	8	3
上 海	Shanghai		2	14	3
江 苏	Jiangsu	5	15	15	7
浙 江	Zhejiang	1	13	12	5
安 徽	Anhui	1	15	16	4
福 建	Fujian		4	7	
江 西	Jiangxi	2	7	5	
山 东	Shandong	1	12	9	4
河 南	Henan		13	8	13
湖 北	Hubei	2	8	7	1
湖 南	Hunan	1	9	3	2
广 东	Guangdong	32	14	11	10
广 西	Guangxi	2	3	6	
海 南	Hainan			1	
重 庆	Chongqing		8	27	1
四 川	Sichuan	11	5	8	
贵 州	Guizhou		2	6	2
云 南	Yunnan		4	10	5
西 藏	Tibet				
陕 西	Shaanxi			5	1
甘 肃	Gansu	15	23	13	6
青 海	Qinghai			7	
宁 夏	Ningxia		1	5	
新 疆	Xinjiang		2	4	
新疆兵团	Xinjiang Production and Construction Corps				
黑龙江垦区	Heilongjiang Land Reclamation Area				

4-8-1 续表 3 Continued 3

地 区	Region	文化 Cultural Activities 省级 At Provincial Level 公共图书馆盲文及盲人有声读物图书室 Reading Rooms with Braille and Audio Reading Materials in Public Library (个 unit)	残疾人文化周 Cultural Week for PWDs (场次 time)	残疾人文化艺术类比赛及展览 Cultural or Artistic Competitions and Exhibitions of PWDs (次 time)	残疾人艺术团 Arts Groups of PWDs (个 unit)
全 国	**Nationwide**	**28**	**160**	**174**	**22**
北 京	Beijing		1	7	1
天 津	Tianjin	2	4	18	4
河 北	Hebei	1	12	4	
山 西	Shanxi	1	4	1	
内蒙古	Inner Mongolia	1	1	1	
辽 宁	Liaoning	1	6	3	
吉 林	Jilin	2	12	3	
黑龙江	Heilongjiang	1	2	2	1
上 海	Shanghai	1	12	6	1
江 苏	Jiangsu	1	3	1	
浙 江	Zhejiang	1	1	4	1
安 徽	Anhui	1	3		
福 建	Fujian	2	4	5	1
江 西	Jiangxi	1	6	3	
山 东	Shandong		1		1
河 南	Henan	1	1	4	1
湖 北	Hubei	1	2		1
湖 南	Hunan			2	
广 东	Guangdong	1	3	4	1
广 西	Guangxi	1	2		1
海 南	Hainan	1	8	4	2
重 庆	Chongqing	1	14	82	1
四 川	Sichuan		30	1	1
贵 州	Guizhou	1	10	1	
云 南	Yunnan	1	1		
西 藏	Tibet		3		
陕 西	Shaanxi	1	1		1
甘 肃	Gansu	1	6	5	
青 海	Qinghai	1	3	3	1
宁 夏	Ningxia	1	1	9	1
新 疆	Xinjiang		1	1	1
新疆兵团	Xinjiang Production and Construction Corps		1		
黑龙江垦区	Heilongjiang Land Reclamation Area		1		

4-8-1 续表 4 Continued 4

地 区	Region	文化 Cultural Activities					
		地市级 At Municipal Level				县级 At County Level	
		公共图书馆盲文及盲人有声读物图书室 Reading Rooms with Braille and Audio Reading Materials in Public Library	残疾人文化周 Cultural Week for PWDs	残疾人文化艺术类比赛及展览 Cultural or Artistic Competitions and Exhibitions of PWDs	残疾人艺术团 Arts Groups of PWDs	公共图书馆盲文及盲人有声读物图书室 Reading Rooms with Braille and Audio Reading Materials in Public Library	残疾人文化周 Cultural Week for PWDs
		个 unit	场次 time	次 time	个 unit	个 unit	场次 time
全 国	**Nationwide**	**273**	**780**	**489**	**261**	**823**	**6991**
北 京	Beijing					7	442
天 津	Tianjin					6	20
河 北	Hebei	15	22	32	9	14	325
山 西	Shanxi	7	16	4	7	10	138
内蒙古	Inner Mongolia	9	19	11	5	20	119
辽 宁	Liaoning	16	47	40	15	32	353
吉 林	Jilin	9	18	16	8	42	126
黑龙江	Heilongjiang	11	60	21	12	36	173
上 海	Shanghai					36	327
江 苏	Jiangsu	17	67	43	19	39	522
浙 江	Zhejiang	12	28	23	30	65	739
安 徽	Anhui	14	27	2	6	40	230
福 建	Fujian	6	11	32	1	38	101
江 西	Jiangxi	8	20	16	7	18	111
山 东	Shandong	12	41	46	30	53	316
河 南	Henan	16	43	16	5	58	147
湖 北	Hubei	11	23	18	3	21	123
湖 南	Hunan	9	34	42	26	9	147
广 东	Guangdong	17	91	50	39	31	522
广 西	Guangxi	10	30	7	4	21	144
海 南	Hainan	1					9
重 庆	Chongqing					41	303
四 川	Sichuan	18	15	10	9	34	346
贵 州	Guizhou	7	25	3	1	18	171
云 南	Yunnan	13	13	5	6	23	247
西 藏	Tibet						5
陕 西	Shaanxi	7	36	4	9	42	126
甘 肃	Gansu	14	44	25	4	41	221
青 海	Qinghai	4	9	8		7	71
宁 夏	Ningxia	5	7	12	2	17	53
新 疆	Xinjiang	4	14	3	4	4	120
新疆兵团	Xinjiang Production and Construction Corps	1	17				165
黑龙江垦区	Heilongjiang Land Reclamation Area		3				29

九、体育
Sports

4–9–1 体 育
Sports

地 区	Region	省级 At Provincial Level					
		残疾人群众体育健身活动 Fitness Sports Activities for PWDs	残疾人群众体育健身活动参加人次 Participants of Fitness Sports Activities for PWDs	新增残疾人健身示范点 Exemplary Bases for Fitness Sports of PWDs Established in 2018	新增残疾人社会体育指导员 Coaches for Fitness Sports of PWDs in 2018	残疾人体育比赛 Sports Events for PWDs	参赛残疾人运动员 Disabled Athletes Who Participated in the Sports Events
		次 time	人次 person-time	个 unit	人 person	次 time	人次 person-time
全 国	**Nationwide**	**284**	**86948**	**982**	**12939**	**319**	**36572**
北 京	Beijing	30	8000	36		25	200
天 津	Tianjin	9	3800	251	2663	12	119
河 北	Hebei	64	14184	68	528	87	4441
山 西	Shanxi	2	300	15	433	14	430
内蒙古	Inner Mongolia	3	300		3	1	598
辽 宁	Liaoning	1	100			26	1200
吉 林	Jilin	4	1000	10	80	3	210
黑龙江	Heilongjiang	2	2000		15	1	462
上 海	Shanghai	32	11174	38	80	26	11174
江 苏	Jiangsu	2	1523	166	3323	1	1102
浙 江	Zhejiang	3	3000	5	73	18	1283
安 徽	Anhui	3	356	8	115	14	685
福 建	Fujian	45	5941	34	294	6	336
江 西	Jiangxi	2	102	28	1	1	71
山 东	Shandong	1	305		1	2	1600
河 南	Henan	6	512	252	4254	3	1243
湖 北	Hubei	2	408		2	6	703
湖 南	Hunan	3	466	9	68	1	527
广 东	Guangdong	11	1020	2	95	6	726
广 西	Guangxi	2	347	1	127	1	549
海 南	Hainan	3	600			6	200
重 庆	Chongqing	4	19500	5	82	10	325
四 川	Sichuan			3		1	1840
贵 州	Guizhou	1	100		9	1	430
云 南	Yunnan	1	120		40	1	960
西 藏	Tibet				1		
陕 西	Shaanxi	20	2300	6	86	20	1600
甘 肃	Gansu	7	2860	9	18	3	2108
青 海	Qinghai	10	5200	23	355	11	1300
宁 夏	Ningxia	7	1000	1	1	12	150
新 疆	Xinjiang	1	100				
新疆兵团	Xinjiang Production and Construction Corps	3	330	12	192		
黑龙江垦区	Heilongjiang Land Reclamation Area						

4-9-1 续表 Continued

地　区	Region	省级 At Provincial Level		地市级 At Municipal Level				残疾人康复体育关爱家庭服务 Delivery of Rehabilitative Sports to Families with PWDs
		残疾人体育训练基地 Sports Training Bases for PWDs	聘任教练员 Contracted Coaches	残疾人群众体育健身活动 Fitness Sports Activities for PWDs	残疾人群众体育健身活动参加人数 Participants of Fitness Sports Activities for PWDs	新增残疾人体育健身示范点 Exemplary Bases for Fitness Sports of PWDs Established in 2018	新增残疾人社会体育指导员 Coaches for Fitness Sports of PWDs in 2018	
		个 unit	人 person	次 time	人次 person-time	个 unit	人 person	户 household
全　国	**Nationwide**	**251**	**797**	**4132**	**164135**	**391**	**5167**	**52367**
北　京	Beijing	6	42					3100
天　津	Tianjin	2	15					1000
河　北	Hebei	10	53	3312	77366	1	436	3945
山　西	Shanxi	3	18	6	763	11	105	6000
内蒙古	Inner Mongolia	2	2	7	762	30	33	1000
辽　宁	Liaoning	31	58	43	4585	14	115	
吉　林	Jilin	16	20	61	7520	133	873	355
黑龙江	Heilongjiang	5	12	6	595	2	3	
上　海	Shanghai	5	160					340
江　苏	Jiangsu	2		52	4235	3	13	13268
浙　江	Zhejiang	9	48	44	8747	10	338	6437
安　徽	Anhui	10	18	35	6142	1	55	
福　建	Fujian	15	22	22	1550	3	18	100
江　西	Jiangxi	11	30	24	2153	1	3	1732
山　东	Shandong	12	35	115	11020	17	12	970
河　南	Henan	6	31	34	1345	15	135	2000
湖　北	Hubei	4	8	34	2620	101	1927	
湖　南	Hunan	4	12	48	1548	13	150	1300
广　东	Guangdong	8	30	112	11559	3	501	3130
广　西	Guangxi	1	28	9	840	1	25	
海　南	Hainan	13	25	2	25	1		
重　庆	Chongqing	8	8			8	24	1
四　川	Sichuan	16	50	13	3536		1	4688
贵　州	Guizhou	6	14	10	1446	1	2	
云　南	Yunnan	4	17	24	1276	1	348	
西　藏	Tibet							
陕　西	Shaanxi	31	20	11	1900			1000
甘　肃	Gansu	3	7	92	10716	1		1001
青　海	Qinghai	1	2	6	349	11	22	
宁　夏	Ningxia	1	4	5	1200	2		
新　疆	Xinjiang	6	8	1	25	6	27	
新疆兵团	Xinjiang Production and Construction Corps			4	312	1	1	1000
黑龙江垦区	Heilongjiang Land Reclamation Area							

十、维权
Rights Protection

4-10-1 法规体系
Legal System

地 区	Region	制定或修改关于残疾人的专门法规、规章 Disability-specific Laws and Regulations Enacted or Reviewed for PWDs	省级 At Provincial Level	地市级 At Municipal Level	制定或修改保障残疾人权益的规范性文件 Polices Enacted or Reviewed for PWDs	省级 At Provincial Level	地市级 At Municipal Level	县级 At County Level
		个 unit	个 unit	个 unit	个 unit	个 unit	个 unit	个 unit
全 国	**Nationwide**	**24**	**15**	**9**	**228**	**19**	**61**	**148**
北 京	Beijing				1	1		
天 津	Tianjin	1	1		6	6		
河 北	Hebei				12	2	1	9
山 西	Shanxi				3			3
内蒙古	Inner Mongolia	1	1		1			1
辽 宁	Liaoning				3		2	1
吉 林	Jilin				1		1	
黑龙江	Heilongjiang	1		1	1		1	
上 海	Shanghai	1	1		4			4
江 苏	Jiangsu				11		4	7
浙 江	Zhejiang	1	1		20		1	19
安 徽	Anhui				12		4	8
福 建	Fujian				13	1	7	5
江 西	Jiangxi				5	1	3	1
山 东	Shandong	3	2	1	16	3	2	11
河 南	Henan				7		3	4
湖 北	Hubei	1	1		5		1	4
湖 南	Hunan				9		1	8
广 东	Guangdong	2	1	1	13	1	10	2
广 西	Guangxi				1	1		
海 南	Hainan	1		1	5		1	4
重 庆	Chongqing				6			6
四 川	Sichuan	1		1	15		5	10
贵 州	Guizhou				18	2	1	15
云 南	Yunnan				2		1	1
西 藏	Tibet				2		2	
陕 西	Shaanxi	1	1		5	1	1	3
甘 肃	Gansu	9	6	3	24		5	19
青 海	Qinghai	1		1	3		2	1
宁 夏	Ningxia				2		2	
新 疆	Xinjiang				2			2
新疆兵团	Xinjiang Production and Construction Corps							
黑龙江垦区	Heilongjiang Land Reclamation Area							

4-10-2 执法检查
Law Enforcement Inspection

地区	Region	人大执法检查或专题调研 Inspections and Researches by People's Congresses	省级 At Provincial Level	地市级 At Municipal Level	县级 At County Level
		次 time	次 time	次 time	次 time
全国	**Nationwide**	**294**	**10**	**56**	**228**
北京	Beijing	3			3
天津	Tianjin	1	1		
河北	Hebei	15		1	14
山西	Shanxi	14		1	13
内蒙古	Inner Mongolia	4			4
辽宁	Liaoning	3		2	1
吉林	Jilin	6		1	5
黑龙江	Heilongjiang	13		2	11
上海	Shanghai	2	1		1
江苏	Jiangsu	14		3	11
浙江	Zhejiang	50		8	42
安徽	Anhui	11		2	9
福建	Fujian	7		2	5
江西	Jiangxi	8		1	7
山东	Shandong	22	1	8	13
河南	Henan	9		4	5
湖北	Hubei	10		1	9
湖南	Hunan	17		4	13
广东	Guangdong	14	3	4	7
广西	Guangxi	3	1	1	1
海南	Hainan	3	1		2
重庆	Chongqing	8			8
四川	Sichuan	13	1	3	9
贵州	Guizhou	4			4
云南	Yunnan	4		1	3
西藏	Tibet				
陕西	Shaanxi	8		2	6
甘肃	Gansu	19		4	15
青海	Qinghai	2			2
宁夏	Ningxia	5	1	1	3
新疆	Xinjiang	2			2
新疆兵团	Xinjiang Production and Construction Corps				
黑龙江垦区	Heilongjiang Land Reclamation Area				

4-10-2 续表 Continued

地 区	Region	政协视察或专题调研 Inspections and Researches by People's Political Consultative Conferences	省级 At Provincial Level	地市级 At Municipal Level	县级 At County Level
		次 time	次 time	次 time	次 time
全 国	**Nationwide**	**280**	**6**	**47**	**227**
北 京	Beijing	2			2
天 津	Tianjin				
河 北	Hebei	14		1	13
山 西	Shanxi	8		2	6
内蒙古	Inner Mongolia	3			3
辽 宁	Liaoning	4		2	2
吉 林	Jilin	3			3
黑龙江	Heilongjiang	6		1	5
上 海	Shanghai				
江 苏	Jiangsu	14		4	10
浙 江	Zhejiang	51	1	5	45
安 徽	Anhui	14	1	4	9
福 建	Fujian	6			6
江 西	Jiangxi	14		3	11
山 东	Shandong	18	1	3	14
河 南	Henan	5			5
湖 北	Hubei	13		2	11
湖 南	Hunan	19		5	14
广 东	Guangdong	7		5	2
广 西	Guangxi	2			2
海 南	Hainan				
重 庆	Chongqing	17			17
四 川	Sichuan	17	1	1	15
贵 州	Guizhou	2			2
云 南	Yunnan	12		5	7
西 藏	Tibet				
陕 西	Shaanxi	2		1	1
甘 肃	Gansu	21		3	18
青 海	Qinghai	3	1		2
宁 夏	Ningxia	3	1		2
新 疆	Xinjiang				
新疆兵团	Xinjiang Production and Construction Corps				
黑龙江垦区	Heilongjiang Land Reclamation Area				

4-10-3 法制宣传
Publicity on Laws

地 区	Region	省级 At Provincial Level			
		普法宣传教育活动 Activities for Law Publicity and Education	普法宣传教育活动参加人数 Participants of Activities for Law Publicity and Education	残疾人工作者法律培训班 Law Trainings for Staff Working for PWDs	法律培训班参加人数 Trainees of Law Trainings
		次 time	人 person	个 unit	人 person
全 国	**Nationwide**	**309**	**35835**	**59**	**4051**
北 京	Beijing	200	4000	30	1678
天 津	Tianjin	2	225	2	190
河 北	Hebei	4	1300	2	270
山 西	Shanxi	3	360	2	190
内蒙古	Inner Mongolia	1	20		
辽 宁	Liaoning	21	2200		
吉 林	Jilin			1	50
黑龙江	Heilongjiang	2	533	1	167
上 海	Shanghai	2	260	2	70
江 苏	Jiangsu	1	120	1	30
浙 江	Zhejiang	3	190	1	50
安 徽	Anhui	3	410	1	130
福 建	Fujian	9	453	3	206
江 西	Jiangxi	7	510	3	180
山 东	Shandong	5	570	2	196
河 南	Henan				
湖 北	Hubei	2	200	2	140
湖 南	Hunan				
广 东	Guangdong	1	18000		
广 西	Guangxi	3	150	1	44
海 南	Hainan	1	102		
重 庆	Chongqing	4	680	1	100
四 川	Sichuan	2	300	1	80
贵 州	Guizhou	2	400	1	120
云 南	Yunnan				
西 藏	Tibet	9	710		
陕 西	Shaanxi	4	600		
甘 肃	Gansu	3	600		
青 海	Qinghai	4	2100		
宁 夏	Ningxia	5	450		
新 疆	Xinjiang	5	260	2	160
新疆兵团	Xinjiang Production and Construction Corps				
黑龙江垦区	Heilongjiang Land Reclamation Area	1	132		

4-10-4 法律救助
Legal Aid

地 区	Region	建立残疾人法律救助协调组织 Legal Assistance and Coordination Organization for PWDs			
		建立残疾人法律救助工作协调机构 Legal Assistance and Coordination Organization for PWDs	省级 At Provincial Level	地市级 At Municipal Level	县级 At County Level
		个 unit	个 unit	个 unit	个 unit
全 国	**Nationwide**	**1988**	**27**	**256**	**1705**
北 京	Beijing	13	1		12
天 津	Tianjin	17	1		16
河 北	Hebei	162	1	11	150
山 西	Shanxi	21	1	4	16
内蒙古	Inner Mongolia	67		5	62
辽 宁	Liaoning	81	1	14	66
吉 林	Jilin	69	1	10	58
黑龙江	Heilongjiang	21	1	3	17
上 海	Shanghai	18	1		17
江 苏	Jiangsu	98	1	12	85
浙 江	Zhejiang	102	1	11	90
安 徽	Anhui	53	1	10	42
福 建	Fujian	63	1	9	53
江 西	Jiangxi	58	1	7	50
山 东	Shandong	82	1	11	70
河 南	Henan	127	1	18	108
湖 北	Hubei	75	1	11	63
湖 南	Hunan	114	1	14	99
广 东	Guangdong	55	1	16	38
广 西	Guangxi	43	1	9	33
海 南	Hainan	23		3	20
重 庆	Chongqing	29			29
四 川	Sichuan	121	1	13	107
贵 州	Guizhou	78	1	6	71
云 南	Yunnan	40	1	7	32
西 藏	Tibet				
陕 西	Shaanxi	101	1	9	91
甘 肃	Gansu	102	1	15	86
青 海	Qinghai	47	1	6	40
宁 夏	Ningxia	23		4	19
新 疆	Xinjiang	75	1	9	65
新疆兵团	Xinjiang Production and Construction Corps	4		4	
黑龙江垦区	Heilongjiang Land Reclamation Area	6	1	5	

4-10-4 续表 1 Continued 1

地区	Region	残疾人法律救助工作站 Legal Assistance Stations for PWDs			
		残疾人法律救助工作站 Legal Assistance Stations for PWDs	省级 At Provincial Level	地市级 At Municipal Level	县级 At County Level
		个 unit	个 unit	个 unit	个 unit
全　国	**Nationwide**	**1814**	**22**	**230**	**1562**
北　京	Beijing	4			4
天　津	Tianjin	17	1		16
河　北	Hebei	156	1	11	144
山　西	Shanxi	17		3	14
内蒙古	Inner Mongolia	77		4	73
辽　宁	Liaoning	74	1	14	59
吉　林	Jilin	66	1	10	55
黑龙江	Heilongjiang	13		2	11
上　海	Shanghai	17	1		16
江　苏	Jiangsu	93	1	12	80
浙　江	Zhejiang	102	1	11	90
安　徽	Anhui	44		8	36
福　建	Fujian	54	1	9	44
江　西	Jiangxi	46	1	6	39
山　东	Shandong	82	1	11	70
河　南	Henan	116	1	14	101
湖　北	Hubei	65	1	10	54
湖　南	Hunan	108	1	14	93
广　东	Guangdong	43	1	13	29
广　西	Guangxi	39	1	8	30
海　南	Hainan	23		3	20
重　庆	Chongqing	29			29
四　川	Sichuan	98	1	12	85
贵　州	Guizhou	67	1	3	63
云　南	Yunnan	36	1	7	28
西　藏	Tibet				
陕　西	Shaanxi	93	1	9	83
甘　肃	Gansu	102	1	15	86
青　海	Qinghai	43	1	6	36
宁　夏	Ningxia	22		4	18
新　疆	Xinjiang	65	1	8	56
新疆兵团	Xinjiang Production and Construction Corps	3		3	
黑龙江垦区	Heilongjiang Land Reclamation Area				

4-10-4 续表 2 Continued 2

地 区	Region	残疾人法律救助工作站 Legal Assistance Stations for PWDs			
		残疾人法律救助工作站办理的案件 Cases Handled by Legal Assistance Stations for PWDs	省级 At Provincial Level	地市级 At Municipal Level	县级 At County Level
		件 case	件 case	件 case	件 case
全 国	**Nationwide**	**3532**	**285**	**339**	**2908**
北 京	Beijing	34			34
天 津	Tianjin	585	182		403
河 北	Hebei	97		17	80
山 西	Shanxi	27			27
内蒙古	Inner Mongolia	52			52
辽 宁	Liaoning	163	10	38	115
吉 林	Jilin	55		8	47
黑龙江	Heilongjiang	11		4	7
上 海	Shanghai	144			144
江 苏	Jiangsu	182	22	47	113
浙 江	Zhejiang	496	1	61	434
安 徽	Anhui	20		5	15
福 建	Fujian	73	14	16	43
江 西	Jiangxi	23			23
山 东	Shandong	188	1	17	170
河 南	Henan	68		23	45
湖 北	Hubei	108	10	10	88
湖 南	Hunan	219		23	196
广 东	Guangdong	58		31	27
广 西	Guangxi	22			22
海 南	Hainan	4		2	2
重 庆	Chongqing	220			220
四 川	Sichuan	105	7	9	89
贵 州	Guizhou	98	1		97
云 南	Yunnan	93	12		81
西 藏	Tibet				
陕 西	Shaanxi	45	25	3	17
甘 肃	Gansu	111		6	105
青 海	Qinghai	97		1	96
宁 夏	Ningxia	92		18	74
新 疆	Xinjiang	42			42
新疆兵团	Xinjiang Production and Construction Corps				
黑龙江垦区	Heilongjiang Land Reclamation Area				

4–10–5 参政议政
Participation of Persons with Disabilities in Administration and Discussion of State Affairs

地区	Region	残联协助提出建议、议案和提案 Bills,Suggestions and Proposals Submitted with Assistance of Disabled Persons' Federations		残联办理人大政协建议、提案 Suggestions and Proposals Handled by Disabled Persons' Federations	
		协助人大代表提出议案、建议 Bills and Suggestions Submitted to People's Congresses	协助政协委员提出提案 Proposals Submitted to People's Political Consultative Conferences	办理人大建议 Suggestions of People's Congresses Handled	办理政协提案 Proposals of People's Political Consultative Conferences Handled
		件 case	件 case	件 case	件 case
全国	**Nationwide**	**305**	**528**	**399**	**682**
北京	Beijing	3	5	9	19
天津	Tianjin			8	9
河北	Hebei	11	18	14	14
山西	Shanxi	15	19	11	19
内蒙古	Inner Mongolia		6	1	5
辽宁	Liaoning	19	25	14	25
吉林	Jilin	4	6	6	7
黑龙江	Heilongjiang	3	8	3	4
上海	Shanghai	1	3	21	15
江苏	Jiangsu	12	20	23	34
浙江	Zhejiang	64	111	97	132
安徽	Anhui	1	14	12	30
福建	Fujian	2	17	9	31
江西	Jiangxi	9	29	3	18
山东	Shandong	44	19	11	42
河南	Henan	2	9	7	11
湖北	Hubei	12	34	28	25
湖南	Hunan	11	18	7	11
广东	Guangdong	6	16	44	72
广西	Guangxi	5	10	5	18
海南	Hainan	4	3		
重庆	Chongqing	28	36	26	42
四川	Sichuan	12	25	15	33
贵州	Guizhou	2	8	1	2
云南	Yunnan	6	12	2	4
西藏	Tibet				
陕西	Shaanxi	7	5	9	20
甘肃	Gansu	13	21	5	17
青海	Qinghai	6	10	4	11
宁夏	Ningxia		9	3	7
新疆	Xinjiang	3	11	1	5
新疆兵团	Xinjiang Production and Construction Corps		1		
黑龙江垦区	Heilongjiang Land Reclamation Area				

4-10-6 无障碍环境建设与残疾人机动轮椅车燃油补贴
Promotion of Accessible Environments and Gas Subsidy for Motorized Wheelchairs

地 区	Region	无障碍建设与管理法规、政府令 Regulations and Decrees on Accessible Environments Building and Management	无障碍建设领导协调组织 Leading and Coordinating Bodies for Building Accessible Environments	系统开展无障碍建设市、县 Cities and Counties Carrying Out Systematic Accessibitity Construction	地市级 At Municipal Level	县级 At County Level
		个 unit	个 unit	个 unit	个 unit	个 unit
全 国	**Nationwide**	**475**	**1315**	**1702**	**210**	**1492**
北 京	Beijing	1	17	16		16
天 津	Tianjin	1	17	16		16
河 北	Hebei	43	128	186	11	175
山 西	Shanxi	13	44	72	11	61
内蒙古	Inner Mongolia	12	20	67	9	58
辽 宁	Liaoning	3	49	8	5	3
吉 林	Jilin	17	30	13	4	9
黑龙江	Heilongjiang	1	11	36	2	34
上 海	Shanghai	2	34	16		16
江 苏	Jiangsu	26	78	56	13	43
浙 江	Zhejiang	45	68	99	11	88
安 徽	Anhui	6	29	81	16	65
福 建	Fujian	7	51	48	9	39
江 西	Jiangxi	6	14	127	11	116
山 东	Shandong	38	83	58	7	51
河 南	Henan	92	41	60	5	55
湖 北	Hubei	8	23	83	13	70
湖 南	Hunan	10	44	5		5
广 东	Guangdong	27	30	145	21	124
广 西	Guangxi		126	125	14	111
海 南	Hainan	1	4	4	2	2
重 庆	Chongqing	5	32	38		38
四 川	Sichuan	25	67	66	11	55
贵 州	Guizhou	2	19	28	3	25
云 南	Yunnan	15	62	56	3	53
西 藏	Tibet					
陕 西	Shaanxi	21	23	50	3	47
甘 肃	Gansu	39	69	101	15	86
青 海	Qinghai	3	39	11	3	8
宁 夏	Ningxia	3	17	24	4	20
新 疆	Xinjiang	1	31	5	2	3
新疆兵团	Xinjiang Production and Construction Corps		1			
黑龙江垦区	Heilongjiang Land Reclamation Area	2	14	2	2	

4-10-6 续表 Continued

地　区	Region	残疾人家庭无障碍改造 Accessibility Renovation for Homes of PWDs	无障碍建设检查 Inspections on Accessibility	无障碍培训 Trainings on Accessibility	残疾人机动轮椅车燃油补贴 Subsidy for Gas Used by Motorized Wheelchairs of PWDs
		户 household	次 time	人次 person-time	人 person
全　国	**Nationwide**	**1157900**	**2929**	**37530**	**651328**
北　京	Beijing	31238	40	4202	24445
天　津	Tianjin	13299	59	661	19003
河　北	Hebei	34653	47	346	12502
山　西	Shanxi	21469	26	601	8189
内蒙古	Inner Mongolia	15291	53	162	24317
辽　宁	Liaoning	20534	91	4512	14001
吉　林	Jilin	9604	10	72	11030
黑龙江	Heilongjiang	16375	6	20	10685
上　海	Shanghai	31140	709	2016	21174
江　苏	Jiangsu	36663	187	2979	20753
浙　江	Zhejiang	153943	556	3071	11545
安　徽	Anhui	74563	46	527	24034
福　建	Fujian	17694	35	1779	3079
江　西	Jiangxi	33372	18	157	22076
山　东	Shandong	157668	104	1426	15654
河　南	Henan	103272	50	903	48824
湖　北	Hubei	34309	34	400	38302
湖　南	Hunan	60902	64	851	77786
广　东	Guangdong	23832	323	1841	22719
广　西	Guangxi	21422	102	1101	9875
海　南	Hainan	5385	3	270	6534
重　庆	Chongqing	19259	47	2311	4211
四　川	Sichuan	10740	75	5308	20527
贵　州	Guizhou	63587	14	284	31148
云　南	Yunnan	39480	48	844	23545
西　藏	Tibet	2358	2	21	4116
陕　西	Shaanxi	41761	31	290	11492
甘　肃	Gansu	14449	54	175	31791
青　海	Qinghai	5136	28	23	15939
宁　夏	Ningxia	5916	31	158	13952
新　疆	Xinjiang	37072	35	161	40437
新疆兵团	Xinjiang Production and Construction Corps	1323			6153
黑龙江垦区	Heilongjiang Land Reclamation Area	191	1	58	1490

4–10–7 残疾人信访
Petitions from Persons with Disabilities

地 区	Region	来信 Petition Letters					
		总计 Subtotal	涉法涉诉类 Regarding Legal Lawsuits	医疗康复类 Medical Rehabilitation	教育类 Education	就业扶贫类 Employment and Poverty Alleviation	社会保障类 Social Security
		件 case	件 case	件 case	件 case	件 case	件 case
全 国	**Nationwide**	**27862**	**1174**	**5099**	**1713**	**4543**	**6269**
北 京	Beijing	7039	454	863	168	1416	1485
天 津	Tianjin	283	2	18	4	17	99
河 北	Hebei	463	77	64	16	165	50
山 西	Shanxi	1770	13	736	78	134	399
内蒙古	Inner Mongolia	91	1	22	4	38	11
辽 宁	Liaoning	256	4	45	27	41	69
吉 林	Jilin	85	12	6		10	35
黑龙江	Heilongjiang	97		10	8	20	30
上 海	Shanghai	839	40	65	36	111	153
江 苏	Jiangsu	614	37	55	23	100	96
浙 江	Zhejiang	1402	98	104	26	90	556
安 徽	Anhui	197	7	16	12	29	32
福 建	Fujian	265	54	26	9	29	43
江 西	Jiangxi	918	72	250	54	131	150
山 东	Shandong	378	23	22	4	36	84
河 南	Henan	435	14	46	36	57	119
湖 北	Hubei	1757	63	217	50	375	510
湖 南	Hunan	2409	81	429	174	472	791
广 东	Guangdong	1624	25	321	318	240	242
广 西	Guangxi	985	9	382	128	165	199
海 南	Hainan	47		16	2	5	15
重 庆	Chongqing	822	27	53	42	58	106
四 川	Sichuan	1086	12	133	76	244	233
贵 州	Guizhou	187	4	27	12	27	26
云 南	Yunnan	1186	14	334	193	158	282
西 藏	Tibet						
陕 西	Shaanxi	403	20	112	12	44	92
甘 肃	Gansu	1546	4	656	164	205	294
青 海	Qinghai	88	2	16	11		24
宁 夏	Ningxia	39	4	7		1	14
新 疆	Xinjiang	547	1	48	26	123	28
新疆兵团	Xinjiang Production and Construction Corps						
黑龙江垦区	Heilongjiang Land Reclamation Area	4				2	2

4-10-7 续表 1 Continued 1

地 区	Region	来信 Petition Letters				
		权益保障类 Rights and Interest Protection	控告检举类 Accusation and Disclosure	意见建议类 Opinions and Suggestions	非残类 Unrelated with Disability	其他类 Others
		件 case	件 case	件 case	件 case	件 case
全 国	**Nationwide**	**2126**	**307**	**937**	**1568**	**4126**
北 京	Beijing	93	68	69	1262	1161
天 津	Tianjin	45	26	8	2	62
河 北	Hebei	44	5	28	5	9
山 西	Shanxi	144	13	39	105	109
内蒙古	Inner Mongolia	4		2		9
辽 宁	Liaoning	33	1	1	3	32
吉 林	Jilin	3	2	12		5
黑龙江	Heilongjiang	18	1	4	3	3
上 海	Shanghai	163	10	51	25	185
江 苏	Jiangsu	93	35	64	19	92
浙 江	Zhejiang	167	29	23	12	297
安 徽	Anhui	20	3	29	1	48
福 建	Fujian	50	10	2	3	39
江 西	Jiangxi	88	8	102	13	50
山 东	Shandong	39	6	3	1	160
河 南	Henan	106	2	13	1	41
湖 北	Hubei	120	8	53	13	348
湖 南	Hunan	232	12	119	23	76
广 东	Guangdong	212	25	60	11	170
广 西	Guangxi	30	3	4	10	55
海 南	Hainan	2				7
重 庆	Chongqing	73	7	54		402
四 川	Sichuan	128	17	52	28	163
贵 州	Guizhou	5	2	9	5	70
云 南	Yunnan	92	2	31	9	71
西 藏	Tibet					
陕 西	Shaanxi	29	5	12	5	72
甘 肃	Gansu	68	6	89	5	55
青 海	Qinghai	1				34
宁 夏	Ningxia	5	1		2	5
新 疆	Xinjiang	19		4	2	296
新疆兵团	Xinjiang Production and Construction Corps					
黑龙江垦区	Heilongjiang Land Reclamation Area					

4-10-7 续表 2 Continued 2

地区	Region	来访 Petition Visits					
		总计 Subtotal	涉法涉诉类 Regarding Legal Lawsuits	医疗康复类 Medical Rehabilitation	教育类 Education	就业扶贫类 Employment and Poverty Alleviation	社会保障类 Social Security
		人次 person-time	人次 person-time	人次 person-time	人次 person-time	人次 person-time	人次 person-time
全 国	**Nationwide**	**158597**	**6192**	**31073**	**9207**	**26158**	**42345**
北 京	Beijing	4669	1286	285	59	487	977
天 津	Tianjin	2128	453	136	78	203	564
河 北	Hebei	3151	100	692	190	552	776
山 西	Shanxi	12280	169	3432	416	2189	4652
内蒙古	Inner Mongolia	1860	18	393	288	379	508
辽 宁	Liaoning	7278	507	776	187	1103	2942
吉 林	Jilin	2402	79	252	81	235	665
黑龙江	Heilongjiang	1833	32	276	157	343	443
上 海	Shanghai	3094	262	217	82	328	595
江 苏	Jiangsu	3764	120	496	174	566	688
浙 江	Zhejiang	5516	182	887	601	845	1132
安 徽	Anhui	6786	103	1109	529	1156	1031
福 建	Fujian	3181	84	561	405	657	744
江 西	Jiangxi	5552	133	1202	317	1464	1154
山 东	Shandong	2457	325	228	148	327	547
河 南	Henan	1982	63	313	101	362	352
湖 北	Hubei	10545	349	1403	425	1521	4253
湖 南	Hunan	12693	942	2035	1009	2220	3165
广 东	Guangdong	7703	149	2917	575	1086	1348
广 西	Guangxi	4710	25	1369	444	841	1170
海 南	Hainan	172		13	15	39	67
重 庆	Chongqing	3698	125	226	98	637	843
四 川	Sichuan	15556	253	3006	541	2619	3543
贵 州	Guizhou	7535	73	1928	192	587	3141
云 南	Yunnan	10246	92	1902	874	1880	2964
西 藏	Tibet	11				3	
陕 西	Shaanxi	6427	81	1153	397	1376	1900
甘 肃	Gansu	2657	50	859	258	478	488
青 海	Qinghai	323	5	96	40	38	72
宁 夏	Ningxia	3666	92	1860	124	806	492
新 疆	Xinjiang	2394	40	710	167	412	342
新疆兵团	Xinjiang Production and Construction Corps	2290		336	233	415	781
黑龙江垦区	Heilongjiang Land Reclamation Area	38		5	2	4	6

4-10-7 续表 3 Continued 3

地 区	Region	来访 Petition Visits				
		权益保障类 Rights and Interest Protection	控告检举类 Accusation and Disclosure	意见建议类 Opinions and Suggestions	非残类 Unrelated with Disability	其他类 Others
		人次 person-time	人次 person-time	人次 person-time	人次 person-time	人次 person-time
全 国	**Nationwide**	**16524**	**1132**	**4814**	**2132**	**19020**
北 京	Beijing	714	103	62	356	340
天 津	Tianjin	167	113	31	8	375
河 北	Hebei	500	18	163	59	101
山 西	Shanxi	347	28	57	51	939
内蒙古	Inner Mongolia	67		19	1	187
辽 宁	Liaoning	495	36	159	103	970
吉 林	Jilin	532	16	186	46	310
黑龙江	Heilongjiang	116		49	21	396
上 海	Shanghai	828	22	215	153	392
江 苏	Jiangsu	747	92	262	101	518
浙 江	Zhejiang	420	25	609	68	747
安 徽	Anhui	551	13	131	23	2140
福 建	Fujian	339	22	40		329
江 西	Jiangxi	496	2	211	290	283
山 东	Shandong	539	12	50	7	274
河 南	Henan	302	2	105	7	375
湖 北	Hubei	1169	8	408	58	951
湖 南	Hunan	1250	155	445	132	1340
广 东	Guangdong	565	69	140	74	780
广 西	Guangxi	531	2	138	33	157
海 南	Hainan	38				
重 庆	Chongqing	612	13	149	34	961
四 川	Sichuan	1874	170	383	120	3047
贵 州	Guizhou	834	3	436	251	90
云 南	Yunnan	718	1	91	56	1668
西 藏	Tibet	8				
陕 西	Shaanxi	671	22	87	13	727
甘 肃	Gansu	351	5	74	29	65
青 海	Qinghai	15		2		55
宁 夏	Ningxia	180	6	35	9	62
新 疆	Xinjiang	167	174	50	29	303
新疆兵团	Xinjiang Production and Construction Corps	380		7		138
黑龙江垦区	Heilongjiang Land Reclamation Area	1		20		

十一、组织建设
Disabled Persons' Organizations

4–11–1 省(自治区、直辖市)级残联
Disabled Persons' Federations at Provincial Level

地 区	Region	省市县乡残联实有人员 Staff of Disabled Persons' Federations at Provincial,Municipal, County and Township Level	省级残联机关 Disabled Persons' Federations at Provincial Level		省级残联事业单位 Affiliated Institutions at Provincial Level		
			实有人员 Staff	残疾人干部 Staff with Disability	单位 Affiliated Institutions	实有人员 Total Staff	残疾人 Staff with Disability
		人 person	人 person	人 person	个 unit	人 person	人 person
全 国	**Nationwide**	**111056**	**1558**	**155**	**153**	**7091**	**267**
北 京	Beijing	1280	70	9	11	267	22
天 津	Tianjin	955	47	4	9	167	22
河 北	Hebei	5380	52	3	4	141	7
山 西	Shanxi	4729	62	6	8	413	9
内蒙古	Inner Mongolia	3053	34	4	4	98	5
辽 宁	Liaoning	3405	37	6	1	249	5
吉 林	Jilin	2632	38	6	4	104	9
黑龙江	Heilongjiang	3022	41	5	3	563	5
上 海	Shanghai	1144	39	6	7	267	12
江 苏	Jiangsu	4605	55	10	5	67	4
浙 江	Zhejiang	4895	43	5	6	407	6
安 徽	Anhui	3470	50	6	4	184	10
福 建	Fujian	2723	39	2	4	182	26
江 西	Jiangxi	3939	55	2	6	120	3
山 东	Shandong	6009	48	3	5	279	6
河 南	Henan	7995	54	7	3	184	6
湖 北	Hubei	3365	50	4	6	89	7
湖 南	Hunan	4807	45	3	6	94	4
广 东	Guangdong	7877	49	5	5	213	9
广 西	Guangxi	3568	55	5	5	198	7
海 南	Hainan	703	70	3	2	80	3
重 庆	Chongqing	1900	34	1	3	153	5
四 川	Sichuan	8961	45	10	3	641	2
贵 州	Guizhou	3266	51	8	3	111	7
云 南	Yunnan	3843	60	9	8	258	26
西 藏	Tibet	329	26	2	2	77	
陕 西	Shaanxi	4203	66	3	5	441	2
甘 肃	Gansu	4208	78	5	9	564	6
青 海	Qinghai	1291	42	4	2	72	1
宁 夏	Ningxia	875	56	3	2	208	10
新 疆	Xinjiang	2302	50	5	5	182	19
新疆兵团	Xinjiang Production and Construction Corps	92	11	1	2	14	1
黑龙江垦区	Heilongjiang Land Reclamation Area	230	6		1	4	1

4-11-1 续表 Continued

地区	Region	干部队伍综合培训情况 Training of Staff						志愿者助残情况 Volunteers	
		省级举办综合培训班 Provincial-level General Trainings	参加省级综合培训人次 Trainees on Provincial-level Trainings	省级举办残疾人干部培训班 Provincial-level Trainings for Staff with Disability	参加省级残疾人干部培训人次 Trainees on Provincial-level Trainings for Staff with Disability	参加全国培训人次 Trainees on State-level Trainings	参加全国残疾人干部培训人次 Trainees on State-level Trainings for Staff with Disability	志愿者登记在册 Registered Volunteers	受助残疾人 PWDs Helped by Volunteers
		期 session	人次 person-time	期 session	人次 person-time	人次 person-time	人次 person-time	人 person	人次 person-time
全　国	**Nationwide**	**68**	**8099**	**43**	**4310**	**147**	**86**	**7027**	**83439**
北　京	Beijing	4	191	4	191			54	871
天　津	Tianjin	1	272	1	102				
河　北	Hebei	1	222					796	946
山　西	Shanxi	1	120			1	1	60	500
内蒙古	Inner Mongolia								
辽　宁	Liaoning	1	50	25	3400				
吉　林	Jilin							320	2566
黑龙江	Heilongjiang	5	560						
上　海	Shanghai	7	775	2	45			245	47160
江　苏	Jiangsu	2	135						
浙　江	Zhejiang	2	250			30	72		
安　徽	Anhui	4	1100	1	70				
福　建	Fujian	1	120						
江　西	Jiangxi	1	120			40	2		
山　东	Shandong							10	190
河　南	Henan	2	145	1	53			108	648
湖　北	Hubei	3	350	2	120			5100	22800
湖　南	Hunan	1	46	1	125				
广　东	Guangdong					11	3	3	1000
广　西	Guangxi	3	550						
海　南	Hainan	2	102						
重　庆	Chongqing	1	80	1	80				
四　川	Sichuan	2	500					1	3
贵　州	Guizhou	2	180						
云　南	Yunnan								
西　藏	Tibet					1	1	25	75
陕　西	Shaanxi	3	430	1	28	35	5	5	680
甘　肃	Gansu	4	680	1	60				
青　海	Qinghai	4	415						
宁　夏	Ningxia	2	300					300	6000
新　疆	Xinjiang	4	200			29	2		
新疆兵团	Xinjiang Production and Construction Corps	4	56	3	36				
黑龙江垦区	Heilongjiang Land Reclamation Area	1	150						

4-11-2 地市级残联
Disabled Persons'Federations at Municipal Level

地 区	Region	残联 Disabled Persons' Federations	配备了残疾人领导干部的残联 Disabled Persons' Federations Whose Leadership Include PWDs	残联机关 Disabled Persons' Federations		
				实有人员 Staff	残疾人领导干部 Leaders with Disability	残疾人干部 Ordinary Staff with Disability
		个 unit	个 unit	人 person	人 person	人 person
全 国	**Nationwide**	**361**	**236**	**4912**	**265**	**429**
北 京	Beijing					
天 津	Tianjin					
河 北	Hebei	11	9	242	10	12
山 西	Shanxi	11	6	160	6	10
内蒙古	Inner Mongolia	12	11	181	13	25
辽 宁	Liaoning	14	13	291	14	28
吉 林	Jilin	10	5	144	5	12
黑龙江	Heilongjiang	13	8	166	8	14
上 海	Shanghai					
江 苏	Jiangsu	13	7	275	7	15
浙 江	Zhejiang	11	10	174	11	22
安 徽	Anhui	16	9	194	9	11
福 建	Fujian	9	9	131	10	13
江 西	Jiangxi	11	8	126	8	11
山 东	Shandong	17	13	276	13	19
河 南	Henan	18	8	259	9	14
湖 北	Hubei	13	5	136	6	12
湖 南	Hunan	14	8	178	8	13
广 东	Guangdong	21	15	336	17	25
广 西	Guangxi	15	11	177	11	16
海 南	Hainan	3	2	44	4	4
重 庆	Chongqing					
四 川	Sichuan	21	13	276	13	24
贵 州	Guizhou	10	9	121	10	15
云 南	Yunnan	16	13	208	16	25
西 藏	Tibet	7	2	70	2	5
陕 西	Shaanxi	11	10	153	15	15
甘 肃	Gansu	15	11	230	13	23
青 海	Qinghai	8	4	84	4	12
宁 夏	Ningxia	5	4	46	4	7
新 疆	Xinjiang	14	12	179	16	26
新疆兵团	Xinjiang Production and Construction Corps	12	1	37	3	1
黑龙江垦区	Heilongjiang Land Reclamation Area	10		18		

4-11-2 续表 Continued

地 区	Region	事业单位 Affiliated Institutions			干部队伍综合培训情况 Training of Staff				志愿者助残情况 Volunteers	
		单位 Institutions	实有人员 Total Staff	残疾人 Staff with Disability	地市级举办综合培训班 City-level General Trainings	参加地市级培训人次 Trainees on City-level General Trainings	地市级举办残疾人干部培训班 City-level Trainings for Staff with Disability	参加地市级残疾人干部培训人次 Trainees on City-level Trainings for Staff with Disability	志愿者登记在册 Registered Volunteers	受助残疾人 PWDs Helped by Volunteers
		个 unit	人 person	人 person	期 session	人次 person-time	期 session	人次 person-time	人 person	人次 person-time
全 国	**Nationwide**	**694**	**10188**	**466**	**422**	**24061**	**159**	**8605**	**67200**	**915835**
北 京	Beijing									
天 津	Tianjin									
河 北	Hebei	24	336	17	15	545	5	313	448	3709
山 西	Shanxi	40	604	40	30	1173	4	198	53	13558
内蒙古	Inner Mongolia	26	195	5	8	913	2	60	95	10931
辽 宁	Liaoning	9	236	9	33	2520	15	947	4283	14297
吉 林	Jilin	22	265	16	7	294	2	8	430	8585
黑龙江	Heilongjiang	25	203	12	21	866	7	135	436	197
上 海	Shanghai									
江 苏	Jiangsu	34	448	17	13	1551	6	770	3566	97780
浙 江	Zhejiang	25	589	24	16	2028	6	492	2579	32959
安 徽	Anhui	29	255	7	26	1517	7	304	330	5203
福 建	Fujian	24	235	18	9	714	1	100	24451	63654
江 西	Jiangxi	17	96	5	16	472	7	186	154	2588
山 东	Shandong	42	725	44	15	1124	4	193	1077	4250
河 南	Henan	45	848	9	18	1328	10	506	20824	152107
湖 北	Hubei	27	207	14	6	21	4	21	1175	23458
湖 南	Hunan	31	161	7	11	596	7	189	261	6129
广 东	Guangdong	76	2784	102	37	1548	4	583	1189	315545
广 西	Guangxi	33	465	15	10	453	3	161	284	2538
海 南	Hainan	4	35	2	6	130	2	60	371	930
重 庆	Chongqing									
四 川	Sichuan	34	328	16	41	2311	22	1393	187	15887
贵 州	Guizhou	16	72	4	2	64			70	266
云 南	Yunnan	27	134	10	12	581	3	431	825	6534
西 藏	Tibet	5	50							
陕 西	Shaanxi	16	205	47	8	442	9	101	140	4069
甘 肃	Gansu	24	490	19	18	1549	12	644	3469	124129
青 海	Qinghai	6	64		3	30	5	190	10	730
宁 夏	Ningxia	6	55	1	13	652	4	390	116	659
新 疆	Xinjiang	17	79	5	18	207	4	150	121	159
新疆兵团	Xinjiang Production and Construction Corps	10	24	1	8	307	2	54	248	4956
黑龙江垦区	Heilongjiang Land Reclamation Area				2	125	2	26	8	28

4-11-3 县(县级市、市辖区)级残联
Disabled Persons' Federations at County/District Level

地 区	Region	残联 Disabled Persons' Federations	配备了残疾人干部的残联 Disabled Persons' Federations with Disabled Staff	残联机关 Disabled Persons' Federations 实有人员 Staff	残疾人干部 Staff with Disability
		个 unit	个 unit	人 person	人 person
全 国	**Nationwide**	**3097**	**1499**	**26689**	**2195**
北 京	Beijing	16	14	186	21
天 津	Tianjin	16	11	146	19
河 北	Hebei	171	125	1478	139
山 西	Shanxi	119	68	1194	91
内蒙古	Inner Mongolia	108	53	923	103
辽 宁	Liaoning	108	74	620	84
吉 林	Jilin	70	24	704	38
黑龙江	Heilongjiang	133	33	561	42
上 海	Shanghai	16	5	186	6
江 苏	Jiangsu	102	45	1243	57
浙 江	Zhejiang	94	56	1142	74
安 徽	Anhui	115	56	832	67
福 建	Fujian	89	30	553	35
江 西	Jiangxi	109	56	939	87
山 东	Shandong	160	60	1680	73
河 南	Henan	171	84	2243	109
湖 北	Hubei	106	35	939	64
湖 南	Hunan	126	64	1321	87
广 东	Guangdong	137	42	1188	54
广 西	Guangxi	111	53	828	82
海 南	Hainan	20	6	153	6
重 庆	Chongqing	40	21	310	32
四 川	Sichuan	186	94	1492	130
贵 州	Guizhou	90	61	856	110
云 南	Yunnan	134	93	1285	161
西 藏	Tibet	74	10	104	12
陕 西	Shaanxi	115	59	1142	110
甘 肃	Gansu	86	72	1042	144
青 海	Qinghai	46	17	287	36
宁 夏	Ningxia	21	12	173	16
新 疆	Xinjiang	95	54	733	91
新疆兵团	Xinjiang Production and Construction Corps	2	1	4	1
黑龙江垦区	Heilongjiang Land Reclamation Area	111	11	202	14

4-11-3 续表 Continued

地 区	Region	事业单位 Affiliated Institutions			干部队伍综合培训情况 Training of Staff		志愿者助残情况 Volunteers	
		单位 Institutions	实有人员 Total Staff	残疾人 Staff with Disability	县级举办综合培训班累计 County-level General Trainings	参加县级培训 Trainees on County-level General Trainings	志愿者登记在册 Registered Volunteers	受助残疾人 PWDs Helped by Volunteers
		个 unit	人 person	人 person	期 session	人次 person-time	人 person	万人次 10,000 person-times
全 国	**Nationwide**	**2718**	**15273**	**1034**	**3802**	**167532**	**637158**	**925.8**
北 京	Beijing	41	390	30	73	7265	268	1.9
天 津	Tianjin	26	207	23	74	3235	2338	2.6
河 北	Hebei	93	668	32	124	6123	45354	98.5
山 西	Shanxi	143	717	39	120	4760	2423	6.2
内蒙古	Inner Mongolia	65	302	43	78	2908	3347	4.8
辽 宁	Liaoning	69	300	19	168	8077	5670	9.2
吉 林	Jilin	59	400	13	95	3876	72082	126.3
黑龙江	Heilongjiang	78	263	23	95	2850	106786	76.5
上 海	Shanghai	22	203	24	50	1928	1117	11.5
江 苏	Jiangsu	140	830	40	207	5950	17145	23.7
浙 江	Zhejiang	155	823	71	279	15131	18916	58.2
安 徽	Anhui	63	283	19	132	7225	6151	16.8
福 建	Fujian	141	431	37	124	7128	30687	37.9
江 西	Jiangxi	95	389	30	119	3502	3151	10.9
山 东	Shandong	120	906	52	134	5004	12741	17.1
河 南	Henan	203	1487	35	158	4104	76644	107.2
湖 北	Hubei	123	652	35	135	2707	2847	3.4
湖 南	Hunan	143	923	32	80	2738	3684	8.0
广 东	Guangdong	183	1080	58	195	5283	7803	60.7
广 西	Guangxi	100	446	51	154	5563	6323	5.3
海 南	Hainan	12	82	9	36	1510	1386	5.5
重 庆	Chongqing	42	197	15	113	6041	20514	47.6
四 川	Sichuan	132	832	39	340	23567	14002	25.5
贵 州	Guizhou	85	408	42	73	3826	1667	18.8
云 南	Yunnan	117	384	56	122	5204	2368	9.5
西 藏	Tibet	1	2	1	4	14		
陕 西	Shaanxi	93	716	68	170	10199	7114	11.3
甘 肃	Gansu	66	298	29	139	6142	153448	102.9
青 海	Qinghai	29	240	20	60	1652	979	5.1
宁 夏	Ningxia	8	97	5	34	965	1973	1.6
新 疆	Xinjiang	70	315	43	101	2892	6596	8.5
新疆兵团	Xinjiang Production and Construction Corps	1	2	1	4	25	475	1.7
黑龙江垦区	Heilongjiang Land Reclamation Area				12	138	1159	1.1

4-11-4 乡(镇、街道)残联
Disabled Persons'Federations at Township Level

地区	Region	乡(镇、街道)已建残联 Disabled Persons' Federations Established in Townships (Towns, Sub-districts)	残联机关 Disabled Persons' Federation			
			实有人员 Total Staff	专职残联理事长 Full-time Presidents	兼职残联理事长 Part-time Presidents	残疾人专职委员 Full-time Commissioners on Disability Issues
		个 unit	人 person	人 person	人 person	人 person
全国	**Nationwide**	**38584**	**45209**	**10227**	**11023**	**66639**
北京	Beijing	326	367	249	46	1496
天津	Tianjin	240	388	212	17	246
河北	Hebei	2292	2463	500	726	3821
山西	Shanxi	1479	1579	111	593	3495
内蒙古	Inner Mongolia	1032	1317	113	285	1626
辽宁	Liaoning	1525	1669	378	1136	2387
吉林	Jilin	879	977	161	375	1139
黑龙江	Heilongjiang	1212	1225	107	342	1699
上海	Shanghai	220	449	49	128	1158
江苏	Jiangsu	1317	1687	726	207	2004
浙江	Zhejiang	1375	1717	1220	75	2371
安徽	Anhui	1516	1669	520	372	2381
福建	Fujian	1114	1149	271	398	1960
江西	Jiangxi	1630	2212	398	444	2659
山东	Shandong	1793	2087	514	383	2118
河南	Henan	2397	2907	876	811	5487
湖北	Hubei	1142	1276	346	261	1786
湖南	Hunan	1893	2083	472	446	4777
广东	Guangdong	1644	2221	459	282	2325
广西	Guangxi	1249	1392	162	608	2609
海南	Hainan	225	239	11	137	313
重庆	Chongqing	1029	1206	324	342	1386
四川	Sichuan	4109	5339	409	1433	7322
贵州	Guizhou	1412	1615	538	200	2303
云南	Yunnan	1404	1507	446	461	1475
西藏	Tibet					1
陕西	Shaanxi	1264	1475	167	112	2996
甘肃	Gansu	1369	1506	387	214	1507
青海	Qinghai	384	502	7	53	480
宁夏	Ningxia	237	240	17	12	343
新疆	Xinjiang	876	746	77	124	842
新疆兵团	Xinjiang Production and Construction Corps					89
黑龙江垦区	Heilongjiang Land Reclamation Area					38

4-11-4 续表 Continued

地区	Region	干部队伍综合培训情况 Training of Staff		志愿者助残情况 Volunteers	
		乡镇级举办综合培训班 Township-level General Trainings	参加乡镇级培训人次 Trainees on Township-level Trainings	志愿者登记在册 Registered Volunteers	受助残疾人 PWDs Helped by Volunteers
		期 session	人次 person-time	万人 10,000 persons	万人次 10,000 person-times
全 国	**Nationwide**	**17784**	**288274**	**122.2**	**942.2**
北 京	Beijing	556	10898	0.5	21.6
天 津	Tianjin	225	2660	7.5	23.1
河 北	Hebei	648	4888	12.2	43.1
山 西	Shanxi	299	6084	0.2	3.0
内蒙古	Inner Mongolia	243	2952	0.3	2.0
辽 宁	Liaoning	560	7489	1.4	11.2
吉 林	Jilin	274	2495	5.2	41.3
黑龙江	Heilongjiang	406	3864	16.5	93.7
上 海	Shanghai	289	3224	0.2	59.0
江 苏	Jiangsu	855	13681	4.0	109.7
浙 江	Zhejiang	1019	25221	1.2	31.6
安 徽	Anhui	628	5639	0.8	7.9
福 建	Fujian	321	2823	2.7	29.0
江 西	Jiangxi	563	3037	0.4	5.0
山 东	Shandong	469	72285	2.0	18.9
河 南	Henan	928	10367	16.9	170.4
湖 北	Hubei	613	4158	0.3	5.0
湖 南	Hunan	466	4237	1.1	12.3
广 东	Guangdong	1019	6917	21.9	12.5
广 西	Guangxi	461	4244	0.3	3.4
海 南	Hainan	152	1069	0.1	3.2
重 庆	Chongqing	877	10658	2.6	38.7
四 川	Sichuan	2862	38334	3.7	40.6
贵 州	Guizhou	497	8302	0.1	12.6
云 南	Yunnan	503	7291	0.5	16.8
西 藏	Tibet				
陕 西	Shaanxi	788	11246	0.6	6.5
甘 肃	Gansu	614	7298	18.3	106.4
青 海	Qinghai	356	2994	0.1	4.8
宁 夏	Ningxia	52	643	0.1	1.5
新 疆	Xinjiang	241	3276	0.4	3.9
新疆兵团	Xinjiang Production and Construction Corps			0.1	3.7
黑龙江垦区	Heilongjiang Land Reclamation Area				0.1

4−11−5　村(社区)残疾人组织
Disabled Persons' Federations at Village /Community Level

地　区	Region	已建残协 Associations of PWDs 村 In Villages	已建残协 Associations of PWDs 社区 In Communities	残协情况 Associations 已建残疾人活动室 Recreational Rooms for PWDs	残协情况 Associations 村 In Villages	残协情况 Associations 社区 In Communities
		个 unit	个 unit	个 unit	个 unit	个 unit
全　国	**Nationwide**	**482323**	**67110**	**240227**	**203049**	**37178**
北　京	Beijing	3754	2235	3491	2269	1222
天　津	Tianjin	3085	1178	4267	3090	1177
河　北	Hebei	48138	3212	35646	33007	2639
山　西	Shanxi	22775	2047	7914	6900	1014
内蒙古	Inner Mongolia	11077	1764	2425	1827	598
辽　宁	Liaoning	11779	3917	13504	10177	3327
吉　林	Jilin	9155	1562	2990	2425	565
黑龙江	Heilongjiang	6202	1933	3124	1982	1142
上　海	Shanghai	1295	2802	2966	984	1982
江　苏	Jiangsu	15069	4576	16251	12300	3951
浙　江	Zhejiang	20382	2693	16806	14504	2302
安　徽	Anhui	14078	2096	5918	5012	906
福　建	Fujian	13924	1902	4625	4051	574
江　西	Jiangxi	15309	2232	7891	6729	1162
山　东	Shandong	45393	3702	15526	14039	1487
河　南	Henan	43105	3322	27400	24706	2694
湖　北	Hubei	18797	2407	5351	4651	700
湖　南	Hunan	22856	2946	11033	9518	1515
广　东	Guangdong	18661	4845	6545	4358	2187
广　西	Guangxi	14252	1466	3083	2719	364
海　南	Hainan	2114	213	351	264	87
重　庆	Chongqing	8947	2094	5268	3867	1401
四　川	Sichuan	39928	3854	14923	13409	1514
贵　州	Guizhou	13178	1062	1507	1402	105
云　南	Yunnan	12503	1582	4775	4095	680
西　藏	Tibet					
陕　西	Shaanxi	20568	1948	5165	4505	660
甘　肃	Gansu	16075	1087	9405	8722	683
青　海	Qinghai	3962	373	348	313	35
宁　夏	Ningxia	1608	385	225	73	152
新　疆	Xinjiang	4354	1606	1487	1134	353
新疆兵团	Xinjiang Production and Construction Corps		1			
黑龙江垦区	Heilongjiang Land Reclamation Area		68	17	17	

4-11-5 续表 Continued

地 区	Region	残疾人专职委员选聘情况 Full-time Commissioners on Disability Issues			志愿者助残情况 Volunteers	
		残疾人专职委员 Full-time Commissioners on Disability Issues	村 In Villages	社区 In Communties	志愿者登记在册 Registered Volunteers	受助残疾人 PWDs Assisted by Volunteers
		人 person	人 person	人 person	万人 10,000 persons	万人次 10,000 person-times
全 国	**Nationwide**	**520833**	**456930**	**63903**	**108.3**	**902.7**
北 京	Beijing	5161	3559	1602	0.4	15.8
天 津	Tianjin	4036	2944	1092	7.1	19.8
河 北	Hebei	48074	45087	2987	9.9	43.7
山 西	Shanxi	20691	18854	1837	0.2	2.5
内蒙古	Inner Mongolia	12757	11010	1747	0.4	3.0
辽 宁	Liaoning	14782	10980	3802	3.0	30.0
吉 林	Jilin	10022	8526	1496	7.6	104.4
黑龙江	Heilongjiang	4451	1930	2521	12.0	68.5
上 海	Shanghai	3360	1216	2144	0.1	16.1
江 苏	Jiangsu	18414	14223	4191	5.1	68.5
浙 江	Zhejiang	21324	18196	3128	0.7	16.4
安 徽	Anhui	15756	13528	2228	1.1	14.4
福 建	Fujian	15519	13507	2012	1.0	5.6
江 西	Jiangxi	12911	11246	1665	0.4	8.4
山 东	Shandong	66943	60956	5987	1.4	9.9
河 南	Henan	41584	38232	3352	19.9	195.0
湖 北	Hubei	17408	15429	1979	0.9	18.4
湖 南	Hunan	19163	16630	2533	1.1	14.5
广 东	Guangdong	21551	17739	3812	12.8	5.2
广 西	Guangxi	13803	12564	1239	0.4	3.6
海 南	Hainan	2521	2213	308	0.1	2.0
重 庆	Chongqing	10124	8055	2069	3.0	37.1
四 川	Sichuan	51419	48105	3314	4.5	37.0
贵 州	Guizhou	10803	9771	1032	0.3	10.1
云 南	Yunnan	13723	12172	1551	0.3	5.1
西 藏	Tibet					
陕 西	Shaanxi	22501	20443	2058	0.9	6.8
甘 肃	Gansu	17235	16129	1106	12.3	103.7
青 海	Qinghai	1658	1470	188	0.1	4.6
宁 夏	Ningxia	983	710	273	0.2	1.3
新 疆	Xinjiang	2133	1506	627	1.1	28.8
新疆兵团	Xinjiang Production and Construction Corps	5		5		2.2
黑龙江垦区	Heilongjiang Land Reclamation Area	18		18		0.1

十二、残疾人服务设施建设
Service Facilities for Persons with Disabilities

4-12-1 残疾人综合服务设施
Comprehensive Service Facilities for Persons with Disabilities

地区	Region	已竣工 Completed Projects		
		本年度新竣工 Projects Completed in 2018		
		项目个数 Projects	建设规模 Construction Area	总投资 Total Investment
		个 unit	平方米 square meter	万元 10,000 yuan
全 国	**Nationwide**	**68**	**343951**	**137633.8**
北 京	Beijing	1	16450	13737.1
天 津	Tianjin	2	34490	18780.6
河 北	Hebei	2	1600	2080.0
山 西	Shanxi	1	4300	520.0
内蒙古	Inner Mongolia	4	6470	1846.4
辽 宁	Liaoning	2	2700	750.0
吉 林	Jilin			
黑龙江	Heilongjiang	2	1490	441.0
上 海	Shanghai			
江 苏	Jiangsu	1	140	15.0
浙 江	Zhejiang	2	3949	557.5
安 徽	Anhui	6	33133	8393.8
福 建	Fujian	5	45749	20909.6
江 西	Jiangxi	2	6839	1146.0
山 东	Shandong	2	14009	7237.0
河 南	Henan	1	900	106.0
湖 北	Hubei			
湖 南	Hunan			
广 东	Guangdong	2	48145	23877.1
广 西	Guangxi			
海 南	Hainan	1	1000	345.0
重 庆	Chongqing	1	8000	3000.0
四 川	Sichuan	16	100012	30517.0
贵 州	Guizhou	1	600	60.0
云 南	Yunnan	4	4823	768.2
西 藏	Tibet	2	4903	1530.0
陕 西	Shaanxi	1	1300	350.0
甘 肃	Gansu	4	1594	344.0
青 海	Qinghai			
宁 夏	Ningxia			
新 疆	Xinjiang	3	1355	322.5
新疆兵团	Xinjiang Production and Construction Corps			
黑龙江垦区	Heilongjiang Land Reclamation Area			

4-12-1 续表 1 Continued 1

地 区	Region	已竣工 Completed Projects 累计已竣工 Completed Projects in Total 项目个数 Projects	建设规模 Construction Area	总投资 Total Investment
		个 unit	平方米 square meter	万元 10,000 yuan
全 国	**Nationwide**	**2364**	**5783330**	**1768882.7**
北 京	Beijing	8	95721	63880.2
天 津	Tianjin	23	117338	62904.0
河 北	Hebei	138	140667	28553.1
山 西	Shanxi	52	146370	35051.6
内蒙古	Inner Mongolia	64	87249	21709.3
辽 宁	Liaoning	118	269976	96342.9
吉 林	Jilin	46	84150	23137.9
黑龙江	Heilongjiang	99	114717	36708.0
上 海	Shanghai	17	23896	11782.1
江 苏	Jiangsu	77	431187	161311.2
浙 江	Zhejiang	93	612105	260300.8
安 徽	Anhui	89	234579	55603.8
福 建	Fujian	84	264716	89946.2
江 西	Jiangxi	76	88402	20377.6
山 东	Shandong	121	320632	80295.6
河 南	Henan	141	224399	39234.9
湖 北	Hubei	85	186037	36545.7
湖 南	Hunan	98	118633	22995.9
广 东	Guangdong	108	678155	224477.2
广 西	Guangxi	102	147128	26088.8
海 南	Hainan	12	18022	5664.0
重 庆	Chongqing	28	87819	26289.2
四 川	Sichuan	162	457312	131315.7
贵 州	Guizhou	57	61979	11676.9
云 南	Yunnan	127	165426	32399.3
西 藏	Tibet	40	50637	16653.0
陕 西	Shaanxi	78	172921	38019.5
甘 肃	Gansu	94	99659	31254.5
青 海	Qinghai	19	39067	12781.7
宁 夏	Ningxia	15	30450	7685.2
新 疆	Xinjiang	78	202848	56363.3
新疆兵团	Xinjiang Production and Construction Corps	9	6183	925.0
黑龙江垦区	Heilongjiang Land Reclamation Area	6	4949	608.6

4-12-1 续表 2 Continued 2

地 区	Region	在建项目 Projects under Construction 项目个数 Projects	建设规模 Construction Area	总投资 Total Investment
		个 unit	平方米 square meter	万元 10,000 yuan
全 国	**Nationwide**	**94**	**901283**	**339166.1**
北 京	Beijing			
天 津	Tianjin			
河 北	Hebei	1	500	200.0
山 西	Shanxi	3	11526	4362.0
内蒙古	Inner Mongolia	8	69898	27636.6
辽 宁	Liaoning	1	11989	3556.0
吉 林	Jilin	1	2000	600.0
黑龙江	Heilongjiang	4	9014	5394.5
上 海	Shanghai			
江 苏	Jiangsu	3	33910	30500.0
浙 江	Zhejiang	5	60939	29266.0
安 徽	Anhui	5	29308	8807.0
福 建	Fujian	3	14364	4445.0
江 西	Jiangxi	2	4752	730.0
山 东	Shandong	4	144200	52160.0
河 南	Henan	4	122194	31754.0
湖 北	Hubei	3	44200	8190.0
湖 南	Hunan	4	27618	8300.0
广 东	Guangdong	5	79781	52765.0
广 西	Guangxi	4	10247	1796.0
海 南	Hainan			
重 庆	Chongqing			
四 川	Sichuan	9	28878	7918.0
贵 州	Guizhou	2	41500	18220.4
云 南	Yunnan	5	12041	3047.0
西 藏	Tibet			
陕 西	Shaanxi	4	32157	8965.0
甘 肃	Gansu	1	6778	1356.0
青 海	Qinghai	7	63965	20240.0
宁 夏	Ningxia	1	5616	1800.0
新 疆	Xinjiang	5	33909	7157.7
新疆兵团	Xinjiang Production and Construction Corps			
黑龙江垦区	Heilongjiang Land Reclamation Area			

4-12-1 续表 3 Continued 3

地 区	Region	筹建项目 Projects under Discussion and Preparation		
		项目个数 Projects	建设规模 Construction Area	总投资 Total Investment
		个 unit	平方米 square meter	万元 10,000 yuan
全 国	**Nationwide**	**17**	**121938**	**60592.0**
北 京	Beijing			
天 津	Tianjin			
河 北	Hebei			
山 西	Shanxi			
内蒙古	Inner Mongolia	1	1786	730.0
辽 宁	Liaoning	1	3000	570.0
吉 林	Jilin			
黑龙江	Heilongjiang			
上 海	Shanghai			
江 苏	Jiangsu	1	3000	1500.0
浙 江	Zhejiang			
安 徽	Anhui	1	4000	660.0
福 建	Fujian	1	4000	5000.0
江 西	Jiangxi			
山 东	Shandong			
河 南	Henan	1	500	50.0
湖 北	Hubei	1	2035	1000.0
湖 南	Hunan	2	4200	1420.0
广 东	Guangdong	6	82639	43942.0
广 西	Guangxi			
海 南	Hainan	1	16428	5717.0
重 庆	Chongqing			
四 川	Sichuan			
贵 州	Guizhou			
云 南	Yunnan			
西 藏	Tibet			
陕 西	Shaanxi			
甘 肃	Gansu	1	350	3.0
青 海	Qinghai			
宁 夏	Ningxia			
新 疆	Xinjiang			
新疆兵团	Xinjiang Production and Construction Corps			
黑龙江垦区	Heilongjiang Land Reclamation Area			

4—12—2 残疾人康复设施
Rehabilitation Service Facilities for Persons with Disabilities

地 区	Region	已竣工 Completed Projects 本年度新竣工 Projects Completed in 2018 项目个数 Projects		
		项目个数 Projects	建设规模 Construction Area	总投资 Total Investment
		个 unit	平方米 square meter	万元 10,000 yuan
全 国	**Nationwide**	**84**	**536232**	**167117.4**
北 京	Beijing			
天 津	Tianjin			
河 北	Hebei			
山 西	Shanxi	4	10197	2887.0
内蒙古	Inner Mongolia	4	26068	13969.0
辽 宁	Liaoning			
吉 林	Jilin			
黑龙江	Heilongjiang	3	22000	4640.0
上 海	Shanghai			
江 苏	Jiangsu	3	6327	3070.0
浙 江	Zhejiang	1	7562	3812.0
安 徽	Anhui	3	38356	7585.0
福 建	Fujian	1	8158	1830.0
江 西	Jiangxi	6	35188	7315.0
山 东	Shandong	10	78770	29747.0
河 南	Henan	8	57459	14467.5
湖 北	Hubei	2	12005	2130.0
湖 南	Hunan	2	12500	2950.0
广 东	Guangdong	5	26127	18556.0
广 西	Guangxi	4	19418	5665.0
海 南	Hainan	2	8894	3190.0
重 庆	Chongqing			
四 川	Sichuan	6	39485	14824.6
贵 州	Guizhou	3	20071	4200.0
云 南	Yunnan	1	10676	3398.3
西 藏	Tibet	2	9999	3603.0
陕 西	Shaanxi	1	8000	1500.0
甘 肃	Gansu	7	39492	7938.0
青 海	Qinghai	1	6000	1780.0
宁 夏	Ningxia	1	5310	1797.0
新 疆	Xinjiang	2	8170	2363.0
新疆兵团	Xinjiang Production and Construction Corps	2	20000	3900.0
黑龙江垦区	Heilongjiang Land Reclamation Area			

4-12-2 续表 1 Continued 1

地 区	Region	已竣工 Completed Projects 累计已竣工 Completed Projects in Total 项目个数 Projects 个 unit	建设规模 Construction Area 平方米 square meter	总投资 Total Investment 万元 10,000 yuan
全 国	**Nationwide**	**914**	**3449352**	**1111543.0**
北 京	Beijing	3	13221	8273.7
天 津	Tianjin	10	18720	10886.0
河 北	Hebei	9	58041	17146.1
山 西	Shanxi	42	115498	31704.5
内蒙古	Inner Mongolia	19	93235	32712.0
辽 宁	Liaoning	20	98671	23758.3
吉 林	Jilin	10	39502	15758.0
黑龙江	Heilongjiang	5	33246	7267.0
上 海	Shanghai	5	100462	45136.9
江 苏	Jiangsu	64	247453	98788.2
浙 江	Zhejiang	40	273995	109011.7
安 徽	Anhui	21	122836	44094.4
福 建	Fujian	219	62931	16747.6
江 西	Jiangxi	13	119067	20935.0
山 东	Shandong	106	652391	188371.2
河 南	Henan	24	162947	37752.1
湖 北	Hubei	14	68327	21154.4
湖 南	Hunan	36	97281	21465.5
广 东	Guangdong	46	196441	65192.7
广 西	Guangxi	10	64792	17082.0
海 南	Hainan	4	11099	3714.7
重 庆	Chongqing	13	81191	30407.5
四 川	Sichuan	46	206503	88203.9
贵 州	Guizhou	9	63296	16072.0
云 南	Yunnan	7	42726	11967.3
西 藏	Tibet	13	22290	8283.0
陕 西	Shaanxi	40	87277	26179.7
甘 肃	Gansu	16	82393	19912.7
青 海	Qinghai	6	33858	13590.0
宁 夏	Ningxia	6	51314	20928.2
新 疆	Xinjiang	23	45060	11252.0
新疆兵团	Xinjiang Production and Construction Corps	10	44287	13914.8
黑龙江垦区	Heilongjiang Land Reclamation Area	5	39000	13880.0

4-12-2 续表 2 Continued 2

地 区	Region	在建项目 Projects under Construction		
		项目个数 Projects	建设规模 Construction Area	总投资 Total Investment
		个 unit	平方米 square meter	万元 10,000 yuan
全 国	**Nationwide**	**260**	**2071353**	**632677.8**
北 京	Beijing			
天 津	Tianjin			
河 北	Hebei	7	98447	50331.0
山 西	Shanxi	5	33595	10246.5
内蒙古	Inner Mongolia	11	53831	15070.0
辽 宁	Liaoning	1	11517	2800.0
吉 林	Jilin	4	38070	9628.9
黑龙江	Heilongjiang	4	28300	7300.0
上 海	Shanghai			
江 苏	Jiangsu	2	29085	13960.0
浙 江	Zhejiang	3	64354	39566.1
安 徽	Anhui	3	26578	6300.0
福 建	Fujian			
江 西	Jiangxi	19	162998	40523.5
山 东	Shandong	11	92888	28331.1
河 南	Henan	14	108232	29612.6
湖 北	Hubei	23	176202	62258.3
湖 南	Hunan	17	158420	38642.0
广 东	Guangdong	5	21147	5576.0
广 西	Guangxi	15	91078	22641.1
海 南	Hainan	3	11117	4899.4
重 庆	Chongqing	7	74459	25549.0
四 川	Sichuan	3	21000	5500.0
贵 州	Guizhou	28	254484	63918.6
云 南	Yunnan	12	107698	29460.4
西 藏	Tibet	4	23869	9800.8
陕 西	Shaanxi	11	89078	21432.0
甘 肃	Gansu	19	122944	31796.3
青 海	Qinghai	2	8000	2520.0
宁 夏	Ningxia	15	92921	29209.2
新 疆	Xinjiang	10	57043	12505.0
新疆兵团	Xinjiang Production and Construction Corps	2	14000	13300.0
黑龙江垦区	Heilongjiang Land Reclamation Area			

4-12-2 续表 3 Continued 3

地 区	Region	筹建项目 Projects under Discussion and Preparation		
		项目个数 Projects	建设规模 Construction Area	总投资 Total Investment
		个 unit	平方米 square meter	万元 10,000 yuan
全 国	**Nationwide**	**38**	**302647**	**101846.3**
北 京	Beijing			
天 津	Tianjin			
河 北	Hebei	1	2000	360.0
山 西	Shanxi	1	3640	728.0
内蒙古	Inner Mongolia	2	7470	2124.0
辽 宁	Liaoning			
吉 林	Jilin			
黑龙江	Heilongjiang			
上 海	Shanghai			
江 苏	Jiangsu	1	3000	300.0
浙 江	Zhejiang	2	51084	28198.4
安 徽	Anhui			
福 建	Fujian	1	6350	2095.5
江 西	Jiangxi	1	5100	1020.0
山 东	Shandong	2	30000	4450.0
河 南	Henan	4	22873	4378.0
湖 北	Hubei	3	16579	4250.0
湖 南	Hunan	5	38483	9790.0
广 东	Guangdong	2	5930	956.0
广 西	Guangxi	3	22500	5540.0
海 南	Hainan	1	7225	3405.4
重 庆	Chongqing	1	37977	23216.0
四 川	Sichuan			
贵 州	Guizhou	1	6000	1755.0
云 南	Yunnan	1	5257	1620.0
西 藏	Tibet			
陕 西	Shaanxi			
甘 肃	Gansu	4	19600	4530.0
青 海	Qinghai			
宁 夏	Ningxia			
新 疆	Xinjiang	2	11579	3130.0
新疆兵团	Xinjiang Production and Construction Corps			
黑龙江垦区	Heilongjiang Land Reclamation Area			

4-12-3 残疾人托养设施
Institutional Care Service Facilities for Persons with Disabilities

地 区	Region	已竣工 Completed Projects		
		本年度新竣工 Projects Completed in 2018		
		项目个数 Projects	建设规模 Construction Area	总投资 Total Investment
		个 unit	平方米 square meter	万元 10,000 yuan
全 国	**Nationwide**	**118**	**333466**	**85391.4**
北 京	Beijing			
天 津	Tianjin			
河 北	Hebei	5	11805	1936.3
山 西	Shanxi	4	9688	2447.0
内蒙古	Inner Mongolia	6	14456	4374.0
辽 宁	Liaoning	1	2000	300.0
吉 林	Jilin	1	6500	3446.0
黑龙江	Heilongjiang	6	12137	2496.5
上 海	Shanghai			
江 苏	Jiangsu			
浙 江	Zhejiang	7	42633	15708.0
安 徽	Anhui	2	4915	1160.0
福 建	Fujian	2	10736	3527.0
江 西	Jiangxi	5	10000	1900.0
山 东	Shandong	5	17332	3609.9
河 南	Henan	8	27103	5566.0
湖 北	Hubei	4	10278	2091.0
湖 南	Hunan	11	27606	7211.8
广 东	Guangdong			
广 西	Guangxi	2	3887	690.0
海 南	Hainan			
重 庆	Chongqing	1	2200	784.0
四 川	Sichuan	7	21554	4150.0
贵 州	Guizhou	8	18151	3310.0
云 南	Yunnan	9	21426	6007.9
西 藏	Tibet			
陕 西	Shaanxi	4	17500	4474.0
甘 肃	Gansu	9	20493	4675.0
青 海	Qinghai	1	2000	570.0
宁 夏	Ningxia	3	6682	2227.0
新 疆	Xinjiang	4	8284	1880.0
新疆兵团	Xinjiang Production and Construction Corps	3	4100	850.0
黑龙江垦区	Heilongjiang Land Reclamation Area			

4-12-3 续表 1 Continued 1

地 区	Region	已竣工 Completed Projects 累计已竣工 Completed Projects in Total 项目个数 Projects	建设规模 Construction Area	总投资 Total Investment
		个 unit	平方米 square meter	万元 10,000 yuan
全 国	**Nationwide**	**791**	**2148422**	**578492.3**
北 京	Beijing			
天 津	Tianjin	16	11333	3891.0
河 北	Hebei	26	86934	16912.0
山 西	Shanxi	15	36619	8334.7
内蒙古	Inner Mongolia	24	48568	12985.6
辽 宁	Liaoning	24	84984	36501.2
吉 林	Jilin	10	31469	9507.0
黑龙江	Heilongjiang	20	44911	9843.0
上 海	Shanghai	12	7260	1593.0
江 苏	Jiangsu	59	321284	102675.4
浙 江	Zhejiang	36	241450	95684.7
安 徽	Anhui	14	36784	8868.3
福 建	Fujian	47	74914	15472.6
江 西	Jiangxi	24	67177	13934.5
山 东	Shandong	43	139599	37773.9
河 南	Henan	31	93390	18300.0
湖 北	Hubei	25	50885	10245.6
湖 南	Hunan	65	84467	15171.3
广 东	Guangdong	11	61722	12805.1
广 西	Guangxi	15	29944	5440.4
海 南	Hainan			
重 庆	Chongqing	6	21658	8519.3
四 川	Sichuan	26	59622	15659.0
贵 州	Guizhou	38	118390	26118.1
云 南	Yunnan	13	30440	8800.1
西 藏	Tibet	3	12309	3865.8
陕 西	Shaanxi	52	125760	20041.0
甘 肃	Gansu	22	47422	11935.3
青 海	Qinghai	30	57545	16531.2
宁 夏	Ningxia	7	14682	4328.0
新 疆	Xinjiang	39	41174	9542.2
新疆兵团	Xinjiang Production and Construction Corps	34	53207	10436.3
黑龙江垦区	Heilongjiang Land Reclamation Area	4	12521	6777.0

4-12-3 续表 2 Continued 2

地区	Region	在建项目 Projects under Construction		
		项目个数 Projects	建设规模 Construction Area	总投资 Total Investment
		个 unit	平方米 square meter	万元 10,000 yuan
全国	**Nationwide**	**253**	**888927**	**259499.2**
北京	Beijing			
天津	Tianjin			
河北	Hebei	6	17501	4096.6
山西	Shanxi	6	18725	5181.6
内蒙古	Inner Mongolia	16	39213	12511.8
辽宁	Liaoning	4	7700	1660.0
吉林	Jilin	3	7956	2052.0
黑龙江	Heilongjiang	10	31800	7245.8
上海	Shanghai			
江苏	Jiangsu	1	6000	2800.0
浙江	Zhejiang	16	118048	53727.3
安徽	Anhui	4	19785	5510.6
福建	Fujian	1	3026	1000.0
江西	Jiangxi	12	25563	4305.0
山东	Shandong	1	3500	669.0
河南	Henan	11	43757	11707.5
湖北	Hubei	10	33822	6446.2
湖南	Hunan	12	49578	20172.9
广东	Guangdong	3	15950	6873.0
广西	Guangxi	12	36759	7304.4
海南	Hainan	4	11939	4468.6
重庆	Chongqing	5	18751	5349.0
四川	Sichuan	9	35959	9232.0
贵州	Guizhou	41	153128	40132.9
云南	Yunnan	22	57487	14853.0
西藏	Tibet	1	5748	2095.0
陕西	Shaanxi	6	13805	2915.0
甘肃	Gansu	12	43209	11302.9
青海	Qinghai	1	2226	1013.0
宁夏	Ningxia	5	16132	5049.0
新疆	Xinjiang	12	35860	6620.2
新疆兵团	Xinjiang Production and Construction Corps	7	16000	3205.0
黑龙江垦区	Heilongjiang Land Reclamation Area			

4-12-3 续表 3 Continued 3

地　区	Region	筹建项目 Projects under Discussion and Preparation		
		项目个数 Projects	建设规模 Construction Area	总投资 Total Investment
		个 unit	平方米 square meter	万元 10,000 yuan
全　国	**Nationwide**	**28**	**102872**	**34496.0**
北　京	Beijing			
天　津	Tianjin			
河　北	Hebei	2	9500	1900.0
山　西	Shanxi			
内蒙古	Inner Mongolia			
辽　宁	Liaoning	1	1200	600.0
吉　林	Jilin	1	2000	792.0
黑龙江	Heilongjiang			
上　海	Shanghai			
江　苏	Jiangsu			
浙　江	Zhejiang	3	31950	13973.0
安　徽	Anhui			
福　建	Fujian	1	3000	990.0
江　西	Jiangxi			
山　东	Shandong	1	3500	680.0
河　南	Henan	2	6806	1261.0
湖　北	Hubei			
湖　南	Hunan	2	3250	1200.0
广　东	Guangdong	1	3000	2875.0
广　西	Guangxi	2	5601	1535.0
海　南	Hainan			
重　庆	Chongqing	1	4606	1381.0
四　川	Sichuan	2	8573	2131.0
贵　州	Guizhou			
云　南	Yunnan	5	11387	3098.0
西　藏	Tibet			
陕　西	Shaanxi	1	2000	700.0
甘　肃	Gansu			
青　海	Qinghai			
宁　夏	Ningxia			
新　疆	Xinjiang	2	5000	1080.0
新疆兵团	Xinjiang Production and Construction Corps	1	1500	300.0
黑龙江垦区	Heilongjiang Land Reclamation Area			

十三、信息化建设
Application of IT

4-13-1 残疾人事业信息化建设
Application of IT in the Work for Persons with Disabilities

地区	Region	门户网站 Websites	省级 At Provincial Level	地市级 At Municipal Level	县级 At County Level	本年度省级统计工作培训情况 Training for Statistics and Management at Provincial Level in 2018: 举办统计工作培训班 Trainings for Statistics and Management	参加统计工作培训班 Participants of Trainings
		个 unit	个 unit	个 unit	个 unit	期 session	人次 person-time
全国	**Nationwide**	**1155**	**31**	**261**	**863**	**36**	**2436**
北京	Beijing	15	1		14	2	150
天津	Tianjin	4	1		3	2	200
河北	Hebei	56	1	10	45	1	45
山西	Shanxi	26	1	7	18	1	46
内蒙古	Inner Mongolia	39	1	8	30	1	158
辽宁	Liaoning	30	1	13	16	1	60
吉林	Jilin	25	1	8	16	1	100
黑龙江	Heilongjiang	13	1	5	7		
上海	Shanghai	16	1		15	1	120
江苏	Jiangsu	80	1	13	66	1	60
浙江	Zhejiang	68	1	11	56	1	110
安徽	Anhui	73	1	16	56	1	40
福建	Fujian	102	1	9	92	1	40
江西	Jiangxi	43	1	8	34	2	110
山东	Shandong	71	1	17	53	1	25
河南	Henan	58	1	18	39	1	65
湖北	Hubei	42	1	13	28	1	135
湖南	Hunan	35	1	14	20	1	160
广东	Guangdong	61	1	20	40	1	50
广西	Guangxi	61	1	10	50	1	69
海南	Hainan	7	1	1	5	1	40
重庆	Chongqing	16	1		15	1	50
四川	Sichuan	63	1	18	44	1	25
贵州	Guizhou	14	1	3	10	1	130
云南	Yunnan	32	1	9	22	1	60
西藏	Tibet	1	1			1	70
陕西	Shaanxi	37	1	9	27	1	63
甘肃	Gansu	36	1	10	25	1	35
青海	Qinghai	13	1	4	8	1	75
宁夏	Ningxia	7	1	3	3	2	70
新疆	Xinjiang	11	1	4	6	1	40
新疆兵团	Xinjiang Production and Construction Corps					1	20
黑龙江垦区	Heilongjiang Land Reclamation Area					1	15

5

分省统计报告

Provincial Statistical Reports

2018 年北京市残疾人事业发展统计公报

2018 年，全市各级残联认真贯彻习近平总书记关于残疾人事业的重要论述和中国残联第七次全国代表大会精神，认真落实市委、市政府关于残疾人事业的决策部署，以庆祝改革开放 40 周年、残联成立 30 周年为契机，坚持首善标准推进残疾人小康进程，高质量完成市政府为民办实事项目，推动 24 项政策落地实施，1.58 亿人次刷卡享受服务，残疾人获得感幸福感安全感不断增长。

一、康复

康复服务覆盖全生命周期。发布全国第一本省级残疾预防工作报告，协调、督促 34 个部门落实残疾预防责任。市政府办公厅印发《关于完善残疾儿童康复服务制度的意见》，进一步完善了 0-15 岁残疾儿童的康复服务体系。出台全国首个非医疗康复保障政策，16 周岁以上残疾人康复可获得 60%至 90%补贴。落实政府实事项目，为 5388 名残疾人提供居家和社区康复服务，一批长年难以走出家门的残疾人健康状况得以改善，满意度达到 99.37%。修订残疾人辅助器具购买补贴目录，扩充产品、提高标准、简化流程，辅具平台注册率达到 83%。

2018 年，258653 名残疾儿童及持证残疾人得到基本康复服务，其中包括 0-6 岁残疾儿童 1420 人。得到康复服务的持证残疾人中，有视力残疾人 26075 名、听力残疾人 18460 名、言语残疾人 513 名、肢体残疾人 153448 名、智力残疾人 17496 名、精神残疾人 27493 名、多重残疾人 15165 名。全年共为 198838 残疾人提供各类辅助器具适配服务。

截至 2018 年底，有残疾人康复机构 127 个，其中，10 个机构提供视力残疾康复服务，26 个提供听力言语残疾康复服务，25 个提供肢体残疾康复服务，43 个提供智力残疾康复服务，20 个提供精神残疾康复服务，32 个提供孤独症儿童康复服务，8 个提供辅助器具服务。康复机构在岗人员 3774 人，其中，管理人员 534 人，专业技术人员 2592 人，其他人员 648 人。

二、教育

融合教育覆盖全年龄段。推动落实特殊教育二期提升计划，非教育类辅助性服务试点成效明显，为残疾学生高考提供便利服务。支持北京联合大学开展高等院校融合教育试点。率先编制盲文、手语网络课程，推广国家通用盲文、手语。

残疾人事业专项彩票公益金助学项目的实施，为 6 名家庭经济困难的残疾儿童享受普惠性学前教育提供资助。多渠道争取资金支持，对 315 名残疾儿童给予学前教育资助。

共有特殊教育普通高中班（部）2 个，在校生 287 人，其中聋生 198 人，盲生 89 人。残疾人中等职业学校（班）3 个，在校生 340 人，毕业生 72 人。有 97 名残疾人被普通高等院校录取，122 名残疾人进入特殊教育学院学习。

三、就业

“充分就业”取得重大突破。印发《关于进一步促进本市残疾人就业工作的若干措施》（京残发〔2018〕26 号），把促进残疾人就业增收与优化营商环境统筹考虑，突出用人单位招用残疾人和残疾人自主创业就业两条主线，统筹城乡残疾人就业政策待遇，加大对“三类就业困难人群”和残疾人学生的就业支持，强化职业培训和精准帮扶服务两大支撑，有力促进城乡残疾人平等充分就业。开展“岗位定制”，建立帮扶性就业基地 127 个，2324 名残疾人与企业签订劳动合同实现就业，其中智力、精神、重度肢体三类残疾人 1036 名，辐射带动 14897 人。党政机关定向招录工作取得突破性进展，市区两级拿出 22 个公务员岗位，不设工作经历、专业限制，降低身体条件、学历要求，定向招录残疾人，551 名残疾人通过资格初审，458 人参考。

切实落实减税降费要求，会同有关部门印发《北京市残疾人就业保障金征收使用管理办法》（京财税〔2018〕1271 号），将残疾人就业保障金征收标准上限，由上一年度本市社会平均工资的 3 倍降低至2倍，进一步缓解部分企业缴费过高问题。

培训盲人保健按摩人员153名、盲人医疗按摩人员119名；保健按摩机构达到434个，医疗按摩机构达到3个；24人获得盲人医疗按摩人员初级职务任职资格，10人获得中级职务任职资格。

四、社会保障

社会保障水平稳步提高。推动残疾人保障政策应保尽保，所有残疾人免费参加城乡基本医疗保险，为5955名残疾人购买居家服务，为100名重度残疾人提供喘息式服务，获得社会普遍赞誉。加大残疾人特殊帮扶力度，会同有关部门出台成年无业重度残疾人单独施保政策，将托养机构运营补贴范围扩大到所有年龄段残疾人。

截至2018年底，残疾居民参加城乡社会养老保险人数90236名，42098名60岁以下参保重度残疾人中，42098名得到政府的参保扶助，享受代缴比例达到100.0%。23631名非重度残疾人享受了个人缴费资助政策。

残疾人托养服务工作稳步推进，残疾人托养服务机构达到99个，其中寄宿制托养服务机构85个，综合性托养服务机构14个，为1383名残疾人提供了托养服务。117138名残疾人接受居家服务。312名托养服务管理和服务人员接受了各级各类专业培训。

五、扶贫

扶贫协作工作成效显著。把帮扶受援地残疾人脱贫作为光荣的政治任务、义不容辞的责任和分内之事，印发《关于做好东西部贫困残疾人扶贫协作工作的实施意见》，启动实施“五个一批”帮扶行动，牵头统筹各区残联，分别与内蒙古、河北省残联、结对旗县密切对接，建立日常联系机制，签订帮扶框架协议，并通过专题会、联席会等方式适时调度，初步实现了从被动接受到主动担当、从点滴切入到全面铺开、从泛泛帮扶到精准聚焦、从分散助力到形成整体合力的转变。

32家助残增收基地辐射1054名残疾。

六、宣传文化体育

多次参加外事才艺展示活动，麦秸秆画入选市政府外事礼品目录，展现风采。1944人参加职业技能竞赛，弘扬工匠精神。我市选手夺得全球残疾青少年IT精英挑战赛计算机操作冠军，我市运动员在国内外赛事中获得61金54银45铜，为首都增光添彩。创编主题话剧《北极光》，举办“我梦最美”第九届社区（村）残疾人艺术汇演，一批文艺骨干和原创作品受到好评。举办首都残疾人事业30年发展成就展，进一步营造了全社会关心关爱残疾人的氛围。编纂完成第一本残疾人事业地方志，填补了本市残疾人事业历史记述的空白。

冬残奥会筹办任务扎实推进。《2022年冬奥会和冬残奥会北京市筹办工作任务书》涉及残联主责任务14项、协办任务29项，实施《北京市残联冬残奥会行动计划》。立足“找准需求、抓好监督”职能定位，把规划建设无障碍环境作为一件要事、急事、实事，牵头开展全市无障碍摸底调查，推动重大项目无障碍同步设计、同步施工。《北京市村庄规划导则》明确无障碍标准，居家环境无障碍改造实现精准服务，“互联网+随手拍”无障碍监督平台做到随时发现、随时整改。立足中国特色、北京特点，积极推进市区两级残疾人职业康复和托养服务中心建设。立足群众体育与竞技体育齐头并进，落实“3亿人上冰雪”要求，开展残疾人冰雪体验活动，组织6支冰雪运动队科学训练。由我市担任主力的国家轮椅冰壶队，在平昌冬残奥会上夺得历史首枚奖牌、首枚金牌，为祖国赢得了荣誉。

截至2018年底，共有市级残疾人专题广播节目1个、电视手语栏目2个；地市级残疾人电视手语栏目3个。市、区两级公共图书馆共设立盲文及盲文有声读物阅览室7个。

七、维权

残疾人法律服务工作得到加强。2018年，深入社区村开展“庭院式”法律服务活动527场次，参与的残疾人及家属达到17200余人次。代理法律救助案件80件。为23名残疾人提供公证。为100人次提供法律手语翻译服务。开展北京市残疾人法律服务工作、心智残疾人监护调研，完成《无障碍出行手册—首都大型购物中心篇》。

2018年，制定或修改保障残疾人权益的市级规范性文件1个。人大开展《中华人民共和国残疾人保障法》执法检查和专题调研3次；政协开展视察和专题调研 2 次。开展市级普法宣传教育活动 200 次，4000 人参加；举办市级法律培训班 30 个，1678 人参加。

残疾人参政议政工作得到加强，各级残联协助人大代表、政协委员提出议案、建议、提案 8 件，办理议案、建议、提案 28 件。

无障碍建设法规、标准进一步完善。出台了 1 个市级无障碍环境建设与管理法规、政府令和规范性文件；16 个区级残联系统开展无障碍环境建设；开展无障碍环境建设检查 40 次，无障碍培训 4202 人次。

八、组织建设

服务基层持续深入。将村级温馨家园建设纳入乡村振兴计划，就近就便为残疾人提供服务。残疾人需求采集和服务响应实现常态化，需求响应率达 99.8%。妥善关停下属盲人保健按摩企业，实现事企分开。建立专门协会意见建议办理机制，126 项意见建议按期办结。全面停发纸质残疾人证，全流程服务电子档案逐渐建立。推进业务系统整合统筹，42 个市级残疾人服务事项精简至 25 个，7 个事项纳入市政务服务大厅集中办理，残疾人服务纳入“一刻钟社区服务圈”建设目录，全市惠民便民地图新增 1278 个残疾人服务机构标注，残疾人服务事项实现“能上尽上”，残疾人“一门一网一次”办事格局加快形成。

2018 年，市区乡镇（街道）共成立残联 342 个，区级残联已建 16 个，乡镇（街道）残联已建 326 个；已建社区（村）残协 5989 个。

市区乡镇（街道）残联工作人员 1280 人，乡镇（街道）、村（社区）选聘残疾人专职委员总计 6657 名。区级残联配备了残疾人干部 14 人。

共建立市级及以下各类残疾人专门协会 85 个，其中市级专门协会已建 5 个，区级专门协会已建 80 个。助残社会组织共有 190 个。

九、服务设施

截至 2018 年底，已竣工的各级残疾人综合服务设施 8 个，总建设规模 95721.1 平方米，总投资 63880.2 万元；已竣工的各级残疾人康复设施 3 个，总建设规模 13221.4 平方米，总投资 8273.7 万元。

十、信息化

2018 年，北京市残联通过业务梳理、服务上网和信息融合，打通残疾人服务的“最后一公里”，完善残疾人服务的便捷化、精准化和个性化，实现了残疾人服务管理工作创新。首次以事项的方式理清了各项残疾人服务，形成了上报市级事项清单、待完善事项清单和各委办局服务事项清单三大清单百余项服务事项列表。其中 48 项服务事项形成办事指南，于 2018 年底前在市残联网站公开。持续推进残疾人服务事项上网和优化。累计完成了残疾人证、康复、辅具、教育、就业、社会保障、养护照料、交通出行等 8 大类 31 项服务在线办理，实现残疾人服务事项“能上尽上”互联网。拓展残疾人网上服务渠道，加强部门间信息融合，让服务不仅上网，而且多渠道便捷可达，与首都之窗合作建设了“残疾人服务频道”，整合了十多个委办局提供的五十多项涉残服务；在政务地图增加残疾人服务资源 1278 个，实现了线上多渠道的服务拓展和信息融合。截至 2018 年底，市区两级残联开通网站 15 个。积极拓宽数据采集渠道，通过帮扶基地、居家社区康复开展两个服务全采集试点，累计采集各类服务数据 80 余万条；大力开展与其他涉残单位的数据共享工作，目前已于市公安局、市人社局、市民政局、市地税局、市经信局、市农委等 13 个合作单位，共享 29 类 230 项数据，累计获取数据 3.7 亿条；完成市残联数据资源的梳理，共梳理核心数据 2901 项，初步形成数据目录，统一了数据标准。为实现“一数一源”“一源多用”奠定基础。截至 2018 年底，市区两级残联开通网站 15 个。

2018 年天津市残疾人事业发展统计公报

2018 年，在市委、市政府的正确领导和中国残联的有力指导下，在各区、各部门和社会各界的共同支持下，天津市全面完成了残疾人事业各项工作的年度任务，积极推进残疾人社会保障、康复、教育、培训、就业、扶贫、维权、无障碍环境建设、托养、重残护理、文化体育、福利基金、组织建设、服务设施和信息化建设等工作，取得了新的成效和新的突破，残疾人物质和文化生活状况得到进一步改善，各领域服务水平得到进一步提升，现根据 2018 年度残疾人事业统计数据和实际情况，进行分析，并公报如下：

一、残疾人康复工作精准提升

积极推进残疾人社区康复工作。截至 2018 年底，在 16 个市辖区开展了社区康复工作，全市共有社区康复协调员 3970 人，康复服务设施 227 个。

2018 年，实施了天津市残疾人精准康复实施方案和残疾预防行动计划，全年共有 52564 名残疾人得到了基本康复服务，并实现了不同程度的康复。在得到基本康复服务的残疾人中，各类别残疾人数及占比如下：

1. 视力残疾人共 3436 人，约占 7%。接受复明手术、定向行走等训练 306 人；接受盲杖、助视器等辅具适配服务 1930 人。

2. 听力残疾人为 2433 人、言语残疾人为 167 人，两个类别共约占 5%。接受人工耳蜗、助听器适配服务 1906 人。

3. 肢体残疾人共 31865 人，约占 61%。有 710 名肢体残疾人接受矫治手术、运动功能训练等服务；接受假肢、矫形器等辅具适配服务 12587 人。

4. 智力残疾人共 5784 人，约占 11%。接受认知及适应性训练 104 人。

5. 精神残疾人共 7139 人，约占 14%。接受药物治疗及作业疗法训练 5126 人。

6. 多重残疾人共 1673 人，约占 3%。

截止 2018 年底，全市共建立残疾人康复服务机构 89 个，按机构属性划分：残联办最多，共计 21 个；按残疾类别划分，精神康复机构最多，共计 45 个。

二、残疾人教育工作进展稳定

2018 年，继续认真落实《天津市第二期特殊教育提升计划（2017-2020）实施方案》，全面精准掌握本市适龄入学残疾儿童少年接受各类教育情况。为接受各阶段教育的残疾学生和贫困残疾人在校健全子女发放助学金，残疾人整体素质有所提高。全市各特教学校义务教育阶段对残疾学生继续实施“三免一补”（免交杂费、教科书费、住宿费，补贴生活费）政策，实现义务教育阶段免费教育。全面落实残疾考生参加普通高考工作，为残疾考生提供便利。残疾人特殊教育事业发展稳定。开办特殊教育普通高中 2 所，在校生 105 人。其中聋生 74 人，盲生 31 人。有 65 名残疾人被普通高等院校录取，121 名残疾人进入特殊教育学院学习。

三、残疾人就业工作稳步推进

2018 年，加强残疾人就业服务，多种方式促进残疾人就业，多渠道促进残疾人高校毕业生就业创业。

城乡残疾人就业总人数为 83272 人。就业形式主要集中在按比例就业、个体就业和农村种植养殖加工业，其中：按比例就业为 49558 人，个体就业为 11500 人，农村种植养殖加工业为 19225 人。

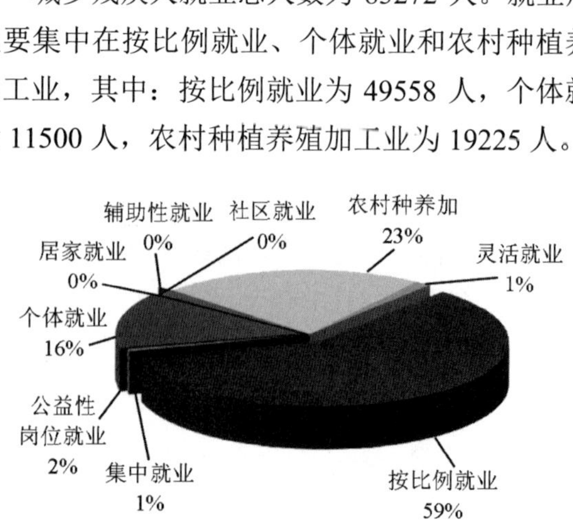

图 3-1　2018 年就业状况

本年度加大对盲人按摩人员培训及培养力度，

培训盲人保健按摩人员 90 人，培养盲人医疗按摩人员 72 人；保健按摩机构数 162 个，与去年持平，医疗按摩机构 5 个，比去年增加 1 个，10 人获得盲人医疗按摩人员初级职务任职资格。

四、残疾人社会保障工作成效显著

2018 年，全面落实残疾人医疗参保、医疗救助、大病救助政策，推进残疾人积极纳入全民参保计划，提高残疾人参加城乡居民基本养老保险参保率。全市实际参保的残疾居民为 75823 人，较 2017 年增加了 241 人。其中领取待遇的有 51105 人[1]，较 2017 年增加了 1145 人。60 周岁以下参保残疾居民 24718 人。

残疾人托养服务工作稳步推进，有需求且符合条件的托养服务对象基本实现了全覆盖。残疾人托养服务机构达到 60 个，托养残疾人总数 40534 人，其中享受居家托养服务残疾人 39700 人，较 2017 年增加了 176 人。

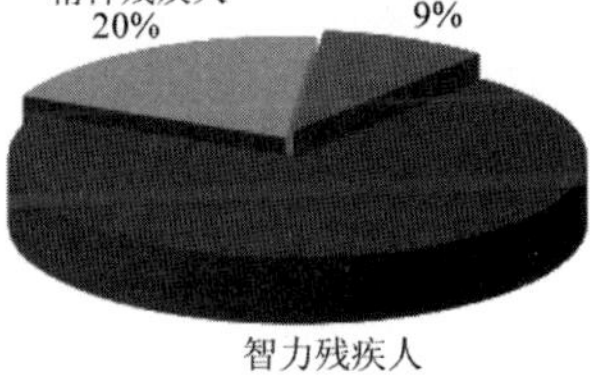

图 4-1　2018 年在托养服务机构中托养的残疾人情况

五、残疾人扶贫工作快速精准

2018 年，积极动员机关、企事业单位、志愿者组织及党员、干部、学生、街坊邻里等社会各界，采取多种形式，进行“帮、包、带、扶”，并充分发挥工会、共青团、妇联等团体和组织在残疾人扶贫工作中的作用。贫困残疾人生产生活状况得到进一步改善，社会帮扶效果显著，结对帮扶受益残疾人 240 人。加大农村贫困残疾人危房改造力度，本年度完成 459 户农村贫困残疾人危房改造，较 2017 年增加 210 户，投入危房改造资金 1217.8 万元。

六、残疾人维权工作迈出新步伐

2018 年，制定或修改保障残疾人权益的规范性文件 6 个；各级人大、政协的检查或专题调研 1 次，对残疾人保障法的贯彻实施起到了重要的推动作用。

已建立残疾人法律救助工作协调机构 17 个，建立残疾人法律救助工作站 17 个，办理案件 585 件。残联办理人大建议、政协提案 17 件，残疾人参政议政工作得到加强。

《天津市无障碍环境建设管理办法》已正式施行，全市无障碍环境建设法规基础得到进一步夯实。截止 2018 年底，建立无障碍环境建设领导协调组织 17 个，全市 16 个区全部系统开展无障碍建设，大力实施各类无障碍建设项目，全市大多数新建主要城市道路、公共建筑物、居住建筑都建设了相应的无障碍设施，同时加强了无障碍改造和对已建无障碍设施的管理，我市城市无障碍设施建设得到进一步加强，大大方便了广大残疾人、老年人、妇女、儿童、伤病人和全体社会成员参与社会生活。

2018 年，全市各级残联信访部门共处理来信 283 件，接待来访 2128 人次。完善天津市“助残一键通”和法规政策信息平台建设，残疾人 12385 维权热线运转良好，拓宽残疾人诉求表达渠道，为残疾人维护自身合法权益提供便捷途径，接听和解答残疾人来电 8132 通。

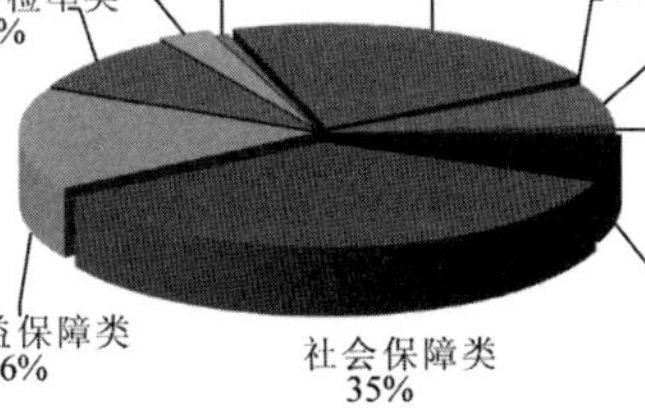

图 6-1　2018 年残疾人来信（件）情况

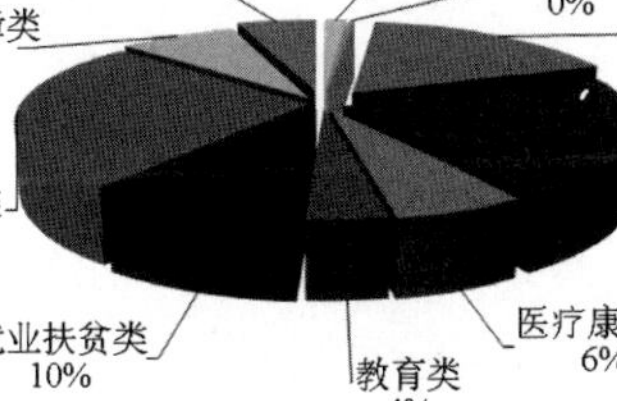

图 6-2　2018 年残疾人来访（人次）情况

七、宣传文化体育工作广泛深入

2018 年，组织新闻发布会 2 次。全市公共图书馆共设立盲文及盲文有声读物阅览室 8 个。开展丰富多彩的群众性残疾人文化活动，举办残疾人文化

[1] 领取待遇的人员为 60 周岁以上的参加养老保险的人员，60 周岁以下人员未领取。

周活动24场次，残疾人参加文化活动13920人次。

八、残疾人组织建设进一步加强

天津市共有各类残疾人57万，其中持证残疾人34万，占残疾人总数的60%。截至2018年底，全市共建立残联256个，其中：已建区残联16个，乡镇（街道）残联240个；已建村（社区）残协4263个，已建残疾人活动室4267个。全市残联系统实有工作人员共955人，乡镇（街道）、村（社区）选聘残疾人专职委员总计4282名。全市共建立各类残疾人专门协会85个，助残社会组织共有6个[2]。各专门协会认真履行职责，各级残联组织全面开展干部职工和专职委员培训工作，基层组织队伍建设得到进一步加强，越来越多的残疾人得到不同程度的帮助。

九、残疾人工作信息化建设稳步提高

残疾人信息化建设队伍不断壮大，全市各级残联均配备统计工作人员。各级残联独立建立网站2个，搭载上级残联、同级政府网站2个。重点加大信息化基础设施建设、技术保障和安全投入，提高了残疾人工作信息化水平。

[2] 6个社会助残组织为：天津市残疾人体育协会；天津市残疾人福利基金会；天津市南开区残疾人福利基金会；天津市杨兆兰慈善基金会；宝坻区助残志愿者联络站；蓟州区残疾人联合会（志愿者服务队）

2018 年河北省残疾人事业发展统计公报

2018 年，在省委、省政府的正确领导下，省残联以习近平新时代中国特色社会主义思想为指导，全面贯彻落实党的十九大精神，按照党的群团改革精神要求，以保障和改善残疾人民生为目标，以更实的举措，全力推进贫困残疾人脱贫攻坚，统筹推进残疾人各项工作，残疾人事业取得新成效。

一、康复工作

2018 年，493290 名残疾儿童及持证残疾人得到基本康复服务，其中包括 0-6 岁残疾儿童 4737 人。得到康复服务的持证残疾人中，有视力残疾人 40973 名、听力残疾人 26397 名、言语残疾人 3198 名、肢体残疾人 332435 名、智力残疾人 31303 名、精神残疾人 35558 名、多重残疾人 22711 名。全年共为 153604 残疾人提供各类辅助器具适配服务。

截止 2018 年底，有残疾人康复机构 431 个，其中，41 个机构提供视力残疾康复服务，97 个提供听力言语残疾康复服务，185 个提供肢体残疾康复服务，157 个提供智力残疾康复服务，87 个提供精神残疾康复服务，79 个提供孤独症儿童康复服务，62 个提供辅助器具服务。康复机构在岗人员 12570 人，其中，管理人员 1611 人，专业技术人员 8893 人，其他人员 2066 人。

二、教育工作

实施残疾人事业专项彩票公益金助学项目，为 914 名家庭经济困难的残疾儿童享受普惠性学前教育提供资助。多渠道争取资金支持，对 2 名肢体残疾儿童给予其他项目学前教育资助。

全省共有特殊教育普通高中班（部）10 个，在校生 804 人，其中聋生 578 人，盲生 185 人，其他 41 人。残疾人中等职业学校（班）4 个，在校生 376 人，毕业生 153 人，毕业生中 37 人获得职业资格证书。有 187 名残疾人被普通高等院校录取。

继续实施《“十三五”残疾青壮年文盲扫盲行动方案》，871 名残疾青壮年文盲接受了扫盲教育。

三、就业工作

截止 2018 年底，全省城乡持证残疾人就业人数为 613526 人，其中按比例就业 16856 人，本年新增 912 人；集中就业 7378 人，本年新增 72 人；个体就业 19432 人，本年新增 765 人；社区就业 2208 人，本年新增 100 人；公益性岗位就业 1567 人，本年新增 131 人；辅助性就业 3352 人，本年新增 77 人；居家就业 67396 人，本年新增 398 人；从事农业种养加 433142 人，本年新增 5089 人；灵活就业 62195 人，本年新增 2560 人。

全年共培训盲人保健按摩人员 963 名、盲人医疗按摩人员 1349 名；保健按摩机构达到 397 个，医疗按摩机构达到 56 个；在专业技术职务资格评审中，有 148 人获得盲人医疗按摩人员初级职务任职资格，14 人获得中级职务任职资格。

2018 年，由省残联、省人力资源和社会保障厅、省总工会、团省委和省妇联共同主办的河北省第六届残疾人职业技能竞赛在石家庄举行，来自河北各地的 314 位参赛选手围绕信息通讯技术、美术专业、手工业等 5 大类 23 项职业技能展开竞赛。通过比赛，石家庄市、廊坊市、秦皇岛市分获团体总分前三名；保定市和邯郸市代表队分别获得优秀组织奖。

四、扶贫工作

2018 年，贫困残疾人得到有效扶持，其中 59561 名残疾人通过扶贫开发退出建档立卡；残疾人接受实用技术培训 30085 人次。

176 名农村残疾人获得康复扶贫贴息贷款扶持。187 个残疾人扶贫基地安置 2657 名残疾人就业，扶持带动 6939 户残疾人家庭。

完成 1590 户农村贫困残疾人家庭危房改造，投入危房改造资金 12343631.7 元。

五、社会保障工作

截止 2018 年底，城乡残疾居民参加城乡社会养老保险人数达到 1430933 名，309696 名 60 岁以下参保重度残疾人中，300987 名得到了政府的参保扶助，享受代缴养老保险比例达到 97.2%。有 193767 名非重度残疾人享受了个人缴费资助政策。512834 人领取养老金。

残疾人托养服务工作稳步推进，残疾人托养服务机构达到 214 个，其中寄宿制托养服务机构 116 个，日间照料机构 35 个，综合性托养服务机构 63 个，为 12304 名残疾人提供了托养服务。5070 名残疾人接受居家服务。410 名托养服务管理和服务人员接受了各级各类专业培训。

六、宣传文化工作

通过微信公众号及时传达最新助残政策、残疾人事业发展最新成果，微信公众号的关注用户已达到 47000 多人。组织河北省残疾人事业好新闻评选和第十三届全省广播电视台残疾人专题广播节目展播，举办河北省第七届特教学校学生艺术汇演，实施残疾人“文化进社区”、“文化进家庭五个一”工程，丰富了残疾人文化生活。

截止 2018 年底，共有省级残疾人专题广播节目 1 个；市级残疾人专题广播节目 8 个、电视手语栏目 10 个。

截止 2018 年底，省市县三级公共图书馆共设立盲文及盲文有声读物阅览室 30 个，共开展残疾人文化周活动 359 场次；省市两级残联共举办残疾人文化艺术类的比赛及展览 36 次，共有各类残疾人艺术团 9 个。

七、体育工作

成功举办省第九届残疾人运动会暨第五届特殊奥林匹克运动会，全省各地的 14 个代表团的 1028 名运动员参赛，共决出金牌 459 枚。成功举办第二届“冰雪河北•快乐你我”残疾人冰雪运动季活动，9 万人次残疾人参与冰雪运动。完成康复体育进家庭 14200 户、培养残疾人社会体育指导员 4011 名，新获批 10 个国家级残疾人体育健身示范点。我省开展的残疾人健身周、残疾人冰雪运动季品牌活动，被列为中国残联示范活动。

全力备战 2022 年冬残奥会和国内外重大赛事。一是参加平昌冬残奥会实现新突破。我省 4 名运动员首次参加冬残奥会，取得了 1 个第九名、1 个第十名和 2 个第十一名好成绩，为备战 2022 年冬残奥会积累了经验、增添了信心。二是以赛代训提升竞技水平。承办首届全国残疾人高山滑雪和单板滑雪两项锦标赛。首次将冬季项目比赛纳入省残运会，组织举办省第九届残疾人运动会四个冬季项目的比赛，来自 12 个市代表队的 131 名运动员参加了比赛，选拔出优秀运动员苗子，为我省冬残奥人才储备奠定了基础。三是全力推进省级运动队外训。组织冬残奥 4 个雪上项目分别在黑龙江、内蒙古等多地转场集训和拉练；组织越野滑雪队赴俄罗斯外训，学习借鉴俄罗斯冬残奥项目夏训经验；组织高山滑雪和单板滑雪队赴新西兰反季节雪上训练，熟悉掌握国外雪场和高山滑雪技巧，取得良好训练效果。四是做好冬季项目运动员人才的选拔、培养、试训、输送力度。为国家队培养输送冬残奥运动员教练员 67 人，入选国家队运动员人数第一，完成了省残联与中国残联签定的输送优秀体育人才责任书任务。配合北京冬奥组委、省冬奥办做好 2022 北京冬残奥会各项筹办工作。五是参加国际国内赛事成绩显著，组队参加全国残疾人锦标赛、亚锦赛、亚残运会等赛事，全年共取得 115 金、68 银、47 铜的好成绩。其中，全国残疾人锦标赛，共取得 63 金、49 银、34 铜的好成绩，举重项目打破 1 项世界记录 3 项全国记录，射击项目打破 1 项世界纪录；亚残运会，共获得 26 枚金牌、8 枚银牌、8 枚铜牌，打破 3 项世界纪录、2 项亚残运会纪录，金牌数全国排位第二名，受到省委、省政府领导亲切接见和鼓励。参加 2018 年全国残疾人冰壶、越野滑雪、冬季两项锦标赛，成绩全国第一。

八、维权工作

2018 年，制定或修改保障残疾人权益的省级规范性文件 2 个、市级 1 个、县级 9 个。全省县级以上人大开展《中华人民共和国残疾人保障法》执法检查和专题调研 15 次；政协开展视察和专题调研 14 次。开展省级普法宣传教育活动 4 次，1300 人参加；举办省级法律培训班 2 个，270 人参加。

截止 2018 年底，全省成立残疾人法律救助工作协调机构 162 个，建立残疾人法律救助工作站 162 个。

“12385”残疾人服务热线全年处理残疾人来

电、微信、短信等 20773 件次。会同有关部门出台《关于优惠扶助残疾人家庭安装使用有线数字电视的指导意见》，降低残疾人消费支出成本。会同司法部门印发《“法援惠民生•关爱残疾人”法律援助品牌建设实施方案》，为残疾人及时提供法律援助。

残疾人参政议政工作得到加强，各地残联协助人大代表、政协委员提出议案、建议、提案 29 件，办理议案、建议、提案 28 件。

无障碍建设法规、标准进一步完善。共出台了 43 个省、市、县级无障碍建设环境建设与管理法规、政府令和规范性文件；186 个市、县系统开展无障碍环境建设；开展无障碍环境建设检查 47 次，无障碍培训 346 人次。

九、残疾人组织建设

2018 年，市县乡共成立残联 2474 个，各市已建残联 13 个，县（市、区）残联已建 169 个，乡镇（街道）残联已建 2292 个；已建社区（村）残协 51350 个。

省市县乡残联工作人员 5380 人，乡镇（街道）、村（社区）选聘残疾人专职委员总计 51895 名。9 个市级残联配备了残疾人领导干部，125 个县级残联配备了残疾人干部。

共建立省级及以下各类残疾人专门协会 898 个，其中省级专门协会已建 5 个，市级专门协会已建 65 个，县级专门协会已建 828 个。全省各级助残社会组织共有 27 个。

十、综合服务设施建设

截止 2018 年底，已竣工的各级残疾人综合服务设施 138 个，总建设规模 140667 平方米，总投资 28553.1 万元；已竣工的各级残疾人康复设施 9 个，总建设规模 58040.6 平方米，总投资 17146.1 万元；已竣工的各级残疾人托养服务设施 26 个，总建设规模 86933.7 平方米，总投资 16912 万元。

十一、信息化建设

截止 2018 年底，10 个市、45 个县级残联开通网站。

2018年山西省残疾人事业发展统计公报

2018年，在省委、省政府的坚强领导和中国残联的正确指导下，山西省残联坚持以习近平新时代中国特色社会主义思想为指导，深入学习贯彻党的十九大精神和习近平总书记关于残疾人事业的重要论述，围绕实现“全面建成小康社会，残疾人一个也不能少”的目标，着力打赢打好贫困残疾人脱贫攻坚战，锐意进取，扎实工作，努力开创新时代残疾人事业发展新局面。

一、康复

2018年，216779名残疾儿童及持证残疾人得到基本康复服务，其中包括0-6岁残疾儿童3135人。得到康复服务的持证残疾人中，有视力残疾人17328名、听力残疾人9959名、言语残疾人9名、肢体残疾人136610名、智力残疾人18832名、精神残疾人25003名、多重残疾人7890名。全年共为115400名残疾人提供各类辅助器具适配服务。

截至2018年底，有残疾人康复机构327个，其中，48个机构提供视力残疾康复服务，51个提供听力言语残疾康复服务，164个提供肢体残疾康复服务，134个提供智力残疾康复服务，73个提供精神残疾康复服务，50个提供孤独症儿童康复服务，64个提供辅助器具服务。康复机构在岗人员9784人，其中，管理人员929人，专业技术人员7266人，其他人员1589人。

二、教育

残疾人事业专项彩票公益金助学项目的实施，为793名家庭经济困难的残疾儿童享受普惠性学前教育提供资助。多渠道争取资金支持，对10名残疾儿童给予学前教育资助。

共有特殊教育普通高中班（部）7个，在校生588人，其中聋生529人，盲生59人。残疾人中等职业学校（班）2个，在校生163人，毕业生21人，毕业生中4人获得职业资格证书。有377名残疾人被普通高等院校录取。

548名残疾青壮年文盲接受了扫盲教育。

三、就业

城乡持证残疾人就业人数为285137人，其中按比例就业5973人，集中就业6158人，个体就业10392人，公益性岗位就业1104人，辅助性就业1092人，灵活就业（含社区、居家就业）40207人，从事农业种养加220211人。

培训盲人保健按摩人员826名、盲人医疗按摩人员867名；保健按摩机构达到551个，医疗按摩机构达到44个；5人获得盲人医疗按摩人员初级职务任职资格，13人获得中级职务任职资格。

四、社会保障

截至2018年底，残疾居民参加城乡社会养老保险人数946207名，168671名60岁以下参保重度残疾人中，155800名得到政府的参保扶助，享受代缴比例达到92.4 %。75298名非重度残疾人享受了个人缴费资助政策。436401人领取养老金。

残疾人托养服务工作稳步推进，残疾人托养服务机构达到115个，其中寄宿制托养服务机构32个，日间照料机构52个，综合性托养服务机构31个，为4740名残疾人提供了托养服务。8680名残疾人接受居家服务。54名托养服务管理和服务人员接受了各级各类专业培训。

五、扶贫

贫困残疾人得到有效扶持，44694名残疾人退出建档立卡；残疾人接受实用技术培训11569人次。

49个残疾人扶贫基地安置1184名残疾人就业，扶持带动1350户残疾人家庭。

共完成298户农村贫困残疾人危房改造，投入资金1069562.4元。

六、宣传文化

截至 2018 年底，共有省级残疾人专题广播节目 1 个、电视手语栏目 1 个；地市级残疾人专题广播节目 11 个、电视手语栏目 7 个。

省地县三级公共图书馆共设立盲文及盲文有声读物阅览室 18 个，共开展残疾人文化周活动 158 场次；省地两级残联共举办残疾人文化艺术类的比赛及展览 5 次，共有各类残疾人艺术团 7 个。

七、维权

2018 年，制定或修改保障残疾人权益的县级规范性文件 3 个。县级以上人大开展《中华人民共和国残疾人保障法》执法检查和专题调研 14 次；政协开展视察和专题调研 8 次。开展省级普法宣传教育活动 3 次，360 人参加；举办省级法律培训班 2 个，190 人参加。

截至 2018 年底，成立残疾人法律救助工作协调机构 21 个，建立残疾人法律救助工作站 17 个。

残疾人参政议政工作得到加强，各地残联协助人大代表、政协委员提出议案、建议、提案 34 件，办理议案、建议、提案 30 件。

无障碍建设法规、标准进一步完善。共出台了 13 个省、地市、县级无障碍环境建设与管理法规、政府令和规范性文件；72 个地市、县系统开展无障碍环境建设；开展无障碍环境建设检查 26 次，无障碍培训 601 人次。

八、组织建设

2018 年，市县乡共成立残联 1609 个，各地市已建残联 11 个，县（市、区）残联已建 119 个，乡镇（街道）残联已建 1479 个；已建社区（村）残协 24822 个。

省市县乡残联工作人员 4729 人，乡镇（街道）、村（社区）选聘残疾人专职委员总计 24186 名。地市级配备了残疾人领导干部的残联 6 个，县级配备了残疾人干部的残联 68 个。

共建立省级及以下各类残疾人专门协会 643 个，其中省级专门协会已建 5 个，市级专门协会已建 55 个，县级专门协会已建 583 个。助残社会组织共有 14 个。

九、服务设施

截至 2018 年底，已竣工的各级残疾人综合服务设施 52 个，总建设规模 146369.8 平方米，总投资 35051.6 万元；已竣工的各级残疾人康复设施 42 个，总建设规模 115497.9 平方米，总投资 31704.5 万元；已竣工的各级残疾人托养服务设施 15 个，总建设规模 36618.6 平方米，总投资 8334.7 万元。

十、信息化

截至 2018 年底，7 个地市、18 个县级残联开通网站。

2018年内蒙古自治区残疾人事业发展统计公报

2018年，全区残联系统认真学习习近平总书记关于残疾人事业的重要论述，紧紧围绕实现“全面建成小康社会，残疾人一个也不能少”的目标，着力打赢打好贫困残疾人脱贫攻坚战，努力开创新时代残疾人事业发展新局面。

一、康复

2018年，13.42万名残疾儿童及持证残疾人得到基本康复服务，其中包括0至6岁残疾儿童1419人。在得到康复服务的持证残疾人中，有视力残疾人1.24万名、听力残疾人1.16万名、言语残疾人92名、肢体残疾人8.07万名、智力残疾人7062名、精神残疾人1.62万名、多重残疾人5791名。全年共为6.8万名残疾人提供各类辅助器具适配服务。

截至2018年底，全区共有残疾人康复机构211个，其中，46个机构提供视力残疾康复服务，52个提供听力言语残疾康复服务，100个提供肢体残疾康复服务，59个提供智力残疾康复服务，26个提供精神残疾康复服务，42个提供孤独症儿童康复服务，66个提供辅助器具服务。康复机构在岗人员5067人，其中管理人员740人，专业技术人员3262人，其他人员1065人。

二、教育

在全区范围实施残疾人事业专项彩票公益金助学项目，为214名家庭经济困难的残疾儿童享受普惠性学前教育提供资助。多渠道争取资金支持，对64名残疾儿童给予学前教育资助。

2018年，全区共有特殊教育普通高中班（部）6个，在校生329人，全为聋生。残疾人中等职业学校（班）2个，在校生65人，毕业生23人。有436名残疾人被普通高等院校录取。791名残疾青壮年文盲接受了扫盲教育。

三、就业

截止2018年底，城乡持证残疾人就业人数为23.58万人，其中，按比例就业1.15万人，集中就业6795人，个体就业2.35万人，公益性岗位就业1625人，辅助性就业1209人，灵活就业（含社区、居家就业）6.62万人，从事农业种养业12.5万人。

全区共培训盲人保健按摩人员514名、盲人医疗按摩人员179名；保健按摩机构达到297个，医疗按摩机构达到108个；65人获得盲人医疗按摩人员初级职务任职资格。

四、社会保障

截至2018年底，残疾居民参加城乡社会养老保险人数45.09万名，10.87万名60岁以下参保重度残疾人中有10.23万名得到政府的参保扶助，享受代缴比例达到94.1%。4.73万名非重度残疾人享受了个人缴费资助政策。20.23万人领取养老金。

2018年，残疾人托养服务工作稳步推进，残疾人托养服务机构达到169个，其中寄宿制托养服务机构110个，日间照料机构12个，综合性托养服务机构47个，为3688名残疾人提供了托养服务。5907名残疾人接受居家服务。147名托养服务管理和服务人员接受了各级各类专业培训。

五、扶贫开发

2018年，各类贫困残疾人得到有效扶持，3.4万名残疾人退出建档立卡；残疾人接受实用技术培训2万人次。

2392名农村残疾人获得康复扶贫贴息贷款扶持。116个残疾人扶贫基地安置1363名残疾人就业，扶持带动1719户残疾人家庭。共完成1477户农村贫困残疾人危房改造，投入资金647.89万元。

六、宣传文化

截至2018年底，自治区本级残疾人电视手语栏目1个；盟市级残疾人专题广播节目2个、电视手语栏目8个。

自治区、盟市、旗县三级公共图书馆共设立盲文及盲文有声读物阅览室 30 个，开展残疾人文化周活动 139 场次；自治区和盟市两级残联共举办残疾人文化艺术类的比赛及展览 12 次，有各类残疾人艺术团 5 个。

七、体育

残疾人群众体育活动日益活跃，残疾人竞技体育水平不断提高。在乌兰察布市举办了全区第五届残运会，展现了我区残疾运动员自强不息的精神风貌，实现了与全运会同城举办，同样精彩。参加各类国际残疾人体育赛事，获得 2 金 2 银 1 铜，参加各类全国残疾人体育赛事，获得 4 金 6 银 3 铜，我区举重运动员徐立立两次打破世界纪录。

八、维权

2018 年，制定或修改自治区级关于残疾人的专门法规、规章 1 个；制定或修改保障残疾人权益的旗县级规范性文件 1 个。旗县级以上人大开展《中华人民共和国残疾人保障法》执法检查和专题调研 4 次；政协开展视察和专题调研 3 次。开展省级普法宣传教育活动 1 次，20 人参加。

截至 2018 年底，全区成立残疾人法律救助工作协调机构 67 个，建立残疾人法律救助工作站 77 个。

残疾人参政议政工作得到加强，各地残联协助人大代表、政协委员提出议案、建议、提案 6 件，办理议案、建议、提案 6 件。

无障碍建设法规、标准得到了进一步完善。自治区、盟市、旗县三级共出台了无障碍环境建设与管理法规、政府令和规范性文件 12 个；系统开展无障碍环境建设市、县 67 个；开展无障碍环境建设检查 53 次，无障碍培训 162 人次。

九、组织建设

全区共成立残联 1153 个，其中自治区残联 1 个，盟市级残联 12 个，旗县（市、区）残联 108 个，乡镇（街道）残联 1032 个；已建社区（村）残协 12841 个。

全区残联工作人员 3053 人，乡镇（街道）、村（社区）选聘残疾人专职委员总计 14383 名。盟市残联配备残疾人领导干部的残联 11 个，县级残联配备了残疾人干部的残联 53 个。

全区共建立自治区级及以下各类残疾人专门协会 564 个，其中自治区级专门协会 5 个，盟市级专门协会已建 60 个，旗县（市、区）县级专门协会 499 个。助残社会组织共有 28 个。

十、服务设施

截至 2018 年底，全区已竣工的各级残疾人综合服务设施 64 个，总建设规模 87249.0 平方米，总投资 21709.3 万元；已竣工的各级残疾人康复设施 19 个，总建设规模 93235.1 平方米，总投资 32712.0 万元；已竣工的各级残疾人托养服务设施 24 个，总建设规模 48568.1 平方米，总投资 12985.6 万元。

十一、信息化

截至 2018 年底，全区有 8 个盟市、30 个旗县（市、区）级残联开通网站。全区残疾人人口基础数据库持证残疾人 78.9 万人。

2018 年辽宁省残疾人事业发展统计公报

2018 年，辽宁省残联以习近平新时代中国特色社会主义思想为指引，深入贯彻落实习近平总书记在辽宁考察时和在深入推进东北振兴座谈会上重要讲话精神，按照“五位一体”总体布局和“四个全面”战略布局总体要求，扎实贯彻新发展理念和“四个着力”“三个推进”，着力补齐残疾人民生短板，加快推进残疾人小康进程，推动新时代辽宁省残疾人事业高质量发展。

一、康复

深度融入公共卫生服务体系，残疾康复服务不断加强。

2018 年，全省已累计有 25.2 万残疾儿童及持证残疾人得到基本康复服务，其中有视力残疾人 2.9 万、听力残疾人 1.4 万、言语残疾人 0.1 万名、肢体残疾人 13.6 万、智力残疾人 2 万、精神残疾人 3.7 万、多重残疾人 1.4 万。

截至 2018 年底，全省已有残疾人康复机构 376 个，其中，提供视力残疾康复服务的机构 52 个，提供听力言语残疾康复服务的机构 57 个，提供肢体残疾康复服务的机构 164 个，提供智力残疾康复服务的机构 94 个，提供精神残疾康复服务的机构 79 个，提供孤独症儿童康复服务的机构 73 个，提供辅助器具服务的机构 115 个。康复机构在岗人员 9682 人，其中，管理人员 1297 人，专业技术人员 6829 人，其他人员 1556 人。

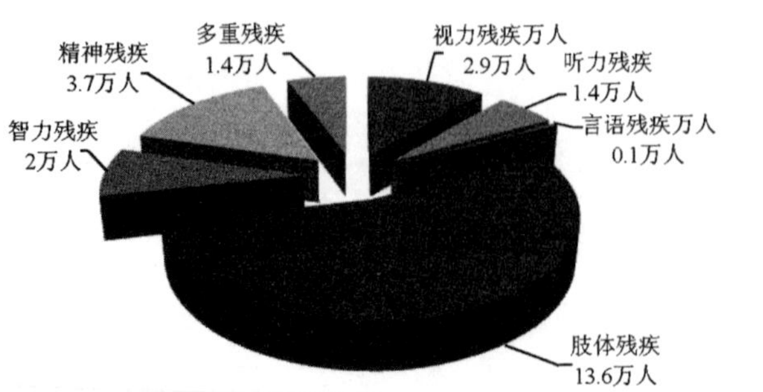

图 1-1　2018 年残疾人接受康复服务情况（单位：万人）

二、教育

实施二期特殊教育提升计划，促进残疾人享受公平而有质量的教育。

实施残疾人事业专项彩票公益金助学项目，为全省 1082 名家庭经济困难的残疾儿童享受普惠性学前教育提供资助。本年度残疾人事业彩票公益金助学项目资助新入园 340 人。

2018 年全省共有特殊教育普通高中班（部）5 个，在校生 74 人。残疾人中等职业学校（班）6 个，在校生 444 人，毕业生 86 人，毕业生中 23 人获得职业资格证书。有 243 名残疾人被普通高等院校录取，19 名残疾人进入特殊教育学院学习。

172 名残疾青壮年文盲接受了扫盲教育。

三、就业

发挥省级残疾人就业机构引领示范作用，促进残疾人就业创业。

2018 年城乡持证残疾人就业总人数合计 28.3 万，其中按比例就业 4.1 万，集中就业 1.6 万，个体就业 1.8 万，公益性岗位就业 0.7 万，辅助性就业 0.8 万，灵活就业（含社区、居家就业）4.3 万，从事农业种养加 15 万。

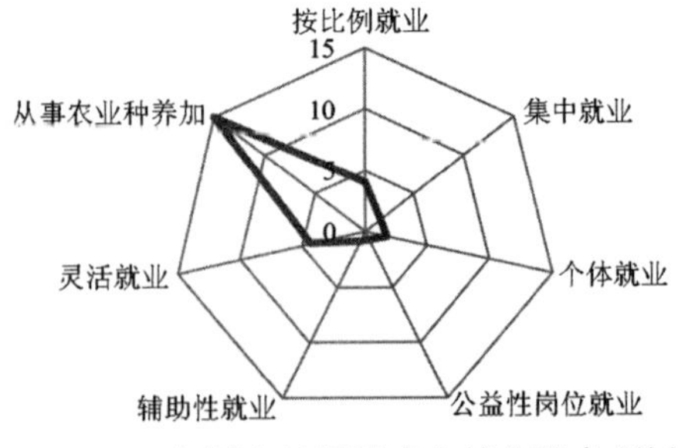

图 3-1　2018 年城乡持证残疾人就业形式（单位：万人）

培训盲人保健按摩人员 568 名、盲人医疗按摩人员 218 名；保健按摩机构达到 564 个，医疗按摩机构达到 27 个；在专业技术职务资格评审中，8 人获得盲人医疗按摩人员初级职务任职资格，8 人获得中级职务任职资格。

四、社会保障

扩大社会保障覆盖面，残疾人民生不断改善。

截至 2018 年底，残疾居民参加城乡社会养老保险人数达到 43 万名，60 岁以下的参保残疾人中有 9.6 万名重度残疾人得到了政府的参保扶助，代缴养老保险费比例达到 91.6%。领取养老金待遇的人数达到 18.1 万人。

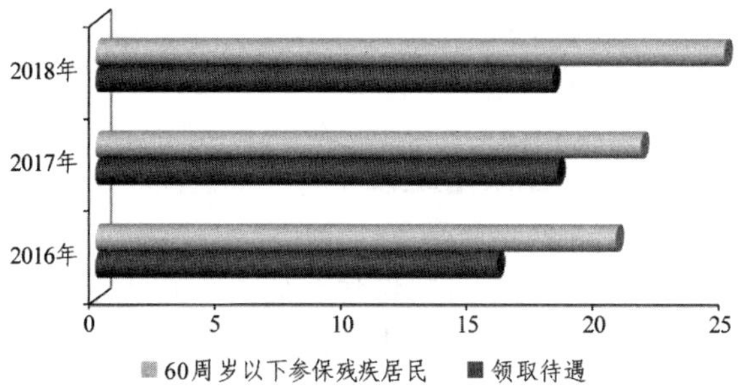

图 4-1　2016-2018 年实际参保残疾居民（单位：万人）

残疾人托养服务工作稳步推进，残疾人托养服务机构达到 180 个，其中寄宿制托养服务机构 100 个，日间照料机构 54 个，综合性托养服务机构 26 个，共为 6754 名残疾人提供了托养服务。13152 名残疾人接受居家服务。全年共有 921 名托养服务管理和服务人员接受了各级各类专业培训。

五、扶贫

聚焦因残致贫家庭突出困难，贫困残疾人脱贫攻坚取得新进展。

2018 年，贫困残疾人得到有效扶持，其中接受实用技术培训的残疾人达到 1.2 万人次。19 个残疾人扶贫基地安置 234 名残疾人就业，扶持带动 359 户残疾人家庭。

六、宣传文化

加强宣传文化工作，促进残疾人广泛参与社会生活。

截至 2018 年底，省市两级残联组织新闻发布会 8 次，共有残疾人专题广播节目 12 个、电视手语栏目 17 个。

省市县三级公共图书馆共设立盲文及盲文有声读物阅览室 49 个，共开展残疾人文化周活动 406 场次，5.1 万人次参加。省市两级残联共举办残疾人文化艺术类的比赛及展览 43 次。

七、体育

辽宁省第十三届残疾人运动会暨首届特殊奥林匹克运动会于 2018 年 9 月在盘锦市举办，首次实现了残运会与省运会同城举办，“两个运动会同样精彩”的目标。开展“全国第二届残疾人冰雪运动季”辽宁站等群众体育活动，促进残疾人群众体育与竞技体育协调发展。

八、维权

加强无障碍环境建设，提升残疾人生活质量。完善法规制度，维护残疾人合法权益。

全省县级以上人大开展《中华人民共和国残疾人保障法》执法检查和专题调研 3 次；政协开展视察和专题调研 4 次。开展省级普法宣传教育活动 21 次，2200 人参加。

截至年底，全省成立残疾人法律救助工作协调机构 81 个，建立残疾人法律救助工作站 74 个。

残疾人参政议政工作得到加强，各地残联协助人大代表、政协委员提出议案、建议、提案 44 件，办理议案、建议、提案 39 件。

无障碍建设法规、标准进一步完善。全省共出台了 3 个无障碍环境建设与管理法规、政府令和规范性文件；系统开展无障碍环境建设市、县、区 8 个；开展无障碍环境建设检查 91 次，无障碍培训 4512 人次。

表 1　2018 年度全省残疾人法律救助情况

级别	法律救助协调机构（个）	法律救助	
		工作站（个）	办理案件（件）
省　级	1	1	10
地市级	14	14	38
县　级	66	59	115
总　计	81	74	163

表 2　2018 年度全省残疾人参政议政情况

级　别	人大			政协		
	人大代表（人）	协助人大代表提出议案、建议（件）	办理人大建议（件）	政协委员（人）	协助政协委员提出提案（件）	办理政协提案（件）
省　级	0	5	2	1	5	3
地市级	13	10	10	27	12	17
县　级	118	4	2	100	8	5
总　计	131	19	14	128	25	25

九、组织建设

圆满完成换届工作，提升各级残联组织为残疾人服务能力。

截至 2018 年底，市县乡共成立残联 1647 个，其中各市已建残联 14 个，县（市、区）含开发区已建残联 108 个，乡镇（街道）已建残联 1525 个；社区（村）已建残协 15696 个。已建率达到 100%。

省市县乡残联实有人员 3405 人，乡镇(街道)、村（社区）选聘残疾人专职委员总计 1.7 万名。市级配备了残疾人领导干部的残联 13 个，县级配备了残疾人干部的残联 74 个。全省共有助残志愿者 5.4 万人，受助残疾人 51.8 万人次。

全省共建立各级残疾人专门协会 600 个，其中省级专门协会 5 个，市级专门协会 70 个，县级专门协会 525 个。助残社会组织共有 36 个。

十、服务设施

截至 2018 年底，全省已竣工的各级残疾人综合服务设施 118 个，总建设规模 27 万平方米，总投资 9.6 亿元；已竣工的各级残疾人康复设施 20 个，总建设规模 9.9 万平方米，总投资 2.4 亿元；已竣工的各级残疾人托养服务设施 24 个，总建设规模 8.5 万平方米，总投资 3.7 亿元。

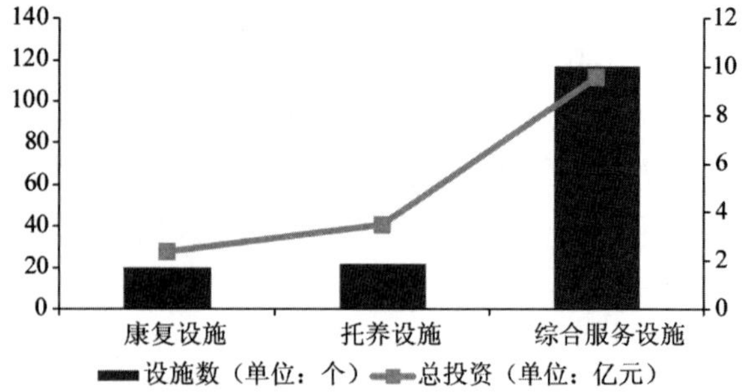

图 10-1　2018 年度全省残疾人服务设施建设情况

十一、信息化建设

促进互联网、大数据在残疾人工作中的运用，以需求为导向加强和改进残疾人服务。稳步推进第三代残疾人证（智能化）试点工作，为建设“智慧残联”，推广“互联网+助残服务”奠定基础。推进市级残联网站无障碍建设，提升网站服务能力。推进市、县残联党政外网物理接入，打造安全网络环境。

截止 2018 年底，辽宁省残联已建立省级门户网站 1 个，市级 13 个，县级 16 个，在政务公开和为残疾人提供在线服务方面发挥积极作用。

2018 年吉林省残疾人事业发展统计公报

2018 年，吉林省残联认真贯彻落实习近平新时代中国特色社会主义思想和党的十九大精神，按照省委十一届三次、四次全会精神和省政府确定的重点任务，全面加强残联组织建设，认真履行“代表、管理、服务”职能，进一步改进残联干部作风，不断加强残疾人服务，民生实事等重点任务圆满完成，全省残疾人事业继续健康稳定发展。

一、康复

2018 年，216952 名残疾儿童及持证残疾人得到基本康复服务，其中包括 0-6 岁残疾儿童 1915 人。得到康复服务的持证残疾人中，有视力残疾人 21924 名、听力残疾人 10631 名、言语残疾人 525 名、肢体残疾人 140027 名、智力残疾人 13578 名、精神残疾人 23649 名、多重残疾人 6024 名。全年共为 56234 残疾人提供各类辅助器具适配服务。

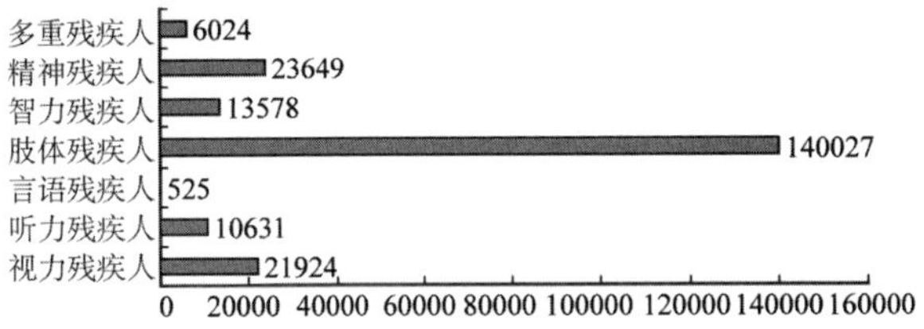

图 1-1　得到康复服务的持证残疾人（数量：人）

截至 2018 年底，有残疾人康复机构 294 个，其中，82 个机构提供视力残疾康复服务，29 个提供听力言语残疾康复服务，155 个提供肢体残疾康复服务，93 个提供智力残疾康复服务，89 个提供精神残疾康复服务，43 个提供孤独症儿童康复服务，46 个提供辅助器具服务。康复机构在岗人员 11225 人，其中，管理人员 1551 人，专业技术人员 7276 人，其他人员 2398 人。

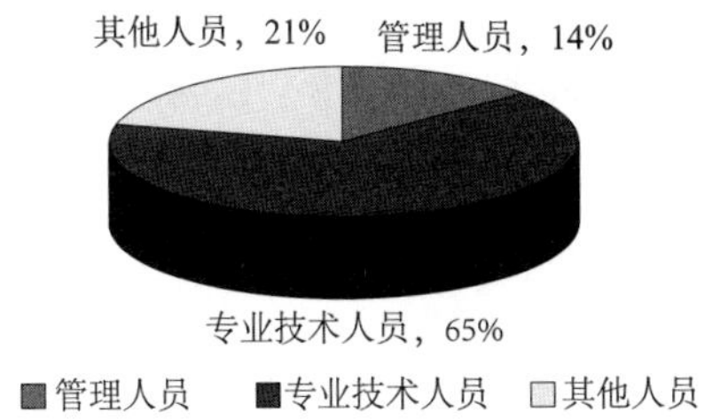

图 1-2　2018 年残疾人康复机构在岗人员情况

二、教育

残疾人事业专项彩票公益金助学项目的实施，为 204 名家庭经济困难的残疾儿童享受普惠性学前教育提供资助。多渠道争取资金支持，对 16 名残疾儿童给予学前教育资助。

共有特殊教育普通高中班（部）5 个，在校生 227 人，其中聋生 227 人。残疾人中等职业学校（班）3 个，在校生 567 人，毕业生 187 人。有 268 名残疾人被普通高等院校录取，200 名残疾人进入特殊教育学院学习。

626 名残疾青壮年文盲接受了扫盲教育。

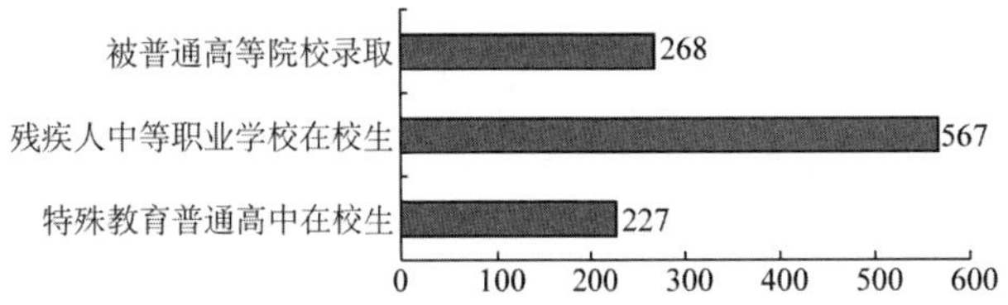

图 2-1　教育情况（数量：人）

三、就业

城乡持证残疾人就业人数为 201192 人，其中按比例就业 6124 人，集中就业 5631 人，个体就业 21783 人，公益性岗位就业 2718 人，辅助性就业 1177 人，灵活就业（含社区、居家就业）46962 人，从事农业种养加 116797 人。

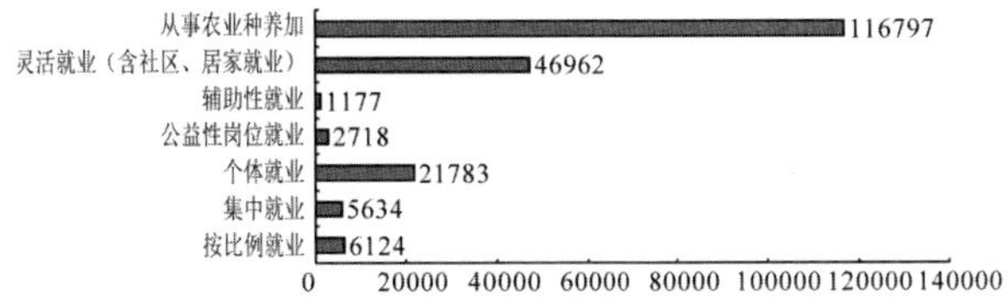

图 3-1　就业情况（数量：人）

培训盲人保健按摩人员 375 名、盲人医疗按摩人员 608 名；保健按摩机构达到 713 个，医疗按摩机构达到 84 个；67 人获得盲人医疗按摩人员初级职务任职资格。

四、社会保障

截至 2018 年底，残疾居民参加城乡社会养老保险人数 328479 名，100551 名 60 岁以下参保重度残疾人中，98991 名得到政府的参保扶助，享受代缴比例达到 98.4%。70388 名非重度残疾人享受了个人缴费资助政策。104432 人领取养老金。

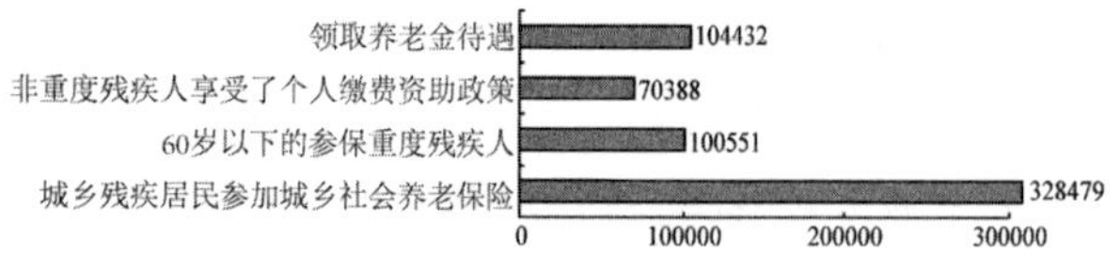

图 4-1　社会保障情况

残疾人托养服务工作稳步推进，残疾人托养服务机构达到 71 个，其中寄宿制托养服务机构 49 个，日间照料机构 14 个，综合性托养服务机构 8 个，为 1800 名残疾人提供了托养服务。6811 名残疾人接受居家服务。16 名托养服务管理和服务人员接受了各级各类专业培训。

五、扶贫

贫困残疾人得到有效扶持，27265 名残疾人退出建档立卡；残疾人接受实用技术培训 11558 人次。

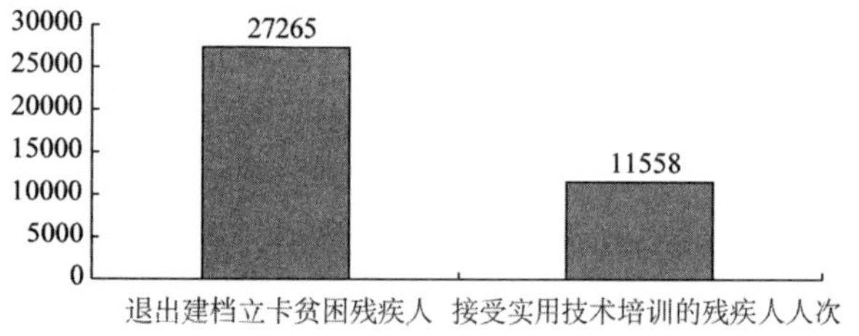

图 5-1　扶贫

27 名农村残疾人获得康复扶贫贴息贷款扶持。192 个残疾人扶贫基地安置 1396 名残疾人就业，扶持带动 4216 户残疾人家庭。

配合住建等有关部门，共扶持 262 户农村贫困残疾人完成危房改造，各级残联投入相关扶持资金 256000 元。

六、宣传文化

截至 2018 年底，共有省级残疾人专题广播节目 1 个、电视手语栏目 1 个；地市级残疾人专题广播节目 2 个、电视手语栏目 7 个。

省地县三级公共图书馆共设立盲文及盲文有声读物阅览室 53 个，共开展残疾人文化周活动 156 场次；省地两级残联共举办残疾人文化艺术类的比赛及展览 19 次，共有各类残疾人艺术团 8 个。

七、维权

2018 年，全国县级以上人大开展《中华人民共和国残疾人保障法》执法检查和专题调研 6 次；政协开展视察和专题调研 3 次。举办省级法律培训班 1 个，50 人参加。

截至 2018 年底，全国成立残疾人法律救助工作协调机构 69 个，建立残疾人法律救助工作站 66 个。

残疾人参政议政工作得到加强，各地残联协助人大代表、政协委员提出议案、建议、提案 10 件，办理议案、建议、提案 13 件。

无障碍建设法规、标准进一步完善。共出台了 17 个省、地市、县级无障碍环境建设与管理法规、政府令和规范性文件；13 个地市、县系统开展无障碍环境建设；开展无障碍环境建设检查 10 次，无障碍培训 72 人次。

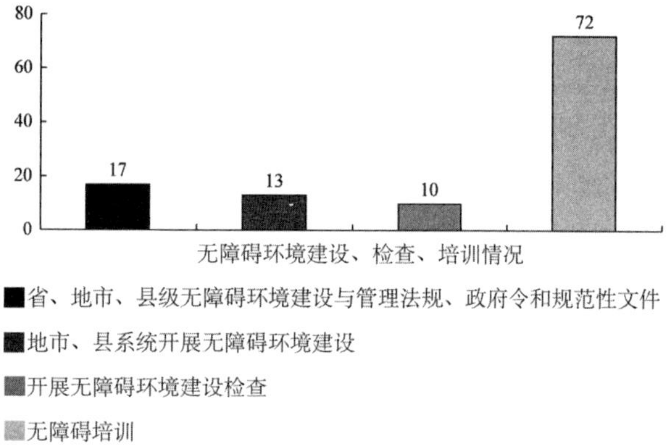

图 7-1　无障碍环境建设、检查、培训情况

八、体育

2018 年，残疾人群众体育活动日益活跃，残疾人竞技体育水平不断提高。继续实施残疾人“康复体育关爱工程”和“自强健身工程”，组织开展了第八届“残疾人自强健身周”、第三届“中国残疾人冰雪运动季”等群众体育活动。

积极组队参加全国残疾人体育赛事，共获得了 12 枚金牌、17 枚银牌、18 枚铜牌。参加了 2019 年天津全国第十届残运会暨第七届特奥会 4 个项目集体项目和群体项目预赛，其中五人制聋人足球项目、三人制聋人篮球项目、盲人跳绳项目、旱地冰壶项目入围决赛圈。

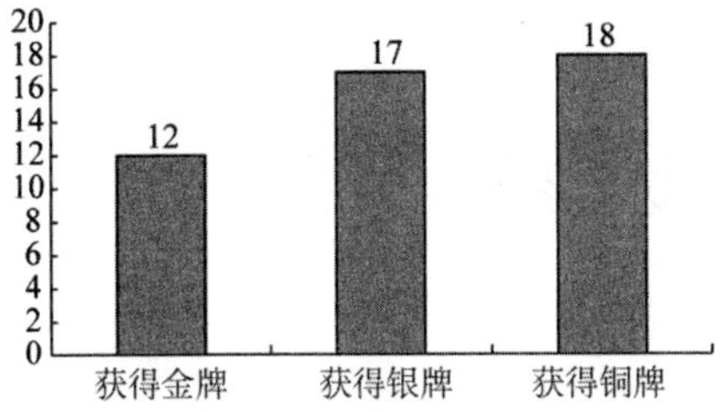

图 8-1　参加全国残疾人体育赛事获奖情况（数量：个）

九、组织建设

2018 年，市县乡共成立残联 959 个，各地市已建残联 10 个，县（市、区）残联已建 70 个，乡镇（街道）残联已建 879 个；已建社区（村）残协 10717 个。

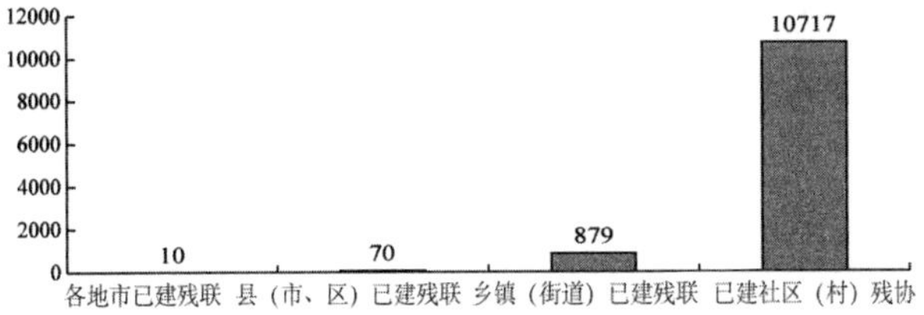

图 9-1　组织建设情况

省市县乡残联共有工作人员 2632 人，乡镇（街道）、村（社区）选聘残疾人专职委员总计 11161 名。配备了残疾人领导干部的地市级残联 5 个，配备了残疾人干部的县级残联 24 个。

共建立省级及以下各类残疾人专门协会 367 个，其中省级专门协会已建 5 个，市级专门协会已建 49 个，县级专门协会已建 313 个。助残社会组织共有 60 个。

十、服务设施

截至 2018 年底，已竣工的各级残疾人综合服务设施 46 个，总建设规模 84150.2 平方米，总投资 23137.9 万元；已竣工的各级残疾人康复设施 10 个，总建设规模 39501.7 平方米，总投资 15758.0 万元；已竣工的各级残疾人托养服务设施 10 个，总建设规模 31468.8 平方米，总投资 9507.0 万元。

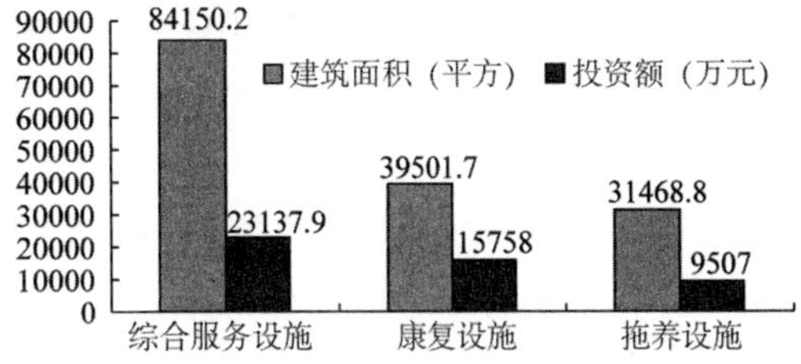

图 10-1　吉林省残疾人综合服务设施建设情况

十一、信息化

截至 2018 年底，8 个地市、16 个县级残联开通网站。省残联门户网站发布各类信息 5660 条，省残联官方微博发布各类信息 470 条。省残联微信公众号发布 1124 条，多篇文章得到网友热情追评，反响热烈，先后 5 次登上全国省级残联微信公众号传播指数十佳榜，2 次位列前五。省残联有 3 个直属事业单位，全省有 9 个市、县残联开通微信公众号，省残联系统微信矩阵初步形成。

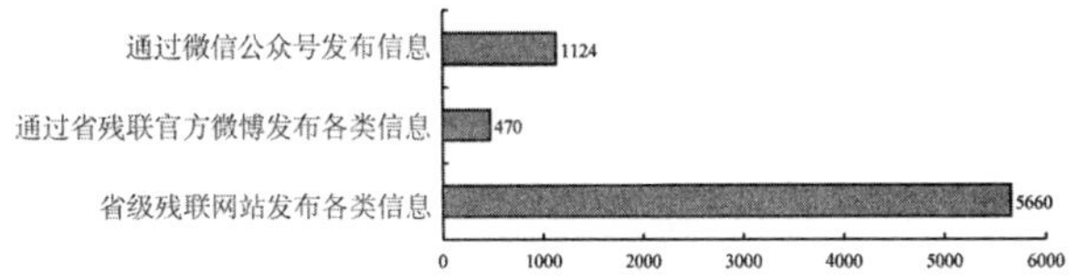

图 11-1　信息化情况

省残联与中国联通吉林省分公司开展信息扶贫战略合作，推出了“三同卡”+“一平台”+“N 服务”深度合作，共同推进残疾人信息扶贫战略实施和智慧残联建设。通过“同梦、同行、同心”助残专属 4G 卡和“智慧残联”移动端生态平台，给全省残疾人提供了最优惠的通讯资费套餐，极大降低了残疾人通信支出，减轻了负担，推动了残疾人服务的数字化、信息化、智能化进程。

2018年黑龙江省残疾人事业发展统计公报

2018年，全省残联系统认真学习习近平总书记关于残疾人事业的重要论述，围绕实现“全面建成小康社会，残疾人一个也不能少”的目标，着力打赢打好贫困残疾人脱贫攻坚战，努力开创新时代残疾人事业发展新局面。

一、康复

2018年，全省共有160552名残疾儿童及持证残疾人得到基本康复服务，其中包括0-6岁残疾儿童2716人。得到康复服务的持证残疾人中，有视力残疾人18061名、听力残疾人7143名、言语残疾人13名、肢体残疾人105119名、智力残疾人9655名、精神残疾人15633名、多重残疾人3557名。全年共为80378名残疾人提供各类辅助器具适配服务。

截至2018年底，全省共有残疾人康复机构252个，其中，46个机构提供视力残疾康复服务，39个提供听力言语残疾康复服务，154个提供肢体残疾康复服务，70个提供智力残疾康复服务，24个提供精神残疾康复服务，51个提供孤独症儿童康复服务，24个提供辅助器具服务。康复机构在岗人员6130人，其中，管理人员663人，专业技术人员4448人，其他人员1019人。

二、教育

残疾人事业专项彩票公益金助学项目的实施，为326名家庭经济困难的残疾儿童享受普惠性学前教育提供资助。

2018年，全省共有特殊教育普通高中班（部）1个，在校生25人，其中聋生25人。残疾人中等职业学校（班）5个，在校生210人，毕业生76人，毕业生中32人获得职业资格证书。有206名残疾人被普通高等院校录取。

全省共有671名残疾青壮年文盲接受了扫盲教育。

三、就业

全省共有城乡持证残疾人就业人数为253914人，其中按比例就业15891人，集中就业6659人，个体就业27750人，公益性岗位就业6505人，辅助性就业2325人，灵活就业(含社区、居家就业)80399人，从事农业种养加114385人。

全省培训盲人保健按摩人员415名、盲人医疗按摩人员373名；保健按摩机构达到272个，医疗按摩机构达到48个；18人获得盲人医疗按摩人员初级职务任职资格，4人获得中级职务任职资格。

四、社会保障

截至2018年底，全省残疾居民参加城乡社会养老保险人数419386名，80572名60岁以下参保重度残疾人中，77596名得到政府的参保扶助，享受代缴比例达到96.3%。49930名非重度残疾人享受了个人缴费资助政策。159494人领取养老金。

全省残疾人托养服务工作稳步推进，残疾人托养服务机构达到96个，其中寄宿制托养服务机构59个，日间照料机构8个，综合性托养服务机构29个，为14981名残疾人提供了托养服务。6337名残疾人接受居家服务。279名托养服务管理和服务人员接受了各级各类专业培训。

五、扶贫开发

全省贫困残疾人得到有效扶持，30791名残疾人退出建档立卡；残疾人接受实用技术培训10464人次。

全省82个残疾人扶贫基地安置1454名残疾人就业，扶持带动1749户残疾人家庭。

共完成6155户农村贫困残疾人危房改造，投入资金77876912.6元。

六、宣传文化

截至2018年底，共有省级残疾人专题广播节目1个、电视手语栏目2个；地市级电视手语栏目8个。

省市（地）县三级公共图书馆共设立盲文及盲文有声读物阅览室 48 个，共开展残疾人文化周活动 235 场次；省地两级残联共举办残疾人文化艺术类的比赛及展览 23 次，共有各类残疾人艺术团 13 个。

2018 年，制定或修改地市级关于残疾人的专门法规、规章 1 个；制定或修改保障残疾人权益的地市级规范性文件 1 个。县级以上人大开展《中华人民共和国残疾人保障法》执法检查和专题调研 13 次；政协开展视察和专题调研 6 次。开展省级普法宣传教育活动 2 次，533 人参加；举办省级法律培训班 1 个，167 人参加。

七、体育

继续实施残疾人“康复体育关爱家庭计划”和残疾人“体育健身示范点”创建工作，残疾人群众体育参与率得到提高，深入开展“残疾人体育健身周”、“中国残疾人冰雪运动季”活动。与省运动会同城同年举办了第七届黑龙江省残疾人运动会，400 余名运动员共同参与了田径、游泳、乒乓球等 7 个大项的全省比赛，实现了全省残运会与全省运动会同城同年举办。全年 124 名运动员参加了 11 项全国比赛，共取得 10 枚金牌、11 枚银牌、3 枚铜牌。韩淼雨、吴晴 2 名运动员代表国家参加雅加达亚残运会，共获得 1 枚金牌和 1 枚铜牌。以王海涛、刘微、张强为主力阵容的中国轮椅冰壶队在 2018 年平昌冬季残奥会上取得金牌，实现了历史性突破。全年共承担全国体育赛事及活动 4 次，圆满地完成了中国残联交办的各项赛事活动及集训任务。

八、维权

各级残联维权组织建设进一步加强，残疾人事业法律法规体系更加完善，无障碍环境建设取得新突破，残疾人维权工作全面开展。

截至 2018 年底，全省成立残疾人法律救助工作协调机构 21 个，建立残疾人法律救助工作站 13 个。

残疾人参政议政工作得到加强，各地残联协助人大代表、政协委员提出议案、建议、提案 11 件，办理议案、建议、提案 7 件。

无障碍建设法规、标准进一步完善。共出台了 1 个省、地市、县级无障碍环境建设与管理法规、政府令和规范性文件；36 个地市、县系统开展无障碍环境建设；开展无障碍环境建设检查 6 次，无障碍培训 20 人次。

九、组织建设

2018 年，市县乡共成立残联 1358 个，各地市已建残联 13 个，县（市、区）残联已建 133 个，乡镇（街道）残联已建 1212 个；已建社区（村）残协 8135 个。

省市县乡残联工作人员 3022 人，乡镇（街道）、村（社区）选聘残疾人专职委员总计 6150 名。地市级配备了残疾人领导干部的残联 8 个，县级配备了残疾人干部的残联 33 个。

共建立省级及以下各类残疾人专门协会 720 个，其中省级专门协会已建 5 个，市级专门协会已建 65 个，县级专门协会已建 650 个。助残社会组织共有 16 个。

十、服务设施

截至 2018 年底，已竣工的各级残疾人综合服务设施 99 个，总建设规模 114717 平方米，总投资 36707.9 万元；已竣工的各级残疾人康复设施 5 个，总建设规模 33245.8 平方米，总投资 7267 万元；已竣工的各级残疾人托养服务设施 20 个，总建设规模 44911.2 平方米，总投资 9843 万元。

十一、信息化建设

截至 2018 年底，5 个地市、7 个县级残联开通网站。

2018 年上海市残疾人事业发展统计公报

2018 年，上海市残联系统认真贯彻落实中央和市委、市政府的决策部署，扎实推进群团改革，圆满完成换届任务，深入开展市委“大调研”活动，着力办好残疾人民生实事，加快推进残疾人小康进程。

一、康复

推动《上海市人民政府关于本市建立残疾儿童康复救助制度的实施意见》出台。根据 2018 年全国残疾人动态更新数据，上海市有 15.9 万残疾人得到基本康复服务，得到康复服务的持证残疾人中，有视力残疾人 2.9 万名、听力残疾人 1.5 万名、言语残疾人 0.1 万名、肢体残疾人 7.6 万名、智力残疾人 1.5 万名、精神残疾人 1.8 万名、多重残疾人 0.5 万名，有需求的残疾人基本康复服务覆盖率达 99%；有 6.1 万残疾人得到辅助器具适配服务，有需求的残疾人基本辅助器具适配率为 99%。

截至 2018 年底，全市已有残疾人康复机构 1071 个，其中，提供视力残疾康复服务的机构 93 个，提供听力言语残疾康复服务的机构 58 个，提供肢体残疾康复服务的机构 305 个，提供智力残疾康复服务的机构 318 个，提供精神残疾康复服务的机构 273 个，提供孤独症儿童康复服务的机构 61 个，提供辅助器具服务的机构 258 个。康复机构在岗人员 8956 人，其中，管理人员 1306 人，专业技术人员 4712 人，其他人员 2938 人，培训康复管理和业务类人员共计 1.8 万人。

二、教育

进一步完善特殊教育体系，加快特殊职业教育发展，建立健全特殊职业教育管理机制，使残疾学生享有优质的职业教育。全市设立了 18 个特殊职业教育办学点，其中 1 个特殊教育普通高中（班），在校盲人学生 172 人。残疾人中职教育（班）17 个，在校生 515 人，已毕业 82 人，其中有 35 人获得职业资格证书。

全年有 15 名残疾人被特殊高等教育机构录取，77 名残疾人进入普通高等院校学习。全年有 1197 名残疾人学生和生活困难残疾人家庭子女获得助学补贴。

上海开放大学残疾人教育学院开设本科、专科和中专学历教学，2018 年有 1319 名残疾人在校就读。

三、就业与扶贫

2018 年，全市持证残疾人新增就业 6528 人。其中城镇就业新增 5476 人，农村城镇就业新增 1052 人。

全市持证残疾人就业年龄段内（男：16 岁～59 岁，女：16 岁～54 岁）就业人数为 8.6 万人，其中按比例就业 4.4 万人，集中就业 1.8 万人，个体就业 812 人，公益性岗位就业 3532 人，辅助性就业 4663 人，灵活就业（含社区、居家就业）8888 人，从事农业种养加 5699 人。

全年培训盲人保健按摩人员 185 人、盲人医疗按摩人员 73 人，有 5 人获得初级专业技术职称。全市共有医疗按摩机构 1 家，保健按摩机构 84 家。

2018 年，上海市残联正式纳入全市东西部扶贫协作和对口支援大局，成为上海市对口支援和合作交流工作领导小组成员单位。全年继续开展“帮扶 5000 名农村困难残疾人劳动增收”项目，积极扶持涉残涉农经济组织，全市有 267 个残疾人扶贫基地，2.2 万人次残疾人得到实用技术培训，安置 4145 名残疾人就业。114 户农村困难残疾人家庭得到无障碍改造，受益残疾人 162 人。

四、社会保障

截至 2018 年底，城乡残疾居民参加城乡社会养老保障人数达到 7.5 万名，60 周岁以下的参保残疾人中有 4.0 万名重度残疾人。

落实残疾人“两项补贴”制度，享受“两项补贴”的残疾人总数为 28.4 万人，其中享受困难残疾人生活补贴 8.4 万人，享受重度残疾人护理补贴 20.0

万人。

截至 2018 年底，残疾人托养机构达到 796 个，其中寄宿制托养服务机构 364 家，日间照料托养服务机构 432 家，有 4.2 万名残疾人接受了托养服务，其中寄宿制机构托养残疾人 0.6 万人，日间照料机构托养残疾人 1.0 万人，享受居家托养服务残疾人 2.6 万人。全市建有 222 个阳光之家、214 家阳光心园。全年有 5639 名托养服务管理和服务人员接受专业培训。

五、宣传文化

举办第 28 次“全国助残日”、第 19 个“上海助残周”、第 2 个全国“残疾预防日”、国际残疾人日暨“上海市残联成立 30 周年座谈会”等系列活动。拍摄《让阳光照亮残疾人心灵》宣传视频，编印《阳光梦想》和《阳光下》宣传画册。截至 2018 年底，全年共组织新闻发布会 10 次，全市残疾人专题广播节目 1 个、电视手语栏目 1 个；区级残疾人专题广播节目 2 个、电视手语栏目 14 个。通过政务新媒体拓展宣传渠道，全年门户网站发布 696 条信息，其中政策发布 50 条；微信公众号发布 615 条信息，其中视频 19 条；微博发布 10 条信息，其中视频 1 条。

继续推进公共图书馆盲人阅览室建设、残疾人艺术人才培养基地建设。截至 2018 年底，全市共设立 37 个盲文及盲人有声读物图书馆，撰写社区无障碍电影剧本 50 余部，配音和制作合成 40 多部；开展残疾人文化周活动 339 场次；商业影院放映 200 余场无障碍电影，惠及全市 2 万多人次残疾人；全年有 6.6 万多人次残疾人参加各级各类文化活动。

六、体育

全年累计开展各类残疾人群众体育活动 32 次，残疾人群众体育健身活动参与人数达到 1.1 万人次，全市设立残疾人自强健身示范点达到 209 个，聘任教练员 160 名，累计培养残疾人体育社会指导员 1018 人，为 1700 户残疾人家庭提供康复体育关爱家庭服务，全市共设 5 个残疾人体育训练基地，全年残疾人运动员在全国各项锦标赛上取得 31 金、24 银、23 铜，在国际赛事上获得 23 金、8 银、15 铜的成绩。

在 2018 年亚残运会上，上海共有 20 名残疾人运动员、4 名教练员、5 名工作人员入选中国体育代表团，分别在坐式排球、田径、轮椅击剑等 3 个大项中斩获 15 枚金牌、5 枚银牌和 6 枚铜牌。以上海队为班底组建的中国女子坐式排球队实现亚残运会三连冠。

七、维权

2018 年，全市加快推进残疾人小康进程和法治残联建设，制定修改关于残疾人的专门法规、规章 1 个，制定或修改保障残疾人权益的规范性文件 4 个。区级以上人大开展《中华人民共和国残疾人保障法》执法检查和专题调研 2 次，开展市级普法宣传教育活动 2 次，260 人参加；举办市级法律培训班 2 个，70 人参加。

2018 年，全市成立残疾人法律救助工作协调机构 18 个，建立残疾人法律救助工作站 17 个。开设手语视频服务的政府服务热线。全年共受理残疾人群众来信 839 件，来电 9539 通接待残疾人群众来访 3094 人次（含集访），均得到妥善处理。

截至 2018 年底，全市残联系统人大代表 30 人，其中市级代表 4 人，区级及以下代表 27 人；本市残联系统政协委员 12 人，其中市级委员 2 人，区级及以下委员 10 人。残疾人参政议政工作得到加强，全市残联系统协助人大代表、政协委员提出议案、建议、提案 4 件，办理议案、建议、提案 36 件。

2018 年，共出台了 2 个市、区级无障碍环境建设与管理法规、政府令和规范性文件；16 个区系统开展无障碍环境建设；开展无障碍环境建设检查 709 次，无障碍培训 2016 人次。

八、组织建设

规范基层组织建设，市、区、街镇三级 237 个残联全部完成换届任务，其中：市级 1 个、区级 16 个、街镇级 220 个。全市 175 个街镇残联建立执行理事会，占 79.5%；130 个街镇残联成立残疾人专门协会，占 59.1%。已建居（村）残协 4097 个。

全市残联系统实有人员达 1144 人，市、区残联领导班子已配备 26 名兼职副理事长，其中区残联 24 名。乡镇（街道）、居（村）选聘残疾人专职委员总计 3360 名。

共建立市级及以下各类残疾人专门协会85个，其中市级已建5个，区级已建80个，助残社会组织160个。

九、服务设施建设

截至2018年底，全市累计投入使用的各级残疾人综合服务设施17个，总建设规模为2.4万平方米，总投资额1.2亿元。累计已投入使用的各级残疾人托养设施12个，总建设规模为7260平方米，总投资额为1593万元。累计已投入使用的各级残疾人康复设施5个，总建设规模为10.1万平方米，总投资额4.5亿元。

十、信息化建设

截至2018年底，全市残联系统建立局域网1个、16个网站，1个OA办公系统。圆满完成残疾人基本服务状况和需求信息数据动态更新，实名制获取了52.6万名持证残疾人、6160个居（村）动态信息，信息采集入户率为97.38%。全市残疾人人口基础数据库持证残疾人54.9万人，新增持证残疾人5.1万人。

2018年，全市残疾人工作13个事项分3批接入上海市“一网通办”办事平台，其中盲人医疗按摩人员从事医疗按摩资格审核属于行政审批，其他12项属下沉事项，完成率达100%。听力言语残疾人信息卡套餐服务申请、视力残疾人固话优惠申请、《上海市盲人证》申请等3个事项“一网通办”可实现直接全程网办，申请人可以一次不用跑，其他10个事项也实现了申请人只跑一次的工作目标。

2018 年江苏省残疾人事业发展统计公报

2018 年，全省残联系统以习近平新时代中国特色社会主义思想为指导，深入学习贯彻党的十九大精神，认真落实省委推动高质量发展走在前列的决策部署，聚焦打赢打好残疾人脱贫攻坚战，不断完善残疾人社会保障和服务体系，着力推进残联组织建设和改革，较好地完成了年度各项工作任务。农村贫困残疾人家庭建立分布式光伏电站、实现全省乡镇（街道）“残疾人之家”全覆盖、为残疾人提供托养服务、加强残疾人就业工作、基本实现全省建档立卡贫困残疾人家庭基本家电全覆盖等 5 项工作，被省政府纳入重点民生实事项目。

一、康复

紧抓精准康复服务主线，加强绩效管理，康复服务取得新突破。以省政府名义印发《关于完善残疾儿童康复救助制度的实施意见》，扩宽救助范围和救助标准。制定《江苏省残疾人辅助器具适配补贴办法》，引入知名品牌。成功举办江苏省第二届听障儿童演讲比赛，省内主流媒体以及网络媒体持续关注，超过 30 万网民在线观看并积极互动，社会效应显著。

2018 年，全省 35.9 万名残疾儿童及持证残疾人得到基本康复服务，其中包括 0-6 岁残疾儿童 2.3 万人。得到康复服务的持证残疾人中，有视力残疾人 3.6 万名、听力残疾人 1.3 万名、言语残疾人 110 名、肢体残疾人 17.8 万名、智力残疾人 3.1 万名、精神残疾人 7.6 万名、多重残疾人 8084 名。全年共为 14.98 万残疾人提供各类辅助器具适配服务。

截至 2018 年底，全省有残疾人康复机构 435 个，其中，93 个机构提供视力残疾康复服务，83 个提供听力言语残疾康复服务，149 个提供肢体残疾康复服务，127 个提供智力残疾康复服务，78 个提供精神残疾康复服务，111 个提供孤独症儿童康复服务，74 个提供辅助器具服务。康复机构在岗人员 1.4 万人，其中，管理人员 1513 人，专业技术人员 9699 人，其他人员 2465 人。

二、教育

教育工作扎实推进。会同省教育厅先后出台了《江苏省特殊教育第二期提升计划（2017-2020 年）》《关于建立特殊教育指导中心制度的通知》《关于建立特殊教育联席会议制度的通知》等文件，共同研究解决未入学残疾儿童少年义务教育问题。

残疾人事业专项彩票公益金助学项目的实施，为全省 586 名家庭经济困难的残疾儿童享受普惠性学前教育提供资助。各地对 401 名残疾儿童给予了学前教育资助。

2018 年，全省共有特殊教育普通高中学校（班）4 个，在校生 588 人，其中聋生 550 人，盲生 23 人，其他 15 人。残疾人中等职业学校（班）11 个，在校生 1544 人，毕业生 442 人，毕业生中 142 人获得职业资格证书。全省有 368 名残疾人被普通高等院校录取，124 名残疾人进入特殊教育学院学习。

继续实施《“十三五”残疾青壮年文盲扫盲行动方案》。2178 名残疾青壮年文盲接受了扫盲教育。

三、就业

就业服务取得新成绩。组织开展残疾人就业援助月专项活动，组织残疾人专场招聘会 183 次。参加全国创业创新大赛专项赛并获全国大赛第一名。组织举办江苏省第六届残疾人职业技能竞赛暨残疾人就业创业成果展，展现了广大残疾人劳动者的职业技能和工匠精神。

全省城乡持证残疾人就业人数为 45.2 万人，其中按比例就业 9.1 万人，集中就业 4.3 万人，个体就业 1841 人，公益性岗位就业 3.95 万人，辅助性就业 9080 人，灵活就业（含社区、居家就业）15.3 万人，从事农业种养加 11.5 万人。

全省培训盲人保健按摩人员 705 名、盲人医疗按摩人员 602 名；保健按摩机构达到 1054 个，医疗按摩机构达到 39 个；44 人获得盲人医疗按摩人员职务任职资格。

四、社会保障

会同人社部门出台《精准实施城乡居民基本养老保险扶贫工作的意见》，建档立卡残疾人资助参加基本养老和基本医保 100%。配合民政部门落实“两项补贴”，领取困难残疾人生活补贴 54.5 万名，护理补贴 43.7 万名。大力推动“单人保”实施，部分地区将“两项补贴”范围扩大到三、四级智力、精神残疾人，护理补贴发放范围覆盖到一二级听力残疾人。新建“残疾人之家”634 家，累计建成 1817 家，实现全省乡镇（街道）“残疾人之家”全覆盖。加强残疾人辅助性就业安全规范，完善辅助性就业补贴制度。

截至 2018 年底，残疾居民参加城乡社会养老保险人数 114.7 万名，30 万名 60 岁以下参保重度残疾人中，29.4 万名得到政府的参保扶助，享受代缴比例达到 98.0%。21 万名非重度残疾人享受了个人缴费资助政策。48 万人领取养老金。

残疾人托养服务工作稳步推进，残疾人托养服务机构达到 1756 个，其中寄宿制托养服务机构 81 个，日间照料机构 1130 个，综合性托养服务机构 545 个，为 3 万名残疾人提供了机构托养服务。7346 名残疾人接受居家服务。1228 名托养机构管理和服务人员接受了各级各类专业培训。

五、扶贫开发

聚焦残疾人脱贫攻坚。全面落实省委《关于打赢打好脱贫攻坚战三年行动的实施意见》，会党组专题研究脱贫攻坚工作，会同扶贫办制定《关于打赢打好残疾人脱贫攻坚战三年行动的实施办法》，与省政府扶贫办、省残疾人基本服务状况和需求信息数据对接，全面开展精准帮扶。

全省残疾人接受实用技术培训 8411 人次。933 名农村残疾人获得康复扶贫贴息贷款扶持。207 个残疾人扶贫基地安置 3851 名残疾人就业，扶持带动 4353 户残疾人家庭。全省共完成 839 户农村贫困残疾人危房改造，投入资金 1101.9 万元。2016 年至 2018 年底，累计有 20.9 万建档立卡残疾人脱贫。

六、宣传文化

2018 年制作七代会宣传画册《奋进的五年——江苏省残疾人联合会五年工作回眸》。截至 2018 年底，协调江苏卫视制播了 51 期《残疾人之友》手语新闻，协调江苏电台制播了 12 期《残疾人之声》，微信公众号审核发布 195 次，推文 773 篇，共计 16.54 万人次阅读。截至 2018 年底，全省共有省、市两级残疾人专题广播节目 16 个、电视手语栏目 17 个。

积极推动省残疾人文联加入省文联，并于 2018 年 5 月正式成为省文联团体会员。截止 2018 年底，全省设立盲文及盲文有声读物阅览室 57 个，共开展残疾人文化周活动 592 场次；省市两级残联共举办残疾人文化艺术类的比赛及展览 44 次，共有各类残疾人艺术团 19 个。

七、体育

宣传文体服务取得新进展。组织全省残疾人事业好新闻评选，协助省级媒体办好残疾人专题栏目，各专业文学艺术协会工作活跃。坚持开展文化助残活动，组织残疾人“文化周”“特奥日”“健身周”等活动，不断丰富残疾人精神文化生活。组织参加 19 项全国残疾人体育锦标赛，取得 78 金 59 银 51 铜。组织参加 7 批次国际残疾人体育比赛，获得 43 金 16 银 6 铜的优良成绩。承接承办了全国轮椅击剑锦标赛、全国坐式排球锦标赛，组织举办江苏省第十届残疾人运动会，向社会展示了残疾人自强不息、奋勇拼搏的精神风貌。

八、维权

残疾人维权服务取得新拓展，开展“七五”普法中期检查，举办残疾人学法用法知识竞赛，完成残联系统“十三五”规划实施情况中期评估工作，落实省人大执法检查整改意见，扎实做好全省贫困重度残疾人家庭无障碍改造工作。全省各级残联抓紧推进贫困重度残疾人家庭无障碍改造托底补短工作，将贫困重度残疾人家庭无障碍改造纳入全省残疾人脱贫攻坚三年行动中，下发《江苏省贫困残疾人家庭无障碍改造示范样板户建设工作方案》。

2018 年，全省制定或修改保障残疾人权益的省级规范性文件 11 个。县级以上人大开展《中华人民共和国残疾人保障法》执法检查和专题调研 14 次；政协开展视察和专题调研 14 次。开展省级普法宣传教育活动 1 次，120 人参加；举办省级法律培训班 1

个，30人参加。

截至2018年底，全省成立残疾人法律救助工作协调机构98个，建立残疾人法律救助工作站93个。

残疾人参政议政工作得到加强，各地残联协助人大代表、委员提出议案、建议、提案32件，办理议案、建议、提案57件。

无障碍建设法规、标准进一步完善。全省共出台了26个地市、县级无障碍环境建设与管理法规、政府令和规范性文件；56个地市、县全部实现系统开展无障碍环境建设；开展无障碍环境建设检查187次，无障碍培训2979人次。

九、组织建设

紧紧围绕党要管党、全面从严治党要求，落实领导班子“一岗双责”，加强廉政风险排查和警示教育，全力配合省委巡视省残联党组工作。根据中国残联改革要求，研究制定《江苏省残疾人联合会改革方案》。2018年，各级残联如期完成换届工作任务，残联领导班子和组织建设得到加强。组织举办全省残联系统新任理事长培训班、第十期优秀专职委员培训班。协助承办全国第二届残疾人专职委员知识竞赛，江苏代表队蝉联冠军。下发了《关于迅速开展残疾人工作者违规持有残疾人证彻查清理工作的通知》，对全省各级残联系统工作人员（含退休工作人员）及亲属违规持有残疾人证情况进行清查。

2018年，全省市县乡共成立残联1432个，地市全部建有残联，98.1%的县（市、区）、99.3%乡镇（街道）已建残联；97.8%的社区（村）已建残协，共1.96万个。

各级残联工作人员4605人，乡镇（街道）、村（社区）选聘残疾人专职委员总计20418名。全部省级残联、53.8%的地市级残联配备了残疾人领导干部，44.1%的县级残联配备了残疾人干部。

全省共建立各类残疾人专门协会552个，其中省、地市级专门协会已建比例为100%，县级为92.7%。全省助残社会组织共有366个。

十、服务设施

残疾人服务设施建设得到全面发展。截至2018年底，全省已竣工的各级残疾人综合服务设施77个，总建设规模43.1万平方米，总投资16.1亿元；已竣工的各级残疾人康复设施64个，总建设规模24.7万平方米，总投资9.9亿元；已竣工的各级残疾人托养服务设施59个，总建设规模32.1万平方米，总投资10.3亿元。

十一、信息化建设

截至2018年底，全省13个地市、66个县级残联开通网站。全省残疾人人口基础数据库持证残疾人160万人。智能化残疾人证在苏州市试点成功，并将泰州市作为下一个试点城市。建立共享交换平台，全力打通与中残联的数据接口，对于封闭、落伍的系统进行反复论证后着手与国家系统并轨。

2018年浙江省残疾人事业发展统计公报

2018年，全省残疾人工作以习近平新时代中国特色社会主义思想为指引，全面贯彻党的十九大精神，认真落实省第十四次党代会、省委十四届二次、三次会议决策部署，紧紧围绕残疾人事业高质量发展的时代要求，推进实施我省残疾人事业发展“十三五”规划，圆满完成年度确定的各项任务。

一、康复

2018年，全省66.2万名残疾儿童及持证残疾人得到基本康复服务，其中0—6岁残疾儿童6222人。得到康复服务的残疾人中，视力残疾人6.6万名，听力残疾人7.3万名，言语残疾人5448名，肢体残疾人26.6万名，智力残疾人9.5万名，精神残疾人12.7万名，多重残疾人2.8万名。全年共为12.7万名残疾人提供各类辅助器具适配服务。

截至2018年底，全省有残疾人康复机构206个，其中，提供视力残疾康复服务的机构21个，提供听力言语残疾康复服务的机构41个，提供肢体残疾康复服务的机构84个，提供智力残疾康复服务的机构96个，提供精神残疾康复服务的机构39个，提供孤独症儿童康复服务的机构85个，提供辅助器具服务的机构56个。康复机构在岗人员6434人，其中管理人员663人，专业技术人员4454人，其他人员1317人。

二、教育

实施残疾人事业专项彩票公益金助学项目，资助全省433名家庭经济困难的残疾儿童享受普惠性学前教育。各地积极争取其他资金支持，对326名残疾儿童给予学前教育资助。

2018年，全省共有特殊教育普通高中班（部）6个，在校生370人，其中聋生87人，盲生283人。残疾人中等职业学校（班）12个，在校生458人，毕业生123人，毕业生中46人获得职业资格证书。全省有418名残疾人被普通高等院校录取，317名残疾人进入浙江特殊教育学院学习。

2018年，有2170名残疾青壮年文盲接受了扫盲教育。

三、就业

2018年，全省持证残疾人就业人数为33.8万人，其中按比例就业8.9万人，集中就业4.5万人，个体就业4.7万人，公益性岗位就业5125人，辅助性就业9456人，灵活就业（含社区、居家就业）8.4万人，从事农业种养殖5.9万人。全年新增就业1.6万人。

2018年，全省共培训盲人保健按摩人员431名、盲人医疗按摩人员196名。全省共有保健按摩机构954个，医疗按摩机构85个。获得盲人医疗按摩人员初级职务任职资格27人。

四、社会保障

2018年，全省发放困难残疾人生活补贴43.9万人，发放重度残疾人护理补贴48.9万人。残疾居民参加城乡社会养老保险人数66.4万人，60岁以下参保的重度残疾人全部得到政府参保扶助，代缴比例达到100.0%。20万名非重度残疾人享受了个人缴费资助政策。30.4万人领取养老金。

截至2018年底，全省共有残疾人托养服务机构1197个，其中寄宿制托养服务机构444个，日间照料机构537个，综合性托养服务机构216个，为2.7万名残疾人提供了托养服务。36.8万名残疾人接受居家服务。全年有1792名托养服务管理和服务人员接受了各级各类专业培训。

五、扶贫

2018年，残疾人接受实用技术培训1.3万人次。康复扶贫贴息贷款扶持2403名农村残疾人。965个残疾人扶贫基地安置5853名残疾人就业，扶持带动1.6万户残疾人家庭。

全省共完成2274户农村残疾人危房改造，投入资金2121.6万元。

六、宣传文化

2018 年，组织第 28 次全国助残日、雅加达亚残运会、国际残疾人日、残疾预防日等系列宣传活动。协调中央新闻媒体赴浙江省集中采访，组织新闻发布会 1 场，组织“最美浙江人之最美助残人”评选发布活动。在中央、省级主流媒体上的新闻报道分别达到 22 篇和 90 余篇。省残联官微影响力逐步放大。截至 2018 年底，共有省级残疾人专题广播节目 1 个、电视手语栏目 3 个；市级残疾人专题广播节目 13 个、电视手语栏目 12 个。

省市县三级公共图书馆共设立盲文及盲文有声读物阅览室 78 个，开展残疾人文化周活动 768 场次。省市两级残联共举办残疾人文化艺术类比赛及展览 27 次，共有各类残疾人艺术团 31 个。

七、体育

继续实施“康复体育关爱家庭计划”，全省残疾人文体活动参与率进一步巩固。2018 年共参加 21 项全国锦标赛、2 项特奥比赛和 4 项群众体育比赛，取得 116 金 70 银 51 铜。在第三届亚残运会夺得 29 金 12 银 2 铜，金牌数位居各省（区、市）第一位。杭州市政府在雅加达接过亚残运会会旗，第四届亚残运会正式进入“杭州时间”。成功举办省第十届残运会，首次将特奥、聋奥、残奥三会合一。

八、维权

2018 年，省政府出台《浙江省实施〈无障碍环境建设条例〉办法》。制定或修改保障残疾人权益的规范性文件市级 1 个、县级 19 个。全省共出台 45 个无障碍环境建设与管理的法规和规范性文件。

县级以上人大开展《中华人民共和国残疾人保障法》执法检查和专题调研 50 次，县级以上政协开展视察和专题调研 51 次。各级残联协助人大代表、政协委员提出议案、建议、提案 175 件，办理议案、建议、提案 229 件。

截至 2018 年底，全省成立残疾人法律救助工作协调机构 102 个，建立残疾人法律救助工作站 102 个（含开发区）。省级开展普法宣传教育活动 3 次，190 人参加；省级举办法律培训班 1 个，50 人参加。99 个设区市和县（市、区）系统开展无障碍环境建设，开展无障碍环境建设检查 556 次，无障碍培训 3071 人次。

九、组织建设

2018 年，市县乡共有残联 1480 个，其中，设区市残联 11 个，县（市、区）残联 94 个（含开发区），乡镇（街道）残联 1375 个。村（社区）已建残协 2.3 万个。

省市县乡残联实有人员 4895 人，乡镇（街道）、村（社区）选聘残疾人专职委员 2.4 万名。10 个设区市残联配备残疾人领导干部，56 个县级残联配备残疾人干部。

全省共建立各类残疾人专门协会 495 个，其中，省级 5 个、设区市 55 个、县级 435 个。全省共有助残社会组织 216 个。

十、服务设施

截至 2018 年底，全省已竣工的各级残疾人综合服务设施 93 个，总建设规模 61.2 万平方米，总投资 26 亿元；已竣工的各级残疾人康复设施 40 个，总建设规模 27.4 万平方米，总投资 10.9 亿元；已竣工的各级残疾人托养服务设施 36 个，总建设规模 24.1 万平方米，总投资 9.6 亿元。

十一、信息化

截至 2018 年底，全省 11 个设区市、56 个县级残联开通网站。

2018年安徽省残疾人事业发展统计公报

2018年，安徽省残疾人工作者深入学习贯彻习近平新时代中国特色社会主义思想和习近平总书记关于残疾人事业的重要论述，围绕实现“全面建成小康社会，残疾人一个也不能少”的目标，着力打赢打好贫困残疾人脱贫攻坚战，努力开创新时代残疾人事业发展新局面。

一、康复

2018年，813806名残疾儿童及持证残疾人得到基本康复服务，其中包括0-6岁残疾儿童7601人。得到康复服务的持证残疾人中，有视力残疾人90915名、听力残疾人37292名、言语残疾人5320名、肢体残疾人410208名、智力残疾人74533名、精神残疾人147039名、多重残疾人47606名。全年共为164221名残疾人提供各类辅助器具适配服务。

截至2018年底，有残疾儿童康复机构237个，其中，12个机构提供视力残疾康复服务，79个提供听力言语残疾康复服务，86个提供肢体残疾康复服务，127个提供智力残疾康复服务，10个提供精神残疾康复服务，109个提供孤独症儿童康复服务，42个提供辅助器具服务。康复机构在岗人员5800人，其中，管理人员645人，专业技术人员4449人，其他人员706人。

二、教育

残疾人事业专项彩票公益金助学项目的实施，为871名家庭经济困难的残疾儿童享受普惠性学前教育提供资助。

共有特殊教育普通高中班（部）、中等职业学校（班）5个，在校生1582人，其中聋生662人，盲生252人，肢残生345人，其他323人；毕业生347人。有545名残疾人被普通高等院校录取。

1613名残疾青壮年文盲接受了扫盲教育。

三、就业

城乡持证残疾人就业人数为497301人，其中按比例就业12002人，集中就业7009人，个体就业36747人，公益性岗位就业2634人，辅助性就业10438人，灵活就业（含社区、居家就业）151913人，从事农业种养加276558人。

培训盲人保健按摩人员1557名、盲人医疗按摩人员216名；保健按摩机构达到493个，医疗按摩机构达到65个。

四、社会保障

截至2018年底，残疾居民参加城乡社会养老保险人数1461356名，410034名60岁以下参保重度残疾人中403144名得到政府的参保扶助，享受代缴比例达到98.3%。54859名非重度残疾人享受了个人缴费资助政策。544197人领取养老金。

残疾人托养服务工作稳步推进，残疾人托养服务机构达到305个，其中寄宿制托养服务机构175个，日间照料机构40个，综合性托养服务机构90个，为35658名残疾人提供了托养服务。14194名残疾人接受居家服务。102名托养服务管理和服务人员接受了各级各类专业培训。

五、扶贫开发

贫困残疾人得到有效扶持，100084名残疾人退出建档立卡；残疾人接受实用技术培训20603人次。

213名农村残疾人获得康复扶贫贴息贷款扶持。146个残疾人扶贫基地安置2017名残疾人就业，扶持带动2302户残疾人家庭。

共完成15447户农村贫困残疾人危房改造，投入资金169233026.1元。

六、宣传文化

截至2018年底，共有省级残疾人专题广播节目1个、电视手语栏目1个；市级残疾人专题广播节目15个、电视手语栏目16个。

省市县三级公共图书馆共设立盲文及盲文有声读物阅览室55个，共开展残疾人文化周活动260场次；省市两级残联共举办残疾人文化艺术类的比赛及展览 2 次，共有各类残疾人艺术团 6 个。

七、体育

牵头组织实施安徽省第七届残疾人运动会。启动实施残疾人体育健身示范点和康复体育进家庭项目，加强残疾人群众体育工作。加强残疾人运动员选拔、培训，积极备战全国第十届残疾人运动会暨第七届特奥会。

八、维权

制定或修改保障残疾人权益的规范性文件，市级 4 个、县级 8 个。县级以上人大开展《中华人民共和国残疾人保障法》执法检查和专题调研 11 次；政协开展视察和专题调研 14 次。开展省级普法宣传教育活动 3 次，410 人参加；举办省级法律培训班 1 个，130 人参加。

截至 2018 年底，成立残疾人法律救助工作协调机构 53 个，建立残疾人法律救助工作站 44 个。

残疾人参政议政工作得到加强，各地残联协助人大代表、政协委员提出议案、建议、提案 15 件，办理议案、建议、提案 42 件。

无障碍建设法规、标准进一步完善。共出台了 6 个省市县级无障碍环境建设与管理法规、政府令和规范性文件；81 个市县系统开展无障碍环境建设；开展无障碍环境建设检查 46 次，无障碍培训 527 人次。

九、组织建设

2018 年，市县乡三级共成立残联 1647 个，各市已建残联 16 个，县（市、区）残联已建 115 个，乡镇（街道）残联已建 1516 个。已建村（社区）残协 16174 个。

省市县乡残联工作人员 3470 人，乡镇（街道）、村（社区）选聘残疾人专职委员总计 18137 名。市级配备了残疾人领导干部的残联 9 个，县级配备了残疾人干部的残联 56 个。

共建立省级及以下各类残疾人专门协会 561 个，其中省级专门协会已建 5 个，市级专门协会已建 75 个，县级专门协会已建 481 个。助残社会组织共有 39 个。

十、服务设施

截至 2018 年底，已竣工的各级残疾人综合服务设施 89 个，总建设规模 234578.5 平方米，总投资 55603.8 万元；已竣工的各级残疾人康复设施 21 个，总建设规模 122836.1 平方米，总投资 44094.4 万元；已竣工的各级残疾人托养服务设施 14 个，总建设规模 36783.8 平方米，总投资 8868.3 万元。

十一、信息化建设

截至 2018 年底，16 个市、56 个县（市、区）级残联开通网站。

2018年福建省残疾人事业发展统计公报

2018年，全省残联系统认真学习习近平总书记关于残疾人事业的重要论述，围绕实现“全面建成小康社会，残疾人一个也不能少”的目标，着力打赢打好贫困残疾人脱贫攻坚战，努力开创新时代残疾人事业发展新局面。

一、康复

2018年，16.9万名残疾儿童及持证残疾人得到基本康复服务，其中包括0-6岁残疾儿童7956人。得到康复服务的持证残疾人中，有视力残疾人5739名、听力残疾人9645名、言语残疾人156名、肢体残疾人7.8万名、智力残疾人2.3万名、精神残疾人4.1万名、多重残疾人8253名。全年共为3.5万名残疾人提供各类辅助器具适配服务。

截至2018年底，有残疾人康复机构274个，其中，23个机构提供视力残疾康复服务，29个提供听力言语残疾康复服务，64个提供肢体残疾康复服务，97个提供智力残疾康复服务，56个提供精神残疾康复服务，104个提供孤独症儿童康复服务，55个提供辅助器具服务。康复机构在岗人员6244人，其中，管理人员828人，专业技术人员4236人，其他人员1180人。

二、教育

残疾人教育持续提升。推动出台了《福建省第二期特殊教育提升计划（2018-2020年）》，制定《福建省国家通用手语推广实施方案》《福建省国家通用盲文推广实施方案》，在全省范围内逐步推广使用国家通用手语和国家通用盲文。实施残疾人事业专项彩票公益金助学项目，对420人次家庭经济困难的残疾儿童接受学前教育提供资助，各地也积极多渠道争取资金支持，对274名残疾儿童给予学前教育资助。全省残疾学生全部纳入国家资助政策实施范围，各地广泛开展扶残助学，1.6万多名残疾学生得到就学资助。残疾人受教育权得到了更好保障，进一步提高了特殊教育发展水平。

2018年，全省共有特殊教育普通高中班（部）4个，在校生144人。残疾人中等职业学校（班）7个，在校生213人，毕业生39人。有216名残疾人被普通高等院校录取，35名残疾人进入特殊教育学院学习。797名残疾青壮年文盲接受了扫盲教育。

三、就业

2018年，城乡持证残疾人就业人数为21.6万人，其中按比例就业1.6万人，集中就业5572人，个体就业2.4万人，公益性岗位就业2440人，辅助性就业3479人，灵活就业（含社区、居家就业）6.6万人，从事农业种养加9.9万人。

2018年度，全省共培训盲人保健按摩人员432名、盲人医疗按摩人员148名；保健按摩机构达到290个，医疗按摩机构达到33个；10人获得盲人医疗按摩人员初级职务任职资格，21人获得中级职务任职资格。

四、扶贫

2018年，贫困残疾人得到有效扶持，162名残疾人退出国家建档立卡；残疾人接受实用技术培训5670人次。共有2283名农村残疾人获得康复扶贫贴息贷款扶持。75个残疾人扶贫基地安置999名残疾人就业，扶持带动1192户残疾人家庭。全省共完成1876户农村贫困残疾人危房改造，投入资金3624.9万元。

五、社会保障

截至2018年底，残疾居民参加城乡社会养老保险人数70.5万名。17.2万名60岁以下参保重度残疾人中，17.1万名得到政府的参保扶助，享受代缴比例达到99.1%。15.5万名非重度残疾人享受了个人缴费资助政策。34.2万人领取养老金。

残疾人托养服务工作稳步推进，残疾人托养服务机构达到102个，其中寄宿制托养服务机构43个，日间照料机构49个，综合性托养服务机构10个。

1.6 万名残疾人得到托养服务。全年 194 名托养服务管理和服务人员接受了各级各类专业培训。

六、宣传体育

残疾人宣传文化工作持续推进。截至 2018 年底，全省共有省级电视手语栏目 1 个；地市级残疾人专题广播节目 4 个、电视手语栏目 7 个。开展“文化进家庭五个一”“残疾人活动日”“残疾人健身周”等活动，省残疾人艺术团公益演出近 20 场，残疾人参与度日益提高。

残疾人群众体育活动日益活跃，残疾人竞技体育水平不断提高。组织 221 名（次）残疾人参加国际、全国性体育赛事，获得 116 枚奖牌。特别是我省 11 名运动员参加雅加达亚残运会，荣获 13 金 12 银 5 铜，创我省参加历届亚残运会金牌数、奖牌数的最好成绩，受到省领导的亲切会见。承办第七届全国特奥运动会特奥足球比赛，带动福建省特奥运动的持续发展。

七、维权

各级残联维权组织建设进一步加强，残疾人事业法律法规体系更加完善，无障碍环境建设取得新突破，残疾人维权工作全面开展。

2018 年，制定或修改保障残疾人权益的省级规范性文件 1 个、地市级 7 个、县级 5 个。全省县级以上人大开展《中华人民共和国残疾人保障法》执法检查和专题调研 7 次；政协开展视察和专题调研 6 次。全省开展省级普法宣传教育活动 9 次，453 人参加；举办省级法律培训班 3 个，206 人参加。

残疾人参政议政工作得到加强，各地残联协助人大代表、政协委员提出议案、建议、提案 19 件，办理议案、建议、提案 40 件。

无障碍建设法规、标准进一步完善。共出台了 7 个省、地市、县级无障碍环境建设与管理法规、政府令和规范性文件；48 个地市、县系统开展无障碍环境建设；开展无障碍环境建设检查 35 次，无障碍培训 1779 人次。

八、组织建设

2018 年，市县乡共成立残联 1212 个，各地市已建残联 9 个，县（市、区）残联已建 89 个，乡镇（街道）残联已建 1114 个；已建社区（村）残协 1.6 万个。

省市县乡残联工作人员 2723 人，乡镇（街道）、村（社区）选聘残疾人联络员总计 1.7 万名。地市级配备了残疾人领导干部的残联 9 个，县级配备了残疾人干部的残联 30 个。

共建立省级及以下各类残疾人专门协会 454 个，其中省级专门协会已建 5 个，市级专门协会已建 45 个，县级专门协会已建 404 个。全省助残社会组织共有 78 个。

九、服务设施

截至 2018 年底，已竣工的各级残疾人综合服务设施 84 个，总建设规模 26.5 万平方米；已竣工的各级残疾人康复设施 219 个，总建设规模 6.3 万平方米；已竣工的各级残疾人托养服务设施 47 个，总建设规模 7.5 万平方米。

十、信息化建设

截至 2018 年底，省残联门户网站共发稿 2654 篇，网站页面年浏览量 38 万人次，在残疾人事业新闻宣传、政务公开、信息服务等方面发挥了重要作用。推行电子政务应用，发送政务短信 10038 条，通过政务邮箱向各级残联发送政务文件通知 3824 份（次）。继续推广“福建省残疾人综合信息服务平台”应用，为残疾人提供网络无障碍服务。

注重加强与纵向、横向部门(单位)的沟通协作，实现数据交换共享。与省城乡居民养老保险中心实现了全省所有残疾人参加居民养老保险的数据交换。与省机关养老保险局实现了残疾人参加养老保险数据的交换。与省劳动保险局实现了残疾人参加职工养老保险数据的交换。与省民政厅实现了残疾人低保户的数据交换。

2018 年江西省残疾人事业发展统计公报

2018 年，在省委省政府的正确领导下，在中国残联的精心指导下，省残联围绕年初确定的工作思路和安排，坚持以深入学习贯彻习近平新时代中国特色社会主义思想和党的十九大精神为主线，认真落实省委省政府有关决策部署，各项工作总体进展顺利。

一、康复

2018 年，24.65 万名残疾儿童及持证残疾人得到基本康复服务，其中包括 0-6 岁残疾儿童 0.38 万人。得到康复服务的持证残疾人中，有视力残疾人 2.48 万名、听力残疾人 1.06 万名、言语残疾人 113 名、肢体残疾人 13.73 万名、智力残疾人 1.36 万名、精神残疾人 4.9 万名、多重残疾人 1.07 万名。全年共为 13.57 万名残疾人提供各类辅助器具适配服务。

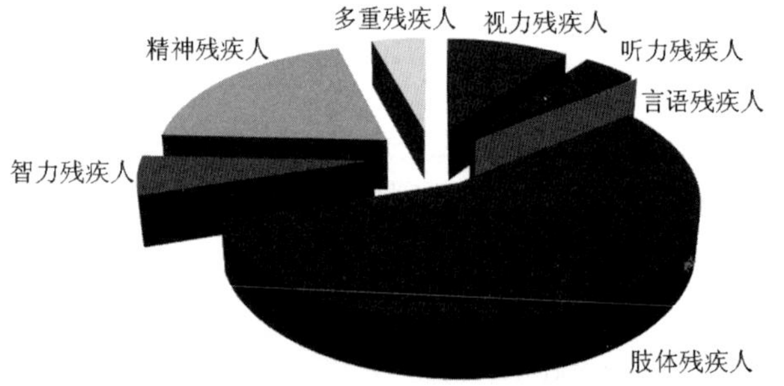

图 1-1　得到康复服务的持证残疾人情况（单位：万名）

截至 2018 年底，有残疾人康复机构 210 个，其中，15 个机构提供视力残疾康复服务，46 个提供听力言语残疾康复服务，65 个提供肢体残疾康复服务，70 个提供智力残疾康复服务，58 个提供精神残疾康复服务，35 个提供孤独症儿童康复服务，35 个提供辅助器具服务。康复机构在岗人员 5982 人，其中，管理人员 834 人，专业技术人员 3714 人，其他人员 1434 人。

二、教育

残疾人事业专项彩票公益金助学项目的实施，为 525 名家庭经济困难的残疾儿童享受普惠性学前教育提供资助。多渠道争取资金支持，对 1287 名残疾儿童给予学前教育资助。

共有特殊教育普通高中班（部）2 个，在校生 355 人，其中聋生 326 人，盲生 29 人。残疾人中等职业学校（班）5 个，在校生 715 人，毕业生 76 人，毕业生中 5 人获得职业资格证书。有 452 名残疾人被普通高等院校录取。538 名残疾青壮年文盲接受了扫盲教育。

三、就业

城乡持证残疾人就业人数为 36.01 万人，其中按比例就业 1.23 万人，集中就业 2.09 万人，个体就业 4.63 万人，公益性岗位就业 0.77 万人，辅助性就业 0.83 万人，灵活就业（含社区、居家就业）13.94 万人，从事农业种养加 12.53 万人。

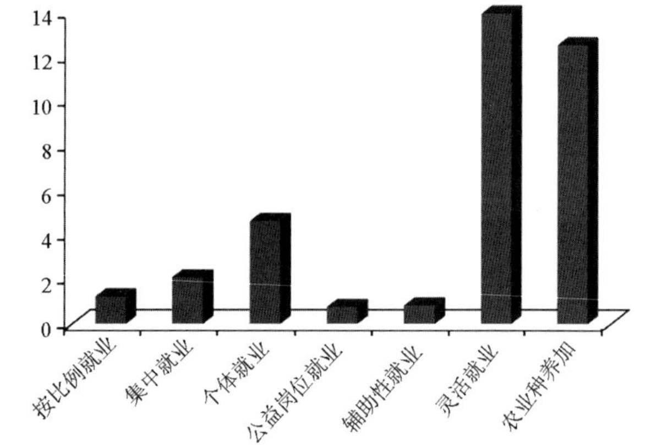

图 3-1　城乡持证残疾人就业情况（单位：万人）

培训盲人保健按摩人员 716 名、盲人医疗按摩人员 238 名；保健按摩机构达到 521 个，医疗按摩机构达到 75 个。

四、社会保障

截至 2018 年底，残疾居民参加城乡社会养老保险人数 87.96 万名，19.43 万名 60 岁以下参保重度残疾人中，18.99 万名得到政府的参保扶助，享受代缴比例达到 97.8%。12.25 万名非重度残疾人享受了个人缴费资助政策。33.23 万人领取养老金。

残疾人托养服务工作稳步推进，残疾人托养服务机构达到 64 个，其中寄宿制托养服务机构 22 个，日间照料机构 23 个，综合性托养服务机构 19 个，为 3807 名残疾人提供了托养服务。4513 名残疾人接受居家服务。152 名托养服务管理和服务人员接受了各级各类专业培训。

五、扶贫

贫困残疾人得到有效扶持，6.77 万名残疾人退出建档立卡;残疾人接受实用技术培训 0.81 万人次。

96 名农村残疾人获得康复扶贫贴息贷款扶持。333 个残疾人扶贫基地安置 2148 名残疾人就业，扶持带动 1895 户残疾人家庭。

共完成 3233 户农村贫困残疾人危房改造，投入资金 3862.56 万元。

六、宣传文化

截至 2018 年底，地市级残疾人专题广播节目 7 个、电视手语栏目 5 个。

省、市、县三级公共图书馆共设立盲文及盲文有声读物阅览室 27 个，共开展残疾人文化周活动 137 场次；省、市两级残联共举办残疾人文化艺术类的比赛及展览 19 次，共有各类残疾人艺术团 7 个。

七、维权

2018 年，制定或修改保障残疾人权益的省级规范性文件 1 个、设区市 3 个、县级 1 个。县级以上人大开展《中华人民共和国残疾人保障法》执法检查和专题调研 8 次;政协开展视察和专题调研 14 次。开展省级普法宣传教育活动 7 次，510 人参加；举办省级法律培训班 3 个，180 人参加。

截至 2018 年底，成立残疾人法律救助工作协调机构 58 个，建立残疾人法律救助工作站 46 个。

残疾人参政议政工作得到加强，各地残联协助人大代表、政协委员提出议案、建议、提案 38 件，办理议案、建议、提案 21 件。

无障碍建设法规、标准进一步完善。共出台了 6 个省、市、县级无障碍环境建设与管理法规、政府令和规范性文件；127 个市、县系统开展无障碍环境建设；开展无障碍环境建设检查 18 次，无障碍培训 157 人次。

八、组织建设

2018 年，市、县、乡共成立残联 1750 个，各设区市已建残联 11 个，县（市、区）残联已建 109 个，乡镇（街道）残联已建 1630 个；已建社区（村）残协 1.75 万个。

省、市、县、乡残联工作人员 0.4 万人，乡镇（街道）、村（社区）选聘残疾人专职委员总计 1.56 万名。市级配备了残疾人领导干部的残联 8 个，县级配备了残疾人干部的残联 56 个。

共建立省级及以下各类残疾人专门协会 463 个，其中省级专门协会已建 5 个，市级专门协会已建 55 个，县级专门协会已建 403 个。助残社会组织共有 25 个。

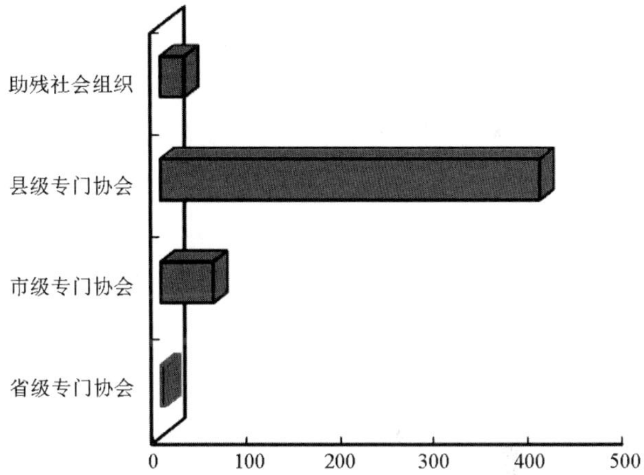

图 8-1 省级及以下各类残疾人专门协会情况（单位：个）

九、服务设施

截至 2018 年底，已竣工的各级残疾人综合服务设施 76 个，总建设规模 8.84 万平方米，总投资 20377.6 万元；已竣工的各级残疾人康复设施 13 个，总建设规模 11.91 万平方米，总投资 20935 万元；已竣工的各级残疾人托养服务设施 24 个，总建设规模 6.72 万平方米，总投资 13934.5 万元。

十、信息化

截至 2018 年底，8 个地市、34 个县级残联开通门户网站。全省残疾人人口基础数据库持证残疾人 110.57 万人。全省 11 个地市全部完成政务外网的搭建。省级完成残疾人数据前置库和电子政务平台（OA）的搭建工作，实现了数据的纵横互通和无纸化办公。

2018 年山东省残疾人事业发展统计公报

2018 年，全省残联组织坚持以习近平新时代中国特色社会主义思想指导，全面贯彻落实习近平总书记视察山东重要讲话、重要指示批示精神，以全方位为残疾人服好务为目标，担当作为，真抓实干，全省残疾人事业实现了新发展。

一、康复

2018 年，全省 77.8 万残疾儿童及持证残疾人得到基本康复服务，其中 0-6 岁儿童 15782 人。得到康复服务的持证残疾人中，有视力残疾人 59190 人、听力残疾人 35861 人、言语残疾人 2333 人、肢体残疾人 497142 人、智力残疾人 58564 人、精神残疾人 85818 人、多重残疾人 37557 人。全年共为 15.9 万名残疾人提供各类辅助器具适配服务。

截至 2018 年底，全省已有残疾人康复机构 564 个，其中，提供视力残疾康复服务的 46 个，提供听力言语残疾康复服务的 75 个，提供肢体残疾康复服务的 247 个，提供智力残疾康复服务的 182 个，提供精神残疾康复服务的 102 个，提供孤独症儿童康复服务的 148 个，提供辅助器具服务的 67 个。康复机构在岗人员达 2.2 万人，其中，管理人员 2063 人，专业技术人员 17291 人，其他人员 2937 人。

二、教育

实施残疾人事业专项彩票公益金助学项目，为 957 名家庭经济困难的残疾儿童享受普惠性学前教育提供资助。各地多渠道争取资金支持，为 198 名残疾儿童提供学前教育资助。

全省共有特殊教育普通高中班（部）5 个，在校生 658 人，其中，聋生 339 人，盲生 319 人。残疾人中等职业学校（班）5 个，在校生 392 人，毕业生 130 人，毕业生中 30 人获得职业资格证书。有 511 名残疾人被普通高等院校录取，261 名残疾人进入特殊教育学院学习。

三、就业

2018 年城乡持证残疾人就业人数为 57.7 万人，其中按比例就业 6.4 万人，集中就业 2.0 万人，个体就业 3.1 万人，公益性岗位就业 0.3 万人，辅助性就业 0.5 万人，灵活就业（含社区、居家就业）10.1 万人，从事农业种养加 35.3 万人。2018 年城乡持证残疾人新增就业 1.6 万人。

全省共培训盲人保健按摩人员 936 名、盲人医疗按摩人员 949 名；保健按摩机构 944 个，医疗按摩机构 95 个；89 人获得盲人医疗按摩人员初级职务任职资格，6 人获得中级职务任职资格。

四、社会保障

截至 2018 年底，残疾居民参加城乡社会养老保险人数 158.6 万；41.7 万名 60 岁以下参保重度残疾人中，40.8 万人得到了政府的参保扶助，享受代缴比例达到 97.8%。11.0 万非重度残疾人享受了个人缴费资助政策。60.9 万人领取了养老金。

全省共有残疾人托养服务机构 377 个，其中寄宿制托养服务机构 207 个，日间照料机构 58 个，综合性托养服务机构 112 个，为 1.1 万名残疾人提供了托养服务。2.8 万名残疾人接受了居家服务。1339 名托养服务管理和服务人员接受了各级各类专业培训。

五、扶贫

贫困残疾人得到有效扶持，4.5 万名残疾人退出建档立卡；残疾人接受实用技术培训 1.7 万人次，扫盲教育 1081 人，地方经费投入 2218.0 万元。421 个残疾人扶贫基地安置 6485 名残疾人就业，扶持带动 0.9 万户残疾人家庭。全省共投入资金 183.4 万元，完成农村贫困残疾人危房改造 563 户。

六、文化体育

截至 2018 年底，省市两级开播残疾人专题广播节目 13 个、电视手语栏目 9 个。省市县三级公共图书馆共设立盲文及盲文有声读物阅览室 65 个，共开展残疾人文化周活动 358 场次。省市两级残联共举办残疾人文化艺术类的比赛及展览 46 次，共有各类残疾人艺术团 31 个。

在雅加达第三届亚残运会上，山东省 8 名运动员获得 8 金 2 银 1 铜的好成绩。按照“同城举办，同样精彩”的要求成功举办省第十届残疾人运动会，全省 1542 名运动员参加了 16 个大项 670 个小项的比赛，充分展示了全省残疾人体育工作成果。

七、政策法规与维权

2018 年，省市两级制定或修改关于残疾人的专门法规、规章 3 个；省市县三级制定或修改保障残疾人权益的规范性文件 16 个。县级以上人大开展《中华人民共和国残疾人保障法》执法检查和专题调研 22 次，政协开展视察和专题调研 18 次。省级开展普法宣传教育活动 5 次，570 人参加。举办省级法律培训班 2 个，196 人参加。

截至 2018 年底，全省成立残疾人法律救助工作协调机构 82 个，建立残疾人法律救助工作站 82 个。

残疾人参政议政工作得到加强，各地残联协助人大代表、政协委员提出议案、建议、提案 63 件，办理议案、建议、提案 53 件。

无障碍建设法规、标准进一步完善。全省共出台 38 个省市县级无障碍环境建设与管理法规、政府令和规范性文件，58 个市县区系统开展无障碍环境建设；全省开展无障碍环境建设检查 104 次，无障碍培训 1426 人次。

八、组织建设

截至 2018 年底，省市县乡四级残联机关和事业单位共有编制 6056 人，实有人员 6009 人。地市级配备了残疾人领导干部的残联 13 个，县级配备了残疾人干部的残联 60 个。乡镇（街道）、村（社区）选聘残疾人专职委员 6.9 万人。

共建立省级及以下各类残疾人专门协会 725 个，其中，市级各专门协会已建率 96.5%，县级各专门协会已建率 93.1%。助残社会组织共有 37 个。

九、服务设施

截至 2018 年底，全省已竣工并投入使用的各级残疾人综合服务设施 121 个，总建设规模 32.1 万平方米，总投资 8.0 亿元。已竣工并投入使用的各级残疾人康复设施 99 个，总建设规模 56.1 万平方米，总投资 17.2 亿元。已竣工并投入使用的各级残疾人托养服务设施 38 个，总建设规模 12.3 万平方米，总投资 3.4 亿元。

十、信息化与统计

截至 2018 年底，全省共有 71 个残联开通了门户网站。《全国残疾人人口基础数据库》中共有持证残疾人 222.8 万人，占全省残疾人总人口的 39.1%，其中：视力残疾 17.6 万人、听力残疾 13.9 万人、言语残疾 2.5 万人、肢体残疾 136.5 万人、智力残疾 20.1 万人、精神残疾 21.4 万人、多重残疾 10.8 万人；一级残疾 31.9 万人、二级残疾 71.3 万人、三级残疾 56.3 万人、四级残疾 63.3 万人。

继续开展残疾人基本服务状况和需求信息数据动态更新工作，全省共入户登记 222.4 万持证残疾人，其中，完成调查 211.2 万人（入户调查 209.9 万人、电话调查 1.3 万人），未完成调查 11.2 万人（查无此人 0.8 万人、已搬迁 2.3 万人、空挂户 1.0 万人、外出 2.1 万人、死亡 5.0 万人）。

2018 年河南省残疾人事业发展统计公报

2018 年，是全面贯彻党的十九大精神的开局之年，也是改革开放 40 周年。一年来，在省委省政府的坚强领导和中国残联有力指导下，河南省残联坚持以习近平新时代中国特色社会主义思想为指导，全面贯彻党的十九大、十九届二中、三中全会精神和省委十届六次、七次全会精神，强化政治引领，积极践行以人民为中心的发展思想，助力打赢贫困残疾人脱贫攻坚战，着力提升残疾人基本公共服务水平，维护残疾人合法权益，切实加强自身建设，全省残疾人事业实现新发展。

一、康复

2018 年，残疾人精准康复服务持续推进。全省 64.1 万名残疾儿童及持证残疾人得到基本康复服务，其中包括 0-6 岁残疾儿童 1.3 万人，康复服务率达到 86.52%。得到康复服务的持证残疾人中，有视力残疾人 6.5 万名、听力残疾人 3.1 万名、言语残疾人 0.4 万名、肢体残疾人 42.1 万名、智力残疾人 5.1 万名、精神残疾人 4.7 万名、多重残疾人 1.7 万名、0-17 岁未持证残疾儿童 0.5 万名。全年共为 25.3 万名残疾人提供各类辅助器具适配服务，服务率为 88.95%。

截至 2018 年底，全省有残疾人康复机构 385 个，其中，40 个机构提供视力残疾康复服务，108 个提供听力言语残疾康复服务，183 个提供肢体残疾康复服务，160 个提供智力残疾康复服务，73 个提供精神残疾康复服务，65 个提供孤独症儿童康复服务，80 个提供辅助器具服务。康复机构在岗人员 1.4 万人，其中，管理人员 1392 人，专业技术人员 1.1 万人，其他人员 1545 人。

二、教育

2018 年全省残疾人事业专项彩票公益金助学项目的实施，为 1536 名家庭经济困难的残疾儿童享受普惠性学前教育提供资助。多渠道争取资金支持，对 15 名残疾儿童给予学前教育资助。

2018 年全省共有特殊教育普通高中班（部）4 个，在校生 268 人，其中聋生 202 人，盲生 66 人。残疾人中等职业学校（班）7 个，在校生 305 人，毕业生 65 人，毕业生中 26 人获得职业资格证书。有 861 名残疾人被普通高等院校录取，386 名残疾人进入特殊教育学院学习。

2018 年全省有 1355 名残疾青壮年文盲接受了扫盲教育。

三、就业

2018 年，全省城乡持证残疾人就业人数为 59.7 万人，其中按比例就业 2.7 万人，集中就业 1.6 万人，个体就业 13.3 万人，公益性岗位就业 3624 人，辅助性就业 1.6 万人，灵活就业（含社区、居家就业）7.2 万人，从事农业种养加 33 万人。

全省培训盲人保健按摩人员 2320 名、盲人医疗按摩人员 977 名；保健按摩机构达到 901 个，医疗按摩机构达到 84 个；13 人获得盲人医疗按摩人员初级职务任职资格，4 人获得中级职务任职资格。

四、社会保障

截至 2018 年底，全省残疾居民参加城乡社会养老保险人数 290.9 万名，50.5 万名 60 岁以下参保重度残疾人中，48.4 万名得到政府的参保扶助，享受代缴比例达到 95.8%。6 万多名非重度残疾人享受了个人缴费资助政策。127.1 万人领取养老金。

全省残疾人托养服务工作稳步推进，残疾人托养服务机构达到 295 个，其中寄宿制托养服务机构 181 个，日间照料机构 21 个，综合性托养服务机构 93 个，为 1.2 万名残疾人提供了托养服务。4546 名残疾人接受居家服务。136 名托养服务管理和服务人员接受了各级各类专业培训。

五、扶贫

2018 年，全省贫困残疾人得到有效扶持。全省残疾人接受实用技术培训 3.5 万人次；170 个残疾人扶贫基地安置 4562 名残疾人就业，扶持带动 8073 户残疾人家庭；全省共完成 4139 户农村贫困残疾人危房改造，投入资金 3091.3 万元。

六、宣传文化

截至 2018 年底，全省共有省级残疾人专题广播节目 1 个、电视手语栏目 1 个；地市级残疾人专题广播节目 13 个、电视手语栏目 8 个。

全省各级公共图书馆共设立盲文及盲文有声读物阅览室 75 个，共开展残疾人文化周活动 191 场次；省市两级残联共举办残疾人文化艺术类的比赛及展览 20 次，全省共有各类残疾人艺术团 6 个。

七、维权

2018 年，全省制定或修改保障残疾人权益的规范性文件地市级 3 个、县级 4 个。全省县级以上人大开展《中华人民共和国残疾人保障法》执法检查和专题调研 9 次；政协开展视察和专题调研 5 次。

截至 2018 年底，全省成立残疾人法律救助工作协调机构 127 个，建立残疾人法律救助工作站 116 个。

残疾人参政议政工作得到加强，各地残联协助人大代表、政协委员提出议案、建议、提案 11 件，办理议案、建议、提案 18 件。

无障碍建设法规、标准进一步完善。全省 92 个省、市、县级出台了无障碍环境建设与管理法规、政府令和规范性文件；60 个地市、县系统开展无障碍环境建设；开展无障碍环境建设检查 50 次，无障碍培训 903 人次。

八、组织建设

2018 年，全省市县乡共成立残联 2586 个，各地市已建残联 18 个，县（市、区）残联已建 171 个，乡镇（街道）残联已建 2397 个；已建社区（村）残协 4.6 万个。

省市县乡残联工作人员 7995 人，乡镇（街道）、村（社区）选聘残疾人专职委员总计 4.7 万名。地市级残联配备了残疾人领导干部 8 人，县级残联配备了残疾人干部 84 人。

全省建立省级及以下各类残疾人专门协会 887 个，其中省级专门协会已建 5 个，市级专门协会已建 90 个，县级专门协会已建 792 个。助残社会组织共有 44 个。

九、服务设施

截至 2018 年底，全省已竣工的各级残疾人综合服务设施 141 个，总建设规模 22.4 万平方米，总投资 39234.9 万元；已竣工的各级残疾人康复设施 24 个，总建设规模 16.3 万平方米，总投资 37752.1 万元；已竣工的各级残疾人托养服务设施 31 个，总建设规模 9.3 万平方米，总投资 18300 多万元。

十、信息化

截至 2018 年底，全省 18 个地市、39 个县级残联开通网站。2018 年省级残联网站发布信息 3483 篇；公众号发布信息 729 篇，总点赞量 3.9 万个。

2018 年湖北省残疾人事业发展统计公报

2018 年，湖北省残联系统坚持以习近平新时代中国特色社会主义思想为指引，深入贯彻党的十九大精神，全面落实中国残联和省委、省政府关于残疾人工作的决策部署，全省残疾人事业在新的历史起点上实现了新发展，取得了新成绩。

一、康复

2018 年，湖北省出台《湖北省残疾儿童康复救助制度》，将救助年龄段拓展到了 10 岁，为残疾儿童接受基本康复服务提供了制度性保障，全年共有 50.6 万名残疾儿童及持证残疾人得到基本康复服务，其中 0-6 岁残疾儿童 6595 人。在得到康复服务的持证残疾人中，视力残疾人 7.1 万、听力残疾人 3.5 万、言语残疾人 1.4 万、肢体残疾人 22.3 万、智力残疾人 4 万、精神残疾人 9 万、多重残疾人 3.1 万。全年共为 10.5 万残疾人提供各类辅助器具适配服务。

截至 2018 年底，全省共有残疾人康复机构 214 个，其中 18 个机构提供视力残疾康复服务，34 个提供听力言语残疾康复服务，67 个提供肢体残疾康复服务，62 个提供智力残疾康复服务，59 个提供精神残疾康复服务，35 个提供孤独症儿童康复服务，55 个提供辅助器具服务。康复机构在岗人员 7256 人，其中，管理人员 732 人，专业技术人员 4828 人，其他人员 1696 人。

二、教育

残疾人事业专项彩票公益金助学项目的实施，为 682 名家庭经济困难的残疾儿童享受普惠性学前教育提供资助。多渠道争取资金支持，对 43 名残疾儿童给予学前教育资助。

共有特殊教育普通高中班（部）6 个，在校生 170 人。残疾人中等职业学校（班）5 个，在校生 4673 人，毕业生 1290 人，毕业生中 38 人获得职业资格证书。有 417 名残疾人被普通高等院校录取。有 1921 名残疾青壮年文盲接受了扫盲教育。

三、就业

截至 2018 年底，全省城乡持证残疾人就业人数 42.9 万人，其中按比例就业 3.4 万人，集中就业 2.3 万人，个体就业 2.7 万人，公益性岗位就业 3849 人，辅助性就业 8004 人，灵活就业（含社区、居家就业）13.2 万人，从事农业种养加 20.1 万人。

2018 年培训盲人保健按摩人员 432 名、盲人医疗按摩人员 60 名；保健按摩机构达到 881 个，医疗按摩机构达到 43 个；64 人获得盲人医疗按摩人员初级职务任职资格，1 人获得中级职务任职资格。

四、社会保障

截至 2018 年底，共有 119.4 万残疾居民参加了城乡社会养老保险。在 32.6 万 60 岁以下参保重度残疾人中，有 32.4 万人得到政府参保扶助，享受代缴比例达 99.3%；有 16 万非重度残疾人享受了个人缴费资助政策。有 41.5 万人领取养老金。

残疾人托养服务工作稳步推进，残疾人托养服务机构达到 192 个，其中寄宿制托养服务机构 71 个，日间照料机构 98 个，综合性托养服务机构 23 个，共为 9720 名残疾人提供了托养服务。584 名托养服务管理和服务人员接受了各级各类专业培训。

五、扶贫

全力助推贫困残疾人脱贫困、奔小康，贫困残疾人得到有效扶持，12.75 万残疾人退出建档立卡。残疾人接受实用技术培训 2.2 万人次。862 名农村残疾人获得康复扶贫贴息贷款扶持。89 个残疾人扶贫基地安置 1346 名残疾人就业，扶持带动 6351 户残疾人家庭。完成 2992 户农村贫困残疾人危房改造。

六、宣传文化

截至 2018 年底，共有省级残疾人专题广播节目 1 个；地市级残疾人专题广播节目 8 个、电视手语栏目 7 个。

省、市、县三级公共图书馆共设立盲文及盲文有声读物阅览室 33 个，共开展残疾人文化周活动 148 场次；省、市两级残联共举办残疾人文化艺术类的比赛及展览 18 次。全省共有各类残疾人艺术团 4 个。

七、体育

举办湖北省第十五届运动会群众体育类（残疾人）暨第十届残疾人运动会，全省 17 支代表队、700 多名残疾人运动员参加了田径、游泳、举重、羽毛球、乒乓球、中国象棋六个大项的比赛，共产生金牌 206 枚。

扎实开展残疾人运动员集训，组队参加全国残疾人体育赛事，共获金牌 6 枚，银牌 26 枚，铜牌 19 枚。

八、维权

2018 年，制定或修改省级关于残疾人的专门法规、规章 1 个；制定或修改保障残疾人权益的规范性文件地市级 1 个、县级 4 个。全国县级以上人大开展《中华人民共和国残疾人保障法》执法检查和专题调研 10 次；政协开展视察和专题调研 13 次。全国开展省级普法宣传教育活动 2 次，200 人参加活动；举办省级法律培训班 2 个，140 人参加培训。

截至 2018 年底，全国成立残疾人法律救助工作协调机构 75 个，建立残疾人法律救助工作站 65 个。

残疾人参政议政工作得到加强，各地残联协助人大代表、政协委员提出议案、建议、提案 46 件，办理议案、建议、提案 53 件。

无障碍建设法规、标准进一步完善。省、市、县三级共出台了 8 个无障碍环境建设与管理法规、政府令和规范性文件；83 个市、县系统开展无障碍环境建设；开展无障碍环境建设检查 34 次，无障碍培训 400 人次。

九、组织建设

2018 年，市县乡共有残联 1261 个，各地市已建残联 13 个，县（市、区）残联已建 106 个，乡镇（街道）残联已建 1142 个；已建社区（村）残协 2.1 万个。

省市县乡残联工作人员 3365 人，乡镇（街道）、村（社区）选聘残疾人专职委员总计 1.9 万人。5 个地市级残联配备了残疾人领导干部，35 个县级残联配备了残疾人干部。

共建立省级及以下各类残疾人专门协会 520 个，其中省级专门协会已建 5 个，市级专门协会已建 65 个，县级专门协会已建 450 个。助残社会组织共有 661 个。

十、服务设施

截至 2018 年底，已竣工的各级残疾人综合服务设施达 85 个，总建设规模 186036.7 平方米，总投资 36545.7 万元；已竣工的各级残疾人康复设施 14 个，总建设规模 68327.2 平方米，总投资 21154.4 万元；已竣工的各级残疾人托养服务设施 25 个，总建设规模 50885.3 平方米，总投资 10245.6 万元。

十一、信息化

截至 2018 年底，13 个地市、28 个县级残联开通网站。主动对接中国残联信息共享平台、省政府政务“一张网”、省纪委“扶贫领域政策落实监察系统”等数据平台、系统，实现湖北政务服务网上线公共服务事项 6 项，“鄂汇办”APP 上线第二代残疾人证查询服务等功能模块。为全省电子证照库和省数据共享交换平台提供了全省持证残疾人基础办证数字化信息、全省残疾人服务机构数字地图信息，与省教育厅、省审计厅、省经信委、省民政厅低保中心等单位共享残疾人业务相关信息。

2018年湖南省残疾人事业发展统计公报

2018年，湖南省残疾人工作在省委省政府正确领导和中国残联指导下，围绕实现“全面建成小康社会，残疾人一个也不能少“的目标，着力完成各项指标任务，努力开创新时代残疾人事业新局面。

一、康复

2018年，541524名残疾人得到基本康复服务，其中包括0-17岁未持证残疾儿童3397名。得到康复服务残疾人中，有视力残疾人69156名、听力残疾人23321名、言语残疾人966名、肢体残疾人316358名、智力残疾人29795名、精神残疾人77650名、多重残疾人20881名。

全省有残疾人康复机构401个，其中，提供视力残疾康复服务的机构55个，提供听力言语残疾康复服务的机构75个，提供肢体残疾康复服务的机构105个，提供智力残疾康复服务的机构123个，提供精神残疾康复服务的机构68个，提供孤独症儿童康复服务的机构71个，提供辅助器具服务的机构112个。康复机构在岗人员达12121人，其中，管理人员1362人，专业技术人员8638人，其他人员2121人。

截至2018年底，共完成复明手术、定向行走等康复训练12493人次，为46058人次视力残疾人进行了配发盲杖、助视器等服务，为其他12808名有视力障碍残疾人进行了康复服务。为30482名听力言语残疾人进行了人工耳蜗手术及助听器适配服务，为356名听力言语残疾人进行了功能训练，为其他3507名听力言语残疾人进行了康复服务。2018年共为46016名肢体残疾人进行了矫治手术和运动功能训练，为215524名肢体残疾人进行了假肢、矫形器等辅具适配服务，为其他68453名肢体残疾人做了不同程度的康复服务。全年共为34710名智力残疾人进行了康复服务。为1632名孤独症儿童沟通及适应训练，为80306名不同程度精神残疾人进行药物治疗及作业疗法训练和其他方式康复服务。

在37个市辖区和93个县（市）开展社区康复，配备24827名社区康复协调员。

二、教育

2018年，残疾人受教育权利得到了更好保障，实施残疾人事业专项彩票公益金助学项目，995名家庭经济困难残疾儿童享受普惠性学前教育提供资助，其中持证残疾儿童814名。

共有特殊教育普通高中班（部）3个，在校生120人，其中聋生120人。残疾人中等职业学校（班）6个，在校生1414人，毕业生207人，有444名残疾学生被普通高等院校录取，117名残疾人进入特殊教育学院（校）学习。

2018年统计台帐有995名学前残疾儿童接受专项彩票公益金助学项目资助，其中视力残疾儿童7名，听力残疾儿童150名，言语残疾儿童66名，肢体残疾儿童113名，智力残疾儿童459名，精神残疾儿童68名，多重残疾儿童132名。

三、就业

2018年，城乡持证残疾人就业人数为417008人，其中按比例就业25574人，集中就业14857人，个体就业35224人，公益性岗位就业2375人，辅助性就业5905人，居家、社区就业71661人，从事农业种养加200377人，灵活就业61035人。

2018年底按摩机构达到1232家，其中盲人保健按摩机构1212家，盲人医疗按摩机构20家。在专业技术职务资格评审中，有23人通过盲人医疗按摩人员初级职称评审。

四、扶贫开发

2018年，贫困残疾人得到有效扶持，贫困残疾人生产生活状况得到改善，接受实用技术培训的残疾人达到21324人次。

全省368个残疾人扶贫基地，安置6005名残疾人就业，扶持带动9421户残疾人家庭，残疾人扶贫基地共获得各级扶持资金1112.0530万元。

本年度实际完成8704户农村贫困残疾人危房

改造，受益残疾人 9489 人，全省各级共投入危房改造资金 11050.1264 万元。

五、社会保障

截至 2018 年底，城乡残疾居民参加城乡社会养老保险人数达到 1268088 名，375836 名 60 岁以下的重度残疾人参保，其中 362406 名得到了政府的参保扶助，代缴养老保险费比例达到 96.4%。有 94186 名非重度残疾人也享受了个人缴费资助政策。499794 人领取养老金。

稳步推进残疾人托养服务工作，残疾人托养服务机构达到 150 个，其中寄宿制托养服务机构 37 个，日间照料机构 80 个，综合性托养服务机构 33 个，为 5319 名残疾人提供了托养服务。15795 名残疾人接受居家服务。全年共有 652 名托养服务管理和服务人员接受了各级各类专业培训。

六、宣传文体

截至 2018 年底，省市县三级公共图书馆共设立盲文及盲文有声读物图书室 8 个，共开展残疾人文化周活动 79 场次；省市两级残联共举办残疾人文化艺术类的比赛及展览 44 次，残疾人事业宣传紧密围绕事业大局，大力弘扬人道主义，营造了良好的舆论氛围。组织省市两级新闻发布会 4 次，残疾人专题广播节目 9 个、电视手语栏目 3 个。

七、维权

2018 年，有 1 个地市和 8 个县区制定或修改保障残疾人权益的规范性文件；地市和县级人大开展执法检查和专题调研 20 次；政协开展视察和专题调研 17 次。

截至 2018 年底，成立残疾人法律救助工作协调机构 114 个，建立残疾人法律救助工作站 108 个，年度为残疾人办理救助案件 219 件。

残疾人参政议政工作稳步开展，全省有各级残疾人、残疾人工作者、残疾人亲属人大代表 91 名，有政协委员 158 名，各级残联协助人大代表、政协委员提出议案、建议、提案 29 件，办理议案、建议、提案 18 件。无障碍建设法规、标准不断完善，出台无障碍建设与管理规范性文件 10 个；开展无障碍建设检查 63 次，无障碍培训 851 人次。

八、组织建设

2018 年，市县乡共建立残联 2033 个，各地市已建残联 14 个，县（市、区）残联已建 126 个，乡镇（街道）残联已建 1893 个；已建社区（村）残协 25802 个。

省市县乡残联实有人员达 4807 人，乡镇（街道）、村（社区）选聘残疾人专职委员总计 23940 名。地市级残联配备了残疾人领导干部 8 人，县级残联配备了残疾人干部 64 人。

共建立省级及以下各类残疾人专门协会 674 个，其中省级专门协会已建 5 个，市级专门协会已建 70 个，县级专门协会已建 599。助残社会组织共有 58 个。

九、服务设施建设

残疾人服务设施建设得到全面发展。截至 2018 年底，已竣工并投入使用的各级残疾人综合服务设施 98 个，总建设规模 118236.8 平方米，总投资 22995.9 万元；已竣工并投入使用的各级残疾人康复设施 36 个，总建设规模 97281 平方米，总投资 21465.5 万元；已竣工并投入使用的各级残疾人托养服务设施 65 个，总建设规模 84467 平方米，总投资 15171.3 万元。

十、信息化建设

全省各级残联共有 155 名统计员，信息化专业人才 198 人，截至 2018 年底，14 个地市、20 个县级残联开通网站。2018 度省残联门户网站共发布信息类稿件 3455 篇。

2018 年广东省残疾人事业发展统计公报

2018 年，在省委、省政府的领导和中国残联的指导下，全省各级残联认真履行“代表、服务、管理”职能，扎实推进残疾人工作，圆满完成“十三五”规划纲要确定的年度任务。

一、残疾人康复

2018 年，全省共 310671 名残疾儿童及持证残疾人得到基本康复服务，其中 0-6 岁残疾儿童 12370 人。得到康复服务的持证残疾人中，有视力残疾人 16916 名、听力残疾人 14478 名、言语残疾人 1087 名、肢体残疾人 116614 名、智力残疾人 23394 名、精神残疾人 118183 名、多重残疾人 16882 名。全年共为 71049 名残疾人提供各类辅助器具适配服务。

截至 2018 年底，全省已有残疾人康复机构 733 个，其中 115 个机构提供视力残疾康复服务、127 个提供听力言语残疾康复服务、302 个提供肢体残疾康复服务、281 个提供智力残疾康复服务、191 个提供精神残疾康复服务、224 个提供孤独症儿童康复服务、106 个提供辅助器具服务。康复机构在岗人员 24871 人，其中管理人员 2437 人，专业技术人员 17706 人，其他人员 4728 人。

二、残疾人教育

残疾人事业专项彩票公益金助学项目的实施，为 1255 名家庭经济困难的残疾儿童享受普惠性学前教育提供资助。各地也多渠道争取资金支持，对 552 名残疾儿童给予学前教育资助。

截止 2018 年底，共有特殊教育普通高中班（部）6 个，在校生 444 人，其中聋生 395 人、盲生 49 人。残疾人中等职业学校（班）11 个，在校生 1307 人、毕业生 376 人、毕业生中 118 人获得职业资格证书。有 565 名残疾人被普通高等院校录取，76 名残疾人进入特殊教育学院学习。3034 名残疾青壮年文盲接受了扫盲教育。

三、残疾人就业

截止 2018 年底，全省城乡持证残疾人就业人数为 288867 人，其中按比例就业 60986 人、集中就业 7087 人、个体就业 12974 人、公益性岗位就业 5442 人、辅助性就业 5984 人、灵活就业（含社区、居家就业）64112 人、从事农业种养加 132282 人。

2018 年度培训盲人保健按摩人员 578 名、盲人医疗按摩人员 674 名；共有保健按摩机构 667 个，医疗按摩机构 10 个；全年有 68 个盲人获得盲人医疗按摩人员初级职务任职资格，4 人获得中级职务任职资格。

四、残疾人社会保障

截至 2018 年底，城乡残疾居民参加社会养老保险人数达 967491 名；60 岁以下参保重度残疾人 364317 名，其中得到政府参保扶助 353344 名，代缴比例达到 97%；112308 名非重度残疾人也享受了全额或部分代缴优惠缴费政策。领取养老金的残疾人达 361668 人。

残疾人托养服务工作稳步推进，残疾人托养服务机构达到 1169 个，其中寄宿制托养服务机构 40 个、日间照料机构 1078 个、综合性托养服务机构 51 个，为 28142 名残疾人提供了托养服务，8208 名残疾人接受居家服务。全年共 1930 名托养管理和服务人员接受了各级各类专业培训。

五、残疾人扶贫

2018 年度，农村实用技术培训残疾人 13185 人次；42 名农村残疾人获得康复扶贫贴息贷款扶持。全省 67 个残疾人扶贫基地安置 2000 名残疾人就业，扶持带动 1653 户残疾人家庭。2018 年度共完成 2195 户农村贫困残疾人危房改造，投入危房改造资金 2874.7 万元。

六、残疾人宣传文化

截至2018年底，共有省级残疾人专题广播节目、电视手语栏目各1个；地市级残疾人专题广播节目共14个、电视手语栏目11个。省地县三级公共图书馆共设立盲文及盲文有声读物阅览室49个。全年共开展残疾人文化节活动616场次；省地两级残联共举办残疾人文化艺术类的比赛及展览54次，共有各类残疾人艺术团40个。

七、残疾人法制建设与维权

2018年，制定或修改省级关于残疾人的专门法规、规章1个、地市级1个；制定或修改保障残疾人权益的省级规范性文件1个、地市级10个、县级2个；县级以上人大开展《中华人民共和国残疾人保障法》执法检查和专题调研14次；政协开展视察和专题调研7次；开展省级普法宣传教育活动1次，18000人参加；截至2018年底，成立残疾人法律救助工作协调机构55个，建立残疾人法律救助工作站43个。

残疾人参政议政工作得到加强，各地残联协助人大代表、政协委员提出议案、建议、提案22件，办理议案、建议、提案116件。

无障碍建设法规、标准进一步完善。共出台了27个省、地市、县级无障碍环境建设与管理法规、政府令和规范性文件；145个地市、县系统开展无障碍环境建设；开展无障碍环境建设检查323次，无障碍培训1841人次。

八、残疾人组织建设

2018年，地市县乡共成立残联1802个，其中各地市已建残联21个、县（市、区）残联已建137个、乡镇（街道）残联已建1644个；已建社区（村）残协23506个。

省市县乡残联工作人员共7877人，乡镇（街道）、村（社区）选聘残疾人专职委员总计23876名。15个地市级残联配备了残疾人领导干部，42个县级残联配备了残疾人干部。

全省共建立各类残疾人专门协会698个，其中省级专门协会已建5个、市级专门协会已建105个、县级专门协会已建588个。助残社会组织共有122个。

九、残疾人服务设施

截至2018年底，已竣工的各级残疾人综合服务设施108个，总建设规模67.82万平方米，总投资22.4亿元；已竣工的各级残疾人康复设施46个，总建设规模19.65万平方米，总投资6.5亿元；已竣工的各级残疾人托养服务设施11个，总建设规模6.17万平方米，总投资1.28亿元。

2018年广西壮族自治区残疾人事业发展统计公报

2018年，广西残疾人事业在中国残联和自治区党委、政府的正确领导下，全区各级残联深入贯彻自治区党委、政府关于全区残疾人事业的新部署新要求，加快推进残疾人小康进程，积极完成“十三五”规划年度目标任务，残疾人事业发展取得良好的成绩，广大残疾人得到更多福祉。现根自治区2018年度残疾人事业统计年报数据和实际情况进行分析，并公报如下：

一、康复

截至2018年底，共有残疾人康复机构363个，其中，79个机构提供视力残疾康复服务，51个提供听力言语残疾康复服务，211个提供肢体残疾康复服务，156个提供智力残疾康复服务，127个提供精神残疾康复服务，53个提供孤独症儿童康复服务，93个提供辅助器具服务。康复机构在岗人员8700人，其中，管理人员1048人，专业技术人员6211人，其他人员1441人。

2018年，236587名残疾儿童及持证残疾人得到基本康复服务，其中包括0-6岁残疾儿童5145人。得到康复服务的持证残疾人中，有视力残疾人25178人、听力残疾人8799人、言语残疾人741人、肢体残疾人134301人、智力残疾人20156人、精神残疾人33917人、多重残疾人11753人。全年共为84177名残疾人提供各类辅助器具适配服务。

二、教育

2018年度实施残疾人事业专项彩票公益金助学项目，为1266名家庭经济困难的残疾儿童享受普惠性学前教育提供资助。各地也积极多渠道争取资金支持，对31名残疾儿童给予学前教育资助。

共有特殊教育普通高中学校（班）2个，在校生91人，都属聋生。有297名残疾人被普通高等院校录取。1053名残疾青壮年文盲接受了扫盲教育。

三、就业

城乡持证残疾人就业人数为326384人，其中按比例就业9631人，集中就业1953人，个体就业14395人，社区就业1230人，公益性岗位就业1948人，辅助性就业2448人，居家就业38220人，灵活就业27558人，从事农业种养加229001人。

培训盲人保健按摩人员599人、盲人医疗按摩人员109；保健按摩机构250个，医疗按摩机构4个。

四、扶贫

2018年，残疾人扶贫开发成效显著，贫困残疾人生产生活状况得到进一步改善。贫困残疾人得到有效扶持，其中56678名残疾人退出建档立卡；接受实用技术培训的残疾人达到25801人次。

残疾人扶贫基地125个，共安置3184名残疾人就业，扶持带动13626名残疾人家庭。

共完成3184户农村贫困残疾人危房改造，各地投入危房资金1928.2万元。

五、社会保障

截至2018年底，残疾居民参加城乡社会养老保险人数1020119名，191559名60岁以下参保重度残疾人中，185798名得到政府的参保扶助，享受代缴比例达到97.0%；85080名非重度残疾人享受了个人缴费资助政策；520091人领取养老金。

残疾人托养服务工作稳步推进，残疾人托养服务机构达到90个，其中寄宿制托养服务机构42个，日间照料机构26个，综合性托养服务机构22个，为4986名残疾人提供了托养服务；33512名残疾人接受居家服务；999名托养服务管理和服务人员接受了各级各类专业培训。

六、宣传文化

截至2018年底，共有省级残疾人专题广播节目

1 个、电视手语栏目 1 个；地市级残疾人专题广播节目 3 个、电视手语栏目 6 个。

省地县三级公共图书馆共设立盲文及盲文有声读物阅览室 32 个，共开展残疾人文化周活动 176 场次；省地两级残联共举办残疾人文化艺术类的比赛及展览 7 次，共有各类残疾人艺术团 5 个。

七、维权

2018 年，省级制定或修改保障残疾人权益的省级规范性文件 1 个；全国县级以上人大开展《中华人民共和国残疾人保障法》执法检查和专题调研 3 次；政协开展视察和专题调研 2 次；全国开展省级普法宣传教育活动 3 次，150 人参加；举办省级法律培训班 1 个，44 人参加。

截至 2018 年底，成立残疾人法律救助工作协调机构 43 个，建立残疾人法律救助工作站 39 个，办理案件 22 件。

残疾人参政议政工作得到加强，各地残联协助人大代表、政协委员提出议案、建议、提案 15 件，办理议案、建议、提案 23 件。

无障碍建设法规、标准进一步完善。125 个地市、县系统开展无障碍环境建设；开展无障碍环境建设检查 102 次，无障碍培训 1101 人次。

各级残联共处理残疾人群众来信 985 件，接待残疾人群众来访 4710 人次，其中集体访 16 批次、126 人次，来电 542 通，网上投诉 2 件。

八、组织建设

2018 年，市县乡共成立残联 1375 个，其中各地市残联已建 15 个，县（市、区）残联已建 111 个，乡镇（街道）残联已建 1249 个；已建社区（村）残协 15718 个。

省市县乡残联实有人员达 3568 人，乡镇（街道）、村（社区）选聘残疾人专职委员总计 16412 名。地市级配备了残疾人领导干部的残联 11 个，县级配备了残疾人干部的残联 53 个。

共建立省级及以下各类残疾人专门协会 628 个，其中省级专门协会已建 5 个，市级专门协会已建 70 个，县级专门协会已建 553 个。助残社会组织共有 19 个。

九、服务设施

残疾人服务设施建设得到全面发展。截至 2018 年底，已竣工的各级残疾人综合服务设施 102 个，总建设规模 147128.3 平方米，总投资 26088.8 万元；已竣工的各级残疾人康复设施 10 个，总建设规模 64792.4 平方米，总投资 17082.0 万元；已竣工的各级残疾人托养服务设施 15 个，总建设规模 29943.8 平方米，总投资 5440.4 万元。

2018年海南省残疾人事业发展统计公报

2018年，在海南省委、省政府正确领导下，在中国残联有力指导下，全省各级残联坚持以习近平新时代中国特色社会主义思想为指导，深入学习宣传贯彻党的十九大精神，认真落实“发展残疾人事业，加强残疾康复服务”总体要求和省委、省政府关于残疾人工作的决策部署，将以人民为中心的发展思想落实到为残疾人提供精准服务之中，团结奋进、攻坚克难，推动全省残疾人事业和残联工作取得了新发展。

一、康复

2018年，6.1万名残疾儿童及持证残疾人得到基本康复服务，其中包括0-6岁残疾儿童1231人。得到康复服务的持证残疾人中，视力残疾人7006名、听力残疾人1649名、言语残疾人100名、肢体残疾人3万名、智力残疾人4780名、精神残疾人1.5万名、多重残疾人2386名。全年共为1.7万残疾人提供各类辅助器具适配服务。

截至2018年底，全省已有残疾人康复机构34个，其中，5个机构提供视力残疾康复服务，4个提供听力言语残疾康复服务，15个提供肢体残疾康复服务，8个提供智力残疾康复服务，7个提供精神残疾康复服务，12个提供孤独症儿童康复服务，3个提供辅助器具服务。康复机构在岗人员1065人，其中管理人员122人，专业技术人员810人，其他人员133人。

二、教育

残疾人事业专项彩票公益金助学项目的实施，为368名家庭经济困难的残疾儿童享受普惠性学前教育提供资助。各地也积极多渠道争取资金支持，对11名残疾儿童给予学前教育资助。共有特殊教育普通高中班（部）1个。有54名残疾人被普通高等院校录取，536名残疾青壮年文盲接受了扫盲教育。

三、就业

2018年，残疾人就业工作在保持稳定的基础上取得了新进展。城乡持证残疾人就业人数为3.6万人，其中按比例就业5222人，集中就业399人，个体就业1136人，公益性岗位就业412人，辅助性就业154人，灵活就业（含社区、居家就业）6927人，从事农业种养加2.2万人。培训盲人保健按摩人员192名、盲人医疗按摩人员31名；保健按摩机构达到217个，医疗按摩机构1个；10人获得盲人医疗按摩人员初级职务任职资格，2人获得中级职务任职资格。

四、社会保障

截至2018年底，残疾居民参加城乡社会养老保险人数20.6万名，5.3万名60岁以下参保重度残疾人中，4.9万名得到政府的参保扶助，享受代缴比例达到90.7%。1.2万名非重度残疾人享受了个人缴费资助政策，1万人领取养老金。

残疾人托养服务工作稳步推进，残疾人托养服务机构达到15个，其中寄宿制托养服务机构14个，综合性托养服务机构1个，为586名残疾人提供了托养服务。2.3万名残疾人接受居家服务。119名托养服务管理和服务人员接受了各级各类专业培训。

五、扶贫

2018年贫困残疾人得到有效扶持，3747名残疾人退出建档立卡；残疾人接受实用技术培训6057人次。32个残疾人扶贫基地安置187名残疾人就业，扶持带动143户残疾人家庭。共完成894户农村贫困残疾人危房改造，投入资金775.5万元。

六、宣传文化

截至2018年底，共有省级残疾人专题广播节目1个、电视手语栏目1个；省、地市、县三级公共图书馆共设立盲文及盲文有声读物阅览室2个，共开展残疾人文化周活动 17 场次；省、地市级残联共举办残疾人文化艺术类的比赛及展览 4 次，共有各类残疾人艺术团 2 个。

七、维权

2018 年制定或修改地市级关于残疾人的专门法规 1 个；制定或修改保障残疾人权益的地市级规范性文件 1 个、县级 4 个。全省县级以上人大开展《中华人民共和国残疾人保障法》执法检查和专题调研 6 次；全省开展普法宣传教育活动 1 次，102 人参加。

截至 2018 年底，全省成立残疾人法律救助工作协调机构 46 个，建立残疾人法律救助工作站 46 个。残疾人参政议政工作得到加强，各地残联协助人大代表、政协委员提出议案、建议、提案 14 件。

无障碍建设法规、标准进一步完善。出台无障碍环境建设与管理法规、政府令和规范性文件 2 个；开展无障碍环境建设的地市县 8 个；开展无障碍环境建设检查 6 次，无障碍培训 540 人次。

八、组织建设

2018 年，市县乡共成立残联 496 个，各地市已建残联 3 个，县（市、区）残联已建 20 个，乡镇（街道）残联已建 225 个；已建社区（村）残协 2327 个。省市县乡残联工作人员 703 人，乡镇（街道）、村（社区）选聘残疾人专职委员总计 5668 名。地市级残联配备了残疾人领导干部 2 人，县级残联配备了残疾人干部 6 人。

共建立省级及以下各类残疾人专门协会 109 个，其中省级专门协会已建 5 个，市级专门协会已建 15 个，县级专门协会已建 89 个。助残社会组织共有 3 个。

九、服务设施和信息化建设

截至 2018 年底，已竣工的各级残疾人综合服务设施 12 个，总建设规模 1.9 万平方米，总投资 5664.0 万元；已竣工的各级残疾人康复设施 4 个，总建设规模 1.1 万平方米，总投资 3714.7 万元；

截至 2018 年底，1 个地市、5 个县级残联开通网站。

2018 年重庆市残疾人事业发展统计公报

2018 年，在重庆市委、市政府的坚强领导下，在中国残联的关怀指导下，在社会各界的关心支持下，重庆市残联深入学习习近平新时代中国特色社会主义思想，以习近平总书记关于残疾人事业发展系列重要指示为根本遵循，突出政治引领，转变工作作风，强化基层基础，狠抓安全稳定，紧紧围绕中心、服务大局，残疾人民生得到明显改善。

一、残疾人康复工作

2018 年，市政府出台了《关于建立残疾儿童康复救助制度的实施意见》。市残联、市财政局等 8 部门联合下发了《关于印发重庆市残疾儿童康复救助制度实施办法的通知》。为 21.2 万名残疾儿童及持证残疾人提供了基本康复服务，其中包括 0-6 岁残疾儿童 3389 人。得到康复服务的持证残疾人中，有视力残疾人 2.7 万名、听力残疾人 9085 名、言语残疾人 380 名、肢体残疾人 9.4 万名、智力残疾人 2 万名、精神残疾人 5.4 万名、多重残疾人 7685 名。全年共为 5.8 万名残疾人提供各类辅助器具适配服务。

推进康复机构规范化管理，完善基层服务网络。全市共有残疾人康复机构 265 个，其中，提供视力残疾康复服务机构 71 个，提供听力言语残疾康复服务机构 62 个，提供肢体残疾康复服务机构 91 个，提供智力残疾康复服务机构 96 个，提供精神残疾康复服务机构 72 个，提供孤独症儿童康复服务机构 31 个，提供辅助器具服务机构 39 个。康复机构在岗人员 7415 人，其中，管理人员 991 人，专业技术人员 4982 人，其他人员 1442 人。

二、残疾人教育工作

残疾人事业专项彩票公益金助学项目的实施，为 373 名家庭经济困难的残疾儿童享受普惠性学前教育提供资助。

全市共有特殊教育普通高中班（部）2 个，在校生 285 人。残疾人中等职业学校（班）1 个，在校生 251 人，毕业生 31 人，毕业生中 27 人获得职业资格证书。有 393 名残疾人被普通高等院校录取，25 名残疾人进入特殊教育学院学习。

2412 名残疾青壮年文盲接受了扫盲教育。

三、残疾人就业工作

大力推进残疾人按比例就业，采取集中就业、个体就业、公益性岗位就业、灵活就业、居家就业、辅助性就业等多种形式就业，促进残疾人就业增收。2018 年，城乡持证残疾人就业 24.6 万人，其中按比例就业 1.7 万人，集中就业 1.1 万人，个体就业 2 万人，公益性岗位就业 2245 人，辅助性就业 3073 人，灵活就业（含社区、居家就业）7.2 万人，从事农业种养加 12.2 万人。

培训盲人保健按摩人员 273 名、盲人医疗按摩人员 133 名；截至 2018 年底，全市共有保健按摩机构 789 个，医疗按摩机构 18 个；5 人获得盲人医疗按摩人员初级职务任职资格，6 人获得中级职务任职资格。

四、社会保障工作

截至 2018 年底，残疾居民参加城乡社会养老保险 56 万人，13.3 万名 60 岁以下参保重度残疾人全部得到政府的参保扶助，享受代缴比例达到 100%。4.2 万名非重度残疾人享受了个人缴费资助政策。22.8 万人领取养老金。

残疾人托养服务工作稳步推进，残疾人托养服务机构达到 81 个，其中寄宿制托养服务机构 26 个，日间照料机构 30 个，综合性托养服务机构 25 个，为 2099 名残疾人提供了托养服务。20590 名残疾人接受居家服务。1439 名托养服务管理和服务人员接受了各级各类专业培训。

五、残疾人扶贫开发工作

按照党中央、国务院和市委、市政府关于打赢打好脱贫攻坚战三年行动计划，市残联专门制定了工作方案。全年完成农村贫困残疾人危房改造 3418 户，投入资金 4871.8 万元。

贫困残疾人得到有效扶持，1.4 万名残疾人退出建档立卡；加大对残疾人的培训力度，做到扶贫与扶志、扶智有机结合，全年接受残疾人实用技术培训 1.2 万人次。

六、残疾人宣传文化工作

加大宣传工作力度。截至 2018 年底，共有市级残疾人专题广播节目 1 个、电视手语栏目 1 个；区级残疾人专题广播节目 8 个、电视手语栏目 27 个。开展人道主义思想宣传活动 35 场，将残疾人事迹、故事、艺术、技艺送进学校、社区、企事业单位，将具有引领、带动性的社会群体请进残疾人人道主义思想宣传基地，搭建社会大众与残疾人互动、交流平台，弘扬残疾人自尊、自信、自立，推动现代社会残疾人观的增强。

残疾人精神文化活动得到新拓展。全市公共图书馆共设立盲文及盲文有声读物阅览室 42 个，开展残疾人文化周活动 317 场次；举办残疾人文化艺术类的比赛及展览 82 次，残疾人艺术团 1 个。继续实施残疾人文化进家庭“五个一”文化项目，实现 2500 户重度、贫困残疾人家庭“读一本书、看一次电影、游一次园、参观一次展览、参加一次文化活动”。

七、残疾人体育工作

加强公共文化体育设施建设，实施“残疾人体育健身计划”，推动残疾人康复体育和健身体育广泛开展，推动残疾人体育进社区、进家庭，加强残疾人运动员队伍建设，全力备战全国第十届残疾人运动会。对全市 13 个区 7900 户不易出户的重度残疾人实施了“康复体育关爱家庭计划”；创建 50 个残疾人文体示范点，推进残疾人社会体育指导员培训；开展健身周、特奥日、冰雪季等主题基层残疾人群众体育活动。组织 154 名残疾人运动员参加 17 项全国锦标赛，获得 18 金 16 银 19 铜，打破三项全国纪录，8 名运动员先后入选国家集训队，6 个群众项目进入第十届残疾人全运会决赛圈；成功举办了“2018 年重庆市残疾人游泳锦标赛”。

八、残疾人维权工作

抓好“大维权、大接访、大稳定”机制的贯彻落实。2018 年，全市制定或修改保障残疾人权益的规范性文件 6 个。县级以上人大开展《中华人民共和国残疾人保障法》执法检查和专题调研 8 次；政协开展视察和专题调研 17 次。开展市级普法宣传教育活动 4 次，680 人参加了活动；举办市级法律培训班 1 期，100 人参加了培训。

截至 2018 年底，成立残疾人法律救助工作协调机构 29 个，建立残疾人法律救助工作站 29 个。

残疾人参政议政工作得到加强，各级残联协助人大代表、政协委员提出议案、建议、提案 64 件，办理议案、建议、提案 68 件。

无障碍建设法规、标准进一步完善。38 个区县系统开展无障碍环境建设；开展无障碍环境建设检查 47 次，无障碍培训 2311 人次。

九、残疾人组织建设工作

残疾人基层组织体系建设更加完善，基层组织实现从“有”向“好”转变，大力加强基层残协和专职委员队伍建设。2018 年，全市共建立各级残联 1069 个，其中，区县残联 40 个，乡镇（街道）残联 1029 个；已建社区（村）残协 1.1 万个。

全市共有残联工作人员 1900 人，乡镇（街道）、村（社区）选聘残疾人专职委员总计 1.2 万名。21 个区县残联配备了残疾人干部。

建立各类残疾人专门协会 199 个，其中市级专门协会 5 个，区县级专门协会 194 个。助残社会组织 54 个。并制定了《重庆市残疾人联合会专门协会管理办法（试行）》。

十、残疾人服务设施建设

截至 2018 年底，已竣工的各级残疾人综合服务设施 28 个，总建设规模 8.8 万平方米，总投资 2.6 亿元；已竣工的各级残疾人康复设施 13 个，总建设规模 8.1 万平方米，总投资 3 亿元；已竣工的各级残疾人托养服务设施 6 个，总建设规模 2.2 万平方米，总投资 0.9 亿元。

十一、残疾人信息化建设

全市共有 15 个区县残联开通了网站，其中：独立建立网站 2 个，搭载上级残联或同级政府网站或集约到同级群团网站 13 个。

截至 2018 年底，全国残疾人人口基础数据库入库重庆籍持证残疾人 84.3 万人。扎实开展残疾人基本服务状况和需求信息动态更新工作，全面掌握残疾人基本服务和需求信息，为业务工作的开展、残疾人精准服务提供了有效数据支撑。与政府相关涉残部门开展数据共享与交换，为整合残疾人服务和管理资源提供了信息保障。

2018 年四川省残疾人事业发展统计公报

2018 年，在四川省委、省政府的正确领导下，在中国残联的大力指导和支持下，在社会各界的热心帮助下，四川省残疾人事业持续深化发展，在残疾人康复、教育、就业、扶贫、组织建设、维权、宣传文化、体育、服务设施建设等业务领域取得了突出的进步和工作成效，为广大残疾人带来了更多的福祉。现将四川省 2018 年度残疾人事业统计数据公报如下：

一、康复

2018 年，通过实施精准康复服务，共为 170.6 万名残疾儿童及持证残疾人提供基本康复服务。其中：视力残疾人 25.8 万名，听力言语残疾人 16.5 万名，肢体残疾人 96 万名，智力残疾人 11.4 万名，精神残疾人 14.5 万名，多重残疾人 6.1 万名。共有 5275 名 0-6 岁残疾儿童得到基本康复服务。

截止 2018 年底，全省共建有残疾人康复机构 278 个，其中，提供视力残疾康复服务的机构 51 个，提供听力言语残疾康复服务的机构 65 个，提供肢体残疾康复服务的机构 131 个，提供智力残疾康复服务的机构 117 个，提供精神残疾康复服务的机构 85 个，提供孤独症儿童康复服务的机构 57 个，提供辅助器具服务的机构 78 个。康复机构在岗人员达 1.1 万人。

二、教育

2018 年，通过实施残疾人事业专项彩票公益金助学项目，为 311 名家庭经济困难的残疾儿童享受普惠性学前教育提供资助；各地也积极多渠道争取资金支持，对 690 名残疾儿童给予学前教育资助。

截止 2018 年底，全省共有特殊教育普通高中班（部）3 个，残疾人中等职业学校（班）2 个；全年共有 583 名残疾考生被普通高等院校录取。

全年共有 1.2 万名残疾青壮年文盲接受了扫盲教育。

三、就业

截止 2018 年底，城乡持证残疾人就业人数为 88.4 万人。其中：按比例就业 2.2 万人，集中就业 1.2 万人，个体就业 5.3 万人，公益性岗位就业 7000 人，辅助性就业 1.7 万人，灵活就业 41.8 万人，从事农业种养加人数 35.5 万。

全年共培训盲人保健按摩人员 703 名、盲人医疗按摩人员 131 名；全省盲人保健按摩机构达到 1191 个，盲人医疗按摩机构达到 28 个。

四、扶贫

全省残疾人扶贫开发成效显著，贫困残疾人生产生活状况得到进一步改善。有效扶持贫困残疾人，有 5.4 万人退出建档立卡；为贫困残疾人提供实用技术培训 12.8 万人次。

全省残疾人扶贫基地达到 255 个，共安置 4102 名残疾人就业，扶持带动 5931 户残疾人家庭。

全年共完成 7162 户农村贫困残疾人危房改造。

五、社会保障

截至 2018 年底，城乡残疾居民参加城乡社会养老保险人数达到 229.8 万名。60 岁以下的参保残疾人中有 44.4 万名重度残疾人，其中 43.7 万名得到了政府的参保扶助，代缴养老保险费比例达到 98.4%。有 29 万名非重度残疾人也享受了全额或部分代缴养老保险费的优惠政策。

全年共为 4.4 万名残疾人提供托养服务，其中：为 6535 名残疾人提供机构托养服务，为 3.8 万名残疾人提供居家托养服务；残疾人托养服务机构达到 164 个；共有 629 名托养服务管理和服务人员接受了专业培训。

六、宣传文化

截止 2018 年底，全省共有残疾人专题广播节目 6 个，电视手语新闻栏目 9 个；共设立盲文及盲文有声读物阅览室 52 个；共有各类残疾人艺术团 10 个。

全年共开展残疾人文化周活动 391 场次；省、市两级举办残疾人文化艺术类比赛及展览 11 次。

七、维权

截至 2018 年底，全省已成立残疾人法律救助工作协调机构 121 个，建立残疾人法律救助工作站 98 个。

残疾人参政议政工作稳步开展，各级残联协助人大代表、政协委员提出议案、建议、提案 37 件，办理议案、建议、提案 48 件。

在无障碍建设领域，全省已有 66 个市、县、区系统开展无障碍建设；全年共开展无障碍建设检查 75 次，无障碍培训 5308 人次。

八、组织建设

截止 2018 年底，市县乡共建立残联 4316 个，其中市级残联 21 个，县级残联 186 个，乡镇（街道）残联已建 4109 个；社区（村）残协已建 43782 个。

省、市、县、乡残联实有人员达到 8961 人，乡镇（街道）、村（社区）选聘残疾人专职委员共计 58741 名。

截止 2018 年底，共建立助残社会组织 153 个。

九、服务设施

深入推进残疾人服务设施建设工作。截至 2018 年底，已竣工的各级残疾人综合服务设施达 162 个，总建设规模 45.7 万平方米；已竣工的各级残疾人康复设施达 46 个，总建设规模 20.7 万平方米；已竣工的各级残疾人托养服务设施达 26 个，总建设规模 6 万平方米。

十、信息化

持续深化“量体裁衣”式残疾人服务工作。根据四川省“量体裁衣”式残疾人服务平台的统计结果显示，2018 年，全省各级残疾人工作者共为 337 万名残疾人提供 3949 万项次的个性化服务。

2018 年贵州省残疾人事业发展统计公报

2018 年，在省委、省政府的领导、中国残联的指导及相关部门的支持下，贵州省残疾人联合会深入学习贯彻党的十九大精神，认真贯彻落实党中央、国务院关于残疾人事业发展的一系列重要部署，主动担当，积极作为，着力加强促进残疾人事业发展的制度建设、民生建设、环境建设和机关建设，大力推进着残疾人事业的各项工作任务，推动残疾人事业持续健康发展。

一、康复

2018 年，共有 23.5 万名残疾儿童及持证残疾人得到基本康复服务，其中包括 0-6 岁残疾儿童 3910 人。得到康复服务的持证残疾人中，有视力残疾人 2.8 万名、听力残疾人 1.3 万名、言语残疾人 1074 名、肢体残疾人 14.8 万名、智力残疾人 1.1 万名、精神残疾人 1.5 万名、多重残疾人 1.6 万名。全年共为 8.9 万名残疾人提供各类辅助器具适配服务。

截至 2018 年底，共有残疾人康复机构 194 个，其中，45 个机构提供视力残疾康复服务，48 个提供听力言语残疾康复服务，62 个提供肢体残疾康复服务，54 个提供智力残疾康复服务，62 个提供精神残疾康复服务，31 个提供孤独症儿童康复服务，42 个提供辅助器具服务。康复机构在岗人员 7014 人，其中，管理人员 880 人，专业技术人员 4687 人，其他人员 1447 人。

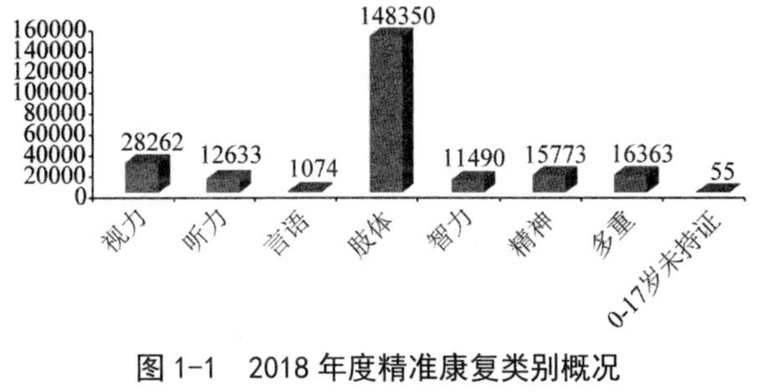

图 1-1　2018 年度精准康复类别概况

二、教育

残疾人事业专项彩票公益金助学项目的实施，为 584 名家庭经济困难的残疾儿童享受普惠性学前教育提供资助。贵州省有 1 所残疾人中等职业学校，在校生 355 人。全省共有 731 名残疾人被普通高等院校和特殊教育学院录取。

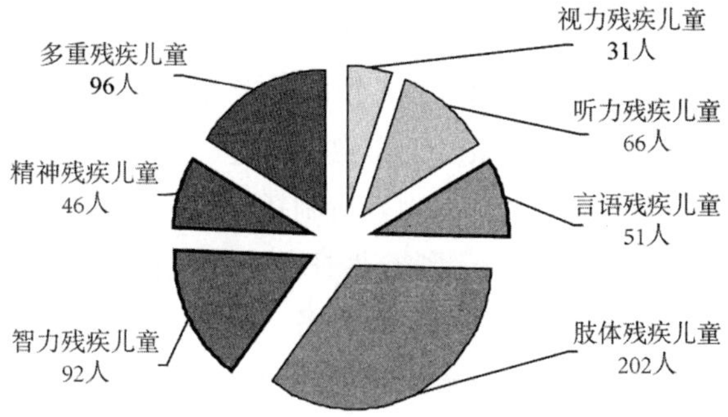

图 2-1　2018 年度接受残疾人事业专项彩票公益金助学项目资情况分析

三、就业

城乡持证残疾人就业人数为 34.4 万人，其中按比例就业 9212 人，集中就业 6137 人，个体就业 1.9 万人，公益性岗位就业 1645 人，辅助性就业 2986 人，灵活就业（含社区、居家就业）10.1 万人，从事农业种养加 20.4 万人。

培训盲人保健按摩人员 717 名、盲人医疗按摩人员 169 名；保健按摩机构达到 571 个，医疗按摩机构达到 23 个；75 人获得盲人医疗按摩人员初级职务任职资格，8 人获得中级职务任职资格。

四、扶贫

残疾人接受实用技术培训 1.2 万人次。210 名农村残疾人获得康复扶贫贴息贷款扶持。171 个残疾

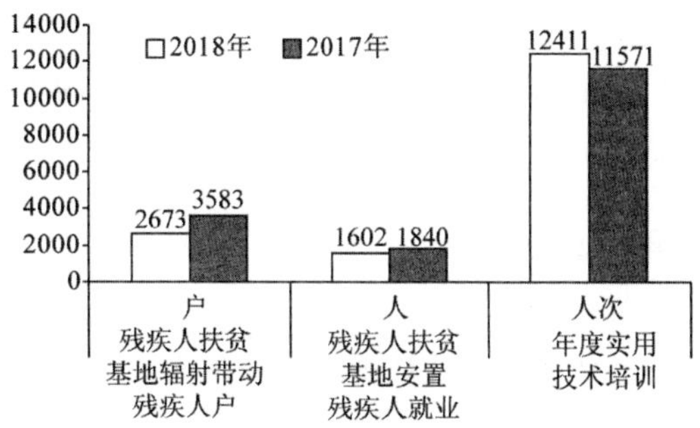

图 4-1　2018 年与 2017 年扶贫情况比较

人扶贫基地安置1602名残疾人就业，扶持带动2673户残疾人家庭。共完成632户农村贫困残疾人危房改造，投入资金170.6万元。

五、社会保障

截至2018年底，残疾居民参加城乡社会养老保险人数83.1万名，15.3万名60岁以下参保重度残疾人中，12.3万名得到政府的参保扶助，享受代缴比例达到80.5%。5.2万名非重度残疾人享受了个人缴费资助政策。40.7万人领取养老金。

残疾人托养服务工作稳步推进，残疾人托养服务机构达到34个，其中寄宿制托养服务机构13个，日间照料机构4个，综合性托养服务机构17个，为2170名残疾人提供了托养服务。6664名残疾人接受居家服务。87名托养服务管理和服务人员接受了各级各类专业培训。

六、宣传文化

截至2018年底，共有省级残疾人专题广播节目2个、电视手语栏目1个；地市级残疾人专题广播节目2个、电视手语栏目6个。

省地县三级公共图书馆共设立盲文及盲文有声读物阅览室26个，共开展残疾人文化周活动206场次；省地两级残联共举办残疾人文化艺术类的比赛及展览4次，共有各类残疾人艺术团1个。

七、体育

2018年，省地县三级共开展残疾人群众体育健身活动139次；参与人数4785人；创建残疾人体育示范点11个；举办全国残疾人羽毛球体育赛事1次；举办省级综合性第六届残疾人运动会，参加人数2000人左右；培训省级第六期残疾人体育健身指导员50名；组队参加国际国内9个残疾人综合体育赛事，共获得金牌28枚、银牌41枚、铜牌19枚、打破2项亚洲纪录。

八、维权

2018年，制定或修改保障残疾人权益的省级规范性文件2个、地市级1个、县级15个。县级以上人大开展《中华人民共和国残疾人保障法》执法检查和专题调研4次；政协开展视察和专题调研2次。开展省级普法宣传教育活动2次，400人参加；举办省级法律培训班1个，120人参加。

截至2018年底，成立残疾人法律救助工作协调机构78个，建立残疾人法律救助工作站67个。

残疾人参政议政工作得到加强，各地残联协助人大代表、政协委员提出议案、建议、提案10件，办理议案、建议、提案3件。无障碍建设法规、标准进一步完善。共出台了2个省、地市、县级无障碍环境建设与管理法规、政府令和规范性文件；28个地市、县系统开展无障碍环境建设；开展无障碍环境建设检查14次，无障碍培训284人次。

九、组织建设

2018年，市县乡共成立残联1512个，各地市已建残联10个，县（市、区）残联已建90个，乡镇（街道）残联已建1412个；已建社区（村）残协1.4万个。

省市县乡残联工作人员3266人，乡镇（街道）、村（社区）选聘残疾人专职委员总计1.3万名。地市级配备了残疾人领导干部的残联9个，县级配备了残疾人干部的残联61个。共建立省级及以下各类残疾人专门协会428个，其中省级专门协会已建5个，市级专门协会已建45个，县级专门协会已建378个。助残社会组织共有14个。

十、服务设施建设

截至2018年底，已竣工的各级残疾人综合服务设施57个，总建设规模6.2万平方米，总投资1.2亿万元；已竣工的各级残疾人康复设施9个，总建设规模6.3万平方米，总投资1.6亿元；已竣工的各级残疾人托养服务设施38个，总建设规模11.8万平方米，总投资2.6亿元。

十一、信息化建设

截至2018年底，3个地市、10个县级残联开通网站。

2018年云南省残疾人事业发展统计公报

2018年，在省委、省政府的坚强领导和中国残联的悉心指导及有关部门的支持下，全省各级残联围绕中心，服务大局，坚定不移以习近平新时代中国特色社会主义思想为指导，全面贯彻落实党的十九大和十九届二中、三中全会精神以及省委十届四次、五次全会精神，进一步贯彻落实习近平总书记对云南发展的重要指示精神，不断健全残疾人事业工作机制，全省残疾人事业取得了长足发展。

一、康复

2018年，全省残联认真贯彻落实《云南省残疾人精准康复服务行动实施方案》，省残联制定下发《云南省残疾人联合会关于进一步加强残疾人精准康复服务行动的指导意见》，强化对全省残疾人精准康复服务行动的指导，全省精准康复服务率大幅度提升。2018年，全省有康复服务需求的残疾人439775人，其中已有387505人获得康复服务。康复服务率为88.11%，辅助器具适配率为84.09%，建档立卡贫困人口康复服务率为91.83%，因病致（返）贫康复服务率为89.01%。中国残联委托第三方开展电话核查，全省残疾人接受康复服务满意率达95.65%。

2018年，全省共有387505名残疾儿童及持证残疾人得到基本康复服务，其中包括0-6岁残疾儿童3993人，7-17岁残疾儿童19416人，60岁以上残疾人131885人。得到康复服务的持证残疾人中，有视力残疾人47600名、听力残疾人26663名，言语残疾人3188名、肢体残疾人205641名、智力残疾人25561名、精神残疾人58167名，其中共有88127名持证残疾人得到各类辅助器具适配。

截止2018年底，全省134个县（市、区）中的116个开展社区康复服务，共建设康复服务设施997个，共有12377个社区配备了12963名社区康复协调员；全省共有残疾人康复机构257个，其中，提供视力残疾康复服务的机构47个，提供听力言语残疾康复服务的机构52个，提供肢体残疾康复服务的机构78个，提供智力残疾康复服务的机构72个，提供精神残疾康复服务的机构80个，提供孤独症儿童康复服务的机构29个，提供辅助器具服务的机构101个；康复机构在岗人员达6929人，其中管理人员794人，业务人员4826人，其他人员1309人；2018年全省共培训康复机构管理人员1765人次，培训康复机构业务人员5834人。

二、教育

2018年，云南省各级特殊教育机构全面划归教育部门管理，各级残联继续配合教育部门实施《云南省特殊教育提升计划实施方案（2017-2020年）》，以期到2020年，全省各级各类特殊教育普及水平全面提高，保障能力全面增强，教育质量全面提升。全年共对1668名家庭贫困在校残疾高中生、残疾大学新生和贫困残疾人子女（在校高中、大学生）进行了资助，组织实施中央彩金助学项目，对339名家庭困难的残疾儿童（学前教育）进行资助。

截止2018年底，全省共有残疾人中等职业技术学校（班）4个，招生850人，在校生1545人，毕业生289人，其中在校生中有盲生203人，聋生348人，肢残生276人，其他718人，共有196名学生获得职业资格证书。

2018年，云南省特殊教育职业学院录取残疾考生25名，共有815名残疾人考生达到普通高等院校招生考试录取分数线，其中有773名残疾人被普通高等院校录取，本科生录取328人，专科（高职）生录取445人。

全省全年通过扫盲培训对3419名残疾青壮年文盲进行了扫盲教育。

三、就业

2018年，省残联积极开展省级机关、事业单位按比例安排残疾人就业情况摸底调查和统计工作，并主动将“按比例安排残疾人就业年审”事项纳入省政府“一部手机办事通”移动政务平台实现上线运行。

2018 年，全省城乡持证残疾人就业人数为 449433 人，其中按比例就业 18259 人，全年新增 521 人；集中就业 7561 人，全年新增 260 人；个体就业 17434 人，全年新增 692 人；社区就业 1048 人，全年新增 33 人；公益性岗位就业 1091 人，全年新增 77 人；辅助性就业 4994 人，全年新增 44 人；居家就业 42637 人，全年新增 350 人；从事农业种养加 301589 人，全年新增 6336 人；灵活就业 54820 人，全年新增 3207 人。

2018 年，省残联继续按照“政府引导，部门组织，企业运作，市场导向，就业为本”的原则，全面开展“助盲脱贫”工作，全省盲人按摩事业发展迅速。2018 年全省培训盲人保健按摩人员 1304 人、盲人医疗按摩人员 357 人；全省保健按摩机构达到 889 个，2018 年完成盲人保健按摩机构规范化建设任务 133 家。2018 年全省注册医疗按摩机构 7 个。机构建设有力促进盲人就业，全年促进盲人保健按摩人员就业 279 人，盲人医疗按摩人员在医疗机构中就业 12 人，在专业技术职务资格评审中，有 34 人获得医疗按摩人员初级资格的评定，2 人获得中级资格评定。

四、扶贫

2018 年，省残联积极主动加强与省级相关部门的沟通衔接，切实把残疾人脱贫攻坚工作纳入全省脱贫攻坚工作大局，贫困残疾人脱贫攻坚取得阶段性成效。全年贫困残疾人户退出建档立卡共 68875 户，涉及残疾人共 80037 人实现脱贫；全省接受实用技术培训的残疾人达到 32946 人次，各级投入培训经费 1131.9 万元。

2018 年，全省残疾人扶贫基地建设稳步推进，共建设 353 个残疾人扶贫基地，安置 2703 名残疾人就业，扶持带动 13811 户残疾人走向脱贫的道路。

2018 年，全省共完成 19516 户农村贫困残疾人危房改造，受益残疾人 22480 人，各地投入危房资金 23464 万元，其中省级资金 19677.1 万元，州（市）资金 408.2 万元，县级资金 3378.7 万元。

五、社会保障与托养

2018 年，全省符合参加城乡社会养老保险条件的残疾居民为 104.4 万人，其中符合参保条件的重度残疾人 37.74 万人，实际参保残疾居民 92.22 万人；其中领取待遇 33.56 万人，重度残疾人领取待遇 12.1 万人；60 周岁以下参保 58.66 万人，其中重度残疾人 20.7 万人，重度残疾人中的 19.1 万人获得全额代缴保险费用，1.1 万人获得部分代缴保险费用。

2018 年，在各级党委、政府的高度重视下，贫困残疾人困难补贴和重度残疾人护理补贴得到全面落实，1 月到 10 月共计发放困难残疾人生活补贴 44 万人，补助资金 1.7 亿元，发放重度残疾人护理补贴 32 万人，补助资金 1.7 亿元。

全省残疾人托养服务工作稳步推进，截止 2018 年底全省共建设残疾人托养服务机构 62 个，其中寄宿制托养服务机构 36 个，托养残疾人 1361 人，日间照料托养服务机构 10 个，托养残疾人 83 人，综合性托养服务机构 16 个，托养残疾人 374 人；享受居家托养服务残疾人 15975 人。全省全年共有 976 名托养服务管理和服务人员接受了各级各类专业培训，其中机构内人员 184 名接受培训，792 名居家人员接受了居家托养服务人员培训。

六、宣传文化

2018 年，全省各级充分利用各主流媒体，大力宣传我省残疾人事业。人民日报刊登了《定制化服务、新设备研发，云南多渠道助残——让残疾人生活更便利》、光明日报刊登了《让更多残疾人共享美好生活》等反映云南省残疾人脱贫攻坚、就业创业成绩的文章，并被广泛转载。在云南省残联第七次代表大会期间，云南新闻联播和云南日报等主流媒体全面报道了大会盛况，发表了题为《心手相携 共筑未来》的评论员文章，引起了社会各界的关注和肯定。省残联持续与云南广播电视台国际频道《Hi 云南》栏目携手创办的宣传残疾人事业的《追梦》节目，现已成为我省大力宣传残疾人事业的主要阵地和重要平台。

截止 2018 年底，全省共有省级残疾人专题电视手语栏目 1 个，新闻促进会 1 个，开通 1 个省级残疾人联合会官方微信；州（市）残联残疾人专题广播节目 4 个、电视手语栏目 10 个，新闻促进会 5 个。

2018 年，全面组织实施残疾人文化服务建设工程，努力保障残疾人平等享有文化公共服务的权益，省、州（市）级公共图书馆普遍建立盲人图书室，县级图书馆普遍设立了盲人图书室或盲人阅览区。

截止 2018 年底，省、州（市）、县（市、区）三级公共图书馆共设立盲文及盲文有声读物阅览室 37 个，共开展残疾人文化周活动 261 场次，其中省级举办 1 次，参与人次 300 人；州（市）残联举办 13 次，参与人次 3296 人；县（市、区）残联举办 247 次，参与人次 20725 人。省、州（市）两级残联共举办残疾人文化艺术类的比赛及展览 5 次，共有各类残疾人艺术团 6 个。

七、体育

2018 年，在云南省临沧市成功举办了省第十一届残疾人运动会暨第五届特殊奥林匹克运动会。本届残运会成为历届省残运会中规模最大的一届运动会，圆满实现了省运会、省残运会“同城举办，同样精彩”的办会目标，得到了各级领导、各有关部门和社会各界的一致好评。2018 年在雅加达举办的第三届亚洲残疾人运动会上，入选中国代表团的 5 名云南籍运动员共获得 3 金 4 银 5 铜的好成绩，为国家争得了荣誉。

八、维权与信访

2018 年，全省共有 1 个州（市）和 1 个县（市、区）制定或修改了保障残疾人权益的规范性文件。县（市、区）以上人大开展《中华人民共和国残疾人保障法》执法检查或专题调研 4 次，政协开展视察或专题调研 12 次。

截止 2018 年底，全省共成立残疾人法律救助工作协调机构 40 个，其中省级 1 个，州（市）残联 7 个，县（市、区）残联 32 个；建立残疾人法律救助工作站 36 个，其中省级 1 个并办理案件 12 件，州（市）残联 7 个，县（市、区）残联 28 个并办理案件 81 件。

全省残疾人参政议政工作稳步开展，全省各级残联共有 79 名残疾人担任人大代表，其中州（市）残联 11 人，县（市、区）残联 68 人；各级共有 135 名残疾人担任政协委员，其中省级 2 人，州（市）残联 15 人，县（市、区）残联 118 人。各级残联协助人大代表提出议案、建议 6 件，协助政协委员提出议案、建议 12 件；办理人大建议 2 件，办理政协提案 4 件。

2018 年，全省各级共有 3 个州（市）和 53 个县（市、区）系统开展无障碍环境建设，进行无障碍环境建设检查 48 次，进行无障碍建设培训 844 人次。

2018 年，省级共接到残疾人来信 1186 件，其中涉及医疗康复类 334 件，涉及教育类 193 件，涉及就业扶贫类 158 件，涉及社会保障类 282 件，涉及权益保障类 92 件；全年共接待残疾人来访 10246 人次，来访中个人访 10235 人次，集体来访 2 批次 11 人，其中涉及医疗康复类 1902 人次，涉及教育类 874 人次，涉及就业扶贫类 1880 人次，涉及社会保障类 2964 人次，涉及权益保障类 718 人次；全年共受理 3972 通来电咨询，41 件网上投诉。

九、组织建设

2018 年，全省州（市）、县（市、区）、乡镇（街道）共建立残联 1555 个。其中省级残联机关 1 个，省级事业单位 7 个，实有人员 258 人。州（市）已建残联机关 16 个，其中 13 个州（市）残联配备了残疾人领导干部，州（市）残联机关共有 208 人，州（市）残联事业单位共 27 个，实有人员 134 人；各州市 2018 年共举办综合培训班 12 期，参加培训人次达 581 人次；共举办残疾人干部培训班 3 期，参加培训人次 431 人次；共有 825 名助残志愿者为 6534 名残疾人提供了志愿助残服务。

全省共有 134 个县（市、区）建立了残联，其中 93 个残联机关配备了残疾人领导干部，县（市、区）残联机关实有人员 1285 人，县（市、区）残联残联事业单位 117 个，实有人员 384 人。各县（市、区）共举办 122 期培训班，参加培训人次 5204 人次；共有 2368 名助残志愿者为 95015 名残疾人提供了志愿助残服务。

全省共有 1404 个乡镇（街道）建立了残联，实有人员 1507 人，其中专职理事长有 446 名，兼职理事长 461 名，残疾人专职委员 1475 名。乡镇（街道）残联共举办培训班 503 期，参加培训人次 7291 人次；共有 5050 名助残志愿者为 167601 名残疾人提供了志愿助残服务。

全省已建村（社区）残协 14085 个，其中城市社区建立残协 1582 个，农村社区建立残协 12503 个，共配备残疾人专职委员 13723 名，其中城市社区配备 1551 名，农村社区配备 12172 名；共有 3455 名助残志愿者为 51266 名残疾人提供了志愿助残服务。

截止到2018年底，全省共建立省级及以下各类残疾人专门协会707个，其中盲人协会省级1个、州（市）残联16个、县（市、区）残联125个，聋人协会省级1个、州（市）残联15个、县（市、区）残联126个，肢残人协会省级1个、州（市）残联16个、县（市、区）残联127个，智力残疾人及亲友协会省级1个、州（市）残联15个、县（市、区）残联111个，精神残疾人及亲友协会省级1个、州（市）残联15个、县（市、区）残联111个。

全省2018年累计有助残社会组织19个，其中残联系统内有9个社会团体、1个基金会、6个社会服务机构，残联系统外助残社会组织3个。

十、服务设施

截止2018年底，全省已竣工并投入使用的各级残疾人综合服务设施127个，总建设规模165425平方米，总投资32399万元；本年度新投入使用项目4个，总建设规模4823平方米，总投资768万元，在建项目5个，建设规模12040平方米，总投资3047万元。

全省已竣工并投入使用的各级残疾人托养服务设施6个，总建设规模13813平方米，总投资4035万元；本年度新投入使用项目4个，总建设规模9980平方米，总投资2652万元，在建项目22个，建设规模57486平方米，总投资14853万元，筹建项目5个，建设规模11387平方米，总投资3098万元。

全省已竣工并投入使用的各级残疾人康复服务设施3个，总建设规模6450平方米，总投资2169万元；在建项目12个，建设规模107698平方米，总投资29460万元，筹建项目1个，建设规模5257平方米，投资1620万元。

十一、信息化建设

2018年，全省各级残联进一步加强残联信息化建设力度，不断构建完善与经济社会和残疾人事业发展相适应的互联网体系，继续优化完善各级残联门户网站、残疾人服务信息发布平台等功能建设，充分利用各级残联和专门协会微博、微信、QQ群等，加强与残疾人沟通交流，主动为残疾人实时提供志愿助残服务、社会帮扶、创业就业、生活服务等信息。在第三代《中华人民共和国残疾人证》试点基础上，2019年将全面推动全省第三代残疾人证的换发工作，同时推进省残联数据中心节点建设工作，深化“放管服”改革，实现各级残联与同级部门间的数据信息共享，提高工作效率，把服务残疾人的工作做得更好。

截止2018年底，全省各级残联共建设32个网站，其中独立建站8个，搭载上级残联或同级政府网站24个；全省持证残疾人137.5万人；全省残疾人事业统计部分数据连续3年纳入省统计局统计年鉴；省残联积极参与省政府“互联网+政务服务”建设工作，2018年将“按比例安排残疾人就业年审”纳入到省政府“一部手机办事通”移动政务平台并实现同步运行。

2018年西藏自治区残疾人事业发展统计公报

2018年，在中国残联的精心指导和大力支持下，在自治区党委、政府的高度重视和亲切关怀下，我区各级残联系统牢牢把握工作重点，加大工作力度，强化工作措施狠抓任务落实，各项工作取得了新的成效。

一、康复

2018年，1153名残疾儿童及持证残疾人得到基本康复服务，其中包括0-6岁残疾儿童28人。得到康复服务的持证残疾人中，有视力残疾人93名、听力残疾人152名肢体残疾人783名、智力残疾人13名、精神残疾人12名、多重残疾人100名。全年共为899名残疾人提供各类辅助器具适配服务。

截至2018年底，全区投入使用的残疾人康复机构6个，其中，省级残疾人康复服务机构1个，地市级残疾人康复服务机构5个。全区残疾人康复机构在岗人员63人，其中省级康复机构40人，地市级康复机构23人。

二、教育、就业

残疾人事业专项彩票公益金助学项目的实施，为102名家庭经济困难的残疾儿童享受普惠性学前教育提供资助。并对4名残疾儿童给予学前教育资助。

2018年，全区共有48名残疾人被普通高等院校录取。其中本科录取11人，专科录取37人。全年共有544名残疾青壮年文盲接受了扫盲教育。

持证残疾人就业人数为16883人，其中按比例就业344人，集中就业300人，个体就业619人，公益性岗位就业115人，辅助性就业54人，灵活就业（含社区、居家就业）9156人，从事农业种养加6295人。

2018年，全区共培训盲人保健按摩人员20人、盲人医疗按摩人员4人；

三、社会保障、扶贫

截至2018年底，残疾居民参加城乡社会养老保险人数38363名，10033名60岁以下参保重度残疾人中，7114名得到政府的参保扶助，享受代缴比例达到70.9%。4004名非重度残疾人享受了个人缴费资助政策。7939人领取养老金。

残疾人托养服务工作稳步推进，残疾人托养服务机构达到2个，其中寄宿制托养服务机构1个，综合性托养服务机构1个，为1299名残疾人提供了托养服务。615名残疾人接受了居家服务。

贫困残疾人得到有效扶持，7760名残疾人退出建档立卡；残疾人接受实用技术培训1167人次。

全年完成39户农村贫困残疾人危房改造，投入资金35790元。

四、宣文、维权、组织建设

2018年共开展残疾人文化周活动8次，参加残疾人文化周活动达536人次。全年开展普法宣传教育活动9次，710人参加。开展无障碍环境建设检查2次，无障碍培训21人次。

2018年，市县乡共成立残联81个，各地市已建残联7个，县（市、区）残联已建74个。

省市县乡残联工作人员329人。地市级配备了残疾人领导干部的残联2个，县级配备了残疾人干部的残联10个。建立省级残疾人专门协会3个。

五、服务设施

截至2018年底，已竣工并投入使用的各级残疾人综合服务设施40个，总建设规模50637.1平方米，总投资16653万元；已竣工的各级残疾人康复设施13个，总建设规模22289.7平方米，总投资8283万元；已竣工的各级残疾人托养服务设施3个，总建设规模12308.5平方米，总投资3865.8万元。

2018年陕西省残疾人事业发展统计公报

2018年，全省残联系统认真学习习近平总书记关于残疾人事业的重要论述，全面贯彻落实中国残联和省残联第七次代表大会精神，围绕“五个聚力”工作思路和建设“三个残联”目标，不断开拓进取、强化措施、真抓实干，为实现残疾人对美好生活的向往做出了新贡献。

一、康复

2018年，396541名残疾儿童及持证残疾人得到基本康复服务，其中包括0-6岁残疾儿童3556人。得到康复服务的持证残疾人中，有视力残疾人46023名、听力残疾人20981名、言语残疾人407名、肢体残疾人218006名、智力残疾人16875名、精神残疾人75181名、多重残疾人17551名。全年共为139865名残疾人提供各类辅助器具适配服务。

截至2018年底，有残疾人康复机构358个，其中，74个机构提供视力残疾康复服务，49个提供听力言语残疾康复服务，246个提供肢体残疾康复服务，72个提供智力残疾康复服务，53个提供精神残疾康复服务，42个提供孤独症儿童康复服务，47个提供辅助器具服务。康复机构在岗人员12597人，其中，管理人员1398人，专业技术人员9482人，其他人员1717人。

二、教育

残疾人事业专项彩票公益金助学项目的实施，为131名家庭经济困难的残疾儿童享受普惠性学前教育提供资助。多渠道争取资金支持，对118名残疾儿童给予学前教育资助。

共有特殊教育普通高中班（部）3个，在校生274人，其中聋生274人。残疾人中等职业学校（班）3个，在校生1051人，毕业生474人，毕业生中414人获得职业资格证书。有217名残疾人被普通高等院校录取。

2086名残疾青壮年文盲接受了扫盲教育。

三、就业

城乡持证残疾人就业人数为263278人，其中按比例就业12292人，集中就业4603人，个体就业14083人，公益性岗位就业4101人，辅助性就业5281人，灵活就业（含社区、居家就业）72481人，从事农业种养加150437人。

培训盲人保健按摩人员1279名、盲人医疗按摩人员275名；保健按摩机构达到589个，医疗按摩机构达到54个；50人获得盲人医疗按摩人员初级职务任职资格。

四、社会保障

截至2018年底，残疾居民参加城乡社会养老保险人数875730名，145009名60岁以下参保重度残疾人中，139718名得到政府的参保扶助，享受代缴比例达到96.4%。208425名非重度残疾人享受了个人缴费资助政策。355055人领取养老金。

残疾人托养服务工作稳步推进，残疾人托养服务机构达到141个，其中寄宿制托养服务机构72个，日间照料机构18个，综合性托养服务机构51个，为33361名残疾人提供了托养服务。13382名残疾人接受居家服务。1541名托养服务管理和服务人员接受了各级各类专业培训。

五、扶贫

贫困残疾人得到有效扶持，60547名残疾人退出建档立卡；残疾人接受实用技术培训24762人次。

136个残疾人扶贫基地安置1990名残疾人就业，扶持带动4354户残疾人家庭。

共完成2968户农村贫困残疾人危房改造，投入资金41776815元。

六、宣传文化

截至2018年底，共有省级残疾人专题广播节目1个、电视手语栏目1个；地市级残疾人电视手语栏目 5 个。

省地县三级公共图书馆共设立盲文及盲文有声读物阅览室 50 个，共开展残疾人文化周活动 163 场次；省地两级残联共举办残疾人文化艺术类的比赛及展览 4 次，共有各类残疾人艺术团 10 个。

七、维权

2018 年，制定或修改省级关于残疾人的专门法规、规章 1 个；制定或修改保障残疾人权益的省级规范性文件 1 个、地市级 1 个、县级 3 个；县级以上人大开展《中华人民共和国残疾人保障法》执法检查和专题调研 8 次；政协开展视察和专题调研 2 次。开展省级普法宣传教育活动 4 次，600 人参加。

截至 2018 年底，成立残疾人法律救助工作协调机构 101 个，建立残疾人法律救助工作站 93 个。

残疾人参政议政工作得到加强，各地残联协助人大代表、政协委员提出议案、建议、提案 12 件，办理议案、建议、提案 29 件。

无障碍建设法规、标准进一步完善。共出台了 21 个省、地市、县级无障碍环境建设与管理法规、政府令和规范性文件；50 个地市、县系统开展无障碍环境建设；开展无障碍环境建设检查 31 次，无障碍培训 290 人次。

八、组织建设

2018 年，市县乡共成立残联 1390 个，各地市已建残联 11 个，县（市、区）残联已建 115 个，乡镇（街道）残联已建 1264 个；社区（村）已建残协 22516 个。

省市县乡残联工作人员 4203 人，乡镇（街道）、村（社区）选聘残疾人专职委员总计 25497 名。地市级配备了残疾人领导干部的残联 10 个，县级配备了残疾人干部的残联 59 个。

共建立省级及以下各类残疾人专门协会 583 个，其中省级专门协会已建 5 个，市级专门协会已建 50 个，县级专门协会已建 528 个。助残社会组织共有 10 个。

九、服务设施

截至 2018 年底，已竣工的各级残疾人综合服务设施 78 个，总建设规模 172921.3 平方米，总投资 38019.5 万元；已竣工的各级残疾人康复设施 40 个，总建设规模 87277 平方米，总投资 26179.7 万元；已竣工的各级残疾人托养服务设施 52 个，总建设规模 125759.7 平方米，总投资 20041 万元。

十、信息化

截至 2018 年底，9 个地市、27 个县级残联开通网站，根据中国残联要求，省残联搭建数据交换站，使用残疾人人口数据与扶贫办建档立卡户数据进行比对。

2018 年甘肃省残疾人事业发展统计公报

2018 年，全省残疾人工作以习近平新时代中国特色社会主义思想为指导，深入学习贯彻党的十九大精神和习近平总书记关于残疾人事业的重要论述，以中国残联、省残联七代会精神为统领，以推进残疾人脱贫攻坚、加快残疾人小康进程为主线，以残联改革和作风建设为抓手，全面实施“十三五”残疾人事业发展规划和各项年度任务，积极争取项目资金投入、着力完善保障服务体系，努力办成了一批利长远、惠民生的实事好事，为加快推进新时代残疾人事业发展，努力创造残疾人更加幸福美好的新生活，迈出了坚实的一步。

一、康复

全面实施精准康复，26.8 万残疾儿童及持证残疾人得到基本康复服务，其中 0-6 岁残疾儿童 0.3 万人。得到康复服务的人中有 3 万视力残疾人、1.7 万听力残疾人、0.4 万言语残疾人、15.7 万肢体残疾人、2.4 万智力残人、1.8 万精神残疾人、2.1 万多重残疾人。全年共为 9.3 万残疾人提供各类辅助器具适配服务。

全省共有残疾人康复机构 129 个，其中残联办 66 个、卫健办 27 个、民政办 4 个、教育办 4 个、民办 23 个、其他 5 个。全省康复机构在岗人员 3094 人，其中，管理人员 458 人，专业技术员 2162 人，其他人员 474 人。

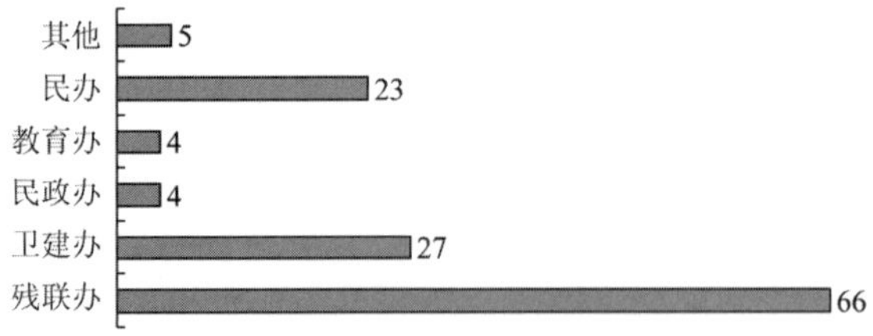

图 1-1　全省残疾人康复机构（单位：个）

二、教育

巩固提升残疾人教育质量实施第二期特殊教育提升计划，积极推进融合教育，着力解决残疾儿童教育问题。实施残疾人事业专项彩票公益金助学项目，为 1137 户家庭经济困难的残疾儿童享受普惠性学前教育提供资助。多渠道争取资金支持，对 182 名残疾儿童给予学前教育资助。

全省共有特殊教育普通高中班（部）2 个。在校生 18 人，毕业生 7 人。残疾人中等职业学校（班）4 个，在校生 371 人，毕业生 71 人，毕业生中 14 人获得职业资格证书。有 594 名被普通高等院校录取。3645 人残疾青壮年文盲接受了扫盲教育。

三、就业

着眼残疾人多形式就业，抓好残疾人按比例就业，完善落实超比例安置残疾人奖励和集中用人单位税收优惠政策；鼓励残疾人自主创业、劳动就业，精准帮扶残疾大学生就业。

全省城乡持证残疾人就业人数为 26.9 万人，其中按比例就业 0.8 万人，集中就业 0.2 万人，个体就业 1.8 万人，公益性岗位就业 0.3 万人，辅助性就业 0.4 万人，灵活就业（含社区、居家就业）6.5 万人，从事农业种养加 17 万人。

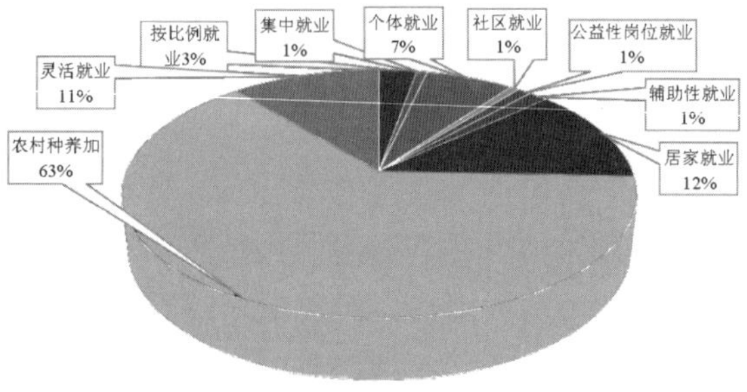

图 3-1　全省城乡持证残疾人就业情况（单位：人）

盲人按摩事业稳步发展，全年培训盲人保健按摩 486 名，盲人医疗按摩 217 名；保健按摩机构达到 334 个，医疗按摩机构达到 23 个。

四、社会保险

全省残疾居民参加城乡社会养老保险人数 108.6 万，24.7 万 60 岁以下参保重度残疾人中，24.2 万得到政府的参保扶助。11 万非重度残疾人享受了个人缴费资助政策。34.8 万残疾人领取养老金。

残疾人托养服务工作稳步推进，残疾人托养服务机构达到94个，其中寄宿制托养服务机构46个，日间照料机构22个，综合性托养服务机构26个，为0.3万残疾人提供了托养服务。2.7万残疾人接受居家服务。64名托养服务管理和服务人员接受了各级各类专业培训。

五、扶贫

贫困残疾人得到有效扶持，4.2万残疾人精准脱贫；残疾人接受实用技术培训2.3万人次。182个残疾人扶贫基地安置0.3万残疾人就业，扶持带动0.5万户残疾人家庭。完成0.6万户农村贫困残疾人危房改造，投入资金1.3亿元。全省东西部扶贫协作落实资金1.3亿元，帮扶建档立卡贫困残疾人1.9万人，帮扶成效显著。

六、宣传文化

组织全省残疾人文化创意精品参加第三届丝绸之路敦煌文博会，全省组织新闻发布会17次，省市级残疾人专题广播节目24个、电视手语栏目14个，省市县三级公共图书馆共设立盲文及盲文有声读物阅览室56个，全省共开展残疾人文化周活动271场次，省市县残联共举办残疾人文化艺术类的比赛及展览30次。

七、体育

2018年举办全省第十届残运会暨第四届特奥运动会。全国残疾人锦标赛我省选手参加了跆拳道、乒乓球、羽毛球、田径，取得了4金7银9铜的成绩，首次参加残奥越野滑雪、冬季两项、高山单板三个冬季项目的比赛，夺得了3金7银7铜的优异成绩。省级组织残疾人体育比赛3次，参加人数2108人。省市县组织残疾人群众体育健身活动430次，参加人数40185人。

八、维权

依法落实惠残政策，贯彻落实“七五”普法规划和“十三五”无障碍建设规划。全省制定或修改省级关于残疾人的专门法规、规章6个，制定或修改保障残疾人权益规范性文件24个。全省县级以上人大开展《中华人民共和国残疾人保障法》执法检查和专题调研19次；政协开展视察和专题调研21次。开展普法宣传教育活动3次。

全省共成立残疾人法律救助工作协调机构102个，建立残疾人法律救助工作站102个。全省残疾人法律救助工作站办理案件111件。

残疾人参政议政工作得到加强，各地残联协助人大代表、政协委员提出议案、建议、提案34件，办理议案、建议、提案22件。

无障碍建设法规、标准进一步完善。省市县无障碍环境建设与管理法规、政府令和规范性文件共出台了39个；101个地市、县开展无障碍环境建设；开展无障碍环境建设检查54次，组织无障碍环境建设工作培训175人次。

九、组织建设

全省市（州）、县（市、区）全部建立残联。乡镇（街道）残联已建1369个，社区（村）残协已建16075个。省市县乡残联工作人员达4208人，乡镇（街道）、村（社区）选聘残疾人专职委员达1.9万。各市州残联配备了残疾人领导干部11人，县级残联配备了残疾人领导干部72人。

全省共建立各类残疾人专门协会510个，其中省级专门协会5个，市级专门协会75个，县级专门协会已建430个。助残社会组织共有43个。

十、服务设施

2018年底，已竣工的综合服务设施（含办公楼）94个，总建筑规模997.6万平方米，总投资3.1亿元；2018年中央预算内投资项目康复设施、托养设施已全部开工建设。

十一、信息化

落实省政府关于“放管服”改革要求，大力推进“网上办事”，为更多的残疾人在网上办理残疾人证，实现了让“数据多跑腿，残疾人少跑路”。全省残疾人人口基础数据库办理残疾人证76.9万，开展了第三代智能化残疾人证换发试点工作。甘肃省残疾人联合会门户网站在全国省级残联网站评测中位列第四。网站全年刊发政务信息2949条，中国残联网站采用2696条，采用率达91%。

2018 年青海省残疾人事业发展统计公报

2018 年，在省委、省政府的坚强领导和中国残联的有力指导下，青海省残联认真学习习近平总书记关于残疾人事业的重要论述，围绕实现“全面建成小康社会，残疾人一个也不能少”的目标，聚焦完成加快残疾人小康进程的各项业务指标，努力推动全省残疾事业再创新业绩。

一、康复

2018 年，7.7 万名残疾儿童及持证残疾人得到基本康复服务，其中包括 0-6 岁残疾儿童 1226 人。得到康复服务的持证残疾人中，有视力残疾人 1.1 万名、听力残疾人 9430 名、言语残疾人 851 名、肢体残疾人 4.3 万名、智力残疾人 5627 名、精神残疾人 2408 名、多重残疾人 4702 名。全年共为 3.1 万残疾人提供各类辅助器具适配服务。

截至 2018 年底，有残疾人康复机构 31 个，其中，9 个机构提供视力残疾康复服务，11 个提供听力言语残疾康复服务，20 个提供肢体残疾康复服务，19 个提供智力残疾康复服务，6 个提供精神残疾康复服务，16 个提供孤独症儿童康复服务，15 个提供辅助器具服务。康复机构在岗人员 405 人，其中，管理人员 73 人，专业技术人员 242 人，其他人员 90 人。

二、教育

残疾人事业专项彩票公益金助学项目的实施，为 207 名家庭经济困难的残疾儿童享受普惠性学前教育提供资助。

共有特殊教育普通高中班（部）1 个，在校生 179 人，其中盲生 179 人。残疾人中等职业学校（班）1 个，在校生 354 人，毕业生 47 人。有 150 名残疾人被普通高等院校录取。

200 名残疾青壮年文盲接受了扫盲教育。

三、就业

城乡持证残疾人就业人数为 4.8 万人，其中按比例就业 1880 人，集中就业 1999 人，个体就业 2976 人，公益性岗位就业 948 人，辅助性就业 582 人，灵活就业（含社区、居家就业）1.5 万人，从事农业种养加 2.5 万人。

培训盲人保健按摩人员 214 名、盲人医疗按摩人员 105 名；保健按摩机构达到 146 个，医疗按摩机构达到 10 个；18 人获得盲人医疗按摩人员初级职务任职资格，3 人获得中级职务任职资格。

四、社保保障

截至 2018 年底，残疾居民参加城乡社会养老保险人数 13 万名，4.4 万名 60 岁以下参保重度残疾人中，4.3 万名得到政府的参保扶助，享受代缴比例达到 99.2%。3 万名非重度残疾人享受了个人缴费资助政策。5.2 万人领取养老金。

残疾人托养服务工作稳步推进，残疾人托养服务机构达到 45 个，其中寄宿制托养服务机构 15 个，日间照料机构 10 个，综合性托养服务机构 20 个，为 1358 名残疾人提供了托养服务。1175 名残疾人接受居家服务。63 名托养服务管理和服务人员接受了各级各类专业培训。

五、扶贫

贫困残疾人得到有效扶持，9355 名残疾人退出建档立卡；残疾人接受实用技术培训 6826 人次。

77 名农村残疾人获得康复扶贫贴息贷款扶持。60 个残疾人扶贫基地安置 877 名残疾人就业，扶持带动 960 户残疾人家庭。

共完成 1307 户农村贫困残疾人危房改造，投入资金 1070 万元。

六、宣传文化

截至 2018 年底，共有省级残疾人专题广播节目 1 个、电视手语栏目 1 个；地市级电视手语栏目 7 个。

省地县三级公共图书馆共设立盲文及盲文有声

读物阅览室12个，共开展残疾人文化周活动83场次；省地两级残联共举办残疾人文化艺术类的比赛及展览11次，共有各类残疾人艺术团1个。

七、维权

2018年，制定或修改关于残疾人的专门法规、规章地市级1个；制定或修改保障残疾人权益的规范性文件地市级2个、县级1个。全省县级以上人大开展《中华人民共和国残疾人保障法》执法检查和专题调研2次；政协开展视察和专题调研3次。开展省级普法宣传教育活动4次，2100人参加。

截至2018年底，全省成立残疾人法律救助工作协调机构47个，建立残疾人法律救助工作站43个。

残疾人参政议政工作得到加强，各地残联协助人大代表、政协委员提出议案、建议、提案16件，办理议案、建议、提案15件。

无障碍建设法规、标准进一步完善。共出台了地市、县级无障碍环境建设与管理规范性文件3个；11个地市、县系统开展无障碍环境建设；开展无障碍环境建设检查28次，无障碍培训23人次。

八、组织建设

2018年，市县乡共成立残联438个，各地市已建残联8个，县（市、区）残联已建46个，乡镇（街道）残联已建384个；已建社区（村）残协4335个。

省市县乡残联工作人员1291人，乡镇（街道）、村（社区）选聘残疾人专职委员总计2138名。地市级残联配备了残疾人领导干部4人，县级残联配备了残疾人干部17人。

共建立省级及以下各类残疾人专门协会267个，其中省级专门协会已建5个，市级专门协会已建40个，县级专门协会已建222个。助残社会组织共有6个。

九、服务设施

截至2018年底，已竣工的各级残疾人综合服务设施19个，总建设规模3.9万平方米，总投资12781.7万元；已竣工的各级残疾人康复设施6个，总建设规模3.4万平方米，总投资13590万元；已竣工的各级残疾人托养服务设施30个，总建设规模5.8万平方米，总投资16531.2万元。

十、信息化

截至2018年底，4个地市、8个县级残联开通网站。

2018 年宁夏回族自治区残疾人事业发展统计公报

2018 年，全区残联系统认真学习贯彻习近平新时代中国特色社会主义思想和习近平总书记关于残疾人事业的重要论述，围绕实现“全面建成小康社会，残疾人一个也不能少”的目标，着力打赢打好贫困残疾人脱贫攻坚战，努力开创新时代残疾人事业发展新局面，推动全区残疾人事业发展取得新进展。

一、康复

2018 年，102905 名残疾儿童及持证残疾人得到基本康复服务，其中 0-6 岁残疾儿童 1511 人。得到康复服务的持证残疾人中，有视力残疾人 13482 名，听力残疾人 10102 名，言语残疾人 1391 名，肢体残疾人 50237 名，智力残疾人 9899 名，精神残疾人 11112 名，多重残疾人 6327 名。40575 残疾人得到各类辅助器具适配服务。

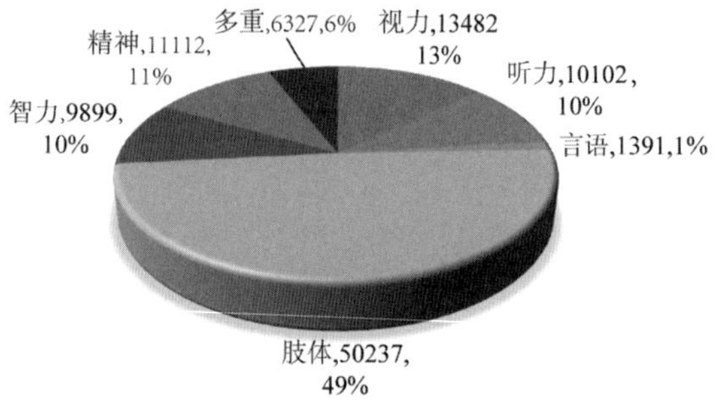

图 1-1　2018 年各类残疾人得到康复服务情况

截至 2018 年底，全区有残疾人康复机构 30 个，其中：8 个机构提供视力残疾康复服务，7 个提供听力言语残疾康复服务，22 个提供肢体残疾康复服务，23 个提供智力残疾康复服务，9 个提供精神残疾康复服务，15 个提供孤独症儿童康复服务，10 个提供辅助器具服务。康复机构在岗人员 567 人，其中：管理人员 89 人，专业技术人员 390 人，其他人员 88 人。

二、教育

2018 年，全区各地实施残疾人事业专项彩票公益金助学项目，多渠道争取资金支持，共资助了 425 名家庭经济困难的学前教育残疾儿童和 179 名大中专学生。有 166 名残疾人被普通高等院校录取，683 名残疾青壮年文盲接受了扫盲教育。

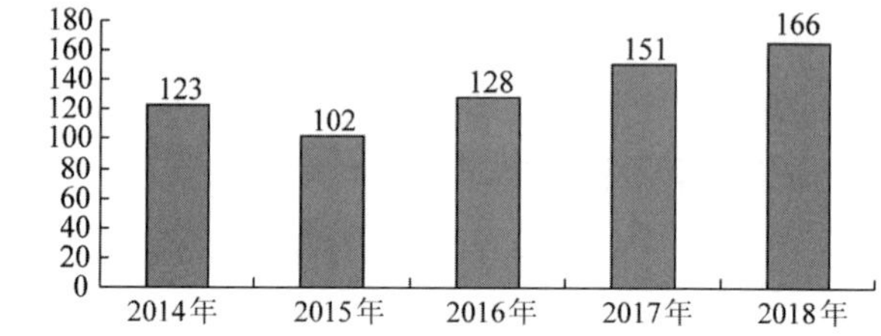

图 2-1　2014—2018 年全国普通高等院校录取残疾考生情况

全区现有特殊教育普通高中学校 1 所，在校生 284 人，其中：聋生 184 人、盲生 100 人。

三、就业

2018 年，城乡持证残疾人新增就业 2494 人，其中，城镇新增就业 813 人，农村新增就业 1681 人；城乡新增培训残疾人 3844 人。

全区城乡持证残疾人就业人数为 62115 人，其中：按比例就业 7306 人、集中就业 1782 人、个体就业 5002 人、公益性岗位就业 646 人、辅助性就业 1266 人、灵活就业（含社区、居家就业）20631 人、从事农业种养加 25482 人。各级残联建立残疾人就业服务机构 20 个，从事就业服务人员 97 人。

截至 2018 年底，全区建立医疗按摩机构 12 个，保健按摩机构 271 个，盲人保健按摩就业 438 人，盲人医疗按摩就业 75 人。2018 年，全区共培训盲人保健按摩人员 119 人，盲人医疗按摩人员 164 人。

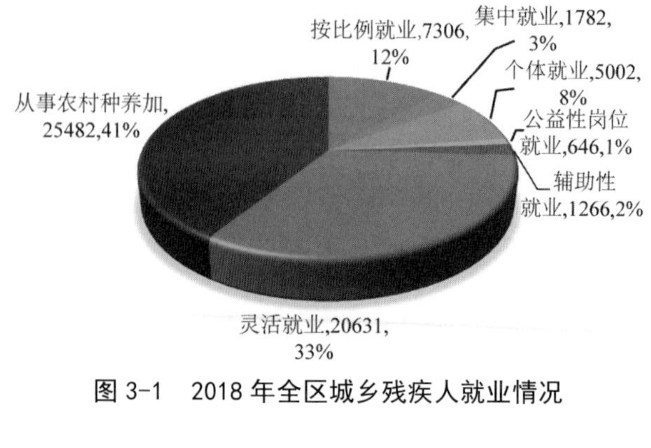

图 3-1　2018 年全区城乡残疾人就业情况

四、社会保障

截至 2018 年底，残疾居民参加城乡社会养老保险人数 214651 名，57044 名 60 岁以下参保重度残疾人中，56940 名得到政府的参保扶助，享受代缴比例达到 99.8%。31469 名非重度残疾人享受了个人缴费资助政策。101754 人领取养老金。

全区残疾人托养服务机构 67 个，其中寄宿制托养服务机构 21 个，日间照料机构 42 个，综合性托养服务机构 4 个，为 1775 名残疾人提供了托养服务，5509 名残疾人接受居家服务。138 名托养服务管理和服务人员接受了各级各类专业培训。

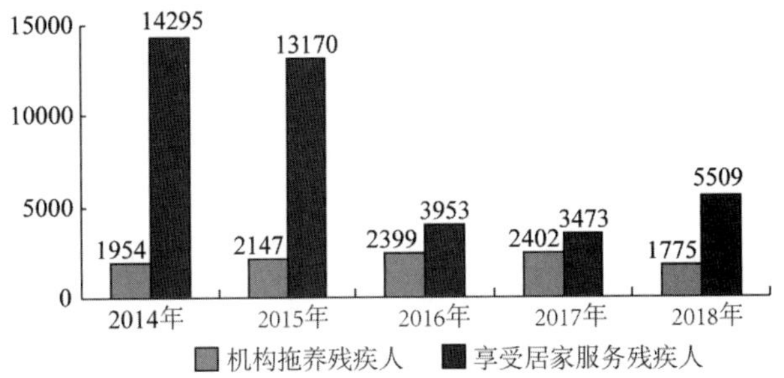

图 4-1　2014—2018 年享受托养和居家服务残疾人情况

五、扶贫开发

2018 年，贫困残疾人得到有效扶持，9485 名残疾人脱贫退出建档立卡；6311 人次残疾人接受实用技术培训；748 名农村残疾人获得康复扶贫贴息贷款扶持；36 个残疾人扶贫基地安置 496 名残疾人就业，扶持带动贫困残疾人家庭 1676 户。

全区共完成农村贫困残疾人危房改造 609 户，其中建档立卡贫困残疾人 252 户，共投入资金 1554.63 万元。

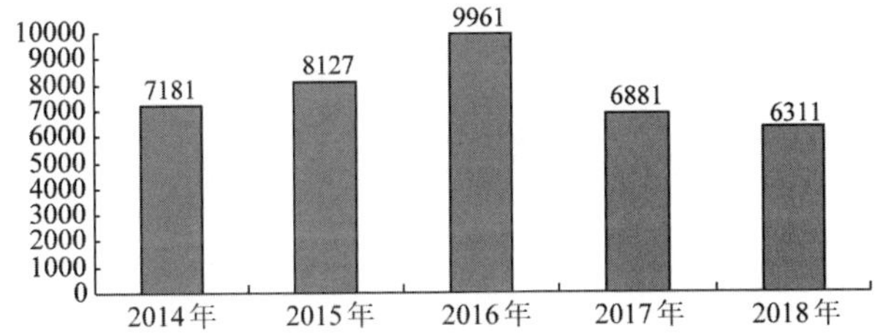

图 5-1　2014—2018 年农村贫困残疾人接受实用技术培训情况

六、宣传文化

截至 2018 年底，共有自治区级广播电台残疾人专题节目 1 个，电视台手语栏目 1 个，残疾人事业新闻宣传促进会 1 个，官方微信 1 个；市级广播电台残疾人专题节目 1 个，电视台手语栏目 5 个。自治区、市、县（区）三级公共图书馆共设立盲文及盲文有声读物阅览室 23 个，共有各类残疾人艺术团 3 个。

2018 年，自治区举行新闻发布会 8 次，各地组织开展残疾人文化周活动 61 场次；自治区、市两级残联共举办残疾人文化艺术类比赛及展览21次。

七、体育

2018 年，全区组织残疾人群众体育健身活动 44 次，参加活动 3937 人次。建立残疾人体育健身示范点 5 个（累计达到 14 个），聘任残疾人体育社会指导员 11 人（累计达到 20 人）、教练员 4 人。参加国内外残疾人体育赛事 12 次，参赛运动员 150 人次，获得 33 金、22 银和 20 铜的好成绩。

八、维权

2018 年，2 个地市级制订出台了保障残疾人权益的规范性文件。自治区、市、县（区）三级人大开展《中华人民共和国残疾人保障法》执法检查或专题调研 5 次，政协视察或专题调研 3 次。自治区组织普法宣传教育活动 5 次，450 人参加了活动。

截至 2018 年底，全区成立残疾人法律救助工作协调机构 23 个，建立残疾人法律救助工作站 22 个。各级残联全年接待残疾人来访 3666 人次，处理来信 39 件、来电 522 个，网上投诉 87 件。

残疾人参政议政工作得到加强，各级选举人大代表 35 人、政协委员 28 人。各地残联全年协助人大代表、政协委员提出议案、建议、提案 9 件，办理议案、建议、提案 10 件。

无障碍建设法规、标准进一步完善。3 个市、县出台了无障碍环境建设与管理规范性文件；24 个市、县（区）系统开展无障碍环境建设；开展无障碍环境建设检查 31 次，无障碍培训 158 人次。2738 户残疾人家庭接受了无障碍改造。14002 人获得机动轮椅车燃油补贴。

九、组织建设

截至 2018 年底，市、县、乡三级共成立残联组织 263 个，各市已全部建立残联，95.5%的县（市、区）、所有乡镇（街道）已建立残联，95.6%的村

（社区）已建残协，共 1993 个。

自治区、市、县、乡残联实有工作人员 875 人，乡镇（街道）、村（社区）选聘残疾人专职委员总计 1326 名，分别占 100%和 47.2%。80%的地市级残联配备了残疾人领导干部，57.1%的县级残联配备了残疾人干部。

全区共建立各类残疾人专门协会 133 个，其中自治区、市级各类专门协会已建比例为 100%，县级为 98.1%。全区助残社会组织共有 40 个。

十、服务设施

截至 2018 年底，全区残疾人综合服务设施累计投入使用项目 15 个，建设规模 30450.28 平方米，总投资 7685.24 万元。在建项目 1 个，建设规模 5616.44 平方米，总投资 1800 万元。

残疾人托养设施建设累计投入使用项目 2 个，建设规模 4000 平方米，总投资 1021 万元。竣工未投入使用设施 5 个，建设规模 10682 平方米，总投资 3307 万元。在建项目 5 个，建设规模 16132 平方米，总投资 5049 万元。

残疾人康复设施建设累计投入使用项目 4 个，建设规模 45204 平方米，总投资 19031 万元。竣工未投入使用设施 2 个，建设规模 6110 平方米，总投资 1897 万元。在建项目 15 个，建设规模 92920.5 平方米，总投资 29209.17 万元。

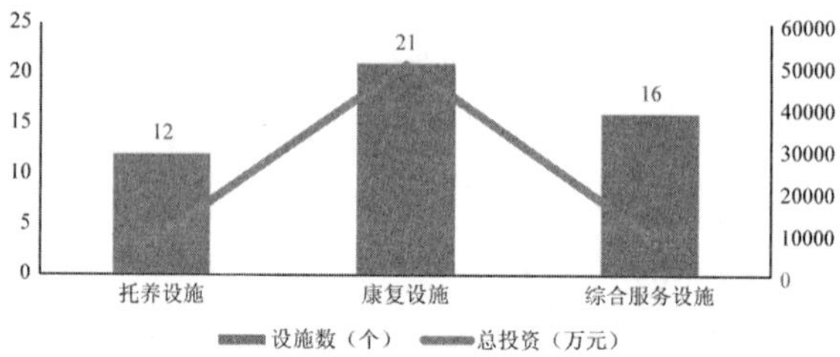

图 10-1　全区残疾人服务设施累计建设情况

十一、信息化

截至 2018 年底，3 个地级市残联、3 个县级残联开通门户网站。全区残疾人人口基础数据库中持证残疾人 227697 人。

2018年新疆维吾尔自治区残疾人事业发展统计公报

2018年，在自治区党委、人民政府的领导和中国残联的指导下，新疆残联紧紧围绕社会稳定和长治久安总目标，按照自治区党委“1+3+3+改革开放”工作部署，着力打赢贫困残疾人脱贫攻坚战，圆满完成各项年度工作任务。

一、康复

2018年，全区全面实施残疾儿童康复救助制度，实施精准康复服务行动，7.8万名残疾儿童及持证残疾人得到基本康复服务，其中0-6岁残疾儿童2342人，得到康复服务的持证残疾人中，有视力残疾人7698名、听力残疾人7131名、言语残疾人420名、肢体残疾人4.2万名、智力残疾人7300名、精神残疾人9536名、多重残疾人4453名。全年共为3.1万名残疾人提供各类辅助器具适配服务。

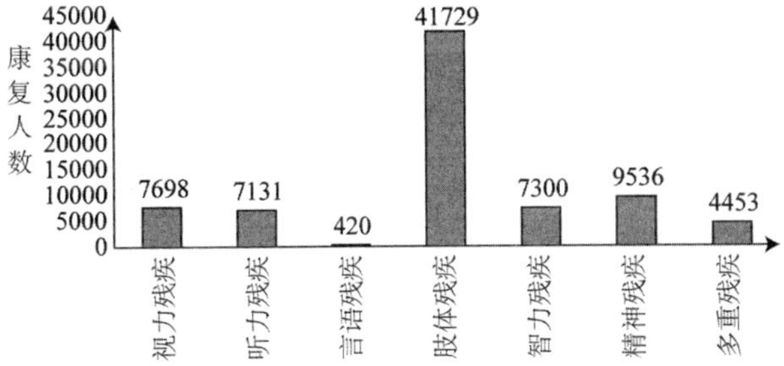

图1-1　各类残疾人接受精准康复服务情况

截至2018年底，全区有残疾人康复机构148个，康复机构在岗人员2486人，其中，管理人员347人，专业技术人员1737人，其他人员402人。

二、教育

全面实施《残疾人教育条例》和《第二期特殊教育提升计划》，有360名残疾人被普通高等院校录取，为180名家庭经济困难的残疾儿童享受普惠性学前教育提供资助。多渠道争取资金支持，对92名残疾儿童给予学前教育资助。

继续实施《“十三五”残疾青壮年文盲扫盲行动方案》，对2767名残疾青壮年进行扫盲教育。

三、就业

截至2018年底，全区城乡持证残疾人就业人数为17.6万人，其中按比例就业2.1万人，集中就业4236人，个体就业1.3万人，公益性岗位就业2752人，辅助性就业1343人，灵活就业（含社区、居家就业）4.2万人，从事农业种养加9.2万人。全区各级残联共走访登记失业残疾人家庭1.8万余户，组织召开残疾人就业援助专场招聘会129场。

开展2018年全国盲人医疗按摩人员资格考试，培训盲人保健按摩人员191名，盲人医疗按摩人员285名；保健按摩机构达到120个，医疗按摩机构达到19个；16人获得盲人医疗按摩人员初级职务任职资格，10人获得中级职务任职资格。

会同人社、扶贫、财政等部门联合制定《自治区助盲就业脱贫行动实施方案》。

四、社会保障

截至2018年底，残疾居民参加城乡社会养老保险人数38万名，9.3万名60岁以下参保重度残疾人中，8.6万名得到政府的参保扶助，享受代缴比例达到92.1%。

残疾人托养服务工作稳步推进，残疾人托养服务机构达到173个，其中寄宿制托养服务机构36个，日间照料机构86个，综合性托养服务机构51个，为6414名残疾人提供了托养服务，有3355名残疾人接受居家服务。15名托养服务管理和服务人员接受各级各类专业培训。

五、扶贫

贫困残疾人得到有效扶持，其中1.7万名残疾人退出建档立卡；接受实用技术培训的残疾人达1.8万人次。

10名农村残疾人获得康复扶贫贴息贷款扶持。全区182个残疾人扶贫基地共安置2078名残疾人就业，扶持带动2557户残疾人家庭。

全年投入资金 15075.1 万元，共完成 1.1 万户农村贫困残疾人危房改造。

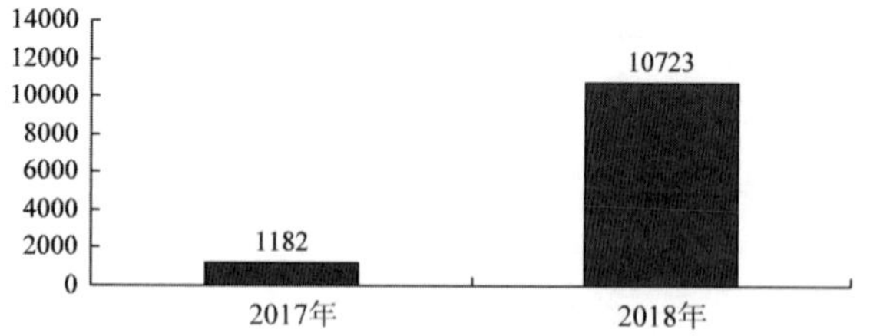

图 5-1　2017-2018 新疆贫困残疾人危房改造情况贫困残疾人危房改革数据（单位：户）

举办了两期全区残联系统扶贫业务培训班，共培训扶贫干部 184 人。与扶贫、民政等部门建立信息共享机制，定期开展基础数据比对，摸清建档立卡贫困残疾人底数。加大督导检查力度，准确掌握建档立卡贫困残疾人实名制纳入、兜底保障、扶贫资金落实情况。

六、宣传文化

截至 2018 年底，共有自治区级残疾人电视手语栏目 1 个，在新疆卫视新闻夜班车开启手语解说栏目；地州市级残疾人专题广播节目 2 个、电视手语栏目 4 个。

在全区县级以上公共图书馆共设立盲文及盲文有声读物阅览室 8 个，开展残疾人文化周活动 135 场次；自治区、地州市两级残联共举办残疾人文化艺术类的比赛及展览 4 次，有各类残疾人艺术团 5 个。

利用“全国助残日”、“残疾预防日”等重要节点，组织开展送文化下乡、文化进社区等系列活动，丰富残疾人精神文化生活。

七、体育

积极开展田径、射箭、冰球等项目集训，在全国类赛事中获得 5 个第一、5 个第二、3 个第三名的好成绩；聋人女子篮球队入围第十届残运会决赛比赛资格；1 名运动员入选国家队并参加在荷兰举行的高山滑雪公开赛。开展残疾人“冰雪运动季”、“特奥日”、“康复体育进家庭”等活动，带动更多残疾人参与健身运动。

八、维权

2018 年，制定、修改保障残疾人权益的规范性文件 2 个。县级以上人大开展《中华人民共和国残疾人保障法》执法检查和专题调研 2 次；开展普法宣传教育活动 5 次，260 人参加；举办自治区级法律培训班 2 次，160 人参加。

截至 2018 年底，成立残疾人法律救助工作协调机构 75 个，建立残疾人法律救助工作站 65 个。

残疾人参政议政工作得到加强，各地残联协助人大代表、政协委员提出议案、建议、提案 14 件，办理议案、建议、提案 6 件。

无障碍建设法规、标准进一步完善。出台 1 个规范性文件；5 个地、县开展无障碍环境建设；开展无障碍环境建设检查 35 次，无障碍培训 161 人次。

九、组织建设

全区共成立残联 985 个，地州市残联 14 个，县市区残联 95 个，乡镇（街道）残联 876 个；社区（村）残协 5960 个。

全区残联共有工作人员 2302 人，乡镇（街道）、村（社区）选聘残疾人专职委员总计 2975 名。地州市配备残疾人领导干部的残联 11 个，县市区配备残疾人干部的残联 54 个。

全区共建立各类残疾人专门协会 507 个，其中自治区专门协会 5 个，地州市专门协会 68 个，县市区专门协会 434 个。全区共有助残社会组织 17 个。

各专门协会进一步活跃，先后开展“自强与助残”巡回演讲、“你是我的眼”残健同行公益晚会等活动 30 余次。

全面实施新的《残疾人证管理办法》，在克拉玛依市开展智能化残疾人证试点工作。

十、服务设施

截至 2018 年底，已竣工的各级残疾人综合服务设施 78 个，总建设规模 20.3 万平方米，总投资 56363.3 万元；已竣工的各级残疾人康复设施 23 个，总建设规模 4.5 万平方米，总投资 11252.0 万元；已竣工的各级残疾人托养服务设施 39 个，总建设规模 4.1 万平方米，总投资 9542.2 万元。

十一、信息化

全区门户网站共发布各类信息及工作动态 3130

条，图片2000多张，有4个地市、6个县级残联开通网站；新疆残疾人人口综合服务平台建设项目已基本完成，与自治区扶贫办、卫健委、公安厅、民政厅、人社厅、住建厅、教育厅签署了数据交换共享协议，定期进行数据交换。

2018 年新疆生产建设兵团残疾人事业发展统计公报

2018 年，新疆兵团残联系统认真学习习近平总书记关于残疾人事业的重要论述，围绕实现“全面建成小康社会，残疾人一个也不能少”的目标，着力打赢打好贫困残疾人脱贫攻坚战，努力开创新时代残疾人事业发展新局面。

一、康复

2018 年，10908 名残疾儿童及持证残疾人得到基本康复服务，其中包括 0-6 岁残疾儿童 98 人。得到康复服务的持证残疾人中，有视力残疾人 661 名、听力残疾人 467 名、肢体残疾人 4606 名、智力残疾人 1038 名、精神残疾人 3811 名、多重残疾人 325 名。全年共为 3161 名残疾人提供各类辅助器具适配服务。

截至 2018 年底，有残疾人康复机构 35 个，其中，17 个机构提供视力残疾康复服务，17 个提供听力言语残疾康复服务，30 个提供肢体残疾康复服务，7 个提供智力残疾康复服务，10 个提供精神残疾康复服务，4 个提供孤独症儿童康复服务，7 个提供辅助器具服务。康复机构在岗人员 810 人，其中，管理人员 105 人，专业技术人员 588 人，其他人员 117 人。

二、教育

残疾人事业专项彩票公益金助学项目的实施，为 45 名家庭经济困难的残疾儿童享受普惠性学前教育提供资助。多渠道争取资金支持，对 14 名残疾儿童给予学前教育资助。有 27 名残疾人被普通高等院校录取，155 名残疾青壮年文盲接受了扫盲教育。

三、就业

城乡持证残疾人就业人数为 23827 人，其中按比例就业 10805 人，集中就业 1064 人，个体就业 2817 人，公益性岗位就业 384 人，辅助性就业 305 人，灵活就业（含社区、居家就业）5134 人，从事农业种养加 3318 人。

培训盲人保健按摩人员 2 名、盲人医疗按摩人员 3 名；保健按摩机构达到 17 个，医疗按摩机构达到 2 个；5 人获得中级职务任职资格。

四、社会保障

截至 2018 年底，残疾居民参加城乡社会养老保险人数 21697 名，8190 名 60 岁以下参保重度残疾人中，7616 名得到政府的参保扶助，享受代缴比例达到 93.0%。2866 名非重度残疾人享受了个人缴费资助政策。3340 人领取养老金。

残疾人托养服务工作稳步推进，残疾人托养服务机构达到 49 个，其中寄宿制托养服务机构 24 个，日间照料机构 6 个，综合性托养服务机构 19 个，为 1563 名残疾人提供了托养服务。2353 名残疾人接受居家服务。39 名托养服务管理和服务人员接受了各级各类专业培训。

五、扶贫

贫困残疾人得到有效扶持，1447 名残疾人退出建档立卡；残疾人接受实用技术培训 4676 人次。50 个残疾人扶贫基地安置 606 名残疾人就业，扶持带动 1150 户残疾人家庭。

六、宣传文化

截至 2018 年底，共有省级残疾人专题电视手语栏目 1 个；省地县三级公共图书馆共设立盲文及盲文有声读物阅览室 1 个，共开展残疾人文化周活动 183 场次。

七、维权

截至 2018 年底，成立残疾人法律救助工作协调机构 4 个，建立残疾人法律救助工作站 3 个。

残疾人参政议政工作得到加强，各地残联协助人大代表、政协委员提出议案、建议、提案 1 件。

八、组织建设

2018 年，市县乡共成立残联 14 个，各地市已建残联 12 个，县（市、区）残联已建 2 个，乡镇（街道）残联已建 0 个；社区（村）已建残协 1 个。

省市县乡残联工作人员 92 人，乡镇（街道）、村（社区）选聘残疾人专职委员总计 94 名。地市级配备了残疾人领导干部的残联 1 个，县级配备了残疾人干部的残联 1 个。

共建立省级及以下各类残疾人专门协会 36 个，其中省级专门协会已建 5 个，市级专门协会已建 31 个，助残社会组织共有 1 个。

九、服务设施

截至 2018 年底，已竣工的各级残疾人综合服务设施 9 个，总建设规模 6183.0 平方米，总投资 925.0 万元；已竣工的各级残疾人康复设施 10 个，总建设规模 44287.2 平方米，总投资 13914.8 万元；已竣工的各级残疾人托养服务设施 34 个，总建设规模 53207.0 平方米，总投资 10436.3 万元。

2018年黑龙江垦区残疾人事业发展统计公报

2018年，黑龙江垦区残联以习近平新时代中国特色社会主义思想为指导，深入学习贯彻习近平总书记重要指示，在中国残联和农垦总局党委的领导之下，紧紧围绕实现“全面建成小康社会，残疾人一个也不能少”的目标，着力推进残联各项工作。

一、康复

2018年，1039名残疾儿童及持证残疾人得到基本康复服务，其中包括0-6岁残疾儿童2人。得到康复服务的持证残疾人中，有视力残疾人24名、听力残疾人18名、肢体残疾人637名、智力残疾人10名、精神残疾人329名、多重残疾人21名。全年共为616名残疾人提供各类辅助器具适配服务。

截至2018年底，有残疾人康复机构71个，其中，1个提供听力言语残疾康复服务，54个提供肢体残疾康复服务，3个提供精神残疾康复服务，37个提供辅助器具服务。康复机构在岗人员895人，其中，管理人员140人，专业技术人员616人，其他人员139人。

二、就业

城乡持证残疾人就业人数为10185人，其中按比例就业4249人，集中就业97人，个体就业1045人，公益性岗位就业136人，辅助性就业20人，灵活就业（含社区、居家就业）2559人，从事农业种养加2079人。

保健按摩机构1个，5人获得盲人医疗按摩人员初级职务任职资格，1人获得中级职务任职资格。

三、社会保障

截至2018年底，残疾居民参加城乡社会养老保险人数31名，3名60岁以下参保重度残疾人中，3名得到政府的参保扶助，享受代缴比例达到100%，10人领取养老金。

残疾人托养服务工作稳步推进，残疾人托养服务机构达到11个，其中寄宿制托养服务机构8个，日间照料机构1个，综合性托养服务机构2个，为430名残疾人提供了托养服务。25名残疾人接受居家服务。

四、扶贫

贫困残疾人得到有效扶持，残疾人接受实用技术培训1265人次。

3个残疾人扶贫基地安置14名残疾人就业，扶持带动3户残疾人家庭。

五、维权

2018年，开展省级普法宣传教育活动1次，132人参加；截至2018年底，成立残疾人法律救助工作协调机构6个。

无障碍建设法规、标准进一步完善。共出台了2个省、地市、县级无障碍环境建设与管理法规、政府令和规范性文件；2个地市、县系统开展无障碍环境建设；开展无障碍环境建设检查1次，无障碍培训58人次。

六、组织建设

2018年，市县乡共成立残联121个，各地市已建残联10个，县（市、区）残联已建111个，社区（村）已建残协68个。

省市县乡残联工作人员230人，乡镇（街道）、村（社区）选聘残疾人专职委员总计56名，县级配备了残疾人干部的残联11个。

共建立省级及以下各类残疾人专门协会585个，其中省级专门协会已建5个，市级专门协会已建45个，县级专门协会已建535个。

七、服务设施建设

截至 2018 年底，已竣工的各级残疾人综合服务设施 6 个，总建设规模 4949.4 平方米，总投资 608.6 万元；已竣工的各级残疾人康复设施 5 个，总建设规模 39000.0 平方米，总投资 13880.0 万元；已竣工的各级残疾人托养服务设施 4 个，总建设规模 12520.8 平方米，总投资 6777.0 万元。

6

附 录

Appendix

关于使用2010年末全国残疾人总数及各类、不同残疾等级人数的通知

残联〔2012〕25号

各省、自治区、直辖市及计划单列市残联，新疆生产建设兵团残联，黑龙江农垦总局残联：

根据第六次全国人口普查我国总人口数，及第二次全国残疾人抽样调查我国残疾人占全国总人口的比例和各类残疾人占残疾人总人数的比例，推算了2010年末我国残疾人总人数及各类、不同等级的残疾人数，现通知如下：

全国残疾人总数为8502万人。

各类残疾人的人数分别为：视力残疾1263万人；听力残疾2054万人；言语残疾130万人；肢体残疾2472万人；智力残疾568万人；精神残疾629万人；多重残疾1386万人。

各残疾等级人数分别为：重度残疾2518万人；中度和轻度残疾人5984万人。

以上数据可在工作中使用并对外公开。

中国残疾人联合会

二〇一二年三月五日

中国残联统计调查项目目录

审批项目一览表

统计调查项目名称	批准文号	有效期截止时间
中国残疾人事业统计调查制度	国统制[2018] 82 号	2021 年 6 月
全国残疾人基本服务状况和需求信息数据动态更新	国统制[2019] 16 号	2022 年 1 月
全国残疾人家庭收入状况调查制度	国统制[2018] 60 号	2021 年 5 月

中国残疾人联合会文件

残联发[2006]1 号

关于印发《全国残联系统统计工作管理办法》的通知

各省、自治区、直辖市及计划单列市残联，新疆生产建设兵团残联、黑龙江农垦总局残联：

为了加强统计工作的管理，规范统计调查行为，提高统计调查的整体效益，充分发挥统计工作的服务和监督作用，中国残联依据《中华人民共和国统计法》、《中华人民共和国统计法实施细则》、《部门统计调查管理暂行办法》，结合工作实际，对原有的《中国残联系统统计工作暂行规定》、《中国残联系统专项业务统计调查项目管理暂行办法》、《中国残联机关统计资料管理暂行办法》等进行了修订和整合，制定了《全国残联系统统计工作管理办法》，现予以印发，请遵照执行。

中国残疾人联合会

二〇〇六年一月三日

全国残联系统统计工作管理办法

一、总　则

第一条　为了科学、有效地组织全国残联系统统计工作，规范统计调查行为，提高统计调查的整体效益，充分发挥统计工作的服务和监督作用，依据《中华人民共和国统计法》（以下简称《统计法》）、《中华人民共和国统计法实施细则》（以下简称《实施细则》）、《部门统计调查管理暂行办法》，结合工作实际，制定本办法。

第二条　全国残联系统统计工作的基本任务是：对全国残疾人事业的发展状况和残联系统的业务工作进行统计调查、统计分析、统计预测和统计监督，为国家和各级人民政府制定与残疾人事业相关的政策、法规提供依据，为领导运筹决策和残联系统工作的发展提供有效的服务。

第三条　全国残联系统统计工作由：中国残疾人事业统计年报制度、中国残疾人事业统计快报制度、中国残疾人事业基础统计台账制度、专项业务统计调查工作组成。

第四条　各级残联应加强统计现代化建设，积极利用信息技术手段，使残疾人事业统计数据更加科学、准确、及时，逐步实现残疾人事业统计数据的电子化和统计数据的社会共享与服务。

二、统计机构、职责和统计人员

第五条　全国残联系统统计工作实行统一领导、分级负责。中国残联负责全国残疾人事业统计工作的组织、协调与管理，并对地方残联统计工作进行指导，具体由中国残联设置的统计机构负责组织实施。地方各级残联的统计工作由地方各级残联设置的统计机构或统计主管部门负责管理和组织实施，并接受上级残联统计机构和同级人民政府统计部门的指导、监督与管理。

第六条　中国残联的统计机构设在中国残联信息中心，负责组织、协调和管理全国残联系统的统计工作。其主要职责是：制定残疾人事业统计调查计划和项目，制定统计标准；组织协调各级残联搜集、整理、提供统计资料，管理统计资料的发布，开展统计分析、统计预测和统计监督工作；指导、检查全国残联系统统计工作，组织统计业务经验交流，开展全国残联系统统计科学研究；做好统计人员培训工作；制订全国残联系统统计工作现代化规划。

各省级残联应设置统计机构或明确统计主管部门并设专职统计人员，负责指导本行政区域内各级残联统计工作，组织管理本级残联的统计工作。其主要职责是：在完成好中国残联和上级残联下达的各项统计调查工作的同时，为本级残疾人事业提供各项统计数据，并开展统计调查活动。

各地级市残联应明确统计主管部门并设专（兼）职统计人员，其主要职责是：在完成好中国残联和上级残联下达的各项统计调查工作的同时，为本级残疾人事业提供各项统计数据，并开展统计调查活动。

各县级残联应明确统计工作主管部门或主管负责人，确定兼职统计人员。其主要职责是：做好基础数据工作，建立统计台账，完成好中国残联和上级残联下达的统计调查任务，为本级残疾人事业提供各项统计数据，并开展统计调查活动。

第七条　各级残联统计人员应保持相对稳定。统计人员的调动，应当征得本级统计主管部门或统计工作负责人的同意；省级专职统计人员的调动，应当征得中国残联统计机构的同意。统计人员调动工作或离职，应当由经过统计业务培训、能够胜任统计业务工作的人员接替，并办理交接手续。各级残联的统计人员应取得同级人民政府统计机构颁发的统计上岗证，具有残联系统业务知识和计算机操作能力。

三、统计报表制度的编制、修改与审批

第八条　中国残疾人事业统计年报、快报制度和统计台账制度中的指标、指标涵义、调查范围、

分类目录、计算方法和统计报表表式、统计编码以及报送时间，由中国残联统一规定，按照国家统计局的要求报送国家统计局进行审批备案。按规定程序经国家统计局批准或备案的统计报表，在报表的右上角标明制表机关名称、表号、批准或备案机关名称及其批准文号。被调查的部门、人员应当准确、及时地按报表规定填报。

不符合前款规定的统计报表（包括以搜集数字为主的调查提纲）是非法报表，被调查的部门可以拒绝填报。

第九条　中国残疾人事业统计年报、快报和统计台账应根据中国残疾人事业发展的需要及时进行调整和补充。中国残联各业务部门因工作需要，调整和补充有关指标时，应进行充分论证并与中国残联统计管理部门联系与协商，经中国残联理事会批准后，报国家统计局批准或备案。

四、统计台账管理

第十条　为了规范中国残联系统统计工作，做到依法统计，发挥统计服务和监督作用，根据《中华人民共和国统计法》和国家相关统计工作的规定，中国残联将制定中国残疾人事业统计台账制度，加强统计台账的管理与数据的报送。

第十一条　中国残疾人事业统计台账（卡）充分利用电子网络化的方式、将科学合理、准确实用的动态管理，与中国残疾人事业统计报表制度相衔接。台账填写内容要符合法律法规政策的要求，填写对象真实、准确；先填卡，后建帐，做到由台账中提取统计数字。

第十二条　各级残联必须依据中国残疾人事业统计台账（卡）中的数据，报送中国残疾人事业统计快报、年报和各项专项业务统计调查的统计报表，做到填报统计报表的数据全面、准确、及时、数出一门。

第十三条　中国残疾人事业统计台账在统一格式、统一软件下实施，由各级地方残联统计人员协调业务部门和人员用计算机或纸质台账、台卡方式进行专门管理。统计人员发生变动时，要严格履行交接手续。

第十四条　省级、地（市）级残联都应建立电子化台账。有条件的县级残联也要实行电子化台账，各级残联应积极推动电子化台账建设，加强统计台账的管理工作。在没有实行全面电子化台账之前，将实行电子化台账和纸质台账、台卡的同时保存。

第十五条　中国残疾人事业统计台账、台卡按中国残疾人事业统计报表逐级汇总上报。

五、专项业务统计调查管理

第十六条　中国残联和地方各级残联开展的专项业务统计调查，以及残联各业务部门与其他部门或单位联合组织实施的统计调查，其调查的统计指标与中国残联年报、快报指标交叉重复或需要对外公布统计数据的统计调查，均属于专项业务统计调查管理范畴。

第十七条　中国残联系统各级统计机构统一管理和协调本级业务部门专项业务统计调查。

第十八条　专项业务统计调查项目必须符合国家统计局《部门统计调查项目管理暂行办法》的基本原则与要求。专项业务统计调查项目的立项必须有充分的理由。调查要有明确的目的和资料使用范围。调查项目应当与中国残联职能范围和各项业务工作相对应。

第十九条　中国残联系统各级统计机构通过建立审批备案制度、调查项目公布制度、跟踪检查制度、举报制度，对会内专项业务统计调查进行管理。

第二十条　专项业务统计调查项目中的统计标准和分类必须与政府综合统计机构规定使用的标准和分类相一致。涉及政府综合统计机构规定以外的专业标准和分类，要与国家有关标准或行业标准相一致。尚无国家标准和行业标准的，必须严格按照标准化及分类科学的原则进行归纳和设计，并在使用前征求政府综合统计机构的意见。

第二十一条　中国残联新增设的统计调查项目在制定好统计调查方案后，须提交中国残联统计机构审核，报国家统计局批准后统一组织实施。

地方残联新增设的统计调查项目，由本级残联统计机构统一管理，报上级残联统计机构和同级人民政府统计局批准后组织实施。地方残联制发的统计调查表内容、指标涵义、计算方法、完成期限等，均不得与中国残联制发的有关统计调查表相抵触。

六、统计资料的管理与发布

第二十二条 残联系统统计资料实行归口管理。全国性残联系统 统计资料，由中国残联统计机构统一管理；地方性残联系统统计资料，由地方残联统计机构或统计人员统一管理。统计机构和统计人员必须建立统计工作责任制和统计资料整理、审查、管理制度，不断提高工作质量和工作效率，保证残联系统统计资料的准确、及时。

各级残联的文件、报告、简报、情况反映、信息等引用综合性的统计数字，必须经本级统计机构或统计人员复核。对外提供和公布的统计资料，必须经本级统计机构或统计人员统一复核和办理并由主管理事长批准。任何部门和个人不得擅自公开和使用未经正式公布的残联系统统计资料。

第二十三条 各级残联统计机构、统计人员必须建立健全统计资料档案，对原始记录、统计台账和综合分析等统计资料，按有关规定保管，不得损坏。对于属于国家秘密的残联系统统计资料，要按照《中华人民共和国保守国家秘密法》、国家统计局《统计资料保密管理办法》等有关规定，妥善保管。

七、奖励和惩罚

第二十四条 各级残联对有下列表现之一的残联统计机构或者人员，给予表扬或奖励：

一、在改革和完善残联系统统计制度、统计方法等方面，有重要贡献的；

二、在完成规定的残联系统统计调查任务，保障残联系统统计资料的准确性、及时性方面，做出显著成绩的；

三、在进行残联系统统计分析、统计预测和统计监督方面取得重要成绩的；

四、在运用和推广现代化信息技术方面，有显著效果的；

五、在残联系统统计科学研究方面有所创新的；

六、坚持实事求是，依法办事，同违反统计法规和本办法的行为作斗争，表现突出的。

第二十五条 各级残联对有下列行为之一的机构或者人员，给予批评或处分：

一、虚报、瞒报、拒报残联系统统计资料的；

二、伪造、篡改残联系统统计资料的；

三、无故迟报残联系统统计资料的；

四、侵犯统计机构、统计人员行使统计法规及本办法所规定的职权或打击报复统计人员的；

五、违反统计法规及本办法，未经批准，自行编制发布残联系统统计报表的；

六、违反统计法规及本办法，未经核定批准，擅自对外提供或公布残联系统统计资料的。

八、附　则

第二十六条 本办法由中国残联负责解释。

第二十七条 本办法自发布之日起试行。

中华人民共和国统计法

（1983 年 12 月 8 日第六届全国人民代表大会常务委员会第三次会议通过。根据 1996 年 5 月 15 日第八届全国人民代表大会常务委员会第十九次会议《关于修改〈中华人民共和国统计法〉的决定》修正。2009 年 6 月 27 日第十一届全国人民代表大会常务委员会第九次会议修订。）

第一章　总　则

第一条　为了科学、有效地组织统计工作，保障统计资料的真实性、准确性、完整性和及时性，发挥统计在了解国情国力、服务经济社会发展中的重要作用，促进社会主义现代化建设事业发展，制定本法。

第二条 本法适用于各级人民政府、县级以上人民政府统计机构和有关部门组织实施的统计活动。

统计的基本任务是对经济社会发展情况进行统计调查、统计分析，提供统计资料和统计咨询意见，实行统计监督。

第三条 国家建立集中统一的统计系统，实行统一领导、分级负责的统计管理体制。

第四条 国务院和地方各级人民政府、各有关部门应当加强对统计工作的组织领导，为统计工作提供必要的保障。

第五条 国家加强统计科学研究，健全科学的统计指标体系，不断改进统计调查方法，提高统计的科学性。

国家有计划地加强统计信息化建设，推进统计信息搜集、处理、传输、共享、存储技术和统计数据库体系的现代化。

第六条 统计机构和统计人员依照本法规定独立行使统计调查、统计报告、统计监督的职权，不受侵犯。

地方各级人民政府、政府统计机构和有关部门以及各单位的负责人，不得自行修改统计机构和统计人员依法搜集、整理的统计资料，不得以任何方式要求统计机构、统计人员及其他机构、人员伪造、篡改统计资料，不得对依法履行职责或者拒绝、抵制统计违法行为的统计人员打击报复。

第七条 国家机关、企业事业单位和其他组织以及个体工商户和个人等统计调查对象，必须依照本法和国家有关规定，真实、准确、完整、及时地提供统计调查所需的资料，不得提供不真实或者不完整的统计资料，不得迟报、拒报统计资料。

第八条 统计工作应当接受社会公众的监督。任何单位和个人有权检举统计中弄虚作假等违法行为。对检举有功的单位和个人应当给予表彰和奖励。

第九条 统计机构和统计人员对在统计工作中知悉的国家秘密、商业秘密和个人信息，应当予以保密。

第十条 任何单位和个人不得利用虚假统计资料骗取荣誉称号、物质利益或者职务晋升。

第二章　统计调查管理

第十一条　统计调查项目包括国家统计调查项目、部门统计调查项目和地方统计调查项目。

国家统计调查项目是指全国性基本情况的统计调查项目。部门统计调查项目是指国务院有关部门的专业性统计调查项目。地方统计调查项目是指县级以上地方人民政府及其部门的地方性统计调查项目。

国家统计调查项目、部门统计调查项目、地方统计调查项目应当明确分工，互相衔接，不得重复。

第十二条　国家统计调查项目由国家统计局制定，或者由国家统计局和国务院有关部门共同制定，报国务院备案；重大的国家统计调查项目报国务院审批。

部门统计调查项目由国务院有关部门制定。统计调查对象属于本部门管辖系统的，报国家统计局备案；统计调查对象超出本部门管辖系统的，报国家统计局审批。

地方统计调查项目由县级以上地方人民政府统计机构和有关部门分别制定或者共同制定。其中，由省级人民政府统计机构单独制定或者和有关部门共同制定的，报国家统计局审批；由省级以下人民政府统计机构单独制定或者和有关部门共同制定的，报省级人民政府统计机构审批；由县级以上地方人民政府有关部门制定的，报本级人民政府统计机构审批。

第十三条 统计调查项目的审批机关应当对调查项目的必要性、可行性、科学性进行审查，对符合法定条件的，作出予以批准的书面决定，并公布；对不符合法定条件的，作出不予批准的书面决定，并说明理由。

第十四条 制定统计调查项目，应当同时制定该项目的统计调查制度，并依照本法第十二条的规定一并报经审批或者备案。

统计调查制度应当对调查目的、调查内容、调查方法、调查对象、调查组织方式、调查表式、统计资料的报送和公布等作出规定。

统计调查应当按照统计调查制度组织实施。变更统计调查制度的内容，应当报经原审批机关批准或者原备案机关备案。

第十五条 统计调查表应当标明表号、制定机关、批准或者备案文号、有效期限等标志。

对未标明前款规定的标志或者超过有效期限的统计调查表，统计调查对象有权拒绝填报；县级以上人民政府统计机构应当依法责令停止有关统计调查活动。

第十六条 搜集、整理统计资料，应当以周期性普查为基础，以经常性抽样调查为主体，综合运用全面调查、重点调查等方法，并充分利用行政记录等资料。

重大国情国力普查由国务院统一领导，国务院和地方人民政府组织统计机构和有关部门共同实施。

第十七条 国家制定统一的统计标准，保障统计调查采用的指标涵义、计算方法、分类目录、调查表式和统计编码等的标准化。

国家统计标准由国家统计局制定，或者由国家统计局和国务院标准化主管部门共同制定。

国务院有关部门可以制定补充性的部门统计标准，报国家统计局审批。部门统计标准不得与国家统计标准相抵触。

第十八条 县级以上人民政府统计机构根据统计任务的需要，可以在统计调查对象中推广使用计算机网络报送统计资料。

第十九条 县级以上人民政府应当将统计工作所需经费列入财政预算。

重大国情国力普查所需经费，由国务院和地方人民政府共同负担，列入相应年度的财政预算，按时拨付，确保到位。

第三章 统计资料的管理和公布

第二十条 县级以上人民政府统计机构和有关部门以及乡、镇人民政府，应当按照国家有关规定建立统计资料的保存、管理制度，建立健全统计信息共享机制。

第二十一条 国家机关、企业事业单位和其他组织等统计调查对象，应当按照国家有关规定设置原始记录、统计台账，建立健全统计资料的审核、签署、交接、归档等管理制度。

统计资料的审核、签署人员应当对其审核、签署的统计资料的真实性、准确性和完整性负责。

第二十二条 县级以上人民政府有关部门应当及时向本级人民政府统计机构提供统计所需的行政记录资料和国民经济核算所需的财务资料、财政资料及其他资料，并按照统计调查制度的规定及时向本级人民政府统计机构报送其组织实施统计调查取得的有关资料。

县级以上人民政府统计机构应当及时向本级人民政府有关部门提供有关统计资料。

第二十三条 县级以上人民政府统计机构按照国家有关规定，定期公布统计资料。

国家统计数据以国家统计局公布的数据为准。

第二十四条 县级以上人民政府有关部门统计调查取得的统计资料，由本部门按照国家有关规定公布。

第二十五条 统计调查中获得的能够识别或者推断单个统计调查对象身份的资料，任何单位和个人不得对外提供、泄露，不得用于统计以外的目的。

第二十六条 县级以上人民政府统计机构和有关部门统计调查取得的统计资料，除依法应当保密的外，应当及时公开，供社会公众查询。

第四章　统计机构和统计人员

第二十七条　国务院设立国家统计局，依法组织领导和协调全国的统计工作。

国家统计局根据工作需要设立的派出调查机构，承担国家统计局布置的统计调查等任务。

县级以上地方人民政府设立独立的统计机构，乡、镇人民政府设置统计工作岗位，配备专职或者兼职统计人员，依法管理、开展统计工作，实施统计调查。

第二十八条　县级以上人民政府有关部门根据统计任务的需要设立统计机构，或者在有关机构中设置统计人员，并指定统计负责人，依法组织、管理本部门职责范围内的统计工作，实施统计调查，在统计业务上受本级人民政府统计机构的指导。

第二十九条　统计机构、统计人员应当依法履行职责，如实搜集、报送统计资料，不得伪造、篡改统计资料，不得以任何方式要求任何单位和个人提供不真实的统计资料，不得有其他违反本法规定的行为。

统计人员应当坚持实事求是，恪守职业道德，对其负责搜集、审核、录入的统计资料与统计调查对象报送的统计资料的一致性负责。

第三十条　统计人员进行统计调查时，有权就与统计有关的问题询问有关人员，要求其如实提供有关情况、资料并改正不真实、不准确的资料。

统计人员进行统计调查时，应当出示县级以上人民政府统计机构或者有关部门颁发的工作证件；未出示的，统计调查对象有权拒绝调查。

第三十一条　国家实行统计专业技术职务资格考试、评聘制度，提高统计人员的专业素质，保障统计队伍的稳定性。

统计人员应当具备与其从事的统计工作相适应的专业知识和业务能力。

县级以上人民政府统计机构和有关部门应当加强对统计人员的专业培训和职业道德教育。

第五章　监督检查

第三十二条　县级以上人民政府及其监察机关对下级人民政府、本级人民政府统计机构和有关部门执行本法的情况，实施监督。

第三十三条　国家统计局组织管理全国统计工作的监督检查，查处重大统计违法行为。

县级以上地方人民政府统计机构依法查处本行政区域内发生的统计违法行为。但是，国家统计局派出的调查机构组织实施的统计调查活动中发生的统计违法行为，由组织实施该项统计调查的调查机构负责查处。

法律、行政法规对有关部门查处统计违法行为另有规定的，从其规定。

第三十四条　县级以上人民政府有关部门应当积极协助本级人民政府统计机构查处统计违法行为，及时向本级人民政府统计机构移送有关统计违法案件材料。

第三十五条　县级以上人民政府统计机构在调查统计违法行为或者核查统计数据时，有权采取下列措施：

（一）发出统计检查查询书，向检查对象查询有关事项；

（二）要求检查对象提供有关原始记录和凭证、统计台账、统计调查表、会计资料及其他相关证明和资料；

（三）就与检查有关的事项询问有关人员；

（四）进入检查对象的业务场所和统计数据处理信息系统进行检查、核对；

（五）经本机构负责人批准，登记保存检查对象的有关原始记录和凭证、统计台账、统计调查表、会计资料及其他相关证明和资料；

（六）对与检查事项有关的情况和资料进行记录、录音、录像、照相和复制。

县级以上人民政府统计机构进行监督检查时，监督检查人员不得少于二人，并应当出示执法证件；未出示的，有关单位和个人有权拒绝检查。

第三十六条　县级以上人民政府统计机构履行监督检查职责时，有关单位和个人应当如实反映情况，提供相关证明和资料，不得拒绝、阻碍检查，不得转移、隐匿、篡改、毁弃原始记录和凭证、统计台账、统计调查表、会计资料及其他相关证明和资料。

第六章　法律责任

第三十七条　地方人民政府、政府统计机构或者有关部门、单位的负责人有下列行为之一的，由任免机关或者监察机关依法给予处分，并由县级以上人民政府统计机构予以通报：

（一）自行修改统计资料、编造虚假统计数据的；

（二）要求统计机构、统计人员或者其他机构、人员伪造、篡改统计资料的；

（三）对依法履行职责或者拒绝、抵制统计违法行为的统计人员打击报复的；

（四）对本地方、本部门、本单位发生的严重统计违法行为失察的。

第三十八条 县级以上人民政府统计机构或者有关部门在组织实施统计调查活动中有下列行为之一的，由本级人民政府、上级人民政府统计机构或者本级人民政府统计机构责令改正，予以通报；对直接负责的主管人员和其他直接责任人员，由任免机关或者监察机关依法给予处分：

（一）未经批准擅自组织实施统计调查的；

（二）未经批准擅自变更统计调查制度的内容的；

（三）伪造、篡改统计资料的；

（四）要求统计调查对象或者其他机构、人员提供不真实的统计资料的；

（五）未按照统计调查制度的规定报送有关资料的。

统计人员有前款第三项至第五项所列行为之一的，责令改正，依法给予处分。

第三十九条 县级以上人民政府统计机构或者有关部门有下列行为之一的，对直接负责的主管人员和其他直接责任人员由任免机关或者监察机关依法给予处分：

（一）违法公布统计资料的；

（二）泄露统计调查对象的商业秘密、个人信息或者提供、泄露在统计调查中获得的能够识别或者推断单个统计调查对象身份的资料的；

（三）违反国家有关规定，造成统计资料毁损、灭失的。

统计人员有前款所列行为之一的，依法给予处分。

第四十条 统计机构、统计人员泄露国家秘密的，依法追究法律责任。

第四十一条 作为统计调查对象的国家机关、企业事业单位或者其他组织有下列行为之一的，由县级以上人民政府统计机构责令改正，给予警告，可以予以通报；其直接负责的主管人员和其他直接责任人员属于国家工作人员的，由任免机关或者监察机关依法给予处分：

（一）拒绝提供统计资料或者经催报后仍未按时提供统计资料的；

（二）提供不真实或者不完整的统计资料的；

（三）拒绝答复或者不如实答复统计检查查询书的；

（四）拒绝、阻碍统计调查、统计检查的；

（五）转移、隐匿、篡改、毁弃或者拒绝提供原始记录和凭证、统计台账、统计调查表及其他相关证明和资料的。

企业事业单位或者其他组织有前款所列行为之一的，可以并处五万元以下的罚款；情节严重的，并处五万元以上二十万元以下的罚款。

个体工商户有本条第一款所列行为之一的，由县级以上人民政府统计机构责令改正，给予警告，可以并处一万元以下的罚款。

第四十二条 作为统计调查对象的国家机关、企业事业单位或者其他组织迟报统计资料，或者未按照国家有关规定设置原始记录、统计台账的，由县级以上人民政府统计机构责令改正，给予警告。

企业事业单位或者其他组织有前款所列行为之一的，可以并处一万元以下的罚款。

个体工商户迟报统计资料的，由县级以上人民政府统计机构责令改正，给予警告，可以并处一千元以下的罚款。

第四十三条 县级以上人民政府统计机构查处统计违法行为时，认为对有关国家工作人员依法应当给予处分的，应当提出给予处分的建议；该国家工作人员的任免机关或者监察机关应当依法及时作出决定，并将结果书面通知县级以上人民政府统计机构。

第四十四条 作为统计调查对象的个人在重大国情国力普查活动中拒绝、阻碍统计调查，或者提供不真实或者不完整的普查资料的，由县级以上人民政府统计机构责令改正，予以批评教育。

第四十五条 违反本法规定，利用虚假统计资料骗取荣誉称号、物质利益或者职务晋升的，除对其编造虚假统计资料或者要求他人编造虚假统计资料的行为依法追究法律责任外，由作出有关决定的单位或者其上级单位、监察机关取消其荣誉称号，追缴获得的物质利益，撤销晋升的职务。

第四十六条 当事人对县级以上人民政府统计机构作出的行政处罚决定不服的，可以依法申请行政复议或者提起行政诉讼。其中，对国家统计局在省、自治区、直辖市派出的调查机构作出的行政处罚决定不服的，向国家统计局申请行政复议；对国家统计局派出的其他调查机构作出的行政处罚决定不服的，向国家统计局在该派出机构所在的省、自治区、直辖市派出的调查机构申请行政复议。

第四十七条 违反本法规定，构成犯罪的，依法追究刑事责任。

第七章 附 则

第四十八条 本法所称县级以上人民政府统计机构，是指国家统计局及其派出的调查机构、县级以上地方人民政府统计机构。

第四十九条 民间统计调查活动的管理办法，由国务院制定。

中华人民共和国境外的组织、个人需要在中华人民共和国境内进行统计调查活动的，应当按照国务院的规定报请审批。

利用统计调查危害国家安全、损害社会公共利益或者进行欺诈活动的，依法追究法律责任。

第五十条 本法自 2010 年 1 月 1 日起施行。

部门统计调查项目管理办法

（中华人民共和国国家统计局令第22号）

第一章　总则

第一条　为加强部门统计调查项目的规范性、统一性管理，提高统计调查的科学性和有效性，减轻统计调查对象负担，推进部门统计信息共享，根据《中华人民共和国统计法》及其实施条例和国务院有关规定，制定本办法。

第二条　本办法适用于国务院各部门制定的统计调查项目。

第三条　本办法所称的统计调查项目，是指国务院有关部门通过调查表格、问卷、行政记录、大数据以及其他方式搜集整理统计资料，用于政府管理和公共服务的各类统计调查项目。

第四条　国家统计局统一组织领导和协调全国统计工作，指导国务院有关部门开展统计调查，统一管理部门统计调查。

第五条　国务院有关部门应当明确统一组织协调统计工作的综合机构，负责归口管理、统一申报本部门统计调查项目。

第二章　部门统计调查项目的制定

第六条　国务院有关部门执行相关法律、行政法规、国务院的决定和履行本部门职责，需要开展统计活动的，应当制定相应的部门统计调查项目。

第七条　制定部门统计调查项目，应当减少调查频率，缩小调查规模，降低调查成本，减轻基层统计人员和统计调查对象的负担。可以通过行政记录和大数据加工整理获得统计资料的，不得开展统计调查；可以通过已经批准实施的各种统计调查整理获得统计资料的，不得重复开展统计调查；抽样调查、重点调查可以满足需要的，不得开展全面统计调查。

第八条　制定部门统计调查项目，应当有组织、人员和经费保障。

第九条　制定部门统计调查项目，应当同时制定该项目的统计调查制度。

统计调查制度内容包括总说明、报表目录、调查表式、分类目录、指标解释、指标间逻辑关系，采用抽样调查方法的还应当包括抽样方案。

统计调查制度总说明应当对调查目的、调查对象、统计范围、调查内容、调查频率、调查时间、调查方法、组织实施方式、质量控制、报送要求、信息共享、资料公布等作出规定。

面向单位的部门统计调查，其统计调查对象应当取自国家基本单位名录库或者部门基本单位名录库。

第十条　部门统计调查应当规范设置统计指标、调查表，指标解释和计算方法应当科学合理。

第十一条　部门统计调查应当使用国家统计标准。无国家统计标准的，可以使用经国家统计局批准的部门统计标准。

第十二条　新制定的部门统计调查项目或者对现行统计调查项目进行较大修订的，应当开展试填试报等工作。其中，重要统计调查项目应当进行试点。

第十三条　部门统计调查项目涉及其他部门职责的，应当事先征求相关部门意见。

第三章　部门统计调查项目审批和备案

第十四条　国务院有关部门制定的统计调查项目，统计调查对象属于本部门管辖系统或者利用行政记录加工获取统计资料的，报国家统计局备案；统计调查对象超出本部门管辖系统的，报国家统计局审批。

部门管辖系统包括本部门直属机构、派出机构和垂直管理的机构，省及省以下与部门对口设立的管理机构。

第十五条　部门统计调查项目审批或者备案包括申报、受理、审查、反馈、决定等程序。

第十六条 部门统计调查项目送审或者备案时，应当通过部门统计调查项目管理平台提交下列材料：

（一）申请审批项目的部门公文或者申请备案项目的部门办公厅（室）公文；

（二）部门统计调查项目审批或者备案申请表；

（三）统计调查制度；

（四）统计调查项目的论证报告、背景材料、经费保障等，修订的统计调查项目还应当提供修订说明；

（五）征求有关地方、部门、统计调查对象和专家意见及其采纳情况；

（六）制定机关按照会议制度集体讨论决定的会议纪要；

（七）重要统计调查项目的试点报告；

（八）由审批机关或者备案机关公布的统计调查制度的主要内容；

（九）防范和惩治统计造假、弄虚作假责任规定。

前款第（一）项的公文应当同时提交纸质文件。

第十七条 申请材料齐全并符合法定形式的，国家统计局予以受理。

申请材料不齐全或者不符合法定形式的，国家统计局应当一次告知需要补正的全部内容，制定机关应当按照国家统计局的要求予以补正。

第十八条 统计调查制度应当列明下列事项：

（一）向国家统计局报送的制定机关组织实施统计调查取得的具体统计资料清单；

（二）主要统计指标公布的时间、渠道；

（三）统计信息共享的内容、方式、时限、渠道、责任单位和责任人；

（四）向统计信息共享数据库提供的统计资料清单；

（五）统计调查对象使用国家基本单位名录库或者部门基本单位名录库的情况。

第十九条 国家统计局对申请审批的部门统计调查项目进行审查，符合下列条件的部门统计调查项目，作出予以批准的书面决定：

（一）具有法定依据或者确为部门公共管理和服务所必需；

（二）与现有的国家统计调查项目和部门统计调查项目的主要内容不重复、不矛盾；

（三）主要统计指标无法通过本部门的行政记录或者已有统计调查资料加工整理取得；

（四）部门统计调查制度科学、合理、可行，并且符合本办法第八条、第九条和第十八条规定；

（五）采用的统计标准符合国家有关规定；

（六）符合统计法律法规和国家有关规定。

不符合前款规定的，国家统计局向制定机关提出修改意见；修改后仍不符合前款规定条件的，国家统计局作出不予批准的书面决定，并说明理由。

第二十条 国家统计局对申请备案的部门统计调查项目进行审查，符合下列条件的部门统计调查项目，作出同意备案的书面决定：

（一）统计调查项目的调查对象属于制定机关管辖系统，或者利用行政记录加工获取统计资料；

（二）与现有的国家统计调查项目和部门统计调查项目的主要内容不重复、不矛盾；

（三）部门统计调查制度科学、合理、可行，并且符合本办法第八条、第九条和第十八条规定。

第二十一条 国家统计局在收到制定机关申请公文及完整的相关资料后，在 20 个工作日内完成审批，20 个工作日内不能作出决定的，经审批机关负责人批准可以延长 10 日，并应当将延长审批期限的理由告知制定机关；在 10 个工作日内完成备案。完成时间以复函日期为准。

制定机关修改统计调查项目的时间，不计算在审批期限内。

第二十二条 部门统计调查项目有下列情形之一的，国家统计局简化审批或者备案程序，缩短期限：

（一）发生突发事件，需要迅速实施统计调查；

（二）统计调查内容未做变动，统计调查项目有效期届满需要延长期限。

第二十三条 部门统计调查项目实行有效期管理。审批的统计调查项目有效期为 3 年，备案的统计调查项目有效期为 5 年。统计调查制度对有效期规定少于 3 年的，从其规定。有效期以批准执行或者同意备案的日期为起始时间。

统计调查项目在有效期内需要变更内容的，制定机关应当重新申请审批或者备案。

第二十四条 部门统计调查项目经国家统计局批准或者备案后，应当在统计调查表的右上角标明表号、制定机关、批准机关或者备案机关、批准文号或者备案文号、有效期限等标志。

第二十五条 制定机关收到批准或者备案的书面决定后，在10个工作日内将标注批准文号或者备案文号和有效期限的统计调查制度发送到部门统计调查项目管理平台。

第二十六条 国家统计局及时通过国家统计局网站公布批准或者备案的部门统计调查项目名称、制定机关、批准文号或者备案文号、有效期限和统计调查制度的主要内容。

第四章 部门统计调查的组织实施

第二十七条 国务院有关部门应当健全统计工作流程规范，完善统计数据质量控制办法，夯实统计基础工作，严格按照国家统计局批准或者备案的统计调查制度组织实施统计调查。

第二十八条 国务院有关部门在组织实施统计调查时，应当就统计调查制度的主要内容对组织实施人员进行培训；应当就法定填报义务、主要指标涵义和口径、计算方法、采用的统计标准和其他填报要求，向调查对象作出说明。

第二十九条 国务院有关部门应当按《中华人民共和国统计法实施条例》的要求及时公布主要统计指标涵义、调查范围、调查方法、计算方法、抽样调查样本量等信息，对统计数据进行解释说明。

第三十条 国务院有关部门组织实施统计调查应当遵守国家有关统计资料管理和公布的规定。

第三十一条 部门统计调查取得的统计资料，一般应当在政府部门间共享。

第三十二条 国务院有关部门建立统计调查项目执行情况评估制度，对实施情况、实施效果和存在问题进行评估，认为应当修改的，按规定报请国家统计局审批或者备案。

第五章 国家统计局提供的服务

第三十三条 国家统计局依法开展部门统计调查项目审批和备案工作，为国务院有关部门提供有关统计业务咨询、统计调查制度设计指导、统计业务培训等服务。

第三十四条 国家统计局组织国务院有关部门共同维护、更新国家基本单位名录库，为部门统计调查提供调查单位名录和抽样框。

第三十五条 国家统计局建立统计标准库，为部门统计调查提供国家统计标准和部门统计标准。

第三十六条 国家统计局向国务院有关部门提供部门统计调查项目查询服务。

第三十七条 国家统计局推动建立统计信息共享数据库，为国务院有关部门提供部门统计数据查询服务。

第六章 监督检查

第三十八条 国家统计局依法对部门统计调查制度执行情况进行监督检查，依法查处部门统计调查中的重大违法行为；县级以上地方人民政府统计机构依法查处本级和下级人民政府有关部门和统计调查对象执行部门统计调查制度中发生的统计违法行为。

第三十九条 任何单位和个人有权向国家统计局举报部门统计调查违法行为。

国家统计局公布举报统计违法行为的方式和途径，依法受理、核实、处理举报，并为举报人保密。

第四十条 县级以上人民政府有关部门积极协助本级人民政府统计机构查处统计违法行为，及时向县级以上人民政府统计机构移送有关统计违法案件材料。

第四十一条 县级以上人民政府统计机构在调查部门统计违法行为或者核查部门统计数据时，有权采取《中华人民共和国统计法》第三十五条规定的下列措施：

（一）发出检查查询书，向检查单位和调查对象查询部门统计调查项目有关事项；

（二）要求检查单位和调查对象提供与部门统计调查有关的统计调查制度、调查资料、调查报告及其他相关证明和资料；

（三）就与检查有关的事项询问有关人员；

（四）进入检查单位和调查对象的业务场所和统计数据处理信息系统进行检查、核对；

（五）经本机构负责人批准，登记保存检查单位与统计调查有关的统计调查制度、调查资料、调查报告及其他相关证明和资料；

（六）对与检查事项有关的情况和资料进行记录、录音、录像、照相和复制。

县级以上人民政府统计机构进行监督检查时，监督检查人员不得少于 2 人，并应当出示执法证件；未出示的，有关部门有权拒绝检查。

第四十二条 县级以上人民政府统计机构履行监督检查职责时，有关部门应当如实反映情况，提供相关证明和资料，不得拒绝、阻碍检查，不得转移、隐匿、篡改、毁弃与部门统计调查有关的统计调查制度、调查资料、调查报告及其他相关证明和资料。

第七章 法律责任

第四十三条 县级以上人民政府有关部门在组织实施部门统计调查活动中有下列行为之一的，由上级人民政府统计机构、本级人民政府统计机构责令改正，予以通报：

（一）违法制定、实施部门统计调查项目；

（二）未执行国家统计标准或者经依法批准的部门统计标准；

（三）未执行批准和备案的部门统计调查制度；

（四）在部门统计调查中统计造假、弄虚作假。

第四十四条 县级以上人民政府有关部门及其工作人员有下列行为之一的，由上级人民政府统计机构、本级人民政府统计机构责令改正，予以通报：

（一）拒绝、阻碍对部门统计调查的监督检查和对部门统计违法行为的查处；

（二）包庇、纵容部门统计违法行为；

（三）向存在部门统计违法行为的单位或者个人通风报信，帮助其逃避查处。

第四十五条 县级以上人民政府统计机构在查处部门统计违法行为中，认为对有关国家工作人员依法应当给予处分的，应当提出给予处分的建议，将处分建议和案件材料移送该国家工作人员的任免机关或者监察机关。

第八章 附 则

第四十六条 中央编办管理机构编制的群众团体机关、经授权代主管部门行使统计职能的国家级集团公司和工商领域联合会或者协会等开展的统计调查项目，参照部门统计调查项目管理。

县级以上地方人民政府统计机构对本级人民政府有关部门制定的统计调查项目管理，参照本办法执行。

第四十七条 本办法自 2017 年 10 月 1 日起施行。国家统计局 1999 年公布的《部门统计调查项目管理暂行办法》同时废止。